# RUSSIA'S
*People of Empire*

# RUSSIA'S
## *People of Empire*

## LIFE STORIES FROM EURASIA, 1500 TO THE PRESENT

EDITED BY

### STEPHEN M. NORRIS AND
### WILLARD SUNDERLAND

*Indiana University Press*

BLOOMINGTON & INDIANAPOLIS

This book is a publication of

Indiana University Press
601 North Morton Street
Bloomington, Indiana 47404-3797 USA

iupress.indiana.edu

*Telephone orders*     800-842-6796
*Fax orders*     812-855-7931

Library of Congress Cataloging-in-Publication Data

Russia's people of empire : life stories from Eurasia, 1500 to the present / edited by Stephen M. Norris and Willard Sunderland.
    pages ; cm
    Includes bibliographical references and index.
    ISBN 978-0-253-00176-4 (cloth : alkaline paper) — ISBN 978-0-253-00183-2 (paperback : alkaline paper) — ISBN 978-0-253-00184-9 (ebook) (print)
    1. Russia—Biography. 2. Soviet Union—Biography. 3. Russia (Federation)—Biography. 4. Cultural pluralism—Russia. 5. Cultural pluralism—Soviet Union. 6. Cultural pluralism—Russia (Federation) I. Norris, Stephen M. II. Sunderland, Willard, 1965-
    DK37.R79 2012
    947.009'9—dc23
                                          2011053060

1 2 3 4 5 17 16 15 14 13 12

*In memory of Richard Stites (1931–2010),*
*Beloved teacher, scholar, and friend*

# Contents

# Acknowledgments

We could not have taken on an essay collection of this scope without the support of numerous friends and colleagues. Our first thanks go to our contributors for their essays and their patience as our project came into shape and progressed over the last several years. In 2009, we presented a version of our introduction at the annual meeting of the Midwest Russian History Workshop at the University of Notre Dame. We are grateful to all the faculty and graduate students at the session that day for their helpful suggestions and encouragement, with special thanks to Valerie Kivelson for her insightful comments on the text and Alexander Martin, our gracious host for the event. Janet Rabinowitch, our editor at Indiana University Press, has been remarkable. We thank her for all the enthusiasm, confidence, and editorial insight she has invested in our work since the moment we first spoke with her about the project. Jane Burbank and Robert Crews offered us rich and insightful critiques as readers for the Press—we are very grateful to them for this. Peter Froehlich of Indiana University Press helped us with numerous production questions. In addition, we would like to thank Angela Burton, our managing editor; Dawn Ollila for her talented copyediting of the manuscript; and Bill Nelson for his excellent maps.

Finally, we wish to offer the most special of thanks to one of our contributors who is no longer with us—Richard Stites. Richard passed away before he could see his chapter appear in this book, but we still feel his presence. Over a long and accomplished career of teaching and writing about Russian history, he established himself as a remarkable presence in our field, touching many of us with his love for and deep knowledge of the Russian past—and even more with his generous nature as an intellectual, mentor, and friend. It is telling that neither of us formally studied with Richard, but both of us feel charmed to have known him and to have benefited from his rare blend of erudition and kindness. We so wish he could be here to give us his insightful reflections on all the complex and engaging lives captured in these pages. With great respect and affection, we dedicate this volume to him.

# Chronology of the Russian Empire

*Italics indicate lives explored in this volume*

1689    Treaty of Nerchinsk establishes border between Russia and China
1695–1696    Azov campaigns; second one establishes control over the city
1700–1721    Great Northern War between Russia and Sweden
1703    St. Petersburg founded
1710    Conquest of Estonia and Livonia
*1711–1765    Life of Mikhail Lomonosov*
1722–1723    Persian campaign
1725    Peter dies; his second wife, Catherine, becomes tsarina
1727    Catherine dies; Peter's grandson, Peter II, becomes tsar
*1729–1796    Life of Catherine II, the Great*
1730    Peter II dies; Anna, daughter of Peter I's half-brother, Ivan, becomes tsarina
1731–1742    Kazakh khans swear loyalty oaths to Russia
1734–1740    Bashkir revolts, conquest of the Southern Urals
1740    Anna dies; her grand-nephew, the infant Ivan VI, becomes tsar
1741    Bering's expedition reaches the coast of Alaska
1741    Peter I's daughter, Elizabeth, becomes tsarina in palace coup
1757    Russia becomes involved in the Seven Years' War
1761    Death of Elizabeth; Peter I's grandson, Peter III, becomes tsar
1762    Peter III's wife, Catherine, deposes him as tsar in palace coup
1765    Sloboda Ukraine becomes Russian province
*1765–1812    Life of Petr Ivanovich Bagration*
*1768–1835    Life of Johannes Ambrosius Rosenstrauch*
1768–1774    Russo-Turkish War; Russia acquires areas to the north of the
         Black Sea in Treaty of Kuchuk Kainardji
1772    First Partition of Poland
1773–1774    Rebellion in Volga Region led by Emelian Pugachev
1775    Conquest and dissolution of the Zaporozhian Sich
1783    Russian protectorate over Kingdom of Georgia established
1783    Crimean Khanate annexed by Russia
1784    Vladikavkav founded
1785–1791    Chechen and Dagestani uprisings to Dniestr River
1787–1792    War with Ottoman Empire; Treaty of Jassy establishes Russian control
1793    Second Partition of Poland
1795    Third Partition of Poland
1796    Catherine II dies; her son, Paul I, becomes tsar
*1797–1871    Life of Imam Shamil*
*1798–1855    Life of Adam Mickiewicz*
*1800–1857    Life of Archbishop Innokentii*
1801    Kingdom of Georgia annexed
1801    Paul I deposed in palace coup; his son, Alexander, becomes tsar
1804–1813    Russo-Persian War, conquest of khanates in Azerbaijan
1806–1809    War with Ottoman Empire; Treaty of Bucharest gives Russia Bessarabia
1808–1809    War with Sweden; conquest and annexation of Finland

1809–1852  *Life of Nikolai Gogol*
1812  Russia acquires Bessarabia and northeastern Moldavia
1812  Fort Ross established in California
1812–1813  Napoléon's Russian campaign
1815  Kingdom of Poland created at Congress of Vienna
1818  First Sejm of Poland opened by Alexander I
1822  Annexation of Middle Horde of Kazakhs
1824  Annexation of Small Horde of Kazakhs
1825  Alexander I dies; his brother, Nicholas I, becomes tsar
1825  Decembrist Revolt
1826–1828  Russo-Persian War; Treaty of Turkmanchai gives Russia parts of Armenia
1828–1829  War with Ottoman Empire; Treaty of Adrianople gives Russia parts of Black Sea coast
1829–1864  Caucasian War
1829–1894  *Life of Anton Rubenstein*
1830–1831  Polish Uprising
1833–1887  *Life of Aleksandr Borodin*
1834  Shamil leads uprising in Caucasus
1845  Annexation of Kazakh Inner Horde
1848  Annexation of Kazakh Great Horde
1850  *Life of Kutlu-Muhammed Batyr-Gireevich Tevkelev*
1851–1919  *Life of Petr Badmaev*
1853–1856  Crimean War; Treaty of Paris forces Russia to accept neutral Black Sea
1855  Death of Nicholas I; his son, Alexander II, becomes tsar
1859–?  *Life of Ekaterina Sabashnikova-Baranovskaia*
1860  Vladivostok founded
1863–1864  Polish Uprising
1864  Conquest of west Caucasus
1865  Conquest of Tashkent
1867  Sale of Alaska
1867–1951  *Life of Carl Gustaf Emil Mannerheim*
1867  Establishment of Governor-Generalship of Turkestan
1868  Conquest of Samarkand; Emirate of Bukhara protectorate established
1872–1971  *Life of Matilde Kshesinskaia*
1873  Russian protectorate of Khiva established
1875  Sakhalin Island annexed
1876  Khanate of Kokand annexed
1877–1878  Russo-Turkish War
1878–1953  *Life of Joseph Stalin*
1881  Conquest of Turkmen fortress of Gök Tepe
1881  Alexander II assassinated; his son, Alexander III, becomes tsar
1882  May Laws introduce further legal discrimination against Jews
1889–1966  *Life of Anna Akhmatova*

1891–1903    Construction of Trans-Siberian Railway
*1893–1955    Life of Aleksandr Germano*
*1893–1991    Life of Lazar' Kaganovich*
1894    Alexander III dies; his son, Nicholas II, becomes tsar
*1896–1954    Life of Dziga Vertov*
1897    First census of the Russian Empire
*1897–1961    Life of Mukhtar Auezov*
*1900–1967    Life of Jahon Obidova*
1903    Kishinev pogrom; beginning of a wave of anti-Jewish violence in Russian
        Empire
1904–1905    Russo-Japanese War
1905    "Bloody Sunday" (January 9) in St. Petersburg triggers strikes and demon-
        strations throughout Russia; 1905 Revolution begins
1905    October 17 Manifesto grants civil liberties to imperial subjects and estab-
        lishes Duma elections.
1906    First Duma in session, dissolved by Nicholas II after two months; Petr
        Stolypin becomes Prime Minister
1907    Second Duma in session, dissolved by Nicholas II after three months
1907–1912    Third Duma in session
1914–1917    Great War; in 1915 German offensive, Russia loses Lithuania, Kurland,
        Poland, and western Belorussia; Refugees stream across the Empire; From
        1915–1917, a series of bread riots and draft riots break out across the empire
1917    February revolt in Petrograd lead to Nicholas II's abdication; Provisional
        Government announced
1917    Formation of Ukrainian Central Rada in March; Provisional Government
        recognizes Polish independence in March
1917    October seizure of power by Vladimir Lenin's Bolshevik Party
1917    Finland declares independence in December
1918    Lithuania and Estonia declare independence in February
1918    Treaty of Brest-Litovsk in March ends Great War between Russia and Central
        Powers
1918    Independence declared by Transcaucasian Federative Republic in April;
        followed by Georgia, Armenia, and Azerbaidzhan in May
1918    Latvia declares independence in November
1921    Red Army conquers Georgia
1922    Foundation of the Union of Soviet Socialist Republics
1924    Incorporation of Bukhara and Khiva People's Republics into Soviet Union;
        policy of *korenizatsiia* introduced
1924    Death of Lenin; after power struggle, Joseph Stalin becomes Soviet leader
1927    Hujum campaign in Central Asia
1929–1933    Stalin's First Five-Year Plan of collectivization and industrialization
1932    Politburo issues two decrees criticizing Ukrainianization; leads to scaling
        back of korenizatsiia

1933   Famine in Ukraine
1936   Stalinist Constitution establishes eleven Soviet Republics
*1936   Birth of Olzhas Suleimenov*
1939   Molotov-Ribbentrop Pact; USSR annexes eastern Poland and eastern Galicia
1940   Annexation of Lithuania, Latvia, Estonia, and Bessarabia
1941–1945   Great Patriotic War with Nazi Germany
1941–1944   Enemy nations deported (Germans, Kalmyks, Crimean Tatars, Chechens)
1945–1949   Establishment of communist states in Eastern Europe (Poland, East
        Germany, Hungary, Czechoslovakia, Romania, Bulgaria)
1953   Death of Stalin; after power struggle, Nikita Khrushchev becomes Soviet
        leader
1953   East Berlin workers revolt; Soviet troops restore control
1955   Warsaw Pact created
1956   Twentieth Party Congress and Khrushchev's "Secret Speech" denouncing
        Stalinist excesses
1956   October–November revolt in Hungary; Soviet force invades
*1956   Birth of Grigorii Chkhartishvili*
1961   Yuri Gagarin becomes first man in space
1962   October Cuban Missile Crisis
1964   Khrushchev ousted in coup; Leonid Brezhnev heads new Soviet leadership
*1964   Birth of Vladislav Surkov*
1968   Prague Spring begins in January; in October, Soviet force invades; "Brezhnev
        doctrine" declared
1979   Soviet invasion of Afghanistan leads to nine-year war
1982   Brezhnev dies; Iurii Andropov becomes Soviet leader
1984   Andropov dies; Konstantin Chernenko becomes Soviet leader
1985   Chernenko dies; Mikhail Gorbachev becomes Soviet leader
1986   Chernobyl nuclear power plant disaster
1986   December disturbances in Alma-Ata, Kazakhstan
1988–1990   Soviet republics declare independence
1990   March declaration of independence by Lithuania leads to failed Soviet inter-
        vention
1991   August coup attempt by Kremlin hardliners fails; Gorbachev recognizes in-
        dependence of Baltic States
1991   Soviet Union dissolved December 25; Commonwealth of Independent States
        created
1992   Boris Yeltsin elected President of Russian Federation
1994–1996   First Chechen War
1999   Second Chechen War begins
2000   Vladimir Putin elected president of Russia; re-elected in 2004
2008   South Ossetian War between Russia and Georgia

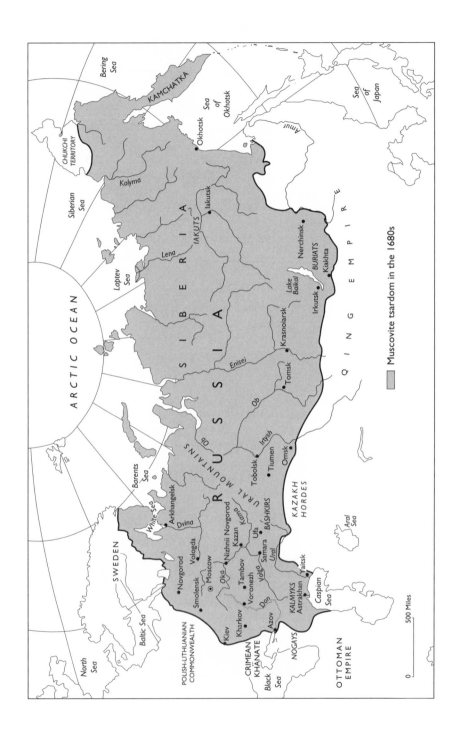

ARCTIC OCEAN

Bering
Sea

Siberian
Sea

CHUKCHI
TERRITORY

KAMCHATKA

Okhotsk

Sea
of
Okhotsk

Sea
of
Japan

Amur

Kolyma

Iakutsk

Nerchinsk

Laptev
Sea

Lena

IAKUTS

BURIATS

Kiakhta

Lake
Baikal

Irkutsk

Barents
Sea

S I B E R I A

Krasnoiarsk

Q I N G   E M P I R E

Enisei

Tomsk

Ob

R U S S I A

Irtysh

White Sea

Arkhangelsk

Dvina

U R A L   M O U N T A I N S

Tiumen

Tobolsk

Omsk

SWEDEN

Novgorod

Vologda

Oka

Nizhnii Novgorod

Kazan

Kama

Ufa

BASHKIRS

KAZAKH
HORDES

Ob

Aral
Sea

Smolensk

Moscow

Tambov

Volga

Samara

Ural

Yaitsk

Baltic Sea

Voronezh

Don

KALMYKS

Astrakhan

Caspian
Sea

North
Sea

POLISH-LITHUANIAN
COMMONWEALTH

Kiev

Kharkov

CRIMEAN
KHANATE

Azov

NOGAYS

OTTOMAN
EMPIRE

Black
Sea

☐ Muscovite tsardom in the 1680s

0          500 Miles

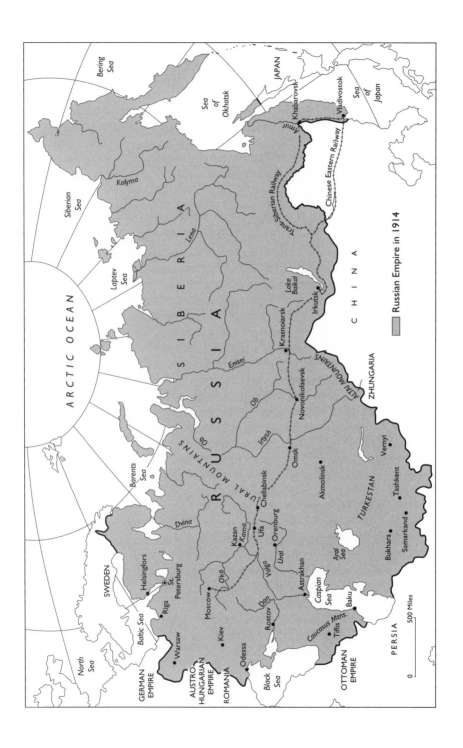

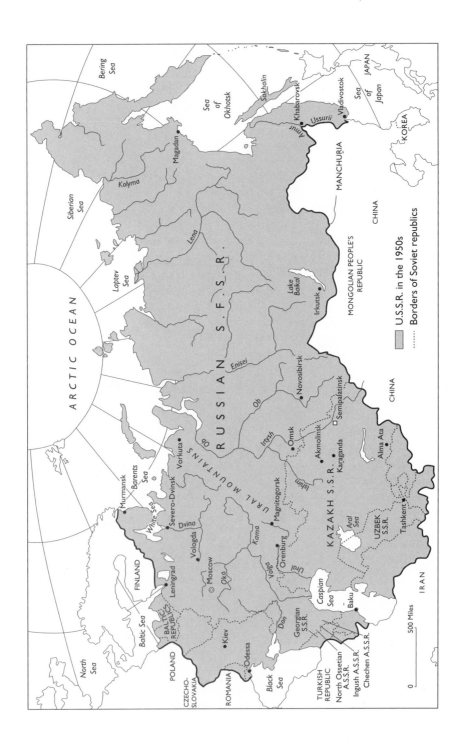

# INTRODUCTION

# Russia's People of Empire

## STEPHEN M. NORRIS AND WILLARD SUNDERLAND

"You are mistaken, my dear grandmamma," Alix wrote in 1900. "Russia is not England. Here we do not need to earn the love of the people. The Russian people revere their Tsars as divine beings, from whom all charity and fortune derive."[1] The grandmother in question was no ordinary one: she was Queen Victoria. And by the time she wrote the letter, Princess Alix had adopted a new name and a new country: she was Empress Alexandra of Russia.

The selected passage reveals several aspects of Alexandra's personality. Born in the German state of Hesse-Darmstadt, Princess Alix grew up an ardent Anglophile. Influenced by her English mother, Alice, and grandmother, Queen Victoria, Alix adored English culture and regularly visited the country. This German attachment to Englishness remained with her for the rest of her life. After meeting and falling in love with the future Nicholas II, tsar of Russia, Alix changed her name to the Russian "Alexandra" and converted to Russian Orthodoxy, but she retained her love for all things British. She and Nicholas spoke and wrote to each other in English; they read English literature together; they decorated their house and garden in the English style.

While Alexandra remained "English" in her temperament and worldview, her marriage and religious conversion added a "Russian" element to her persona. She became a zealous convert to Orthodoxy and a firm supporter of the Russian auto-cratic system, as her letter to Victoria indicates. Alexandra frequently admonished her husband to be strong, making comparisons to such iron-willed rulers of the past as Peter the Great or Ivan the Terrible. She wanted her "Nicky" to embrace a mystical idea of autocratic power that she thought defined the Russian way. Famously, the last ball the royal couple hosted at the Winter Palace in 1903 required everyone to dress in the costumes of the seventeenth century. Nicholas and Alexandra judged the event an unqualified success and even considered requiring seventeenth-century attire at court thereafter.

When not organizing costume balls, Alexandra was acting as Nicholas's right-hand woman and his strongest advocate of the Russian imperial system. During World War I, she urged him to be "the *Samoderzh.* [autocrat] without wh. Russia Cannot exist" and to "show to *all*, that you are the *Master* & *your* will *shall* be obeyed—the time of great indulgence & gentleness is over—now comes yr. reign of will & power, & they shall be *made* to *bow down* before you and listen to yr. orders."[2] These appeals had a powerful effect on Nicholas, redoubling his commitment to rigidly defending his prerogatives as tsar even to the point, eventually, of undermining the monarchy. Indeed, Alexandra's personality, her forceful entreaties, her gossipy letters about politics, and her meetings with Rasputin helped to bring down the very system she defended so vociferously. Mark Steinberg and Vladimir Khrustalev have concluded that "Alexandra's contribution to this tragic history . . . lay less in the pull toward domestic life that she exerted over Nicholas, or even in her damaging interference in government administration, than in her encouragement of Nicholas's anachronistic political convictions."[3]

Alexandra's story is admittedly unique. Not all royal spouses have exerted such influence on their partners. Even the coincidence of Alexandra's German provenance had a crucial impact on history because, as the war against the German powers wore on, rumors began to swirl that she sympathized with the enemy and was secretly sabotaging the Russian war effort. This made it all the easier for a suspicious populace to view her sway over the tsar as proof of the total corruption of the monarchy. Yet Alexandra's basic profile as a non-Russian—in this case, as a foreign princess—who was at the same time a European cosmopolitan *and* a devoted Russian patriot was otherwise not in the least bit unusual. This sort of cultural mixing was common in Russia, for princesses and much humbler souls alike. A famous quip describing Alexandra as a practical Englishwoman on the surface and a mystical Russian underneath, in fact, perfectly captures the multicultural layering that shaped her personality.[4] The empress, in short, was a creation of empire.

The same can be said of one of Alexandra's contemporaries who in every other way would have seemed her polar opposite. Ioseb Jughashvili, better known as Stalin, was, like Alexandra, a non-Russian who became Russian through a long process of cultural transfer and mixing. Stalin grew up in a poor working-class family in Georgia, which was then a province of the Russian Empire. He did not even know Russian until he was ten years old. But like Alexandra, he embraced Russian culture as a form of upward mobility, although in his case, the turn toward Russia became a way of tooling himself to rebel against the autocratic system rather than to defend it (part of this rebellion is reflected in the defiant pseudonym the young Jughashvili chose for himself—"Stalin" derives from *stal'*, the Russian word for steel).

Attracted by Marxism, Stalin joined the Bolsheviks in 1903, when they were still a small underground party. He spent time in and out of Siberian exile, mixing with other radicals, writing papers on socialist theory, becoming ever more "Russian" along the way. Following the October Revolution, he then became the new revolutionary government's first Commissar of Nationalities, a post he obtained in part because he had managed to establish himself as the party's main expert on the "nationality question" but also because he had the right profile. As a non-Russian with a Russian orientation, his very identity seemed to legitimize the Bolsheviks' newly proclaimed agenda to acknowledge and develop the rights of minority peoples. Later, as unrivaled dictator of the USSR, Stalin changed direction and adopted policies that often favored Russians over the other peoples of the state, but in this, too, he acted very much in keeping with his profile as a "man of the borderlands"—he simply shifted the calculation of his interests from his starting point in the periphery to a new one in the center.[5] Like Alexandra, he remained a consummate imperial product.

Alexandra's and Stalin's stories illuminate how the complicated contexts of Russia's condition as a multinational state and society intertwined at the personal level to influence the course of the country's past. The central premise of this volume is that such personal portraits have much to tell us about the Russian experience of empire. Although historians always engage with the lives of people, they usually either gloss over the details or, alternatively, treat the details as important in themselves. Biography tends to assume its own objectives: to document and describe a life, usually by going as deeply as possible into the interior of the subject as possible. But life stories become especially valuable to historians when they are turned *outward* to reveal and explain the contexts around them: lives take on a meaning greater than themselves when they are viewed—and used—as guides to the past, not just as stories of their own.

One of the fundamental dimensions of the Russian experience has been diversity of peoples and cultures, religions and languages, and landscapes and economies—often stitched together in incongruous ways. For centuries, this diversity was contained within the sprawling territories of the Russian Empire and later the Soviet Union, the empire's twentieth-century successor. Today we find it in the still densely interconnected states and societies of the former USSR. In this volume, we set out to explore this enduring world of diversity through life stories. To guide us, we have selected thirty-one individuals. Some, such as Empress Alexandra and Stalin, are well known; others are more obscure. Each shows us the terrain in new and thought-provoking ways.

## THE POWER OF THE PERSONAL

Although there is some debate over when it started, there is no doubt that an "imperial turn" is currently transforming the field of Russian historical studies.[6] The clearest proof is in the rising stack of publications and conference panels related to the history of the empire and the national and regional dimensions of the Soviet past. Alongside the new books and lectures are new journals interested in national questions as well as increased funding for research with a non-metropolitan—that is, a not-exclusively-Russian—focus. This trend is as visible in Russian historiography in Russia as it is in the West.

The good news about this "turn" so far is clear: we now know a great deal more than we did even a generation ago about the varied implications of empire in the Russian past. Research since the 1990s has given us new perspectives on the shaping of imperial borderlands such as Poland and Ukraine, the European steppe, the Middle Volga, Siberia, and Central Asia; the exploration and mapping of imperial territory; and the conflicts and contradictions between imperial and national policies.[7] We have also gained a sounder appreciation of the complexities that shaped modern Russia's two key phases of imperial transition before the Soviet collapse of more recent times—the transition from the Byzantine-Mongol empire of Muscovy to the expressly Europeanized imperial order created by Peter the Great and his successors in the 1700s, and especially the momentous shift from the late tsarist empire to the Soviet Union between the 1910s and the 1930s.[8] Historians are now used to studying the empire as much from the edge as from the center. In keeping with broader trends in general historical scholarship, they have paid great attention to identities and ideologies (some would say too much attention). To a lesser degree, the study of institutions as well as a more traditional focus on social groups and structures has also been a part of the "turn."

What are largely missing from the new historiography, however, are people—or, rather, personalities. Individuals unavoidably appear in the scholarship, but the stuff of their lives is rarely central to the argument historians make about the empire or even the broader picture they draw. Anyone picking up a good history book should hope to take away at least two things: information and understanding—that is to say, we turn to the study of history to find out *what* happened in the past as well as to understand *why* things happened as they did. In the new literature on empire in Russia and the USSR, the history of individuals tends to be used only for the first of these purposes. We read about individual figures, most of them influential personalities of one kind or another, and learn about their lives, but we do not find their experiences used to help us understand the dynamics behind the way the empire was formed, held together, or fell apart.

The generally accepted starting date for the history of the Russian Empire is 1552, the year of Moscow's conquest of Kazan', a Muslim-ruled khanate centered along the Volga River. Moscow had become an ethnically diverse society long before, but the taking of Kazan' was important in that it led to the incorporation into the Russian state of the first large concentrations of non-Russian subjects, and the state's rulers were faced with what would become the persistent challenge of managing and making sense of this diversity. Over the centuries that followed, the Muscovite tsardom and its successor, the Russian Empire, expanded in multiple directions: first, farther south down the Volga and east across the Urals and Siberia; then west into Finland, the Baltic, and Poland; south towards the Black Sea, the Caucasus, and Central Asia; and ultimately farther east to the Sea of Japan. At the time of its unraveling in 1991, the Soviet Union, the heir to the tsarist state, was by far the largest country on earth—stretching for eleven time zones across northern Europe and Asia—and was home to a population of close to three hundred million people belonging to more than a hundred different ethnic groups. Today Russia, although considerably smaller and more ethnically homogenous than the USSR, is still the world's largest state, and diversity remains a basic fact of Russian life. The new post-Soviet national anthem still proudly describes the country as an "age-old union of fraternal peoples."[9]

Russia's expansion was created by tsars, colonists, poets, missionaries, scholars, exiles, commissars, merchants, and soldiers. People of both sexes and of all social classes and estates participated in the process, which was unavoidably multicultural. From its first incarnation in the late Muscovite period, the transcontinental Russian state was the product of the combined efforts of Russians and non-Russians, Orthodox, Muslims, Jews, shamanists, and Buddhists. The resistance that simmered and periodically erupted against Russian state making was also a multiethnic exercise.

Clear lines were drawn at times, with Russians on one side and non-Russians on the other. But more often than not, there was collaboration and cooperation: Russians and non-Russians worked together to build the empire, just as they joined forces in resisting it. The commanding heights of Russian government in the eighteenth century, for example, were controlled by noble families of Polish, German, Russian, and Tatar descent. Meanwhile, far below them on the social ladder, the followers of the Cossack rebel Emelian Pugachev, who advertised himself as tsar Peter III and came close to marching on Moscow in the mid-1770s, were equally diverse. Pugachev's "court" included Russians, Tatars, Bashkirs, Mordvins, Chuvash, and, of course, Pugachev's fellow Cossacks—a frontier people that seemed to some observers of the time to be a "nation" of their own.[10]

Some of the actors in Russia's long multicultural history were self-conscious empire builders. Others were just as determined to destroy the empire. Some in turn were destroyed by it. But what is striking is the sheer number of people who were shaped by the broader pathways of the empire even if they had very little to do with Russian imperialism in an active sense. Russia's history is crowded with individuals who might best be described as imperial products—people whose lives were turned in multicultural directions precisely because of the experiences and combinations that were a part of living in Russian imperial space.

Well before the arrival of Russian imperial power, the varied territories that make up northern Europe and Asia had long been interconnected by networks of movement and exchange, trade and sex, and conflict and negotiation between diverse peoples. When the Russians did arrive, they usually left these "invisible threads" in place,[11] not because they were considerate empire-builders but rather because the connections were useful: these enduring connections often helped the Russians consolidate their imperial authority. Over time, an expanding roster of technologies and institutions—the standing army, the Trans-Siberian Railway, and the Communist Party, to name just a few—built on these deep historical foundations, creating new pathways of multiethnic combination that then augmented or replaced older ones. One of the lasting results of this continuing process of interaction between cultures was the creation of individuals of diversity, men and women who simultaneously lived within several cultures and whose experiences were defined by a certain amount of cross-cultural mediation.

Our volume is the first attempt to bring the reality of these cross-cultural lives into fuller view. The gallery we have assembled is necessarily incomplete and selective; we have had to make subjective decisions about whom to include and whom to leave out. A different team of authors and editors would surely have come up with a different group of personalities. But the cast you will discover in the pages that follow was nonetheless put together with a certain stubborn logic.

First, the lives here are all imperial lives. One way or another they reflect the persistent mixing of cultures that helped to create and was itself a byproduct of imperial dominion. Second, the individuals we have chosen have some relationship to state power or cultural production—or both. Third, they purposefully reflect a mix of the famous and the unknown, the high and the low, and women and men. Fourth, all the lives we have selected overlap in chronological terms, allowing us to offer a broad view of cross-cultural interchanges at work from the late 1500s to the present. Finally, the men and women who appear here have been chosen because their lives have more to tell than just their own individual stories. In each case, our contributors take the approach of the microhistorian: they zoom in tightly on the small scale of a single life—in some cases, even just a single episode within a life—and make it speak to the meaning of larger facts, events, and ideas.

## Getting Down to Scale

The essays here are attempts at a kind of microhistory rather than biography, but this naturally leads to this question: What is the difference?

For one thing, biography is a much older undertaking. Herodotus included biographical treatments of kings and warriors in his *Histories*. Sima Qian, the most influential of the historians of ancient China, based his famous *Shiji* (Records of the Grand Historian) on an interconnecting chain of biographical portraits. Accounts of princes and saints and the great events and instructive lessons of their lives also make up the bulk of medieval European chronicles—and Russian ones as well.

Yet in the West today academic historians have what seems best described as an ambivalent relationship with biography. We acknowledge the compelling effect of studying a single life. As scholars interested in the human condition, we have to appreciate this elemental frame of the human experience. And we know how useful biography can be for making readers and students feel connected to the past. Biography dramatizes history, allowing us to bring past experiences to life in ways that less personal modes of historiography never quite manage to do. But, for all that, there is something limited—some would say even flimsy—about the genre that sits in the craw of most professional historians. Because we know as historians that one cannot really document the complete history of a life, we assume (as one historian has recently admitted) that "biography is closer to fiction than to history."[12] Some of it is surely just guesswork. We also don't trust the form to tell us much about complex historical issues because a single life is simply too particular—too narrow a window through which to take in the larger view.

Finally, historians have been reluctant to trust biography because the genre is also linked—rightly or wrongly—to the assumption that individuals are decisive in shaping the historical process. On the face of it, this is a strange proposition to object to: History is a human process. How could individuals *not* be decisive in shaping it?

But, at least since Marx, historians have been wary of assuming that "men make their history as they please."[13] Instead, like Marx—and, in some cases, directly following his lead—the majority of the most influential historians of the last hundred years have emphasized the power of impersonal forces in producing historical change. History is made by larger entities such as classes or civilizations, and historical developments are set in motion by the impact of geography or swings in population or collective "mentalities" or other such "structures" that are formed and undone over the very long term and are largely, or even completely, beyond the influence of individuals. Even hugely powerful personalities, such as totalitarian dictators, thus impose their sway over only a limited field of events. They are not shaping history in a broader sense.

Ironically, as Marx was proposing a theory of history as class struggle that minimized the importance of individual agency, another historical thinker, Thomas Carlyle, was formulating the completely opposite view. In what came to be known as the Great Man Theory, Carlyle argued, "the history of the world is but the biography of great men."[14] (In keeping with the prejudices of his time, Carlyle ignored great women—and women in general—in his theory.) Judging from the current swell in biography sales, it is clear that the public, by and large, has followed Carlyle. Marx, meanwhile, has ended up with the professors.

Of course, even as academic historians moved away from the practice of biography over the last century or so, they never abandoned the genre. It remained a part of the historian's tool kit, and today we seem to be in a moment of biographical revival, a swing back towards appreciating biography's potential to illuminate the past. Although ambivalence about the genre remains, much of the most recent methodological writing by historians, borrowing on insights from postmodern theory and literary criticism, emphasizes the need to engage with biography and grapple with, rather than reject, its limitations. The traditional role of the historian as biographer was to chronicle a life. Now historians are more likely to see that lives should be interpreted as a performance, and show greater sensitivity to how individuals shape their lives by developing and acting according to multiple identities in specific historical contexts. As a result, we have seen a resurgence of interest in autobiographies, diaries, memoirs, and the issue of individual reflexivity and subjectivity, including in the Russian and Soviet contexts.[15] Historians today are also more likely to accept that biography is not the preserve of only the famous or influential. Ordinary people, even wholly anonymous individuals, also have biographies that historians can attempt to recover.[16]

In its most basic sense, microhistory suggests a focus on the very small—the scale of a single place or locality or individual. Similar to biography, it is premised on the assumption that when historians work only on large canvases of space and time or only with broad aggregates of politics and society, they risk producing unsustainable generalizations and leaving out too much of the particularism and individual agency that shapes the past. But microhistory also brings something to the table that biography, as a rule, does not. As Jill Lepore has argued, "biography is largely founded on a belief in the singularity and significance of an individual's life and his contribution to history," whereas "microhistory is founded upon almost the opposite assumption: however singular a person's life may be, the value of examining it lies not in its uniqueness, but in its exemplariness, in how that individual's life serves as an allegory for broader issues affecting the culture as a whole."[17]

To date, the most influential microhistories have focused on the lives of poor or obscure individuals, the kinds of people—heretics, the marginal, or women—traditionally ignored by biographers.[18] But the methods of microhistory apply just as well to more recognizable figures. In fact, inasmuch as microhistorical research can readily focus on the famous *and* the forgotten and biographers can write about both the humble *and* the proud, the two modes are naturally positioned to meet in the middle. The only meaningful difference lies in the ultimate goal of the undertaking. Biographers tend to assume that the life in question is important unto itself. The microhistorian uses the life as a device to present a picture of the culture.

The essays in this volume begin from the starting point of microhistory. We fully recognize the singularity of each life in our cast of characters, but in the end each of them is presented, indeed, as a character—as a life that allows us to try to grasp the central but frustratingly slippery question of cross-cultural mixing, acceptance, and prejudice in the broader theater of the Russian experience.

With this in mind, we have avoided presenting our essays as potted biographies: birth, life, death, and a concluding paragraph on significance—the kind of entry you might expect to find in an encyclopedia (or on Wikipedia). Instead, our goal has been to use each individual presented herein to open up a view on the long-running effects of what it meant to live in a densely multicultural neighborhood. How did the realities of ethnic and religious diversity shape lives in Russian spaces? How did these factors affect the power of Russian, Soviet, and post-Soviet rulers? What mark did they leave on the country's forms of culture? How has the practical impact of diversity at the individual level changed over time? Which kinds of diversity have been tolerated and which rejected or persecuted, and when, and why? And where might the "diversity question" in Russian Eurasia be pointed in the future?

The basic objective of our undertaking is to answer these questions by considering thirty-one different human portraits. Journeying into the lives of each of our personalities, we reflect on what diversity meant and how it "worked" at the personal level, while at the same time using this personal view to fill in a fuller picture of the whole.

## EMPIRE IN A PERSONAL KEY

We observe a number of overarching themes emerging from the essays. The most basic and important is simply the utter ordinariness and omnipresence of ethnic and religious diversity in Russian life. When historians investigate topics such as diversity or empire, they tend, naturally enough, to categorize. The result is a persistent bifurcation of the Russian past into two parts: "Russian" history on the one hand

and the history of the empire on the other. Diversity in this equation often ends up curiously extracted from Russian life and incorporated instead into the history of the empire, which we often treat as unfolding "over there," in explicitly "imperial" or "non-Russian" areas rather than in Russia proper. Most broad narratives of Russian history still consider the history of the empire as a spatial and thematic addendum, an extension of Russia's history, rather than as a dynamic of diversity and power that turned like a drive shaft through all facets of the country's development. A similar approach holds in the study of the USSR, where we tend to examine "nationality policy" and the "nationality question" as they pertained to and played out in the "national republics," effectively transforming these issues into their own separate subcategories of the Soviet experience.

When we look into the world of individual experience, however, we see how integral diversity was to the way lives were lived in Russian space. Exposure to a range of peoples and faiths shaped the experience of individuals in the center as well as the borderlands, at court and in the Politburo as well as in Cossack settlements and provincial opera houses. Some social spaces of Russia's past were especially marked by diversity—the tsarist officer corps, for example, or the Bolshevik underground. And the variety of possible cultural and ethnic combinations reflected the enormous variety of Russian Eurasia itself. In Ukrainian areas, we see crossroads of Ukrainian, Jewish, and Russian culture, as captured herein in the life of Lazar' Kaganovich, one of Stalin's most loyal (and fawning) subordinates. In the Baltic, looking into the lives of men like Carl Gustaf Mannerheim, we see confluences of Germans, Finns, Russians, and Swedes; three thousand miles away in eastern Siberia, we find similar diversities combining in the life of Petr (Zhamtsaran) Badmaev, a Christianized Buryat "doctor of Tibetan medicine" whose close connections to the imperial court allowed him to become an influential advocate for Russia's supposedly messianic destiny in East Asia.

Diversity was portable and malleable, useful and dangerous. Using the lives here as guides to some of the varied cultural terrains of the Russian state, we get a clearer view of how individuals responded to, shaped, and were shaped by the mixed environments that surrounded them. Some of our figures stand out as textbook cross-cultural "tricksters," such as Timofei Ankudinov, the son of a merchant from northern Russia who fled Moscow after burning his wife to death and made a career out of pretending to be the son of the deposed Russian tsar, Vasilii Shuiskii. For close to a decade in the mid-seventeenth century, Ankudinov made the rounds of foreign courts, looking for support for his claim to the throne. His ploys involved, among other things, converting to Catholicism at the Vatican and promising the Pope that he would help convert all his countrymen once he got back to Russia. (This seems to have been Ankudinov's way of trying to curry favor with the Catholic Poles. Once he got to Ukraine, however, he quickly realized that he was better off being Orthodox, so he hushed up about his "conversion.")

If Ankudinov moved on a path from Russianness to non-Russianness (at least temporarily), other individuals moved in the opposite direction. Many of the figures featured in our essays underscore the enduring allure and usefulness of Russian culture to foreigners from other states as well as to non-Russians whose lands became incorporated into the empire. Before Catherine the Great, for example, was either Catherine or "Great," she was a princess from a relatively minor German principality brought to Russia to marry the tsar (who also, interestingly enough, was a German). Like Empress Alexandra who would follow her a hundred years later, Catherine became Russian by following a crash course in devotion to her new country that involved converting to Orthodoxy, taking a new name, and identifying with Russian culture and history, while at the same time remaining—and excelling at being—European.

Petr Ivanovich Bagration, the son of royalty from the Georgian kingdom of Kartli who became a prominent commander in Russia's war against Napoléon in 1812, offers another example of a foreigner who made a similar journey from the outside in. His Russian contemporaries saw him as "purely Georgian" in his appearance, but Bagration thought of himself as a "pure Russian," by which he meant, in the first order, that he was unswervingly loyal to his Russian sovereign but also moved by and proud of his Russian fatherland (he used the term *otechestvo* repeatedly in his correspondence). By 1812, he had become so Russian in fact that he was associated with the so-called "Russian party" at court and spoke openly of excessive foreign influence in the army. As he put it to one of his patrons in St. Petersburg shortly after the Battle of Smolensk, "For god's sake, send me anywhere else you desire . . . I cannot remain here: the entire headquarters is so filled with Germans a Russian cannot even breathe."

For other individuals, however, the movement towards Russianness was considerably more ambivalent and often carried fateful consequences. The writer Nikolai Gogol went to St. Petersburg as a young man in the 1830s and very quickly became a Russian literary celebrity, but he did so by repackaging himself to suit the nationalist expectations of the Russian elite of the time. This meant dropping the Polish angles of his heritage and giving his Ukrainian background the kind of stylized folkloric tint that made his not-quite-Russian provenance colorful rather than threatening. Gogol effectively became Ukrainian in the Russian manner, yet at the same time, he also tried as best he could to be Russian in *his* manner, which meant articulating a sense of identity as a *Russian* writer who just happened also to be Ukrainian. The ambiguity that resulted from this cross-cultural blending tracked him his whole life and led to prolonged bouts of unresolved soul searching. In public, he presented the profile of the proud Russian patriot and harmonious Russian-Ukrainian hybrid. But more private sources reveal that he saw his in-betweenness in far less comfortable terms.

Jews also felt the painful ambiguity of in-betweenness. Herein we see this reflected in the life of the virtuoso pianist and composer Anton Rubinstein, who acknowledged his family's Jewish roots going back to the shtetl lands of what is now Moldova but otherwise did everything in his power to minimize his Jewishness. Rubinstein thought of himself as a Russian and a Muscovite and spent his creative life building up a conservatory system that helped to institutionalize the international renown of Russian music, but this did not stop his Orthodox Russian critics from using his Jewishness against him when it served their purposes. The famous art critic Vladimir

Stasov went so far as to denounce Rubinstein as a foreigner who was supposedly all but congenitally incapable of understanding the country he lived in.

The antisemitism that Rubinstein encountered is a reminder of the limits of diversity that were also always present in one form or another in the various successive political orders that controlled Russian Eurasia. Diversity proved an advantage for some individuals and communities, while a disadvantage for others, and the rules of multiethnic cohabitation and advancement were flexible and changed over time.

The essays in our collection reveal this process of change in a number of ways. We see it strikingly, for example, in the long trajectory of a family of prominent Muslims, the Tevkelevs of the southern Urals. As early as the late seventeenth century, members of the Tevkelev clan were assisting the Russians as translators in their dealings with Bashkir and Kazakh nomads. Shortly thereafter, some began converting to Orthodoxy. Others remained Muslim but continued serving the Russians as leaders of their community within the imperial system. This mutually beneficial relationship between the Tevkelevs and the empire lasted for the better part of two centuries before changing dramatically for the worse in the last decade or so before 1917 as the family was squeezed out of imperial service by Russification policies driven by official fears of nationalism and separatism within the Muslim community. Kutlu-Mukhammad Tevkelev, the most prominent family member of his generation and a leader of the Muslim faction in the Duma, responded to this anti-Muslim pressure by siding with "the people" and denouncing the government. Once loyal allies of the empire, the Tevkelevs thus found themselves pushed into imperial resistance.

There were other periods of change as well. As Muscovy turned into the Russian Empire during the muddled late seventeenth and early eighteenth centuries, the emerging Petrine order began to favor what would become a new definition of diversity for Russian elites, a model of Russianness that valued the kind of responsible Europeanization that we see in the life of the boyar Boris Kurakin, a diplomat under Peter the Great, who managed to style himself at once as a "honorable person of the Muscovite nation" and a "European minister and prince" during his extensive sojourns in Europe. Then, in the early nineteenth century—as Gogol's case suggests—the acceptable parameters of diversity and Russianness changed again as understandings of Russian cultural nationalism began to grow and the new Russians of the Romantic age, although no less cosmopolitan than their forebears, were expected to be more connected to "true"—that is, supposedly eternal and unchanging—Russian values.

By far the most momentous and rapid change, however, came not during the tsarist era but as the tsarist era unraveled. A number of the personal portraits here open a view on the way in which World War I, the revolution, and the subsequent collapse of the empire profoundly shifted pathways of ethnic identity and practice. Some imperial individuals featured in our essays, like the Russianized Fenno-Swedish nobleman Carl Gustaf Mannerheim, found themselves fundamentally reoriented by the swirl of events—in Mannerheim's case; he went from being a loyal general of the Russian imperial army to becoming the de facto head of the Finnish state in 1918. Others, by contrast, emerged as would-be supranational leaders and patriots of the new Soviet Union. The transformation experienced by these new "Soviet people" was, on the face of it, even stranger than Mannerheim's—if only because the USSR, unlike Finland, was not a national remnant of empire created out of a single, relatively homogenous part of the imperial rubble. Instead it was an expressly anti-imperial multinational socialist state that took over most of the former territory of the empire, profoundly reorganizing it in the process.

The biggest change was the new Soviet state's publicly stated rejection of all national prejudices (such as antisemitism, which was dismissed as being a noxious product of the bourgeois order) and its positive embrace of nationality as a central organizing principle of social life. Soviet leaders, in effect, became champions of diversity, turning multinationality into the equivalent of a public virtue. They promoted national minorities, preserved national languages, and sponsored national folk ensembles. Every Soviet citizen had their nationality of birth—be it Russian, Ukrainian, Tatar, Jewish, Armenian, or Yakut—typed into their internal passport. In this collection, we see the new possibilities created by these policies in the unusual careers of men like Kaganovich and Stalin, the one a Ukrainian Jew who became a Russophilic un-Jewish "internationalist" in charge of virtually all of Soviet industry in the 1930s; and the other, his boss, a Russophilic Georgian who ruled the country as a largely unchallenged dictator for close to a quarter century. Millions of non-Russians became Soviet in large part because the Soviet system created ways for them to identify simultaneously with their own heritage, with Russia, and with a sense of Sovietness.

Yet in the Soviet lives featured herein we also see the paradoxes and profound injustices of the Soviet Union's diversity regime. Like the tsarist empire it replaced, the USSR erected hierarchies of ethnic difference that favored certain peoples and national orientations. Thus, for all the communist cheering about diversity, some diversity was attacked and expunged. "Nationalities" deemed disloyal to the party-state found themselves brutally denationalized. Such was the case, for example, for Soviet Koreans, Germans, Chechens, Ingush, Crimean Tatars, and other "punished" peoples who were deported and stripped of their rights at different points under Stalin. Official anti-Jewish policies continued. Heavy-handed pro-Russian measures of the sort that might have appealed to the supporters of late tsarist Russification also resumed. Multinationality, supposedly effortless and natural, could be a complicated, even painful condition at a personal level. We find some of the ambiguities of Soviet diversity reflected in the experiences of the famous Russian poet Anna Akhmatova and the Kazakh writer Mukhtar Auezov, both of whom moved uneasily among different cultural identities—Russian, Ukrainian, and "Oriental" in the case of Akhmatova; Russian, Kazakh, and "Central Asian" in the case of Auezov—although both were, in different ways, Soviet as well.

Finally, these chapters also lead us into the current moment, another time of transition for understandings and practices of diversity in the Russian zone. What does it mean to be Russian or non-Russian in post-Soviet Russia? How much does the Soviet and broader historical experience of nationality and multinationality weigh on this particular juncture? How much of a transition is actually taking place? Are we seeing a departure from old ways of cultural assimilation and combination toward some new paradigm? Or is today simply an extension of yesterday, repackaged but not substantially changed? It is hard to make out clear answers to these questions because we are in the moment ourselves. What we can see best is the continuing reality of diversity—and its persistent complexity—in Russian lives.

The mystery writer Boris Akunin, arguably the most popular living author in Russia today, is Georgian by birth, culturally Russian *and* Soviet, and, in professional terms, a celebrity product of early-twenty-first-century globalization. Vladislav Surkov, another personality explored herein, is the son of a mixed Russian-Chechen marriage who grew up in Chechnya before cutting a remarkable path from rock-and-roll singer to prominent political advisor to Russian president Vladimir Putin. (Surkov is best known for his strong support of Putin's policies to reduce regional autonomy and reinforce the power of the center, including endorsing a hard line towards his home region of Chechnya.) Born on the periphery, Surkov appears to have seen his future in a bright star shining over the Kremlin and doggedly followed it. In this respect, he moved along a path similar to the ones traveled by countless borderland people before him, taking advantage of the opportunities empire provides (although, as far as we know, he is the first heavy metalist to do so).

## CONCLUSION

The essays of this collection thus invite us to reflect on a key dimension of the Russian experience played out over the long term. Spanning more than five centuries and four political orders, our thirty-one guides show us a rich panorama of cross-cultural diversity, letting us see how questions of ethnic and religious belonging and action "worked" at the personal level. In the process, these life stories help us to see not only how ordinary it was for men and women in Russian space to be multicultural, but also some of the recurring possibilities as well as painful limitations that flowed from this condition. For whatever its particular effect on a given life, cultural diversity invariably carried some sort of meaning. Like all things ordinary, it was at the same time always influential.

In his inventive self-portrait of the Chinese emperor Kangxi, the historian Jonathan Spence quotes French novelist Marcel Proust: "An hour is not just an hour; it is a vase full of perfume, sounds, projects, and moods." Spence notes that the idea captured by Proust in this evocative statement is daunting for historians.[19] Given how much there is to say about a single hour, how can we hope to document the fullness of any past moment, let alone the enormity of a past life, even one that was otherwise uneventful or ordinary? Yet, in a sense, the distance that historians have to cross between the inevitably limited sources they can use to describe a life and the meaning that they can take from it is part of the promise of microhistory—it is the alluring idea that we can, indeed, sometimes step into a cavernous room through the smallest of doorways. In the essays that follow, the room we enter is Russia's remarkably diverse and complex multicultural society. Our doorways are thirty-one lives. Our tour ends in Moscow in the early twenty-first century in the company of a rock star turned Kremlin ideologue. We begin five hundred years earlier, following the eastward journey of a Cossack conqueror.

NOTES

1. Quoted in Orlando Figes, *A People's Tragedy: A History of the Russian Revolution* (New York: Penguin, 1997), 26.

2. Letters from Alexandra to Nicholas from August 22, 1915, and December 4, 1916, reproduced in *Letters of the Tsaritsa to the Tsar, 1914–1916* (Hattiesburg, Miss.: Academic International, 1970), 114, 442. Quoted in Mark Steinberg and Vladimir Khrustalev, "Nicholas and Alexandra, an Intellectual Portrait," in *The Fall of the Romanovs: Political Dreams and Personal Struggles in a Time of Revolution* (New Haven, Conn.: Yale University Press, 1995), 26.

3. Ibid., 5.

4. Ibid., 29.

5. Alfred Rieber, "Stalin, Man of the Borderlands," *American Historical Review* 106, no. 5 (December 2001): 1651–91.

6. See "From the Editors: The Imperial Turn," *Kritika* 7, no. 4 (Fall 2006): 705–12; and Glennys Young, "Fetishizing the Soviet Collapse: Historical Rupture and the Historiography of (Early) Soviet Socialism," *Russian Review* 66, no. 1 (January 2007): 95–122.

7. For an excellent survey of this scholarship, see Nicholas Breyfogle, "Enduring Imperium: Russia/Soviet Union/Eurasia as Multipethnic, Multiconfessional Space," *Ab Imperio* 1 (2008): 75–129. See also the collection issued by the editors of the journal *Ab Imperio*: I Gerasimov, et al., eds., *Novaia imperskaia istoriia postsovetskogo prostranstva* (Kazan', 2004).

8. See, for example, Stephen Kotkin, "Mongol Commonwealth? Exchange and Governance across the Post-Mongol Space," *Kritika: Explorations in Russian and Eurasian History* 8, no. 3 (2007): 487–531; and Mark von Hagen, "Empires, Borderlands, and Diasporas: Eurasia as Anti-Paradigm for the Post-Soviet Era," *American Historical Review* 109, no. 2 (2004): 445–68. On the shift from tsarist to Soviet empire, see the forum in *Slavic Review* 65, no. 2 (2006), "The Multiethnic Soviet Union in Comparative Perspective," which features contributions from Adeeb Khalid, Adrienne Edgar, Peter Blitstein, and Mark Beissinger. Two valuable collections are Ronald Grigor Suny and Terry Martin, eds., *A State of Nations: Empire and Nation-Making in the Age of Lenin and Stalin* (New York: Oxford University Press, 2001); and Jane Burbank, Mark von Hagen, and Anatolyi Remnev, eds., *Russian Empire: Space, People, Power, 1700–1930* (Bloomington: Indiana University Press, 2006).

9. For the text of the anthem, see the Russian government's official site on national symbols: www.gov.ru/main/symbols/gsrf1.html. The same composer—the recently deceased Sergei Mikhalkov—penned the lyrics to both the 1944 Soviet anthem and the current Russian anthem approved in 2000. For the newer version, Mikhalkov simply replaced his original description of the country as a "strong bulwark of the friendship of peoples [*Druzhby narodov nadezhnyi oplot*]!" with "age-old union of fraternal peoples [*Bratskikh narodov soiuz vekovoi*]."

10. See Shane O'Rourke, *The Cossacks* (Manchester, UK: Manchester University Press, 2007).

11. Charles Steinwedel, "Invisible Threads of Empire: State, Religion, and Ethnicity in Tsarist Bashkiriia, 1773–1917" (Ph.D. diss., Columbia University, 1999).

12. Alice Kessler-Harris, "Why Biography?" *American Historical Review* 114, no. 3 (June 2009): 625.

13. See Karl Marx, "The Eighteenth Brumaire of Louis Bonaparte," in *The Marx-Engels Reader,* 2nd ed., ed. Robert C. Tucker (New York: Norton, 1978), 595.

14. See Thomas Carlyle, *On Heroes and Hero Worship and the Heroic in History* (London, 1841).

15. On the Russian context, see Laura Engelstein and Stephanie Sandler, eds., *Self and Story in Russian History* (Ithaca, N.Y.: Cornell University Press, 2000); Sheila Fitzpatrick and Yuri Slezkine, eds., *In the Shadow of Revolution: Life Stories of Russian Women from 1917 to the Second World War* (Princeton, N.J.: Princeton University Press, 2000); Anna Krylova, "In Their Own Words? Soviet Women Writers and the Search for the Self," in Adele Marie Barker and Jehanne M. Gheith, eds., *A History of Women's Writing in Russia* (New York: Cambridge University Press, 2002), 243–63; Jochen Hellbeck and Klaus Heller, eds., *Autobiographical Practices in Russia/Autobiographische Praktiken in Russland* (Göttingen, 2004); Jochen Hellbeck, *Revolution on My Mind: Writing a Diary under Stalin* (Cambridge, Mass.: Harvard University Press, 2006); Alexander Etkind, "Soviet Subjectivity: Torture for the Sake of Salvation?" *Kritika* 6, no. 1 (Winter 2005): 171–86; Julia Herzberg and Christoph Schmidt, eds., *Vom Wir zum Ich: Individuum und Autobiographik im Zarenreich* (Cologne, 2007); David L. Ransel, *A Russian Merchant's Tale: The Life and Adventures of Ivan Alekseevich Tolchënov, Based on his Diary* (Bloomington: Indiana University Press, 2009); and Jochen Hellbeck, "Galaxy of Black Stars: The Power of Soviet Biography," *American Historical Review* 114, no. 3 (June 2009): 615–24.

16. Historians don't even need documents to write a biography of ordinary people in the past; in some cases, bones are enough. See the interesting discussion in Robin Fleming, "Writing Biography at the Edge of History," *American Historical Review* 114, no. 3 (June 2009): 606–14.

17. Jill Lepore, "Historians Who Love Too Much: Reflections on Microhistory and Biography," *The Journal of American History* 88, no. 1 (June 2001): 133.

18. See, for example, Jonathan Spence, *The Question of Hu* (New York: Vintage, 1989); Laurel Thatcher Ulrich, *A Midwife's Tale: The Life of Martha Ballard Based on Her Diary, 1785–1812* (New York: Knopf, 1990); Carlo Ginzburg, *The Cheese and the Worms: The Cosmos of a Sixteenth-Century Miller* (Baltimore: Johns Hopkins University Press, 1993); Paul E. Johnson and Sean Wilentz, *The Kingdom of Matthias* (New York: Oxford University Press, 1994); John Demos, *The Unredeemed Captive: A Family Story from Early America* (New York: Knopf, 1994); and works by Natalie Zemon Davis, including *The Return of Martin Guerre* (Cambridge, Mass.: Harvard University Press, 1983); *Women on the Margins: Three Seventeenth-Century Lives* (Cambridge, Mass.: Harvard University Press, 1995); and *Trickster Travels: A Sixteenth-Century Muslim Between Worlds* (New York: Hill and Wang, 2006).

19. Jonathan D. Spence, *Emperor of China: Self-Portrait of Kang-Hsi* (New York: Vintage, 1988), xxv–xxvi.

Vasilii Surikov, *Ermak's Conquest of Siberia* (1895). Wikimedia Commons.

# 1

# Ermak Timofeevich

## (1530s/40s–1585)

### WILLARD SUNDERLAND

Vasilii Surikov's masterpiece *Ermak's Conquest of Siberia* (1895) takes up an entire wall in St. Petersburg's Russian Museum. It is a typical battle scene, painted in the realist style that made Surikov famous, with the Russians arrayed in the foreground and the native Siberians facing them across a river. Approaching the painting from across the gallery, we need only a moment to realize who will carry the day. The Russians stand like a bristling wall, staring defiantly at the foe, their banners high, and smoke clouding from their muskets. The angle Surikov chose for the scene places us on the Russians' side. The natives, meanwhile, stare back at us from the opposite bank, close enough that we can see the fear in their eyes.

At first, it is hard to locate the hero of the painting, but then we find him, just to the left of the canvas's center: a determined warrior under the banners, outfitted with a steel helmet and a breastplate. He looks out at the natives, his arm outstretched toward the opposite bank, pointing to victory and reaching for the future. This is Ermak.[1]

Or, rather, this is the Ermak of nineteenth-century nationalist myth, Ermak the iconic hero, the great Muscovite conquistador, the Russian Cortés. Almost nothing is known of the real Ermak. We don't know when or exactly where he was born, how he ended up in Siberia, how many men were in his expedition, or even when exactly he "conquered" the region. All we know for certain, it seems, is that he did conquer it—although even this, it turns out, is not quite true. Ermak and his men at most temporarily conquered only the far western part of the region that we now call Siberia. The great conqueror never saw most of the vast territory he supposedly grafted onto the Russian state. The famous battle with the forces of Khan Kuchum depicted in Surikov's painting occurred on the Irtysh River—most historians believe—in October 1582. Ermak died a few years later, in 1585. But the immense spaces of Siberia beyond the Irtysh were acquired by Muscovy, in fits and starts, over the course of the following century.

Ermak, then, is a useful figure to consider as we think about the history of empires and how to study them. Empires are large territories made up of diverse peoples.

They tend to be built by a combination of war, diplomacy, and outright purchase, among other means, and held together through a fluid balance of threats and rewards. The individuals who help to create them, however—especially as we go deeper into the past—are often obscure, and their acts of empire building are rarely as simple as they seem. In Ermak's case, it turns out that most of what we know about him is myth or legend of some sort. But in this respect, too, Ermak is useful; his case reminds us that myth itself is an integral element of empire building. Indeed, the mythical Ermak—or rather, Ermaks, since there are several mythical versions—easily tells us as much about the empire as the historical Ermak ever could.

## ERMAK AND SIBERIA

Our sources on Ermak are limited. The materials of the Siberian expedition have not survived. As a result, with the exception of a few chancellery documents from the period, the only information we have comes from a handful of chronicles, or epic tales, that were composed by scholars and religious men during the century or so following his death. As tools for reconstructing his life, they are woefully incomplete—and inconsistent on top of that. All we have are a few plausible facts on which to hang his story and no way at all of looking into his thoughts.[2]

It's fitting then that we barely know anything about his birth or where he grew up. All we can guess from the chronicles is that he appears to have been between forty and fifty at the time of the Siberian expeditions, which would mean that he was born in the 1530s or early 1540s. One text, supposedly drawing on a statement by Ermak himself, tells us Ermak was the son of a boat builder from the Urals and his true name was Vasilii Alenin. (His father's name was Timofei, hence the patronymic, Timofeevich. In this telling, the name Ermak is simply a nickname, in others it is suggested to have been a corruption of the name German or Ermolai.) The claim that Ermak hailed from the Urals has been disputed by a number of historians, however, and several other locales—from the Don River region in the south to the lands of the White Sea in the north—have been proposed as his place of birth. In fact, the only consistently repeated tidbit on his early life is the allusion to his time—perhaps as much as twenty years—spent on the Volga River, where he lived as an ataman, or leader, of a Cossack band.

This detail hints at the most reliable point we can make about Ermak's life—that he was a product of the frontier, a creation of the limits of Muscovite society. In his time, Cossacks were the ultimate "people of the edge"—mixed bands made up of nomads and peasant runaways who established robber enclaves on the great unclaimed grasslands south of Muscovy. (The term "Cossack" derives from a Turkic word for "freebooter" or "outlaw.") They were largely of Orthodox faith, and their broader culture, reflecting the mixings of the frontier, was a blend of Slavic and Turkic influences. Their most distinctive trait, however, was their independence. Living on the steppe beyond the formal reach of the Muscovite state (or other neighboring states, for that matter), they enjoyed a freedom of movement that peasants and townsmen within

Muscovy typically did not. The tsar was simply too far away and too weak to tell them what to do.[3]

In practical terms, this meant that Cossacks tended to make their living as either mercenaries or pirates. Exactly why Ermak chose this career path and when he made his way to the Volga region is hard to know. In the 1560s and 1570s, the sprawling lands around the river were being incorporated into the empire following Moscow's conquest of the khanates of Kazan' and Astrakhan' a decade or so earlier. The process of incorporation was uneven, however, and there were revolts and sporadic resistance on the part of peoples in the region as well as raids by nomads from the steppe. In this uncertain post-conquest moment, Ermak could easily have served as a mercenary Cossack commander and defended the Muscovite forts that were starting to appear on the river, or he could have emerged as a leader of one of the many outlaw bands that took advantage of the general lawlessness of the times to plunder boats and caravans. It is possible, of course, that he did a bit of both.

What we can say with more certainty is that the world surrounding him on the Volga at the time was a place of diverse peoples and faiths—Muslims, Orthodox, and animists; Slavic, Turkic, and Finnic groups; peasants, Cossacks, and nomads—whose communities intersected in complicated ways. Tension and violence were common, but so, too, was a certain amount of cross-cultural accommodation.[4] Like the frontier Ermak would encounter later in Siberia, the Volga in this period was a "middle ground" characterized by intermittent and fluid relationships between groups, a place of mixed peoples and changing allegiances. Despite the rigid dichotomies suggested by the Church and later nationalist historians, it is difficult to find a consistent dividing line between "Russians" and Orthodox on the one hand, and "non-Russians" and "pagan" peoples and Muslims (*busurmany*) on the other. The state was present but only incompletely so.

That the Volga, the Urals, and Siberia would share basic similarities as fluid frontier zones in the late sixteenth century is not surprising. The regions belonged to a common Eurasian cultural ecosystem; all three had previously been part of the Golden Horde, the westernmost extension of the old Mongol Empire; and each was tied to the other—and to peoples beyond—by longstanding patterns of contact. Russian interaction with the Urals and the western edges of Siberia goes back to the eleventh century, when traders from towns such as Novgorod ventured along northern rivers to points as far east as the lower Ob and Irtysh, where they negotiated with or forced the peoples they found there to pay what later Russians would call *yasak,* or tribute in the form of furs.[5] Ermak's campaign marked a turning point inasmuch as his "conquest" unfolded in the south, which was more populous and politically organized than the northern part of Siberia, where Russian contact had begun. But the general eastward movement that brought him to Siberia in the first place was well underway by the time he appeared.

In fact, as soon as the Muscovites began their takeover of the Volga in the 1550s, the interlocking pathways of the region helped to pull them further east. With the Volga khanates no longer able to protect or pay them, Nogay and Bashkir nomads on the lower reaches of the river and the steppes of the southern Urals realigned their interests and declared their loyalty to Moscow. Meanwhile, Tsar Ivan IV—later, and better, known as Ivan the Terrible—moved swiftly to exploit his advantage beyond the Volga and throughout the Kama River basin and the Urals by doling out huge tracts of land and tax breaks to his servitors; first and foremost among these were the Stroganovs, an enterprising merchant family that would shortly emerge as the leading corporate entity of the region. Soon peasants, serfs as well as runaways, began to arrive on the Kama and in the Urals. Salt works opened. Mines were dug. And furs were collected, as they had been for centuries, the only difference now was that they piled up in the coffers of Moscow rather than in the Golden Horde or Kazan'.

In 1555, Khan Ediger, ruler of Sibir', also requested the protection of Tsar Ivan, dutifully pledging his share of yasak in return. Ediger's realm, which was also known simply as Sibir, was centered in what is now southwestern Siberia, near the confluence of the Irtysh and Tobol rivers. Like Kazan', Astrakhan', and Moscow (as well as the Crimean Khanate), it was a successor state to the Golden Horde, whose population was a hodge-podge of hunter-gatherer and nomadic tribes—Ostiaks (Khanty), Voguls (Mansi), and others—ruled over by a town-based Muslim Tatar elite. Conditions in the khanate were unstable; civil war was raging between Ediger and a rival named Kuchum. In fact, Ediger's readiness to ally with Moscow was motivated at least in part by the hope that the tsar would help him in his struggle. (Kuchum, meanwhile, had the backing of the khan of Bukhara.) In 1563, however, Ediger lost and Kuchum took the throne. At first Kuchum continued his predecessor's policy of rendering yasak to Moscow, but by the 1570s relations had deteriorated, and he stopped sending furs.

In the Russian chronicles, Khan Kuchum's decision to break with Moscow is described as the foulest sort of treachery. If we take a broader view, however, we can see it as a fairly predictable result of the tensions produced by the expansion of Muscovite power. Led in part by the dynamism of the Stroganovs, the Russian presence in the Urals was growing steadily in the 1560s and 1570s, bringing Muscovite outposts ever closer to Kuchum's domains. This was a problem because the two states were vying, in effect, for the same revenue base—the yasak-paying peoples between them. As a result, clashes were all but inevitable, and raids and abuses occurred on both sides. Kuchum, according to the Russian chronicles, plotted to make war on Moscow. Meanwhile, the Stroganovs recruited their own fighting men, which involved making appeals and offering payments to the most obvious pool of nearby military specialists—the Cossacks living near the Volga and Ural rivers. According to at least one chronicle, they specifically called for Ataman Ermak.

Whether this is, in fact, why Ermak appeared in the Stroganovs' domains in the Urals in the late 1570s is impossible to prove. But we have confirmation from all the chronicles that he was there by 1579 and that he was involved in organizing a military attack on Kuchum. The attack was probably conceived at first as a raid and may have been Ermak's own initiative. We have no proof, for example, that Tsar Ivan ordered the "conquest" of Siberia—in fact, it seems more likely that he learned about it after the fact. There is even some doubt that the Stroganovs would have supported such an idea, given the more pressing need to have the Cossacks provide protection for their holdings closer by. Might Ermak have initially intended to make a limited strike, but his plans grew more ambitious as the expedition got under way?

All we know for certain is that the force—about five hundred Cossacks, although the number varies in the different accounts—obtained supplies from the Stroganovs and headed into Kuchum's territory in the summer and fall of 1581 or 1582, traveling by boat and making portages between the rivers as necessary to move eastward. In addition to his Cossacks, the troops under Ermak's command included foreign mercenaries (probably a few Poles or Germans), as well as non-Russian warriors and "guides . . . and interpreters who knew the infidel language." In this sense, Ermak's men may be characterized more accurately as a frontier fighting force rather than a Russian army, as they are often described. (A similar mixture of peoples made up the fighters on Kuchum's side.) Myth has turned the "conquest" into a story of Russians versus natives—in particular, Kuchum's Tatar warriors—but realities on the ground were more complicated than this.

Given the inconsistent dates of the sources, it is difficult to say how long it took Ermak to advance into the khanate—perhaps a year, perhaps as little as a few months. The chronicles all agree, however, that the first part of the campaign culminated in a "great battle" with the "Kuchumites"—the one depicted in Surikov's painting—near the Siberian capital of Kashlyk on the Irtysh River, located some ten miles from the modern city of Tobol'sk. There, according to the *Remezov Chronicle,* as Kuchum looked down from river's hilly bank, "the Cossacks poured forth . . . crying with one voice, 'God is with us!' . . . And all together they went, and there was a great battle. . . . Kuchum shot arrows from the rise, while the Cossacks fired [guns] back upon the pagans. . . . And so they fought for three days without rest."[6] Shortly after the battle, the Cossacks then entered Kashlyk where Ermak formalized his "conquest" in the traditional Eurasian manner by accepting yasak and "gifts" from the defeated Siberians. He also sent messengers to Tsar Ivan in Moscow to relay the news.

This was the high point of the campaign, the famous and later much mythologized "taking of Siberia" (*sibirskoe vziatie*). Not long thereafter, however, things began to go wrong. Although the tsar sent reinforcements that allowed Ermak to renew his campaign and widen his collection of tribute, the expedition in the end proved to be too small and too far away. Kuchum and his allies, who had fled the defeat at Kashlyk, now changed their tactics. Rather than seeking set battles with the Muscovites, they began instead to hound them by fighting a guerrilla war of ambushes and attacks on their supplies. In late 1583, one of Ermak's most notable fellow atamans, Ivan Kol'tso, was killed in a surprise attack. The military governor dispatched to support Ermak died of hunger in the winter of 1584–85, along with many of the men in his force and ordinary Cossacks. Then, finally, in the summer of 1585, Ermak himself met his end by drowning in the Irtysh River as he tried to escape another Tatar ambush. Legend has it that he was, ironically, weighted down by the chain mail he had received from the tsar as a gift after his earlier victory over Kuchum.

Having lost their leader, the remaining men soon decided to abandon the campaign and withdrew from Kashlyk. Of the more than five hundred Cossacks who entered Siberia with Ermak, only ninety or so returned to the Urals in 1585.

## Myth, History, Mythistory

This, as best we can tell, is the life of the historical Ermak. In truth, however, Ermak has been far more important as a mythical figure—particularly as a symbol of Russian conquest. In fact, over the centuries there have been a number of representations of Ermak, each of them speaking to a different dimension of the conquest narrative.

We see this in the first instance in the chronicles where Ermak appears as a valiant warrior and trailblazer for the true faith. As the Esipov Chronicle puts it, the brave ataman may have died before seeing his full victory, but in the aftermath of his "conquest," other Russians arrived and in time "the Siberian land became illuminated by the sun of the Gospels . . . cities were founded, holy churches and monasteries of God were raised . . . [and] having witnessed the Christian faith, many unbelievers were baptized."[7] The chronicles stop short of offering panegyrics to the conquest (such accolades came in later sources), but they clearly present it as a profound turning point, and set up Ermak himself as a kind of Moses figure. He is the courageous prophet who leads the Christians to the brink of Siberia's Orthodox transformation yet falls just short of getting there himself.

In popular legends and songs about Ermak, which date as far back as the earliest Siberian chronicles and abound in Russian folklore, we find a similar pro-conquest tilt, but with a somewhat different emphasis. Rather than touting his achievements as an Orthodox pioneer, the tales evoke the wildness and daring of his background as a would-be outlaw on the Volga and his subsequent transformation into a larger-than-life superhero of conquest who "takes" not only Siberia but Kazan' and Astrakhan' as well. In fact, in some versions of the tales, he comes up with the idea of conquest "on his own" as a way of earning a pardon from the tsar for his earlier robberies and misdeeds. Thus, again his image serves to naturalize conquest, transforming it into a lesson of personal redemption and virtuous loyalty to the tsar.[8]

Yet by far the most influential turn in the myth of Ermak dates to the second half of the eighteenth and especially the nineteenth centuries, when his image changed again to reflect the rising power of Russian national identity (*narodnost'*). In this period, for example, we find the first associations between Ermak and the Spanish conquistadors— including portraits (*parsuny*) in which Ermak appears as a would-be Iberian hidalgo— all as a way of underscoring Russia's place among the great empires of the time. As historian Nikolai Karamzin put it in the 1820s, Ermak was the "Russian Pizarro"—"no less terrifying to the savages than the Spaniard but gentler on humanity."[9]

Over the decades that followed, the association with Russian nationality deepened. Ermak became one of Russia's "most remarkable people," a true "Russian person," a "national figure . . . beloved by the Russian folk"—extolled in textbooks and dramas and celebrated in monuments.[10] For the monarchy, he was a useful symbol of the supposedly time-honored bond between the autocracy and the people. Meanwhile for intellectuals from Romantics to populists, he evoked the daring and fortitude of the common Russian man as well as the panache of the benevolent outlaw and the dependable manly values of pre-Petrine Russia. Not surprisingly, he proved especially popular in places such as the Don Region, where local patriots claimed him as a Don Cossack, and Siberia, where he was turned into a kind of regional founding father. On the tercentenary of the conquest in 1881, one Siberian enthusiast described Ermak as "a personality of powerful character and energy" whose singular achievement was to plant "the first step of popular colonization" on Siberian soil.[11] By the end of the 1800s, Ermak, like other founding fathers elsewhere, had evolved into the sort of familiar and reassuring national figure whose image worked at once high and low. He might feature in Surikov's great painting and just as readily star in an advertisement for farm equipment. In 1898, his name was given to the world's first polar icebreaker, the ship that some Russians dreamed would forge a path through the Arctic all the way to Asia.

With the exception of a few short-lived moments when Ermak was derided as a cruel imperialist by Communist critics, this heroic national image carried over into the Soviet period and is still the dominant representation of Ermak in Russia today. It is easy, of course, to point out that this representation greatly exaggerates and simplifies the historical record. At the same time, it is also true that the record itself is so slight we cannot really be sure what we know. Indeed, so much of the mythmaking about Ermak has arisen precisely because of this uncertainty, and in time the myths have taken on remarkable power. As one historian has put it, "myths gain their potency from their ability to persuade."[12] What Ermak persuades us to see is the rightness of the Russian conquest. His is the great foundation tale, the story that explains why the conquest had to be.[13] In history, frontiers are confusing, and empire building is a complicated business, but in myth they become easier to understand and to believe in.

Making myths can involve outright falsification, but a more innocent form of wishful thinking is often just as important. As Surikov told the poet Maksimilian Voloshin some years after completing his famous *Ermak,* "In a historical painting there's no need to render things exactly as they were, the important thing is the possibility, the idea that things might have been that way." He went on: "The essence of a historical painting is the guesswork [*ugadyvanie*]. . . . When [you depict] everything exactly as it was, it just doesn't feel right [*protivno dazhe*]."[14] In many ways, this statement seems to apply to the whole Ermak story, which has grown and changed so much in the telling over the centuries. The important thing is not so much what may or may not have happened, but rather the guesswork involved.

NOTES

1. On the history of Surikov's painting, see S. V. Korovkevich, *Pokorenie Sibiri Ermakom: Kartina V .I. Surikova* (Leningrad, 1963).

2. The fullest English-language overview of the chronicles relating to Ermak appears in Terence Armstrong, *Yermak's Campaign in Siberia: A Selection of Documents*, Tatiana Minorsky and David Wileman, trans. (London: Hakluyt Society, 1975). The best most recent historical treatments of Ermak as a historical figure are by the noted Russian scholar Ruslan Skrynnikov. See his *Ermak* (Moscow, 2008) and *Sibirskaia ekspeditsiia Ermaka*, 2nd rev. ed. (Novosibirsk, 1986).

3. On Cossacks as peoples shaped by "edge habitats," see Thomas M. Barrett, *At the Edge of Empire: The Terek Cossacks and the North Caucasus Frontier, 1700–1860* (Boulder, Colo.: Westview, 1999), 7–8 and passim.

4. For an interpretation that emphasizes frontier conflict, see Michael Khodarkovsky, *Russia's Steppe Frontier: The Making of a Colonial Empire* (Bloomington: Indiana University Press, 2002), 7–45. On the steppe frontier as a "middle ground" that included both conflict and accommodation, see Brian J. Boeck, *Imperial Boundaries: Cossack Communities and Empire-Building in the Age of Peter the Great* (New York: Cambridge University Press, 2009), 15.

5. On early Russian contact with Siberia, see James Forsyth, *A History of the Peoples of Siberia: Russia's North Asian Colony, 1581–1990* (New York: Cambridge University Press, 1992), 1–27.

6. Semen Ul'ianovich Remezov, "Istoriia sibirskaia: letopis' sibirskaia i kratkaia kungur-skaia," in *Pamiatniki literatury Drevnei Rusi. XVII vek* (Moscow, 1989), 2:558. For an English translation that includes the illustrations that accompany the chronicle, see Armstrong, *Yermak's Campaign in Siberia*, 160–61. The translation here is my own.

7. *Polnoe sobranie russkikh letopisei*, vol. 36, *Sibirskie letopisi*, pt. 1, *Gruppa Esipovskoi letopisi* (Moscow, 1987), 69. For an English translation of the Esipov Chronicle, see Armstrong, *Ermak's Campaign in Siberia*, 62–86.

8. For examples of Ermak tales, see *Biblioteka russkogo fol'klora: Narodnyi teatr* (Moscow, 1991), 111–30; and *Biblioteka russkogo fol'klora: Narodnaia proza* (Moscow, 1991), 73–79.

9. N. M. Karamzin, *Istoriia gosudarstva rossiiskogo*, vol. 9, bk. 3 (Moscow, 1989), 226.

10. For an overview of the various Russian inflections of Ermak in the early to mid-nineteenth century, see A. V. Remnev, "Ermak kak geroi: Ot sibirskikh letopisei do 'pamiatnika tysiacheletiia Rossii'" (unpublished paper).

11. N. Iadrintsev, "Trekhsotletie Sibiri s 26 oktiabria 1581 goda," *Vestnik Evropy* 16, no. 12 (December 1881): 841, 844. On the tercentenary, see A. V. Remnev, "300-letie prisoedinenie Sibiri k Rossii: V ozhidanii 'novogo istoricheskogo perioda,'" *Kulturologicheskie issledovaniia v Sibiri*, 21, no. 1 (2007): 34–50.

12. Paul A. Cohen, *History in Three Keys: The Boxers as Event, Experience, and Myth* (New York: Columbia University Press, 1997), 212.

13. On the importance of such "foundation stories" in a comparative context, see David Day, *Conquest: How Societies Overwhelm Others* (New York: Oxford University Press, 2008), 132–58.

14. Maksimilian Voloshin, "Surikov (materialy dlia biografii)," *Apollon* 6/7 (1916), 62.

Letter from Ivan Groznyi to Simeon Bekbulatovich (1575). RGADA, fond XXVII (razriad Gos. Arkhiva, Tainyi prikaz), delo no. 12.

# 2

## Simeon Bekbulatovich

### (?–1616)

DONALD OSTROWSKI

We can date the beginning of the Russian Empire to 1552 when the tsardom of
Muscovy conquered the Tatar khanate of Kazan´. That initial conquest of a non-
Russian area was followed four years later by the conquest of the khanate of
Astrakhan´; by expansion westward into present-day Estonia, Latvia, and Lithuania
during the Livonian War (1558–83); and then by Muscovite expansion across Siberia,
which resulted in a Russian expedition standing on the shore of the Pacific Ocean at
the Sea of Okhotsk in 1639.

The Tatar princes who came over to the service of the Muscovite ruler were
an essential part of the rise of the Muscovite principality to empire. The military
role of Tatars as commanders of regiments in the Muscovite army had a long tradition. According to the Muscovite chronicles and military registers, in the fifteenth
century a number of them, such as Tsarevich Kasim in 1450 and 1467, Tsarevich
Mehmed Emin in 1487 and 1496, and Tsarevich Saltagan (Saltygan) in 1499, commanded regiments against the Tatars of Kazan´. Others, such as Tsarevich Danyar
in 1473 and Tsarevich Saltagan (Saltygan) in 1491, commanded regiments against
the Great Orda. In yet other cases, Tsarevich Yakup commanded a regiment against
Dmitrii Shemiaka in Kokshenga in 1452, and Tsarevich Danyar commanded a regiment against Novgorod in 1471 and 1478.[1] In the sixteenth century, Tsarevich Kudai
Kul converted to Christianity as Peter Ibramovich in 1505, married the sister of
Grand Prince Vasilii III, and was appointed commander to the main regiment of the
Muscovite army in 1506. For the next seventeen years, Vasilii III and Tsarevich Peter
were inseparable, except when Peter commanded the defense of Moscow against the
Crimean Tatar attack of 1521 (Vasilii fled the city for safety). Their close relationship
led the historian A. A. Zimin to suggest that Vasilii planned to name Peter as his
successor.

Tsarevich Peter's death in 1523 may have prompted Vasilii to divorce his wife
Solomoniia, with whom he had not produced any heirs, and marry Elena Glinskaia,
since he did not want any of his brothers to succeed him.[2]

In the first Muscovite campaign against Livonia in 1558, Tsar Shah-Ali, the former khan of Kazan', commanded the main regiment; Tsarevich Tokhtamysh commanded the vanguard; and Tsarevich Kaibula (Abdulla) commanded the right wing.[3] Shah-Ali continued to command regiments for Muscovy until his death in 1567. Tokhtamysh commanded the vanguard in Smolensk in 1562 and in the Polotsk campaign of 1563. Tsarevich Bekbulat, the brother of Tokhtamysh, commanded Muscovite regiments between 1562 and 1566. Tsarevich Ibak was one of the commanders of the main regiment in 1560 at Pskov, in 1562 at Smolensk, the rear regiment against Polotsk in 1563, and served in the Muscovite army until 1567. Tsarevich Kaibula commanded the left-wing regiment in the Polotsk campaign of 1563.[4] Likewise, Tsar Simeon Kasaevich (formerly Yadigâr Mehmet) commanded Muscovite regiments mainly on the southern frontier after his conversion to Orthodoxy in 1553 until his death in 1565, but also a regiment at Velikie Luki in 1562 and the right-wing regiment in the Polotsk campaign of 1563. Tsar Alexander (formerly Ötemish-Girey) accompanied Ivan IV on the Polotsk campaign, but he was too young to command a regiment.[5]

It is within this context that we can place the ascent of Simeon Bekbulatovich to prominence in Muscovy. He is one of the only Tatars to have commanded regiments in the Muscovite army both before conversion (as Saín Bulat) and after conversion (as Simeon Bekbulatovich), which occurred by July 15, 1573.[6] During his remarkable career he had three identities, each associated with a different name. As Saín Bulat he became khan of the Kasimov Khanate and was, according to a genealogical analysis done in the nineteenth century, a great-grandson of Akhmat, the last khan of the Great Orda, and a descendant of Chinggis Khan through his eldest son, Jochi. As a Muscovite serving prince, Simeon Bekbulatovich was a prominent military and political figure who became involved in one of the more puzzling episodes in Russian history—his replacing Tsar Ivan IV as grand prince of all Rus' in 1575–76. Later he was tonsured and ended his days as the Elder Stefan, and was buried in the Simonov Monastery in Moscow. In certain respects his career paralleled that of his wife's great-grandfather Kudai Kul (Peter Ibraimov) and in other respects went beyond it.

We do not have evidence of when or where Saín was born. The first mention of him in our sources refers to an event in 1561. According to the *Supplement to the Nikon Chronicle*, Tsarevich Saíl [Saín], son of Bulat, came to Moscow in that year in the entourage of his aunt, Princess Kochenei (the sister of his mother Altynchach), when she was baptized Mariia and married to Ivan IV. Our evidence that Saín Bulat had become khan of Kasimov by January 24, 1570, comes from a response by Ivan Novosil'tsev, Muscovite ambassador to the Ottoman Sultan Selim II. The *Military Registers* (*Razriadnie knigi*) provide evidence that from 1572 until 1585—even before he was baptized—whenever he accompanied the Muscovite army, Simeon Bekbulatovich usually led the main regiment (*bol'shoi polk*). A Tatar khan, thus, occupied the position of the second most powerful individual in the Muscovite army (after the tsar) and, by extension, in the Muscovite state.

In 1575, according to one of the *Military Registers*, Ivan IV placed the recently baptized Simeon Bekbulatovich on the throne as the grand prince of all Rus'. Ivan kept for himself the title Tsar (Khan) of Kazan′ and Astrakhan′ as well as the other realms not considered part of "all Rus′." In addition, Ivan carved out an appanage (*udel*) for himself within Simeon's grand principality and called himself "Prince Ivan Vasil′evich of Moscow."[7] Providing a reasonable explanation for Ivan's doing so has challenged both our sources and historians.

First we look at the accounts contemporary to Ivan IV. Daniel Printz von Buchau, the ambassador of the Holy Roman Emperor, in his report to Maximilian II, said that Ivan appointed Simeon because there had been a plot on his life and "because of the deceit of his subjects" (*ob improbitatem subditorum*). Another contemporary source, Daniel Sylvester, says something very similar. Sylvester, an interpreter with the Russia Company, wrote that he had two private talks with Ivan IV, who gave him the reason for making Simeon Bekbulatovich the grand prince of Muscovy. Both talks occurred while Simeon was on the throne. In the first, on November 29, 1575, Ivan cited "the perverse and evill dealinge of our subjects" as the reason for placing the "government . . . into the hands" of Simeon. Like Printz, Sylvester does not name any of the subjects who Ivan thought were doing "perverse and evil" things. During the second talk, on January 29, 1576, Ivan said that he could take back the title of grand prince at any time. Sylvester indicates that Ivan told him that Simeon had not been crowned, nor was he elected.

In a petition dated to October 30, 1575, from Ivan and his sons Ivan and Fëdor to Simeon, Ivan requests that he be allowed to choose servitors "from all the members of the court" without their losing their possessions. The administrative introduction to this petition, a document from 1576, and seventeenth-century chronicles (see below) indicate that Ivan referred to himself as "Prince of Moscow." An immunity charter issued by the Rostov Archbishop Iona on June 27, 1576, refers to "Prince Ivan Vasil′evich of Moscow." But in the petition itself Ivan does not use that title. Although the petition does not provide an explanation for Ivan's action, it does provide evidence for at least part of what Ivan wanted to do once Simeon was grand prince of all Rus′.

A comparison of the reasons given by Printz and reported by Sylvester for Ivan's placing Simeon on the throne with Ivan's declared motivation for establishment of the Oprichnina ten years earlier is instructive. In 1565, Ivan had appointed Ivan Fëdorovich Mstislavskii as head of the Zemshchina. He gave his reasons for leaving Moscow and residing in Aleksandrova sloboda in a 1565 letter to Metropolitan Afanasii. Ivan claimed prelates, in collusion with "boyars, courtiers, *d'iaki*, and all the bureaucrats," would act to thwart the sovereign when he wanted to punish subjects. Thus, the reasons given in contemporaneous sources for placing Simeon Bekbulatovich on the throne coincide with the reasons Ivan gave for setting up the Oprichnina—that is, his desire to punish certain subjects.[8]

We also have at least nine documents issued by Grand Prince of all Rus′ Simeon Bekbulatovich: two immunity charters (*zhalvannye gramoty;* one dated January 1576, and the other dated April 2, 1576), an obedience charter (*poslushnaia gramota;* dated January 7, 1576); three entry charters (*vvoznye gramoty*—the first dated February 9, 1576; the second dated March 29, 1576; and the third dated July 18, 1576); a decree (*ukaznaia gramota;* dated March 14, 1576); a *kormlenie* grant (dated May 23, 1576);

and a deed of purchase (from July 7, 1576).[9] Although none of these documents refers to Ivan or provides any testimony about the placing of Simeon on the throne, they do show that Simeon was officially fulfilling the responsibilities of the grand prince.

Next we turn to those accounts written within a few decades of Ivan's death. Jerome Horsey, an agent of the Russia Company, was in Muscovy more or less continually from 1573 until 1591, so he was there when Simeon Bekbulatovich was ostensibly the grand prince of Rus'. However, Horsey may not have begun writing his *Travels* until 1589 (and possibly not until 1591—after he left Muscovy), and completed the manuscript in 1621. In addition, we have reason to believe Horsey was writing the account of his stay in Muscovy as a means of advancing his own views about England. Horsey describes a financial motivation behind Ivan's placing Simeon Bekbulatovich on the grand princely throne. Horsey wrote that Ivan wanted to transfer monastic wealth to his own treasury. This explanation agrees with that of another Englishman writing at around the same time.

Giles Fletcher, English ambassador to the court of Tsar Fëdor, wrote at the end of the sixteenth century and attributed the placing of Simeon Bekbulatovich on the grand princely throne to an attempt on Ivan's part to get at the wealth of the monasteries and to do so while precluding further hatred for himself. Like Horsey, Fletcher may have been advancing this explanation with an eye to the secularization of Church lands issue in England, since Ivan IV was granting lands to monasteries throughout his reign. In the entry under the year 7081 (1572–73), the early-seventeenth-century *Piskarev Chronicle* proposes two alternative explanations for Ivan's making Simeon grand prince: soothsayers had predicted the grand prince would die in that year, and Ivan wanted to find out what the people were thinking. Jacques Margeret, who served as a mercenary in Russia from 1600 to 1606, also states that by elevating Simeon to the throne Ivan wanted to test the loyalty of his subjects. The *Moscow Chronicle*, which was probably composed after 1613, stated that Ivan found out about "the desire of his son the tsarevich Ivan Ivanovich for the tsardom and wanted to place an obstacle before him; namely, the grand principality of Tsar Simeon Bekbulatovich." The accounts written within a few decades of Ivan's death thus provide various theories for the placing of Simeon Bekbulatovich on the throne.[10] But none of these explanations finds corroboration in the historical record.

Among historical interpretations, the explanations of Zimin and R. G. Skrynnikov come closest to the testimony found in the sources of the time of Ivan IV.[11] Both historians posit an association with the Oprichnina, either to get at the former members of the Oprichnina (Zimin) or to get at those who had escaped the Oprichnina (Skrynnikov). In addition to those associated with the Oprichnina who were executed in the spring and summer of 1575, former oprichniki executed during the reign of Simeon Bekbulatovich included Protasii V. Iur'ev-Zakhar'in, the boyar Ivan A. Buturlin, the okol'nichii Dmitrii A. Buturlin, and the okol'nichii N. V. Borisov-Borozdin. The only prominent execution during 1575–76 that does not involve a former oprichnik was that of Prince P. A. Kurakin, who was also executed when Simeon was on the throne.

If Ivan could have members of the old Oprichnik guard executed while he was tsar and grand prince of all Rus', then why would he need Simeon on the throne as grand prince of all Rus' in order to continue the executions? And how does the execution of Kurakin fit in?

We do not have direct answers to these questions, but one can imagine an explanation that puts the pieces of evidence together within a relatively unified hypothetical framework. At the time, Daniel Printz reported a plan had been hatched with the collusion of some boyars to replace Ivan with the Crimean khan. Such a plan makes sense within the context of steppe political practice. As a non-Chinggisid, Ivan could not be a tsar (khan). If the Muscovite secular ruling elite wanted to maintain a tsar/khan as head of the state, it needed a Chinggisid. The coup plot may have been in response to Ivan's executing a number of those formerly associated with the Oprichnina in the spring and summer of 1575. Ivan's placing Simeon, a Chinggisid khan, on the throne would have thwarted that plot until such time as Ivan could eliminate the coup plotters. If Ivan thought that Kurakin was part of the plot, then that would explain Kurakin's place in the second wave of executions—that is, those that occurred after Simeon was on the throne. Likewise, Ivan's choice of Simeon Bekbulatovich was motivated by more than merely having a loyal subject and friend on the throne of all Rus'. Simeon's being a Chinggisid gave him cachet within the steppe system of political culture, which the Muscovite polity shared, but the Muscovite ruler lacked that cachet.

According to the *Piskarev Chronicle,* Ivan had Simeon marry Anastasiia Ivanovna Mstislavskaia, widow of Mikhail Kaibulin and daughter of Ivan Fëdorovich Mstislavskii, the head of the Zemshchina from 1565 to 1572. Simeon and Anastasiia had six children, three sons—Fëdor, Dmitrii, and Ioann (significantly, the same names as the three sons of Ivan IV)—and three daughters (Evdokhiia, Mariia, and Anastasiia). In the commemoration lists of the Solovki Monastery, the entire family was listed as having prayers paid for them by the Mstislavskiis.[12] Simeon is also listed in prayers in the Trinity St. Sergius Monastery paid for by the Mstislavskiis. Thus, the Mstislavskiis took on the responsibility of care for the soul of a former Tatar khan.

Simeon Bekbulatovich remained a year as grand prince of all Rus', according to the *Moscow Chronicle,* and then Ivan IV took back all the accouterments of that office and "gave Simeon Tver' and Torzhëk as appanage, and ordered him to write 'Grand Prince of Tver' Simeon Bekbulatovich.'" In so doing, Ivan exchanged one of his other titles, "Grand Prince of Tver'," for the title he had given up; that is, "Grand Prince of all Rus'." And Simeon thereby became the last appanage prince in Rus'. Throughout all this, Simeon Bekbulatovich led the main regiment of the Muscovite army or occupied other equally prominent military roles.[13]

After Ivan's death in 1584, Simeon acknowledged his allegiance to the new tsar, Ivan's son Fëdor. In a document addressed to Tsar Fëdor in response to a decree dated May 23, 1585, about the sending of *deti boiarskie,* Simeon Bekbulatovich declared himself a slave (*kholop*) of the tsar and signed it "Grand Prince Simeon Bekbulatovich of Tver'."[14] The historian George Vernadsky saw this as a diminution of Simeon's status as "a sovereign ruler," in that the leaders of "Fëdor's government demanded that

Simeon formally declare himself Tsar Fëdor's subject." But such a formulation was standard for all serving princes and does not necessarily indicate that anyone "demanded" he do so. The nineteenth-century historian N. V. Lileev reported a certificate (*otpis'*) in the Tver' Museum from Ivan Shishkov to Simeon as Grand Prince of Tver'. We also have a petition from one of Simeon's subjects written to him as Grand Prince of Tver'. Finally, we have a certificate (*otpis'*) of an instruction (*nakaz*) of April 1, 1585, from Simeon as Grand Prince of Tver' to Ivan Korsakov and Ivan Shiskov about the taking of *iam* money from the *votchina* of Kuzaz.[15] Then his political fortunes began to decline.

In May 1585, after Simeon Bekbulatovich's father-in-law, Ivan Fëdorovich Mstislavskii, was forced to take monastic vows at the Kirillo-Belozersk Monastery, Simeon was exiled to his estate at Kushalov and deprived of the title "Grand Prince of Tver'." According to the *New Chronicle*, enemies of Simeon went to Boris Godunov in 1595, after the death of Tsarevich Dmitrii Ivanovich, and convinced him to have Simeon blinded. The foreign mercenary Jacques Margeret, who said he heard it from Simeon himself, wrote that Boris Godunov exiled Simeon and sent him Spanish wine for his birthday that caused him to go blind.

In spring 1598, according to a diplomatic report by the Lithuanian governor of Orsha, Andrzej Sapieha, a rumor reached Godunov that Belskii and two Romanov brothers (Fëdor and Aleksandr) were plotting to put Simeon on the throne in place of Boris Godunov. The loyalty oath of September 15, 1598, that Godunov subsequently required forbade recognition of Simeon Bekbulatovich as tsar or any correspondence with him. According to the *New Chronicle*, Rostriga (the first False Dmitrii) brought Simeon to Moscow, but when Simeon would not accept the introduction of Catholicism into Muscovy, Rostriga had him tonsured at the Kirillo-Belozersk Monastery. On March 29 (April 3, according to the *New Chronicle*) 1606, Simeon took the monastic name Stefan.[16] At the same time, his wife, Anastasiia was veiled as the nun Aleksandra. According to a document dated May 29, 1606, Tsar Vasilii Shuiskii ordered the hegumen of the Kirillo-Belozersk Monastery to hand over the Elder Stefan to a certain Fëdor Suponov to take him wherever the tsar ordered. That destination turned out to be the Solovki Monastery on the White Sea.

On June 7, 1607, Simeon's wife died and was buried in the Simonov Monastery. According to the *Donation Book* (*Vkladnaia kniga*) of the Trinity St. Sergius Monastery, she had recently (1605–1606) made a donation of a total of 249 rubles for prayers for her husband, Simeon. In 1612, on the basis of a decree issued by Prince D. M. Pozharskii and "on the advice of all the land" (that is, the Zemskii sobor), the Elder Stefan was sent back to Kirillo-Belozersk Monastery. He returned to Moscow after July 22, 1613, when Mikhail Fedorovich was crowned tsar. On January 5, 1616, the Elder Stefan died and was buried in the Simonov Monastery next to his wife.

We do not have the kind of evidence that would provide any clue as to Simeon's personality. The evidence we do have is indicative of the high-profile role Tatars played not only in the regime of Ivan IV but also in the general rise of Muscovy to empire. As leader of the main regiment of the Muscovite army in the Livonian

War, Simeon could take partial credit for some of the early Muscovite successes of steppe-type strategies and tactics in that war. But by 1578, when the coalition against Muscovy adjusted its own tactics, the tide of the war turned. Yet Simeon remained in favor until after the death of Ivan IV, when Boris Godunov began to see Simeon as a potential rival for the throne, since Simeon was a Chingissid and Boris could not even claim to be a Riurikid. The assertion that Boris Godunov blinded Simeon with poisoned wine is reminiscent of Byzantine emperors' blinding rival claimants.

In terms of empire, Simeon's role in the government and army of Ivan IV demonstrates the importance of kinship relations, since Simeon was Ivan's nephew-in-law just as Tsarevich Peter (Kudai Kul) was the brother-in-law of Grand Prince Vasilii III (1505–33). This implicit comparison was made explicit when Ivan had Simeon marry Anastasiia Ivanovna Mstislavskaia, the great-granddaughter of Tsarevich Peter. This marriage made Simeon a member of the Mstislavskii family, who continued to commemorate his soul after his death. Muscovy gained from having Tatar princes lend their military skills by leading regiments of the Muscovite army.

The status that émigré Jochids held in the Muscovite elite was second only to that of the ruler himself, even above that of the ruler's brothers. Tsarevich Peter, Khan Ötemish, and Simeon Bekbulatovich were companions of the ruler. All this bespeaks a close relationship between the Muscovite ruler and émigré Tatar princes as Muscovy first incorporated other Rus' principalities and then conquered neighboring Tatar khanates and other areas that had never been part of Rus'.

NOTES

1. *Polnoe sobranie russkikh letopisei* (hereafter cited as *PSRL*) (St. Petersburg and Moscow: Arkheograficheskaia komissiia, Nauka, and Arkheograficheskii tsentr, 1841–2005), vols. 6, 12, 13, and 18; A. A. Zimin, ed., *Ioasafovskaia letopis'* (Moscow: Akademiia nauk SSSR, 1957); and M. N. Tikhomirov, ed., *Razriadnaia kniga, 1475–1598,* V. I. Buganov, comp. (Moscow: Nauka, 1966), 17–35.

2. Donald Ostrowski, "The Extraordinary Career of Tsarevich Kudai Kul/Peter in the Context of Relations between Muscovy and Kazan'," in *States, Societies, Cultures: East and West: Essays in Honor of Jaroslaw Pelenski,* ed. Janusz Duzinkiewicz, Myroslav Popovych, Vladyslav Verstiuk, and Natalia Yakovenko (New York: Ross, 2004), 697–719.

3. See George Vernadsky, *A History of Russia,* vol. 5, *The Tsardom of Muscovy 1547–1682* (New Haven, Conn.: Yale University Press, 1969), 94.

4. See Janet Martin, "Tatars in the Muscovite Army during the Livonian War," in *The Military and Society in Russia, 1450–1917,* ed. Eric Lohr and Marshall Poe (Leiden: Brill, 2002), 366–71.

5. See Martin, "Tatars in the Muscovite Army," 368–69.

6. N. M. Karamzin, *Istoriia Gosudarstva Rossiiskogo,* 5th ed. (St. Petersburg: Eduard Prats, 1843), 9: col. 149, citing *Delo Datsk.,* no. 2, fol. 41, that by July 15, 1573, he was called Simeon. Cf. Vel'iaminov-Zernov, *Issledovaniia o kasimovskikh tsariakh* (Moscow, 1853), 2:3, 11–24; and N. V. Lileev, *Simeon Bekbulatovich* (Tver': Tipografiia Gubernskogo Pravleniia, 1891), 17–20.

7. On the composition of Ivan's appanage within Simeon's principality, see S. P. Mordovina and A. L. Stanislavskii, "Sostav osobogo dvora Ivana IV v period 'Velikogo Kniazheniia' Semena Bekbulatovicha," *Arkheograficheskii ezhegodnik za 1976* (Moscow, 1976), 153–92.

8. Daniel Printz, *Moscoviae ortus, et progressus* (Guben, Germany: Christophor Gruber, 1681), 103, as reprinted in *Scriptores Rerum Livonicarum* (Riga and Leipzig: Eduard Franken, 1853), 2:705. Daniel Prinz, "Nachalo i vozvyshenie Moskovii," trans. I. A. Tikhomirov, *Chteniia v Obshchestve istorii i drevnostei rossiiskikh pri Moskovskom universitete,* 1876, no. 3, § 4, 29. Iurii Tolstoi, *Pervyia sorok let snoshenii mezhdu Rossieiu i Anglieiu 1553–1593* (St. Petersburg: A. Transhel, 1875), 179–80, 184–85. Cf. N. C. de Bogoushevsky, "The English in Muscovy in the Sixteenth Century," *Transactions of the Royal Historical Society* 7 (1878): 107. *PSRL* 13:392, 29:342.

9. *Akty, sobrannye v bibliotekakh i arkhivakh Rossiiskoi imperii Arkheograficheskoi ekspeditsiei Imperatorskoi Akademii nauk* (hereafter cited as *AAE*) (St. Petersburg, 1836), 1:355–56, № 290 and 1:356–57, № 292; *Akty sluzhilykh zemlevladel'tsev XV–nachala XVII veka.* *Sbornik dokumentov,* comp. A. V. Antonov and K. V. Baranov (Moscow: Arkheograficheskii tsentr´, 1997), 3:341–42, № 417; 3:205, № 250; 4:234–36, № 317; 4:13–14, № 15; *Akty istoricheskie, sobrannye i izdannye Arkheograficheskoi komissiei* (hereafter cited as *AI*) (St. Petersburg, 1841–1842), 1:360–61, no. 195; *Akty sluzhilykh zemlevladel'tsev XV–nachala XVII veka* 3:126–27, № 148; 1:78–79, № 103; and P. A. Sadikov, "Iz istorii Oprichniny XVI v.," *Istoricheskii arkhiv* 3 (1940): 278–79, № 69.

10. Jerome Horsey, *Travels,* in *Rude and Barbarous Kingdom: Russia in the Accounts of Sixteenth-Century English Voyagers,* ed. Lloyd E. Berry and Robert O. Crummey (Madison: University of Wisconsin Press, 1968), 275. Giles Fletcher, *Of the Russe Commonwealth,* in *Rude and Barbarous Kingdom,* 166–67 [updated spelling]. O. A. Iakovleva, ed., "Piskarevskii letopisets," in *Dokumenty po istorii XV–XVII vv., Materialy po istorii SSSR,* ed. A. A. Novosel'skii, L. V. Cherepnin, and L. N. Pushkarev (Moscow: Akademiia nauk, 1955), 2:81–82. Cf. *PSRL,* 34:192. The so-called *Abbreviated Annal to 1691* (*Sokrashchennyi Vremennik do 1691 g.*) of the eighteenth century reports under the year 7082 (1573–74) provides a shortened form of the information found in the *Piskarev Chronicle.* "Sokrashchennyi vremennik," addendum to "Piskarevskii letopisets," 2:148. The *Abbreviated Annal* is an abbreviation of the *Piskarev Chronicle,* as O. A. Iakovleva concluded in her introduction to the texts. Iakovleva, "Piskarevskii letopisets," 20. Jacques Margeret, *The Russian Empire and Grand Duchy of Muscovy: A 17th-Century Account,* ed. and trans. Chester S. L. Dunning (Pittsburgh: University of Pittsburgh Press, 1983), 16. *PSRL* 34:226. For the proposed time of composition of the *Moscow Chronicle,* see V. I. Buganov, "Predislovie," *PSRL* 34:5.

11. For a survey of historians' interpretations, see Donald Ostrowski, "Simeon Bekbulatovich's Remarkable Career as Tatar Khan, Grand Prince of Rus´, and Monastic Elder," *Russian History/Histoire russe* (forthcoming).

12. Arkhimandrite Dosefei, *Geograficheskoe, istoricheskoe i staticheskoe opisanie stavropigial'nogo pervoklasnogo Solovetskogo monastyria,* 2nd ed. (Moscow: Universitetskaia tipografiia, 1853) 1:118–19. Cf. Russell E. Martin, "Gifts for the Dead: Kinship and Commemoration in Muscovy (The Case of the Mstislavskii Princely Clan)," *Russian History/ Histoire russe* 26 (1999): 196, citing RGADA, *fond* 141, no. 62, fol. 113.

13. The *Moscow Chronicle* reports that in 1580 Simeon led the central regiment along with Fëdor Ivanovich Mstislavskii and Nikita Romanovich Iur'ev. *PSRL* 34:233; Buganov and Koretskii, "Neizvestnii Moskovskii letopisets," 147. The *Pskov Chronicle* reports that Ivan left a reserve army under the command of Simeon Bekbulatovich near Staritsa in August 1581. *Pskovskie letopisi,* ed. A. N. Nasonov (Moscow and Leningrad: Akademiia nauk SSSR, 1941, 1955), 2:263.

14. N. A. Popov, ed., *Akty Moskovskogo gosudarstva,* vol. 1, *Razriadnyi prikaz. Moskovskoi stol 1571–1634* (St. Petersburg: Tipografiia Imperatorskoi Akademii nauk, 1890), 52–56, no. 30.

15. RGADA, f. 210, Moskovskii stol stolbtsy, no. 1131 (22), fols. 17–21: Spisok umianoi velikogo kniazia Seona [*sic*] Bekbulatovicha tverskago stol[']nikom i dvorianom i zhiltsom i detem boiarskim tverich i novgor. . . . [here the text is unclear] dvorovykh i gorodvykh kotorym skazana gosudareva sluzhba v 93-m godu. There follows: fol. 22–23 (new hand): Velikogo kniazia Semeona Bekbulatovicha tverskago deti boiarskie, zhiltsy oklad i pomeste'e po 150 cheti, a deneg po 6 rub[lev] (My thanks to Russell E. Martin for providing me the information about this petition). *Akty sluzhilykh zemlevladel'tsev XV–nachala XVII veka*, 2:358, № 419.

16. *AAE* 2:96–97, no. 41 (March 29, 1606); *PSRL* 14:68 (April 3, 1606).

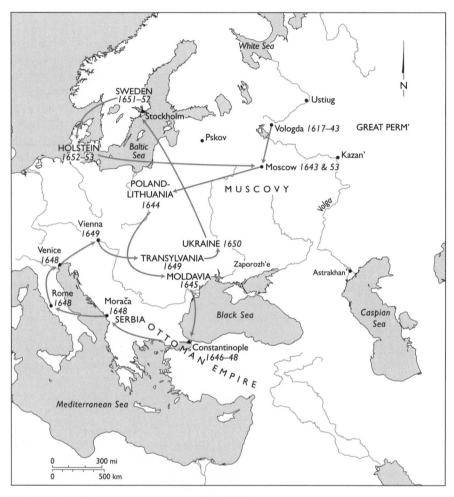

Timofei Ankudinov's travels. Map created by Bill Nelson.

# 3

# Timofei Ankudinov

## (1617?-1653)

MAUREEN PERRIE

In 1646, in the reign of Tsar Aleksei Mikhailovich, a man appeared at the court of the Turkish Sultan Ibrahim in Constantinople (now Istanbul), the capital of the Ottoman Empire. He claimed to be the son of Tsar Vasilii Shuiskii, and the true heir to the Russian throne.

The Turks informed the Russian ambassadors of the arrival of "Tsarevich Ivan Vasil'evich Shuiskii." The Muscovite diplomats knew that Tsar Vasilii Shuiskii had died childless in 1612, and they were convinced that the newcomer was the latest in a series of pretenders who had plagued Russia in the early seventeenth century, falsely claiming the identity of Muscovite tsars or tsareviches. In this assumption they were correct: Ivan Shuiskii was indeed an impostor, and he turned out to be one of the most remarkable of all Russian pretenders.

At first the Russian diplomats in Constantinople were unable to establish the true identity of "Tsarevich" Ivan, but one day their clerk accidentally encountered the impostor's companion and recognized him as Konstantin (Kostka) Koniukhovskii, a clerk from the New Quarter chancellery in Moscow, who had fled from Russia a few years previously. This enabled them to name the pretender as Timofei (Timoshka) Ankudinov (alternate spellings are Ankidinov, Akudinov, or Akidinov), another runaway clerk from the same chancellery. Over the next few years, as Timoshka traveled from Constantinople to various lands including Ukraine, Sweden, and Holstein, Russian envoys supplied the rulers of these countries with compromising information about him. These denunciations constitute our main source of evidence about the pretender's life before his arrival in Constantinople. They are partly confirmed by the confessions which Kostka and Timoshka made under torture in Moscow, in 1652 and 1653, respectively; and can be supplemented by some details provided by Adam Olearius, a German official who interrogated Ankudinov in Holstein in 1653.[1]

The biographical information about Ankudinov in these various sources is somewhat inconsistent, but the following general picture emerges. He was born in Vologda, probably in 1617, the son of trader in canvas Dementii Ankudinov and his wife, Solomonida. Timoshka served as a clerk in Vologda before moving to Moscow, where in 1643 he stole some money from the state treasury, then burned his wife to death (destroying his own house and many others in the process), and fled to Poland-Lithuania with his friend and colleague Kostka. In Poland he called himself Ivan Kirazeiskii (or Karazeiskii), governor of Vologda and vicegerent of Great Perm'. When Tsar Michael sent envoys to Poland in 1644 to demand the return of all Russian pretenders sheltering there, Timoshka decided to flee further. He went first to Moldavia and then to Constantinople, where he began to call himself Tsarevich Ivan (or Ivan-Timofei) Vasil'evich Shuiskii.

Tsar Vasilii Ivanovich Shuiskii, whose son Timoshka claimed to be, had reigned in Muscovy in 1606-10, during the Time of Troubles. This was a period of social and political unrest that witnessed a series of competing claimants to the Russian throne. A number of pretenders called themselves members of the old Muscovite dynasty that had come to an end with the death of Tsar Fëdor Ivanovich in 1598. Tsar Fëdor was succeeded by his brother-in-law, Boris Godunov. But in spite of the fact that Boris was elected by a broadly representative Assembly of the Land, his legitimacy as ruler was never entirely accepted. In 1603 a youth appeared in Lithuania claiming to be Tsar Fëdor's younger half-brother, Tsarevich Dmitrii, who had died under mysterious circumstances in 1591. A devastating famine in the early years of the seventeenth century created many social problems in Russia, and the pretender—generally known to historians as the first False Dmitrii—was able to take advantage of the grievances of the Muscovite population in order to seize the throne in 1605. Doubts persisted, however, about his true identity, and many of the traditional elites were opposed to his policies. He was overthrown in a coup in May 1606 that brought Vasilii Shuiskii to power.

Although the Shuiskii clan could trace its ancestry back to Riurik, the semi-legendary founder of the old dynasty, Tsar Vasilii enjoyed even less legitimacy than had Boris Godunov. Shuiskii's reign was marked by popular uprisings, Polish and Swedish military intervention, and a new crop of pretenders.[2] In 1610 Tsar Vasilii was forced to abdicate, and some of his former supporters swore allegiance to the Polish prince Władysław. The Poles occupied the Moscow Kremlin, and the ex-tsar was taken as a prisoner to Poland, where he died.

The Time of Troubles came to an end in 1613, after the Poles were driven out of Moscow and Michael Romanov was elected tsar by an Assembly of the Land. Michael achieved his electoral success largely because of his family's links by marriage with the old dynasty. But his legitimacy was challenged—not only by Prince Władysław of Poland but also by new impostors, including a false Tsarevich Simeon Vasil'evich Shuiskii who appeared in Moldavia in 1639. He was handed over to a Russian envoy, who killed him on his return journey to Moscow. At around the same time a second false Simeon Shuiskii was rumored to have declared himself in Poland.

The appearance of false Shuiskiis was an innovation in the history of Russian pretendership, since all previous impostors had claimed to belong to the old Muscovite dynasty and to be descendants of Tsar Ivan IV ("the Terrible"). Vasilii Shuiskii, by contrast, had been an unpopular tsar of disputed legitimacy, so that the new pretenders' choice of identity is at first sight somewhat surprising. In 1635, however, Tsar Vasilii's body had been returned from Poland, and given a ceremonial reburial in the Archangel Cathedral in the Moscow Kremlin, the traditional resting-place of the Russian tsars. This event, which represented a form of official posthumous rehabilitation, reminded Russians of the Shuiskii clan, which provided an alternative focus of loyalty for opponents of the new dynasty. In Constantinople, Timoshka Ankudinov developed a strong critique of the Romanovs' legitimacy, presenting them as usurpers who had plotted with the Poles to supplant the true tsar, Vasilii.

Over the next few years Ankudinov produced many different versions of his Shuiskii biography. In Constantinople he claimed that he was born in 1609, and so was only a baby when his father was taken to Poland as a prisoner. Tsar Vasilii had entrusted the infant Tsarevich Ivan to the care of his godfather, Prince Boris Lykov. When Lykov went off on a military expedition he assigned the boy to Varlaam, abbot of the Archangel Monastery in Ustiug, and Varlaam appointed Dementii Ankudinov as his tutor and Solomonida Gorianova as his nanny. Varlaam subsequently became Archbishop of Vologda, and Ivan Shuiskii married his granddaughter. After 1613, when Michael Romanov came to the throne, he made the young man prince of Great Perm' (a remote region to the northeast of Vologda). Later, Tsar Michael brought him to the capital and made him serve in the New Quarter chancellery as a humble clerk, under the false name of Ankudinov. The authorities persecuted him and he fled from Moscow. In Moldavia the ruler tried to kill him, as he had previously killed his elder brother (Timoshka evidently knew about the fate of the false Simeon Shuiskii who had appeared in Moldavia in 1639), and he then fled further, to Turkey.

In Constantinople in 1646, Russian envoys heard that Timoshka had asked the sultan for troops to attack Muscovy and regain his father's throne, promising to cede Astrakhan' to Turkey if they were successful. In a petition to the ambassadors, Ankudinov denied that he had requested Turkish troops, and claimed that he had such unassailable "proof" of his identity, and so much support in Astrakhan', that he did not require foreign military backing. Kostka, however, later stated that Timoshka had asked the sultan for troops to attack both Kazan' and Astrakhan', where he had Russian sympathizers. It seems likely that Timoshka did promise these two cities to the sultan, since they had been the capitals of independent Tatar khanates that were conquered by Moscow only in the mid-sixteenth century. The Turks and their Crimean Tatar allies had made an unsuccessful attempt to capture Astrakhan' in 1569, and they still harbored the aim of regaining these strategically important Volga territories for Islam.

Ankudinov did not inspire much confidence at the sultan's court, but his hosts considered it advantageous to keep him in Constantinople as a potential weapon to use against the tsar, and detained him under house arrest. Timoshka was by now disillusioned with life in Turkey. He fled from Constantinople but was recaptured, and his life was spared only when he promised to become a Muslim (the Turks evidently thought that they could control him better if he converted to Islam). He escaped again before he could be circumcised, but was again recaptured, and on his return to Constantinople he was forced to undergo circumcision. Finally he fled once more, and this time he avoided rearrest.

Timoshka next appeared in Serbia, in the company of two Serbs who had helped him escape from the Turks. The Orthodox Christian community in Serbia at that time was divided. One faction wanted to follow the example of those Orthodox believers in the Polish-Lithuanian Commonwealth who had formed a Uniate Church that accepted the authority of the Pope while continuing to follow Orthodox rites. In February 1648 Timoshka was present at a synod of the Serbian Orthodox Church, held at the monastery of Morača, that decided to send an envoy to Rome to prepare for negotiations about Church union on the Polish model. On his arrival in Serbia, Timoshka had associated with traditional Orthodox believers who opposed the idea of union, but at the Morača synod he sided with the pro-union faction. This shift of allegiance provided him with an opportunity to visit Rome and acquire the support of the Vatican for his claims to the Russian throne. In April 1648 he presented a petition to the Pope, in which he stated that he had been captured in a battle with the Tatars, and taken to Constantinople as a prisoner. He claimed that although he had been born and brought up in the "schismatic Greek" faith, he had always wanted to be received into the Roman Catholic Church, and he promised to do everything he could to bring his people to the light of the true religion. Ankudinov's petition seems to have been successful: Kostka subsequently stated that the pretender had received the sacrament from the Pope.[3]

Timoshka's behavior in Serbia and Rome was rather different from his conduct in Turkey. He did not explicitly present himself as the legitimate heir to the Russian throne, nor seek military support to overthrow Tsar Aleksei Mikhailovich (there was, of course, no way either the Serbs or the Catholic hierarchy in the Vatican could have provided him with troops). He still described himself as the son of Tsar Vasilii, however, thereby making at least an implicit claim to the Muscovite throne.

Timoshka remained in Rome until August 1648. His surviving correspondence provides evidence of influential contacts, and indicates that he enjoyed high-level patronage from the Vatican. It seems likely that the Catholic Church hierarchy hoped to use him to promote its plans for expanding Uniatism in Poland-Lithuania and extending it to Muscovy, and encouraged him to go to Poland in order to further these aims. Timoshka himself may have thought that his conversion to Catholicism would provide him with influence at the Polish court. He doubtless knew that the first False Dmitrii had secretly converted to Roman Catholicism in Poland and had made various promises about the conversion of Muscovy in return for offers of support from the king and the Church.

If Timoshka and his Vatican patrons nourished such hopes, they were thwarted by the outbreak of the Ukrainian revolt against the Polish government at the end of 1648. This rebellion, led by Bohdan Khmel′nyts′kyi, the hetman of the Zaporozhian Cossacks, was largely directed against Church union, in the name of the preservation of Orthodoxy. The political climate in Poland-Lithuania was now distinctly unfavorable to the promotion of Uniatism, and the Polish government was too preoccupied with Khmel'nyts'kyi to consider supporting a pretender to the Muscovite throne.

Thus, instead of going to Poland from Rome, Timoshka traveled via Venice, Vienna, and Transylvania to Ukraine, where his presence was first reported in early 1650.[4] He was no doubt aware of the support some of the pretenders of the Time of Troubles had received from the Zaporozhian Cossacks, and hoped that the Ukrainian hetman would prove to be a more reliable patron than the Polish king. Khmel'nyts'kyi offered Ankudinov his protection, but the Cossacks were reluctant to attack Muscovy at a time when they were bidding for Tsar Aleksei's assistance against the Poles. When he realized that many Ukrainians were indifferent or even hostile to his cause, Ankudinov attempted to negotiate a pardon from the tsar in order to return to Moscow. He now called himself Tsar Vasilii's grandson, rather than his son, and did not make any claim to the throne.

In Ukraine Ankudinov reverted to stressing his Orthodox Christian faith, both initially, when he was trying to gain support from the anti-Catholic and anti-Uniate Cossacks, and later, when negotiating his return to Russia. He wrote to the Patriarch in Moscow to ask him to intercede for him with the tsar, saying that although he had been invited to many lands, he did not want to abandon Orthodox Christianity, and wished to serve Tsar Aleksei. The Russian government feared that Ankudinov's presence in Ukraine would lead to a repetition of the Time of Troubles, and made every effort to bring him to Moscow. But Timoshka's attempts to negotiate his return through Russian intermediaries foundered when they were unable to guarantee that his life would be spared if he went back voluntarily. Diplomatic pressure on Khmel'nyts'kyi was equally unsuccessful: the hetman told the Muscovite envoys to Ukraine that Zaporozhian Cossack custom forbade the extradition of fugitives, and pretenders were no exception to that rule. Eventually, in November 1650, Khmel'nyts'kyi expelled Ankudinov from Zaporozh'e. He sent the pretender back to Transylvania, and from there Timoshka traveled to Sweden.

According to Kostka's confession, Timoshka went to Sweden in order to be close to the town of Pskov, in northwest Russia, where there was an uprising in 1650; Ankudinov planned to ask Queen Christina to let him live near the Russian border, so that he could make contact with the rebels. It is quite possible that Ankudinov heard about the uprising in Pskov while he was in Ukraine, but his information was out of date: the revolt was brought to an end in August 1650.

Ankudinov did not have much success in Sweden. He made another opportunistic conversion, this time to Lutheranism, but this did not endear him to the Queen, who had herself recently become a secret convert to Catholicism. She gave Timoshka financial support, but otherwise did little to promote his cause. As soon as Tsar Aleksei learned of Ankudinov's presence in Sweden, he sent envoys to Stockholm to demand his extradition. In 1652, Kostka Koniukhovskii was returned to Moscow, where he was tortured and interrogated. Timoshka himself managed to avoid extradition from Sweden by fleeing the country. Eventually he was detained in Holstein and extradited to Moscow at the end of 1653. On December 27, he was interrogated in front of the boyars; the next day he was confronted with his mother, Solomonida, and with former colleagues and acquaintances who testified that he was, indeed, the former chancellery clerk Timoshka Ankudinov. He made a partial confession, after which he was executed on Red Square: Olearius reported that he was dismembered alive, and then beheaded.

Timoshka's fate was particularly tragic since he was one of the most talented Russians of his generation, in spite of his humble provincial background. According to Olearius, Dementii Ankudinov had recognized his son's academic potential and sent him to school in Vologda, where he achieved the highest level of education then available in Muscovy. The boy also had a fine voice, and his excellent singing in church services brought him to the attention of Archbishop Varlaam. By the time he reached Holstein in 1652 Timoshka had mastered Latin, Italian, Turkish, and German, and he could write Russian in a variety of styles of handwriting (a skill which served him well when he forged documentary "proof" of his Shuiskii identity). Verses that Ankudinov wrote in Constantinople denouncing the Romanovs had sufficient literary merit that they were anthologized by Soviet scholars.[5] Textual analysis of these verses, and of the many florid letters that he wrote on his travels, shows that he was fully familiar with the Bible, the liturgy, and a number of religious works published in Poland-Lithuania, and that he creatively adapted quotations from them in his own writings. He also studied heraldry and incorporated its symbols into the design of the seals he attached to his letters.[6]

Most of Timoshka's undoubted abilities were devoted to his performance of the role of Tsarevich Ivan Vasil'evich Shuiskii. As well as devising ingenious (if not entirely persuasive) accounts of his biography, Ankudinov backed up his case with a range of evidence of his Shuiskii identity. These included a "royal mark" on his right arm (such marks on the body, supposedly indicating a true tsarevich, were characteristic of many Russian pretenders), and a collection of forged documents, including letters of recommendation from various European rulers and from Tsars Vasilii Shuiskii and Michael Romanov. He also had a portrait that, he claimed, depicted him as a baby with his father, Tsar Vasilii. He performed his role with such self-confidence that many of his hosts were persuaded, at least initially, that he really was a Muscovite tsarevich.

What had prompted Timoshka to adopt the role of Tsarevich Ivan Vasil'evich Shuiskii? In his confession he claimed that when he was a child his mentor, Archbishop Varlaam, had been so impressed by his abilities that he had declared that the boy must be of princely birth, and this remark inspired the young Timoshka with the idea that he was the son of an important man. Ankudinov also said that his father Dementii had suggested that he call himself Prince Shuiskii. Kostka, however, claimed that Timoshka had called himself Tsar Vasilii's son in Constantinople because of the influence of books on astrology and astronomy that he had purchased in Lithuania. It seems most likely that Timoshka decided to call himself Ivan Shuiskii only after learning about the false Simeon Shuiskiis who had appeared in Moldavia and Poland. Before that, he had laid claim only to titles derived from his native region of Vologda.

These date back to his association with Archbishop Varlaam, whose archdiocese (and administrative responsibilities) included Great Perm': Olearius tells us that after Timoshka married the archbishop's granddaughter he sometimes called himself the grandson of the vicegerent of Vologda and Great Perm'. Even after he declared himself to be Tsar Vasilii's son, Timoshka incorporated references to Vologda and Perm' into his titles. He thus preserved an element of his northeast Russian regional identity, even while traveling in foreign lands and constantly reinventing himself.

Timoshka's claims to be Tsarevich Ivan Shuiskii were made outside Russia. The Poles had used pretenders as a pretext for military intervention in Muscovy during the Time of Troubles, and Ankudinov, who was no doubt aware of this precedent, attempted to make use of imperial rivalries in order to promote his own cause. It seems that he placed greater hopes in obtaining military backing from foreign rulers than in recruiting popular support within Muscovy. In 1646 he traveled to Turkey rather than to Astrakhan', despite his claims that he had many supporters there, and in 1650 he chose to go to the Swedish court, rather than to Pskov, although he knew of the uprising in that town.

Ankudinov's series of religious conversions also indicates that he placed his hopes primarily on foreign assistance. If his adoption of Islam was forced upon him by the Turks, his acceptance of Catholicism and Lutheranism was voluntary and calculating, based on the assumption that the Poles and the Swedes would be willing to support only a claimant to the Russian throne who professed their own faith and would promote its spread to Muscovy. His reversion to Orthodoxy in Ukraine follows the same pattern. In an age when international relations were primarily confessional, the pretender had to adopt the religion of each prospective foreign patron in turn, in order to obtain trust.

In spite of his grand tour of the periphery of Russia, Ankudinov was unable to obtain foreign military support. He had misjudged the international situation in the mid-seventeenth century, which was unfavorable to intervention by Russia's enemies. He failed to gain the assistance he sought from the Turks or the Swedes, and the Poles and Ukrainians were too concerned with the Khmel'nyts'kyi rebellion to undertake a campaign on behalf of a Muscovite pretender.

Even if he had acquired foreign backing as an initial impetus for his campaign, it is unlikely that Ankudinov would have acquired significant support within Russia. More successful pretenders, such as the first False Dmitrii and—in the eighteenth century—Emelian Pugachev, were able to tap into broad social grievances against rulers who were widely perceived to be illegitimate (Boris Godunov and Catherine the Great, respectively). But Timoshka's critique of the Romanovs as usurpers and oppressors did not find much resonance in Muscovy. Tsar Michael had achieved a considerable degree of legitimacy by the end of his reign, so the succession of his son Aleksei in 1645 was largely uncontested. A series of uprisings took place in 1648-50 in Moscow and other towns, including Pskov, but these rebellions were directed not against Aleksei himself, but against the evil counselors who had allegedly led the young tsar astray. Thus there was little potential base of support within Russia for a pretender.

Ankudinov's prospects for success inside Muscovy were also undermined by his serial conversions to Islam, Roman Catholicism, and Lutheranism. If he had invaded Russia, his confessional promiscuity would have discredited him in the eyes of the Muscovite population, who—as the Time of Troubles had shown—were staunchly devoted to the notion that a true tsar must be an Orthodox Christian. Timoshka's entire enterprise was thus doomed to failure, but his persistence in playing out his royal role makes him one of the most intriguing and colorful pretenders in Russian history.

Pretenders, of course, provide an extreme example of identity change, and Timoshka's self-transformation from the son of Dementii Ankudinov to the son of Tsar Vasilii Shuiskii was a particularly dramatic one. But he also opportunistically changed his religion on more than one occasion, in the interests of his bids for support from neighboring powers. It seems unlikely that Ankudinov internalized the new confessional identities he adopted, but his constant self-adjustments to the cultural environments within which he found himself have much in common with the strategies employed by other—less colorful—individuals who assumed new personas in order to further their upward mobility in Russian society.

## NOTES

1. On Ankudinov's career, see, for example, S. M. Solov'ev, *Istoriia Rossii s drevneishikh vremen,* kniga V (Moscow, 1961), 464-67, 564-67, 569-71, 607-11; Iu. B. Simchenko, "Lzhe-Shuiskii II. Pravoslavnyi, musul'man, katolik, protestant," in *Russkie: Istoriko-etnograficheskie ocherki* (Moscow, 1997), 14-41; Adam Olearii, *Opisanie puteshestviia v Moskoviiu i cherez Moskoviiu v Persiiu i obratno* (St. Petersburg, 1906), 242-54.

2. On the pretenders of the Time of Troubles, see, Maureen Perrie, *Pretenders and Popular Monarchism in Early Modern Russia: The False Tsars of the Time of Troubles* (Cambridge: Cambridge University Press, 1995).

3. On Ankudinov in Serbia and Rome, see V. A. Moshin, "Iz istorii snoshenii Rimskoi kurii, Rossii i iuzhnykh slavian," in *Mezhdunarodnye sviazi Rossii do XVII v. Sbornik statei* (Moscow, 1961), 491-511.

4. On Ankudinov in Ukraine, see Mykhailo Hrushevsky, *History of Ukraine-Rus': The Cossack Age, 1650-1653,* vol. 1 (Edmonton: Canadian Institute of Ukrainian Studies Press, 2005). Relevant documents are in *Vossoedinenie Ukrainy s Rossiei. Dokumenty i materialy v trekh tomakh,* vols. 2-3 (Moscow, 1953).

5. See *Russkaia sillabicheskaia poeziia XVII-XVIII v.v.,* ed. A. M. Panchenko (Leningrad, 1970), 85-90.

6. V. V. Dubovik, "Ob osobennostiakh tsitatsii v tekstakh Timofeia Akindinova," in *Drevniaia Rus': Voprosy medievistiki* 2 (2003): 83-98; V. V. Dubovik, "Samozvantsy. 'Synov'ia' Shuiskogo i ikh sud'ba," *Rodina* 11 (2005): 31-34.

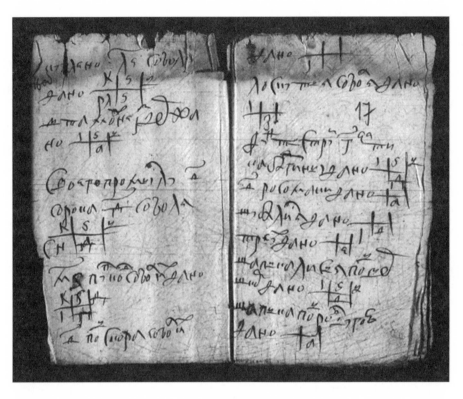

Notebook of Boris Pikalev, one of Gavril Nikitin's agents in Siberia, c. 1690–91. RGADA (Russian State Archive of Ancient Acts), f. 214, stb. 1128, ll. 16ob, 17.

# 4

# Gavril Romanovich Nikitin

## (?–1698)

ERIKA MONAHAN

On October 25, 2003, on the cheerless Siberian tarmac of Novosibirsk, Russian authorities apprehended oil tycoon Mikhail Khodorkovsky's private jet and arrested him on charges of tax evasion and fraud.[1] As this goes to print Khodorkovsky serves his sentence in jail and few doubt that his arrest was politically motivated, although whether he should be considered a victim, visionary, or villain remains a matter of debate. Over three centuries earlier, in 1698, another of Russia's most wealthy businessmen was himself arrested for what looks like politically motivated reasons. That businessman was Gavril Romanovich Nikitin, and this chapter is about him.

Despite the shared circumstances of state heavy-handedness and a national economy undergoing increasing integration and foreign influence, there are many differences between these two inscrutable cases of "riches and ruin." First, Novosibirsk did not exist in 1698, although the river it sits on today, the Ob, was a crucial byway for Nikitin and his men's commercial trafficking. Second, unlike Khodorkovsky's private airplane that zipped through Siberian airspace at blistering speeds, Nikitin's caravans crossed the Siberian forests and steppes far more slowly and at a time when people—those few who cared about such abstractions—considered the Ob rather than the Urals to be the continental divide between Europe and Asia.[2] Third, Khodorkovsky became fabulously rich extremely quickly and mostly as a result of his connections to government. Nikitin's wealth, however, was slow in coming, and he gained government attention and influence after, rather than before, attaining commercial success. And yet both arrests underscore the critical and sometimes precarious relationship between politics and commerce in the early modern and (post)modern Russian worlds. Moreover, by looking at Nikitin's life, we are able to appreciate the now largely forgotten experience of the Siberian merchants of his day, whose work involved navigating the tensions between business and politics in what were then distant and diverse frontier environments.

In many ways, Nikitin's story is that of a self-made man embedded in an ascendant family history. Gavril Romanovich was youngest of eight brothers from a family of "black" peasants from Charonda, a busy village not for from the town of Vologda in the Russian north. Compared to Timofei Ankudinov's outlandish life, of course, Gavril followed a less extraordinary path for a young man from a region distinguished in Russian history for its commercial dynamism. Whether it was the legacy of being in the hinterlands of the medieval Novgorod "republic," whose merchants exploited the northern forests and taiga for their thick-pelted animals, or whether it was influence brought by the sixteenth-century English adventurers who followed the region's rivers in search of imperium and markets, the Russian north produced more than its fair share of Muscovy's leading merchants in the seventeenth century. Nikitin's commercial success in this competitive environment was extraordinary, but understandable. Instead, it was his demise that was bizarre.

Nikitin was probably not the first in his community or family (some of his older brothers who died before he rose to prominence may have traded) to work as a trader, but he was the first to attain the privileged ranks of Russian merchants. We can further surmise that his kin were likely at best petty traders rather than fully established merchants, because Nikitin got his career start not in the family business but working for the elite Moscow merchant, or *gost'*, Ostafii Filat'ev. Filat'ev headed a prominent merchant family; three of his kinsmen and two of his sons attained gost' rank in the last decades of the seventeenth century. To his credit, Nikitin—in an age when kin relations dominated commercial organization—distinguished himself alongside Filat'ev's sons and rose in the ranks of their trade network.[3]

Ostafii Filat'ev did much business in Siberia, the fur-filled lands to the east throughout which the Russian government was extending its reach by building forts and levying tribute on local populations. The state and men of commerce recognized opportunity in these advances, not only for furs, but also as a gateway to the riches of the Far East: silks, gems, and spices. Merchants led caravans laden with various wares—pots, griddles, axes, needles, nails, mirrors, eyeglasses, Russian linens, English woolens, socks, boots, and sometimes books—to Siberia. Eastbound caravans sometimes carried Eastern products such as Persian textiles or Chinese silks that came up the Volga River from Astrakhan'. As Filat'ev's agent (*prikashchik*) in Siberia for much of the 1670s, Nikitin sold such wares for cash or traded them for furs and Eastern goods that he would then cart back to Rus'—either proceeding to Moscow or stopping in the northern towns of Ustiug or Sol'vychegodsk to sell, trade, or store his cargo as the boss directed.[4] In the second half of the seventeenth century, direct Russian trade with China was just beginning and Ostafii Filat'ev, with Nikitin as his agent, was in the vanguard.

In 1674 Nikitin departed from Selenginsk—a wooden fort established in 1665 along the Selenga River near Lake Baikal—with a small party of about forty men bound for Beijing. Their path would take them south toward the "impassable" Mongol steppe and the Gobi Desert. In the eighteenth century this would become the popular Kiakhta route, but at the time no Russian party on record had yet taken this more direct line.[5] In doing so, they shattered long-held myths of the Gobi as a menacing desert marked by extremes of cold and heat and inhabited by man-eating beasts and snakes waiting to devour unsuspecting travelers. Rumors like this were likely spread and embellished by Central Asian merchants. As long-established middlemen in the China trade, they had good reason to discourage their Russian competitors' direct entry into the Chinese market.

To their chagrin, Filat'ev's successful expedition whetted the appetite of Russian merchants for more direct trade with China. This impetus for trade emerged amid tensions brewing between Muscovy and the Qing dynasty over the Amur River valley. In fact, the political situation may have helped because the Qing were on the verge of war with Mongolians, and their desire to court Russian cooperation seems to have trumped tensions over the Amur.[6] At any rate, Filat'ev's success came in the wake of unsuccessful precedents in the short history of Muscovite-Ming relations. The Baikov mission two decades earlier had been an embarrassment for Moscow. It seems that when Russians merchants arrived they pleased the Chinese by performing the kowtow, and the Chinese were happy to consider these hirsute arrivals diplomats. In fact, when Moscow did send diplomats (Baikov in 1654, Spafarii in 1675), they were under strict orders not to perform signs of deference to Chinese officials and their talks with their Chinese counterparts quickly ran aground over quibbles about protocol.[7]

Not so with Nikitin's caravan. Granted, the five-week delay on the Chinese border was inconvenient. Chinese soldiers rode out onto the steppes to satisfy themselves that no Russian army followed behind before allowing the Russian merchants to proceed to Beijing. But the wait was worth it. Nikitin was thrice entertained at the emperor's palace, although he himself never saw the emperor, who remained out of view behind a screen. He and his group were allowed to trade in Beijing's central market for seven weeks, where, in addition to Chinese, they likely encountered Jesuit missionaries, Central Asian merchants, and perhaps even Hindu and Persian visitors. By March 1675, Nikitin had reached Selenginsk again (roughly halfway between Moscow and Beijing), where he paused briefly before continuing on to Moscow with a small fortune in exotic Eastern wares.[8]

About the time that Gavril was preparing for the China expedition, his brother Ivan Romanovich Nikitin, who sometimes also worked for Filat'ev, was having far worse luck in Siberia.[9] Ivan had stored a shipment of pelts, dried fish, and other goods in a warehouse in Verkhotur'e; during a fire they went missing. Fortunately, by April 1674 Ivan Romanov was able to recover the goods, which had been brought to a nearby convent for safekeeping. When Ivan finally reclaimed his goods in Tobol'sk, another of Ostafii Filat'ev's men signed on his behalf because, unlike his brother Gavril, Ivan Romanovich could not write.[10] Given all that could go wrong—elements, enemies, theft, betrayal, rapacious government officials, and spoilage—any successful venture involved some good luck, but one wonders if Ivan's illiteracy explains why he never attained the same success as Gavril. However, one cannot say for sure—although Ivan could not write in 1675 and Gavril could in 1681, we do not know when Gavril learned this skill or whether Ivan might have learned it later.

Gavril Romanovich's success opened doors for him. In 1678, he was still being recorded at the customs post as Ostafii Filat'ev's agent, yet by early 1679, he had been granted membership in the first tier of privileged merchant ranks—the Merchant Hundred—and he soon developed his own team of agents.[11] Then, in 1681, he rose to the membership of the elite gost' corporation, which had a profound effect on his business. Having cut his teeth in trade by crisscrossing the steppes and forests for the Filat'evs, Nikitin would move to Moscow—residence in the capital was required of all gosti—and direct his own network. Being a privileged merchant required performing state service—often in the form of shouldering administrative responsibilities such as heading important customs posts or the Siberian Office. We do not know exactly what Nikitin's service involved, but we can be fairly certain that his work constantly required him to juggle private enterprise and duties to the state. In Moscow he patronized several churches and was a regular donor and supporter of the Church of Georgii of the Old Ponds, in whose parish his Moscow house was located.

At the same time, like most gosti, Nikitin did not forsake ties to his home. He donated monies to his home parish and parents' resting place, the Church of the Supreme Apostles Peter and Paul, and to the Church of the All-Merciful Savior in Sol'vychegodsk—so that the priests there would pray for the souls of his parents. Nor did his relatives forget their roots. Although his wife remarried and remained in Moscow after his death, his nephew returned to Charonda.[12]

By the time he became a privileged merchant, Gavril was the oldest surviving Nikitin brother (he would outlive his two remaining brothers, Ivan and Trifon), which made him patriarch of his own family as well as the head of an extensive trade network. This brought the responsibility of supporting his extended family, which consisted of several orphan nephews and nieces—many of whom received bequests in his will. Several of his orphaned nephews became integral parts of his commercial ventures. Boris, the son of Gavril's deceased brother Kondratii, worked for his uncle Gavril for a while, but later joined government service and worked in metallurgical exploration. His departure from the family business may explain why Nikitin bequeathed only 50 rubles to Boris's sister, Anisiia Kondrat'eva, but 200 and 1,700 rubles to his other nieces.

According to his will—probably a conservative estimate—Nikitin's net worth was just shy of 30,000 rubles in 1697, the year before he died.[13] At the time of his arrest, Gavril's nephew Stepan (the son of the second-oldest brother, Roman) was collecting debts on Gavril's behalf in Siberia while Stepan's two sons, Afanasii and Kirill, were in Moscow helping their great-uncle, Gavril. When Gavril was imprisoned, Kirill brought him meals and tried to negotiate his release. Had the state not confiscated Gavril's property, these two grandnephews would have received the largest single inheritance, 2,000 rubles in cash and 7,000 rubles' worth of Siberian goods.[14] But that is getting ahead of Nikitin's story.

Nikitin's niche was his enterprises in Siberia and China, which placed him among thirteen out of forty-five gosti who were actively involved in Siberian trade during the 1670s and 1680s.[15] He owned and rented trading stalls in Siberian marketplaces such as Eniseisk, Mangazeia, Ilimsk, Irbit, and Tobol'sk. He bought a shop stall in the easternmost Siberian town of Nerchinsk, a stepping-off point to China.

A semi-permanent trading stall in Yakutsk served as a regional base for his people in the field.

At the height of his career, Nikitin was the head of a trade network made up of several dozens of men and women, both kin and non-kin. These people—who could be hired, indentured, contract, or slave labor—acted as the porters, guards, messengers, and cooks that trade caravans needed. Or they might perform any number of tasks necessary to maintain a long distance commercial network. A reliance on family ties obtained throughout all levels of the network. Just as Nikitin's family members worked for him, his hired workers often brought in their own relatives as well, generating a web of family commitments and a system of in-house apprenticeship.

His most key people in the field were his agents and "men." Typically, agents were free individuals while a "man" was a dependent in the boss's household, but their functional duties overlapped and their positions seem to have been determined by merit. After all, with Nikitin overseeing affairs from distant Moscow, micromanagement was not an option. Profit or loss could hinge upon the acumen, judgment, and competence or the complacency and mistakes of these men in the field. Timofei Bozhedomov, Boris Pikalev, Kuz'ma Stepanov, and Vasilii Serebrianikov were among the nine agents and ten "men" Nikitin depended upon to run Siberian and Chinese trade operations. Serebrianikov, who technically began as a dependent but is referred to as an agent in documents, may have been his most trusted helper.

Vasilii Serebrianikov's association with Gavril Nikitin began when his father, Ustiug merchant Grigorii Serebrianikov, could not repay a debt to Nikitin; Vasilii was given over to the Nikitin household in 1681 and remained a part of his household and business for life. In Nikitin's insistent implorations that Vasilii communicate more frequently and quickly and not drink too much, one senses a rapport warmer than a strictly business relationship. It is through surviving letters to Vasilii that we learn of the passing of Gavril's brother Ivan. On September 27, 1688, Gavril wrote Vasilii Serebrianikov,

> From Gavril Nikitin. A letter to my man, Vasilii Serebrianikov. How is God keeping you? I am in Moscow on September 27. God has kept me living. Let it be known to you that by the will of God [my] brother Ivan Romanovich did not rise. He died the night of September 26. Remember him. And write to me, Vasilii, when and which date you arrived to Sol' and what you had with you and give me all your news. And you yourself stay in Sol'vychegodsk until you get a letter and order from me, but I do not know what you have. Ivan Pivovarov and Nikita Gavrilov[16] wrote to me from Eniseisk that you came to Eniseisk and are going to Rus', but what you have and with what you are traveling there was never a letter to me from Eniseisk, and from me to you is this request.[17]

After Ivan's death, Trifon was Gavril's only surviving brother, although, given Trifon's love of drink, Nikitin kept him away from the family business and made his inheritance conditional upon his not getting drunk and carousing.[18] Not long after his brother Ivan died, Nikitin wrote to Vasilii with more sad news: his first wife, Agrippina, had passed away.

As his top-level assistants in the field, Nikitin's agents moved between central Russia, Siberia, and China, and sometimes remained in the field for years at a time. It was not uncommon for agents to work their entire careers for their gosti employer, embedding their networks of kin and staff—including Mongol or Kalmyk slave children, whom they sometimes raised and brought into the business as trusted members of the organization—within his.[19]

The work of an agent in Siberia involved much more than escorting caravans. Procurement, logistics, security, retail, compliance, and staffing were all part of the agent's purview. Warehousing needed to be secured and trade stalls rented and manned in the major Siberian towns. Receipts passed between these men as they handed off goods and money in various Siberian towns make up much of the surviving documentation from the Nikitin archive. On top of all that, credit operations were a standard part of the business.[20]

As was typical of early modern trade, turnover time could be so slow on Siberian endeavors that cash flow was a problem; traders needed to diversify in order to remain solvent. Credit was a component of any major merchant's portfolio, as borrowing and lending were strategies for maintaining solvency first and earning profit second. Merchants engaged in credit operations on both sides of the ledger. They borrowed to finance their own trade missions, and, in the absence of formal lending institutions, merchants functioned as banks for a range of Siberians—soldiers, administrators, churchmen, merchants, trappers, Cossacks, and women—in need of cash.

Unsurprisingly, like any savvy businessman, Nikitin tried to be on the lending side of credit transactions. And it seems he often was, for he acquired not only human labor—for Serebrianikov—as a result of unpaid debts, but also a saltworks in Sol'kamsk. His sale worth 4,100 rubles on credit to a Greek merchant in 1681 reflects a healthy cash flow.[21] In some cases Nikitin's men found themselves needing loans. For example, Timofei Bozhedomov took three loans en route to China, a practice Nikitin roundly discouraged. "Do not take any loans from anyone for any purpose," commands one letter.[22] Indeed, when Bozhedomov died in Siberia, creditors tried to collect by intercepting Nikitin's agents as they returned from a profitable trip to China laden with goods.

Having risen from a humble peasant background, Nikitin could be a harsh boss and was not beyond reminding his agents that he "didn't find this money on the street." Nor did success come overnight for him. Nikitin died a very old man, but he had been a gost' not quite two decades, which indicates that he had worked a long time before attaining an elite status. And so his frugal sense was offended, for example, when he learned that two of his merchants in the field were boarding in separate quarters, thus doubling expenses. "People tell me," Nikitin wrote to an agent in February 1688, "that you and Kusko live separately. Keep joint quarters."[23] On the whole, Nikitin's parsimonious habits served him well. His accounts stood very much in the black at his time of death, but instead of his estate going to his designated inheritors, the state sold his goods through the Siberian Office and profited thereby.

Nikitin's letters from Moscow to his agents in the field illuminate a range of issues, from the mundane to the urgent. Not surprisingly, in many of them we find instructions of one kind or another, although Nikitin was wary of committing all of his plans to paper. Some letters instruct the recipient to get the full instructions on the matter at hand from the bearer of the letter; Nikitin was fearful, obviously, that the letter itself might fall into the wrong hands.[24]

In addition to sending instructions, Nikitin also asked for information. His letters reveal the head of an enterprise conscientiously, anxiously, trying to monitor his investments in a world where certainties were few and mail traveled too slowly. They exude an almost frenetic desire to know what was going on; he repeatedly implored his men in the field to write to him with information and updates. Even his trusted Vasilii Serebrianikov could frustrate the boss with his silences. "I have not heard any news from you," he wrote in one letter, "[H]ow you are living and how is business going? . . . I have sent letters to you with every dispatch but from you to me there has not been one letter last year. Ivan Kozmin informed me that you fired that man Ivan Fedorov on the Kirenga who was useless and drunk."[25]

Nikitin's surviving notes reveal a charming everyday spirituality. They often begin with an inquiry into his agent's health and a report on his own, linking both to the Creator. Written from the center of Russian Orthodoxy in Moscow, these missives reveal none of plaguing doubts that the writings of another Russian merchant—who coincidentally had the same name, although no kinship has been established—the fifteenth-century Afanasei Nikitin revealed when he found himself among proselytizing Muslims and devout Hindus in Persia and India. Far removed from the company of coreligionists and an Orthodox calendar by which to mark days of fasting, Afanasei became plagued with doubt about his standing with God; he worried (as if confession were contagious) that he might become Muslim by keeping their company.

One wonders if Nikitin longed for the concreteness of life in the field. His letters betray the experience of someone who knew all too well the travails and pitfalls of life on the road for a merchant in Siberia. "Keep him from drinking," he admonished one agent about a colleague. Yet there was plenty to keep Nikitin busy in Moscow. He had trading stalls to maintain in the Moscow market. Affairs in the government, not least acquisition of documentation for eastern expeditions, required his attention. Maintaining political relations through favors, gifts, and reciprocity—making sure no hospitality or assistance went unrewarded—was a "core area" of the business. It is said that he had sufficient clout to have matters pertaining to his affairs transferred in the as yet unrationalized Muscovite bureaucracy from the Foreign Office to the Siberian Office, where his connections were stronger. Nikitin also maintained relationships with merchants in trade centers such as Sol'vychegodsk who could be useful in negotiating logistical and political sides of the business. Other merchants sought help from Nikitin in securing transit visas for travel to China. In 1698, when it became known to him that there was an investigation against him, Nikitin tapped his connections to try to learn all he could about the nature of the accusations and the actions being taken.[26]

If Nikitin ever waxed nostalgic for his days traipsing the eastern frontier, such musings must have been tempered by the sobering realities of life in the Eurasian borderlands. His agent Timofei Bozhedomov, traveling to China in 1695 with his brother Dmitrii Bozhedomov and agent Boris Pikalev, died just short of Nerchinsk, never reaching China. Vasilii Serebrianikov also died—"did not rise," as Gavril phrased it— in the field, near the mouth of the Kirenga River on a trading trip to Yakutsk in the winter of 1694. Upon his death, his assistant took over his belongings, which included a metal plated purse containing money, documents and icons, a Mongolian saddle, and a suitcase containing two coats (one of silver fur, the other of dark green homespun), a fancy damask caftan with silver buttons, a short caftan, four red cotton shirts, a pair of red damask pants, two pairs of Moroccan boots (one green, one black), two pistols, some knives, and a pound of tea.[27]

Interestingly, the former assistant who became the custodian of these effects, Aleshka Nikitin, was not Russian but rather a Mongol slave whom Serbrianikov had purchased as a little boy. He received his Russian names at the time of his baptism, and it is no surprise that his last name became that of his owner's boss, as this only underscored the power of family relations in the organization of the business. Trade over long distances is almost cross-cultural by definition, and this was very much the case with Eurasian trade. The steppes and forests were not densely populated but were quite diverse. In the Siberian capital of Tobol'sk, for example, the minarets of mosques shared the skyline with the onion domes of Orthodox churches, and native communities beyond the town practiced varieties of shamanism. Our brief glimpse of Aleshka Nikitin—with his Russian-sounding name—reminds us that life on the ground in Siberia may have been even more diverse than historical records at first suggest.

In the end, life in Moscow proved more perilous for Nikitin than the dangers of the wild forests and steppes. Nikitin was a part of Old Russia reaching out in new ways—he was an elderly man who had made a fortune in eastern endeavors by the time young Tsar Peter began so forcefully turning Russia westward. We do not know for certain what possibilities Nikitin saw in his country's increasing turn to the west. He was a keen businessman who may have recognized opportunity in Russia bridging Eastern supply and Western demand. Yet, we do know that he opposed what he saw as the new tsar's foolhardy attempt to build a southern naval force and expand Russia's influence on the Black Sea.

His criticism of Peter's aggressive maritime priorities may have poised him for a fall from favor. But it was probably personal vindictiveness or opportunism rather than ideological dissonance that catalyzed Nikitin's demise. Seeing an opportunity to rid himself of a debt, one of Nikitin's debtors reported to authorities that Nikitin had criticized Peter's Black Sea adventures—it was, after all, a regime that could look on such pronouncements as treasonous rather than expressions of free speech. The timing was terrible for Nikitin. In the summer of 1698 the musketeers (*strel'tsy*) revolted.

In response, Peter raced home from his famous European embassy and put down the revolt with great brutality. Against the backdrop of these events, the tsar was in no mood to dismiss the report of Nikitin's criticism. On August 30, 1698, just five days after Peter returned to Moscow to suppress the strel'tsy, his officials arrested Nikitin for "disrespectful remarks about the tsar Peter and his favorite Menshikov criticizing state affairs."[28]

Upon his arrest, Nikitin instructed his nephews to appeal to Alexander Menshikov, Peter's all-powerful favorite, to have him released from prison, and he authorized them to spend up to 2,000 rubles to get the job done. Menshikov agreed to a bribe of 2,500 rubles. But bribery would not extricate the merchant, for at the very moment that Kirill Nikitin was bringing the money to Menshikov's home, the tsar appeared and the transaction never took place. Nikitin died in Preobrazhenskii Prison just days later, on September 18, 1698. Thus, even though Tsar Peter had more to worry about than the criticisms of a wealthy old man, he did in the end have a hand in Nikitin's death.

On April 28, 1699, the Siberian Office—the same department that in years past issued orders to let Nikitin's functionaries pass through Siberia unmolested—issued an order to auction off the wares from Nikitin's last expedition to China. Among the bidders was Vasilii Filat'ev, the son of Nikitin's early employer, who had himself risen to gost' rank. One wonders if Filat'ev felt a sense of irony at buying up the wares of a ruined man whose career his father had done so much to launch.[29]

## NOTES

1. David Holley, "Russian Oil Tycoon Khodorkovsky Arrested," *Los Angeles Times*, October 26, 2003, A-3, articles.latimes.com/2003/oct/26/world/fg-khodorkovsky26.

2. K. V. Bazilevich, *V gostiakh u bogdykhana (puteshestviia russkikh v Kitai v XVII veke)* (Leningrad: Izdatel'stvo Brokgauz-Efron, 1927), 19.

3. Gost' was an exclusive title indicating membership granted by the tsar into a small circle of Russia's most elite merchants. The number of gosti ranged from forty-five to sixty-one during the years 1675–99. N. B. Golikova, *Privilegirovannye kupecheskie korporatsii Rossii XVI–pervoi chetverti XVIII v.* (Moscow: Pamiatniki istoricheskoi mysli, 1998), 1:180, 160, 213.

4. In Tiumen' 1672–73, *Tamozhennye knigi Sibirskikh gorodov* (hereafter cited as TKSG), vol. 4, ed. D. Ia. Rezun (Novosibirsk: Ripel Plius, 1997–2001); in Eniseisk 1669–70 or 1671; in Sol'vychegodsk, December 1677 and 1678. S. V. Bakhrushin, "Torgi gostia Nikitina v Sibiri i Kitae," in *Nauchnye trudy*, vol. 3, pt. 1 (Moscow: ANSSSR, 1952–59), 228. This contribution draws heavily on Bakhrushin's original piece on Nikitin.

5. O. N. Vilkov, *Remeslo i torgovlia zapadnoi Sibiri v XVII v.* (Moscow: Nauka, 1967), 209.

6. A. N. Malyshev, "Russia's Early Relations with China: 1619–1792" (Ph.D. diss., University of Colorado, 1967), ch. 5.

7. Fedor Alekseevich Golovin finally bucked that trend when he represented an acquiescent Muscovy in negotiating the 1689 Treaty of Nerchinsk. For a brief summary of early modern Russo-Chinese relations, see George V. Lantseff and Richard A. Pierce, *Eastward to*

*Empire: Exploration and Conquest on the Russian Open Frontier, to 1750* (Montreal: McGill–Queen's University Press, 1973), 159–80. For a more recent, and Sinocentric, treatment, see Peter C. Perdue, *China Marches West: The Qing Conquest of Central Eurasia* (Cambridge, Mass.: Harvard University Press, 2005), chs. 2 and 4.

8. Bazilevich, *V gostiakh u bogdykhana,* 10.

9. Institute of History of the Russian Academy of Sciences, Leningrad Division, (hereafter cited as LOII-SPB), f. 28, op. 1, karton 21, no. 37, l. 4v. (Tobol'sk, 1674); *TKSG* 1:56.

10. LOII-SPB, f. 28, op. 1, karton 21, no. 37, l. 4v. An example of unstable labels: Snishko is named as Filat'ev's agent on l. 1 and as a trading man on l. 4v.

11. Bakhrushin, "Torgi gostia Nikitina v Sibiri i Kitae," 228; Golikova, *Privilegirovannye kupecheskie korporatsii,* 160. For details about Nikitin's operations as a Merchant Hundred, see Rossiiskii gosudarstvennyi arkhiv drevnikh aktov (hereafter cited as RGADA), f. 1111, op. 1, d. 187, ll. 124, 156. On the work of some of his agents, see RGADA, f. 1111, op. 1, d. 187, ll. 124, 126.

12. On these details, see RGADA, f. 214, stb. 1698, ll. 53, 54; and Bakhrushin, "Torgi gostia Nikitina v Sibiri i Kitae," 251. For an excerpt of Gavril Romanovich Nikitin's will, see T. B. Solov'eva and T. A. Lapteva, *Privilegirovannoe kupechestvo Rossii vo vtoroi polovine XVI–pervoi chetverti XVIII v. Sbornik dokumentov,* vol. 1 (Moscow: Rosspen, 2004), no. 109.3, 403.

13. Bakhrushin, "Torgi gostia Nikitina v Sibiri i Kitae," 249.

14. Solov'eva and Lapteva, *Privilegirovannoe kupechestvo Rossii,* vol. 1, no. 109.3, 403.

15. About thirteen out of forty-five gosti were active in the Siberian trade in this period. See Erika Monahan, "Trade and Empire: Merchant Networks, Frontier Commerce, and the State in Western Siberia, 1644–1728" (Ph.D. diss., Stanford University, 2007), 120.

16. Despite the suggestive name, I have encountered no further documentation that Nikita Gavrilov may have been a son of G. R. Nikitin.

17. RGADA, f. 214, stb. 1128, l. 104.

18. Solov'eva and Lapteva, *Privilegirovannoe kupechestvo Rossii,* vol. 1, no. 109.3, 403.

19. For example, Spiridon Iakovlev's agent Ivan Zverev from Viatka. RGADA, f. 214, kn. 892, ll. 49v., 96v., 130. On slaves hired by agents, see RGADA, f. 1111, op. 2, d. 611, l. 174; GATO, f. 47, op. 1, d. 2219, ll. 1–6; Bakhrushin, "Torgi gostia Nikitina v Sibiri i Kitae," 375.

20. See, for example, RGADA, f. 214, stb. 1128, ll. 16–20v.

21. Solov'eva and Lapteva, *Privilegirovannoe kupechestvo Rossii,* vol. 1, no. 81.1, 327; Bakhrushin, "Torgi gostia Nikitina v Sibiri i Kitae," 230–31, 235.

22. RGADA, f. 214, stb. 1128, l. 12; Bakhrushin, "Torgi gostia Nikitina v Sibiri i Kitae," 249.

23. Ibid., 232, 244.

24. Ibid., 236.

25. RGADA, f. 214, stb. 1128, l. 109. The Kirenga River flows from the mountains west of Lake Baikal northward to the Lena River.

26. Bakhrushin, "Torgi gostia Nikitina v Sibiri i Kitae," 236.

27. Ibid., 231, 235.

28. Ibid., 226.

29. On this, see RGADA, f. 214, stb. 1698, l. 55, 78; and op. 5, d. 1495, l. 15.

BORIS PRINCEPS DE KURAKIN,
*EQVES ORDINIS S.<sup>t</sup> ANDREÆ*,
SACRÆ SUÆ CZAREÆ MAJESTATIS MINISTER
Ã SECRETIORIBUS CONCILIIS, COLONELLUS LOCUMTENENS
COHORTIS PRÆTORIANÆ, GENERALIS PRÆFECTUS·
VIGILIARUM. &c. &c.

Kneller pinx.                    S. Gunst sculp.

Portrait of Prince Boris Korybut-Kurakin by Pieter Stevens van Gunst, after original painting by Godfrey Kneller (Holland, after 1717). Line engraving, 37.3 × 28 cm. Hermitage Museum.

# 5

# Boris Ivanovich Korybut-Kurakin

## (1676–1727)

ERNEST A. ZITSER

The autobiographical *Vita del Principe Boris Koribut-Kourakin del familii de Polionia et Litoania* [*sic*],[1] a querulous chronicle of the life of one of the leading diplomats of Peter the Great, is not merely the first eighteenth-century Russian memoir, norsimply an eyewitness account of the reformist reign of Russia's first emperor (r. 1682–1725). It also constitutes a unique, early modern "ego-document,"[2] which expresses how one extraordinary member of Muscovy's hereditary service elite understood and experienced the processes of "modernization" and "secularization" that were the hallmarks of Peter's "cultural revolution."[3] Kurakin's *Vita* not only enriches our understanding of these long-term cultural processes, but also offers an unprecedented opportunity to examine them from the inside out—that is to say, from the point of view of a member of a social group (*dvorianstvo* or *shliakhetstvo*) frequently depicted as a blank slate upon which a reforming tsar and faceless historical forces left their indelible marks. In Kurakin's case, these marks included not only the prominently displayed insignia of the first Russian knightly order or the cravat and perruque that he sports in his personally commissioned engraved portrait,[4] but also the oozing, scorbutic sores and melancholic thoughts concealed in plain sight among all these fashionable trappings of worldly success, like the anamorphic death's-head in Hans Holbein's *The Ambassadors* (1533). Indeed, from a certain angle, Kurakin's complaints can be seen as psychosomatic manifestations of a Muscovite courtier's desperate—and, ultimately, not unsuccessful—attempt to use all the tools at his disposal to reconcile his astrological complexion with his professional aspirations and aristocratic pretensions, and thereby take control of his own fate.[5]

Prince Boris Ivanovich Kurakin (July 20 [July 30, NS], 1676–October 17 [October 28], 1727) was born into one of the greatest princely families in Muscovy, whose members were promoted straight to the Duma rank of *okol'nichii*.[6] Thanks to his familial connections at the court of the Tsar Fëdor Alekseevich (1661–82), the prince was even in line to be the next royal favorite. However, as a result of political upheaval in the wake of Fëdor's early death, he was instead appointed to the retinue of the young Tsar Peter, and thereby consigned to the periphery of Muscovite court life. In 1691, making the most of the hand that he was dealt, Kurakin married the sister of Peter's first wife and thereby became the tsar's brother-in-law (*svoiak*). In 1695–96, he participated in the Azov campaigns and in 1697 he was one of the gentlemen of the chamber (*spal'niki*) to be sent to study navigation in the Venetian Republic, a major maritime power and an important ally in the ongoing struggle against the Ottoman Porte. During this trip Kurakin picked up some Italian, which came to be his language of choice for conveying information or expressing emotions that he did not wish to make known beyond a small circle of intended readers of his writings. At the start of the Northern War against Sweden (1700–21), Kurakin fought in the Semenovskii Life-Guards Regiment. His long and honorable diplomatic career began only in 1707, when the prince was sent to Rome in order to convince the Pope not to recognize the Swedish king's candidate for the Polish throne. In 1709 Kurakin helped to arrange the marriage of his nephew, and Peter's son Tsarevich Aleksei to Sophia Charlotte of Brunswick-Wolfenbüttel, the sister-in-law of the Holy Roman Emperor. From 1708 to 1712, he represented the interests of his sovereign at London, Hanover, and The Hague successively and, in 1713, was the principal Russian plenipotentiary at the peace congress of Utrecht, which ended the War of the Spanish Succession. From 1716 to 1722, Kurakin held the post of ambassador to France, where he successfully participated in negotiations resulting in a French agreement not to provide Sweden with assistance; and, less successfully, in the attempt to arrange the marriage of Peter's daughter Elizabeth (the future empress) to King Louis XV. After the end of the Northern War, when Peter set forth on his Persian campaign (1722–23), Kurakin was appointed supervisor of all the Russian ambassadors accredited to the various European courts, an honor accorded to no other Petrine diplomat. Indeed, by the time he died, in Paris, at the age of fifty-one, Kurakin had largely succeeded in fulfilling Peter's decree that subjects of the Russian Emperor henceforth be known abroad as "Imperial Russians" rather than as members of the "Muscovite nation."[7]

From this brief summary of Kurakin's curriculum vitae, it appears that the polyglot prince embodied the cosmopolitan ideals in the name of which Peter the Great launched his "Westernizing" reforms. However, judging by Kurakin's voluminous writings (most of which remain in manuscript), he was much less sanguine about the changes introduced during Peter's reign than his distinctly European manners and his brilliant diplomatic career would indicate. As the title of his autobiography suggests, being the quintessential "new Russian" did not preclude Kurakin from considering himself as a scion of the princely "family of Poland and Lithuania." Indeed, the desire to be treated simultaneously as a privileged aristocrat and a dutiful imperial subject animated Kurakin's lifelong autobiographical project and informed many of his historical writings, including the unfinished "history" (*gistoriia*) that he intended to write for the "benefit" and "glory" of his "fatherland, the All-Russian Empire" (*v pol'zu moego otechestva Vserossiiskoi imperii*).[8] But its clearest manifestation appears in his personal "book of nativity" (*kniga rozhdeniia* or *libro della mia nascita*),[9] the astrologically inflected memoir that he began to write in 1705 while taking the waters in Carlsbad (Karlovy Vary), where he was sent—on doctors' orders and with the tsar's permission—to restore his health. According to Kurakin's *Vita*, the foreign physicians who served at the Muscovite court had officially diagnosed him with "melancholy (*melankholiia*) and scurvy (*skorbudika*) or [hy]pochondria (*pokhondria*), a disease which is similar to leprosy (*blizhitsia k lepre*), or *prokaza*, as it is called in [Church] Slavonic."[10] It is important to point out that scurvy, a deficiency disease that we now know results from a lack of vitamin C (ascorbic acid) in the diet, was at the time thought to "proceed" from the "putrefaction of Melancholy." Contemporary reference works defined "melancholia," or black choler, as "one of the four humors of the body, the grossest of all the other, which if it abound too much, causes heaviness and sadness of mind." A "windy melancholy," for example, bred "Hypochondriack distempers," so called because "their seat [is] in the Hypochondria, i.e. the upper part of the belly, about the short ribs, from whence a black phlegm arises that infects and troubles the mind proceeded."[11] By this definition, Kurakin was a hypochondriac not because he obsessively wrote about his various ailments, but because he was troubled with an imbalance in the bodily humors, an imbalance that naturally predisposed him to the heaviness of spirit and sadness of mind that caused him to seek a water cure in the first place.

Kurakin was not only sick, but also a disaffected Muscovite courtier: certainly in the obsolete sense of affected with disease, but also in the now rare sense of someone who is disliked, regarded with aversion. Kurakin was very conscious of the fact that after 1698 he was out of favor at the court of Tsar Peter, who had confined his first wife in a convent and had withdrawn his favor from those individuals (like Kurakin) who had belonged to the court clique that put him on the throne. Indeed, after Peter's divorce, the prince was put in the uncomfortable position of being a courtier who had once been related by marriage to the reigning monarch, but who had now, for reasons beyond his control, found himself on the outs with the tsar and his advisers. This is why Kurakin can also be said to be disaffected in the third, much more familiar, sense of the word—namely, estranged in affection or allegiance, or hostile to the government and to constituted authority. As far as we know, Kurakin was never involved in any sort of overt political opposition, and never disloyal. But he was estranged from his former brother-in-law and therefore, by definition, unfriendly to the current constellation of individuals and political clans that made up Peter's inner circle.[12] Kurakin's estrangement is one of the reasons why in the *Vita*, as well as the unfinished chapter of the *Gistoriia* devoted to the "intrigues" at the court of his royal brother-in-law,[13] he attributed many of Peter's reforms to the avarice of low-born "projectors," who rose to positions of power formerly occupied by the likes of the Prince himself— a highly influential (and largely erroneous) interpretation of the social composition of the Petrine court that was part and parcel of what has been called Kurakin's "aristocratic myth of Russian history."[14]

Since the personal was political at the early modern Russian court, Kurakin's disaffection was also expressed in other spheres of his life. Thus, he was a disaffected family man—his first wife (née Ksen'ia Fedorovna Lopukhina) died soon after giving birth to his only son, Aleksandr; and his next marriage, to Princess Mar'ia Fedorovna Urusova, does not appear to have been a happy one, although in the autobiography he purposely refrains from revealing the reasons for his estrangement from his second wife, beyond noting that her behavior caused people to talk and him to feel ashamed. He was also a disaffected military professional. When he first started keeping a separate notebook in which to record his life story, Kurakin was desperately looking for a way out of the army. The year that he received permission to take the waters at Carlsbad marked the tenth year that Kurakin was serving a tour of duty in the ranks, during a military conflict that seemed to be dragging on without end, and which, in fact, would not be resolved for another decade and a half. While the prince was serving in the ranks, many of his peers from the state-mandated study-abroad program of the 1690s had already embarked upon their careers in the diplomatic corps. Scions of other princely families, foreigners, and even men of much lower birth had already landed cushy jobs at the courts of European monarchs while he was still risking his life and endangering his health on the battlefield. This apparent lack of recognition is one of the main themes of the *Vita*. Kurakin felt resentful of the tsar, by whose orders he was subordinated to (and dependent on the whims of) court favorites, and exposed both to constant physical danger and tremendous emotional stress: not just fear of dying a horrible, painful death as a result of combat or disease (to which he is not afraid to admit); but primarily of losing face or bringing dishonor to the family in front of other members of the Muscovite hereditary service elite. The other reason he was so desperate to find a way to leave the Petrine army had less to do with Kurakin's stubborn adherence to the Muscovite notion of precedence ranking (*mestnichestvo*) than his sense of family duty. Earlier in the year he experienced a life event (the death of his brother) by which he inherited the entire family fortune and, in effect, became the eldest representative of the Kurakin clan. As such, he now had to think much more carefully not only about his family's past and his own present, but also the future of his sole son and heir. Indeed, Kurakin's occasional use of direct address makes it clear that the *Vita* was written with an eye to future readers—most likely his only son, who appears to have been the primary member of the intended audience for Kurakin's autobiography.

The *Vita* was, therefore, not merely an act of self-justification designed to counter the impression that he was a shirker of duty. It was also a paternal testament, a writing cure, and a laboratory in which Kurakin could try on a new persona. To the extent that the autobiographical notebook that Kurakin began to keep in Carlsbad may have been intended as his paternal testament, the *Vita* corresponded to the icon of the Savior Not Made by Human Hands (*Spas nerukotvornyi*) with which the prince's own father blessed him shortly before he died: that is, it was a memento mori, a link to family, and a tangible reminder of the power of faith in overcoming earthly pain and injustice. Much like the Russian Orthodox passion bearers (*strastoterptsy*) Boris and Gleb, the heavenly namesakes whose protection Kurakin invoked at the start of his *Vita*, the prince presented himself as a martyr who suffered ill fortune not because of what he did, but simply because of who he was. In his case, who he was had as much to do with his temperament as with the political nation into which he was born and the faith that he professed. Temperament, in this context, referred not to a psychological predisposition but to a person's astrological complexion, which contemporaries believed could be calculated on the basis of one's exact place and time of birth and the corresponding planetary positions, a fateful alignment of the stars that could be depicted in precisely the kind of natal chart (also known as "nativity" or "geniture") that decorated the cover of Kurakin's "book of nativity."[15] The fact that Kurakin begins his autobiography with a depiction of his personal horoscope suggests that (at least to some extent) he also believed that the ups and downs of his health, as well as of his political and personal fortunes, were the result of his predetermined fate and his physical constitution. Far from encouraging resignation, however, this astrological determinism allowed Kurakin's narrative of suffering to lay the foundation for larger social, political, or moral claims (and actions). That is because Kurakin's description of pain (and how he dealt with it) created an emotionally charged community with his reader(s)—his son and future progeny—the community most likely to read this document, and, more importantly, to read it sympathetically. This emotional bond to the actual and imagined readers of the *Vita* drew the readers' attention to the "real" underlying causes of Kurakin's suffering at the court of his former brother-in-law and led them to make the appropriate parallel to the lives of the prince's patron saints, who were martyred on the orders of their royal relatives.

As a writing cure, the *Vita* (retroactively) traced the life path that led Kurakin to his own midlife "crisis"—a crisis not only in the original, medical sense of the word, but also in the personal and professional sense. By tracing how he got to this point in his life, Kurakin could also begin to chart a way to get out. The episodes that Kurakin chose to include in his *Vita* can be seen as the Prince's attempt to demonstrate (first of all to himself) not only that he was constitutionally unfit for war, but also (and more positively) that his astrologically determined temperament predisposed him for more politic pursuits—a career in the Russian foreign service, preferably as an ambassador to the Venetian Republic, where Kurakin had once already been treated like a prince and where he hoped to be well received again. To a certain extent, Kurakin's idealization of the south in general (and Italy in particular) was based as much on an escapist fantasy of the future as on memories of his past experiences in Venice—including of his torrid affair with "Sig-ra Francesia Rotta," a patrician lady (*chitadenka*) whom Kurakin "kept as a mistress [*kotoruiu imel za medresu*]" and to whom he promised to return at the very first opportunity. But it is important to keep in mind that this erotically tinged fantasy about the south also reflected the evolution of the Muscovite prince's political views and his reading of history, and, in particular, about the role of low-born moneyed interests in the decline of the Venetian Republic (an interpretation that early modern Polish historians also projected onto the noble *Rzech Pospolita*).[16] These views explain not only the *Vita*'s numerous vituperative comments about "base" and "plebeian" royal favorites, but also why, in deference to Polish genealogical tradition, Prince Kurakin insisted on calling himself a "Korybut."[17] The Kurakins did indeed trace their roots to "Gedimin, the Grand

Prince of Lithuania" (*velikii kniaz' litovskii*), but so, too, did many other equally proud representatives of princely clans.[18] However, such grandees generally did not choose to hyphenate their names. The hereditary servitors who did resort to this step typically did so because they felt that they had something to prove, and were motivated as much by status anxiety as family pride or personal vanity. And the same can be said for Boris Ivanovich, the "hereditary prince of the Lithuania, from the house of *Korybut-Kurakin*" (*domu* Caributoff Karakinigh, *kniazei nasledstvennykh litovskikh*), a scion of Polish-Lithuanian royalty and would-be diplomat who complained that he "was received with more affection and respect abroad than [he ever experienced] in his own parts [*v svoikh kraiakh*]."[19]

The thrust of Kurakin's autobiographical narrative strongly suggests that a change of climate—both geographical and political (from cold, despotic north [Muscovy] to warm, noble south [Italy]) would alleviate much of his suffering, and help him restore his physical and mental health. Such a change of scenery would finally reconcile Kurakin's astrological complexion with his professional aspirations. Kurakin's invocation of the language of medical astrology is thus not merely a way to understand and describe his own character. It is an attempt to make that character become destiny. This complex interplay between astrological determinism and aristocratic self-fashioning also helps to explain why Kurakin traveled to Carlsbad not as a Muscovite subject but rather as an Italian citizen "by the name of Francisco Damiati."[20] Adopting this nom de guerre was partly a matter of prudence: the Swedish ships that patrolled the waters of the Baltic Sea would certainly not allow a Muscovite subject (even one who was not an enemy combatant) to cross unmolested. But I would argue that there is more to this name change than a desire to travel incognito through enemy territory. An Italian pseudonym gave Prince Kurakin the opportunity to assume a new persona—much like the one that he adopted in the 1690s, when he traveled to Venice as a Muscovite "nobleman" by the name of "Boris Ivanov." This time, however, he was not a student forcibly sent abroad, but a paterfamilias, traveling "by his own will" (*samovol'no*) and on his own personal business.[21] Although this business included a medical component, there was clearly more to it than a desire to seek a cure for his "scorbutic" illness. Judging by Kurakin's travel notebook, which served as one of the primary sources of his autobiographical *Vita*, it appears that the prince himself thought that this trip would be the start of something else, perhaps even a lifetime of travel abroad.[22] It is not too farfetched to suggest that by adopting an Italian pseudonym and repeatedly invoking the language that he had picked up in Venice, Kurakin was not simply paying his respects to the early-eighteenth-century "passion for peppering one's prose with foreign words,"[23] but imagining himself in the role of a professional diplomat traveling incognito—a role that he would get a chance to play in real life just two years later, when he was sent to Rome as Muscovy's secret envoy to the Papal Court.

In sum, the *Vita* can be seen not only as a paternal testament or a writing cure, but as a testing ground for Kurakin's ideas about himself—a private space that provided this self-described diplomat the opportunity to try out a new persona in the relative safety of his own study, before he had to act publicly to convince the tsar and his advisers that he would best be of service to his sovereign abroad. The autobiographical entries written after his visit to Carlsbad demonstrate how assiduously Kurakin worked all possible angles to get a post as the official Russian ambassador to Venice. Although his 1707 mission to Rome was only a partial success, and he was not immediately awarded further diplomatic assignments, Kurakin still hoped that this experience would allow him to parlay his Italian connections and his knowledge of the language into a more permanent position in the Russian diplomatic corps.[24] In hindsight, of course, we know that Kurakin never did become the Russian ambassador to the Venetian Republic. However, more than six years after he began to write in his "nativity book," he did succeed in switching careers. This stroke of good fortune had major repercussions, not least of which was the opportunity to live abroad, away from his estranged wife and his enemies at court—and, more importantly, out of reach of Peter's educational cudgel. In fact, Kurakin's very success may also be the reason why he eventually stopped adding entries to his autobiographical notebook. By 1710–11, he had finally managed to secure a permanent diplomatic appointment abroad, and thereby succeeded in fashioning the life that his *Vita* was intent on exploring. From then on, Kurakin's voluminous diplomatic correspondence, memoranda, and travel notebooks[25]—took over the task of documenting the life of this "Imperial Russian" servitor "of the family of Poland and Lithuania."

## NOTES

1. Two different redactions of the original manuscripts can be found in Gosudarstvennyi istoricheskii muzei (hereafter cited as GIM), f. 3 (Fond Kurakinykh), op. S[taraia], № 6, ll. 184–223 ob., 244–57 ob.; and Nauchno-istoricheskii arkhiv Instituta rossiiskoi istorii Rossiiskoi Akadmii Nauk (hereafter cited as IRI RAN), Koll. 115. Op. 1. № 153. ll. 1–61 ob., 107–21. They were published in the second half of the nineteenth century as "Zhizn' kniazia Borisa Ivanovich Kurakina im samim opsiannaia," in *Arkhiv kn. F. A. Kurakina* (hereafter cited as *Arkhiv*), ed. M. I. Semevskii (St. Petersburg: Tip. V. S. Balasheva, 1890–1902), 1:243–87, Italianate title quoted on 243; and F. A. Ternovskii, ed., "Semeinaia khronika i vospominaniia kniazia Borisa Ivanovicha Kurakina," *Kievskaia starina* 10 (September 1884): 105–28, (November 1884): 478–98, and (December 1884): 621–38.

2. A term coined by the Dutch historian Jacob Presser to describe the multiple literary forms of autobiographical expression and thereby to question the "apriorism and rigid formalism of traditional approaches to the history of autobiography." By expanding the limits of self-testimony beyond "classic manifestations that feature retrospective, chronologically ordered narratives focusing on the development of the inner self," this definition "brings to light a host of new texts and thereby broadens the ranks of autobiographical authors to include greater diversity" of class, race, and gender. See James S. Ameland, "Spanish Autobiography in the Early Modern Era," in *Ego-Dokumente: Annäherung an den Menschen in der Geschichte*, ed. Winfried Schulze [= Selbstzeugnisse der Neuzeit, Bd. 2] (Berlin: Akademie, 1996), 59–71, quotation on 60; and more generally, Winfried Schulze, "Ego-Dokumente: Annäherung an den Menschen in der Geschichte," in ibid., 11–30.

3. This phrase subsumes "the many military, naval, governmental, educational, architectural, linguistic, and other internal reforms enacted by Peter's regime to promote Russia's rise as a major European power." See James Cracraft, "The Russian Empire as a Cultural Construct," *The Journal of the Historical Society* 10, no. 2 (2010): 167–88, quotation on 170.

4. Portrait of Prince Boris Korybut-Kurakin (c. 1717) by Pieter Stevens van Gunst. Line engraving, 37.3 × 28 cm. Available online in The State Hermitage Museum Digital Collection: www.hermitagemuseum.org/fcgi-bin/db2www/browse.mac/category?sellLang=English. For a discussion of Kurakin's iconography, see V. F. Vasilenko, "Neizvestnyi portret kniazia Borisa Ivanovicha Kurakina," in *Kurakinskie chteniia*, ed. Dzh. B. Logashova (Moscow: GU MDN, 2006), 142–66.

5. Ernest A. Zitser, "The *Vita* of Prince Boris Ivanovich 'Korybut'-Kurakin: Personal Life-Writing and Aristocratic Self-Fashioning at the Court of Peter the Great," *Jahrbücher für Geschichte Osteuropas* Band 59, Heft 2 (2011): 163–94. See also Robert Collis, "'Stars Rule Over People, but God Rules Over the Stars': The Astrological World View of Boris Ivanovich Kurakin (1676–1727)," *Jahrbücher für Geschichte Osteuropas* Band 59, Heft 2 (2011): 195–216.

6. On Kurakin, see James Cracraft, "Kurakin, Prince Boris Ivanovich," *The Modern Encyclopedia of Russian and Soviet History*, ed. Joseph L. Wieczynski (Gulf Breeze, Fla.: Academic International Press, 1980), 18:168–70; G. M. Karpov, "Boris Ivanovich Kurakin," *Voprosy istorii* 9 (2007): 18–32; and Iu. V. Trifankova, *B. I. Kurakin: Lichnost' i diplomaticheskaia deiatel'nost'*: diss. . . . kand. ist. nauk (Riazan', 2007).

7. As late as September 1713, in a letter from The Hague, Kurakin complained, "I have an ukaz from His Ts.[arist] M.[ajesty] that in [foreign] newspapers I should be referred to as an Imperial Russian, not as [a member] of the Muscovite nation [*rossiiskim, a ne moskovskoi natsii*], and in the credentials [*bilety*] that are presented on my behalf I am styled as an Imperial Russian. But independent journalists [*korrishpondenty partikuliarnye*] frequently continue to refer to me as a Muscovite. And while I have already commissioned all the newspaper publishers [*vsem kurantirom ot menia zakazano; to make the requisite terminological changes*], it is impossible to establish this in the short term, especially here, in a free country [*v vol'nom pravlenii*]." See Prince B. I. Kurakin to A. D. Menshikov (September 8, 1713), *Arkhiv*, 9:121.

8. *Arkhiv*, 1:41, 79.

9. *Arkhiv*, 5:122, 123.

10. Entry for the twenty-ninth year (July 20, 1704, to July 20, 1705). However, in a personal medical history written in 1718 and intended solely for his doctors, Kurakin attributed his various illnesses to the "dissolute" (*nevozderzhannyi*) lifestyle that he was forced to lead at the court of his brother-in-law and even admitted the possibility that his skin condition may also have been a result of an "unclean disease" (*nechistaia bolezn'*)—a euphemism for the sexually transmitted infection that Kurakin appears to have contracted in Moscow at the age of fifteen. See *Arkhiv*, 3:229.

11. Ian Lancashire, ed., *Lexicons of Early Modern English*, s.vv. "scurvy" and "melancholy" (Toronto: University of Toronto Library and University of Toronto Press, 2011), leme.library. utoronto.ca.

12. In this respect, Kurakin may perhaps best be likened to his more famous French contemporary, Louis de Rouvroy, duc de Saint-Simon (1675–1755), a disaffected and highly rank-conscious courtier who left a memoir chronicling the stultifying pettiness and corruption at the court of King Louis XIV. Saint-Simon, who actually met and befriended Kurakin in 1717, offered the following description of the Prince: "Kourakin was of a branch of that ancient family of the Jagellons, which had long worn the crowns of Poland, Denmark, Norway, and Sweden. He was a tall, well-made man, who felt all the grandeur of his origin; had much intelligence, knowledge of the way of managing men, and instruction. He spoke French and several languages very fairly; he had travelled much, served in war, then been employed in different courts. He was Russian to the backbone, and his extreme avarice much damaged his talents."

*Memoirs of Louis XIV and His Court and of the Regency by The Duke of Saint-Simon*, ed. Jim Manis (Hazleton, Pa.: The Pennsylvania State University, 2003), 726–28, available online at www2.hn.psu.edu/faculty/jmanis/saint-simon/Saint-Simon.pdf. Note that the French courtier's condescending characterization of his foreign interlocutor assumes, and therefore takes for granted, the very conjunction (aristocratic seigneur and royal subject) that the Russian prince was working so hard to realize in his own life, and that he was only able to accomplish in the privacy of his *Vita* and on his trips abroad.

13. See, especially, the chapter of his unfinished history devoted to the intrigues at Peter's court: "Gistoriia o tsare Petre Alekseeviche, 1682–1694," in *Arkhiv,* 1:39–77.

14. This "aristocratic myth" not only presaged the conceptions of Prince M. M. Shcherbatov and "other conservatives of later ages," but also the views of many historians of the reign. Paul Bushkovitch, *Peter the Great: The Struggle for Power, 1671–1725* (Cambridge: Cambridge University Press, 2001), 439. See also Robert O. Crummey, "Peter and the Boyar Aristocracy, 1689–1700," *Canadian-American Slavic Studies* 8, no. 2 (Summer 1974): 274–87, especially 274–75; Brenda Meehan-Waters, "The Russian Aristocracy and the Reforms of Peter the Great," *Canadian-American Slavic Studies* 8, no. 2 (Summer 1974): 288–302; and A. V. Zakharov, *Gosudarev dvor Petra I: publikatsiia i issledovanie massovykh istochnikov razriadnogo deloproizvodstva* (Cheliabinsk: Cheliab. gos. un-t, 2009).

15. The undated ink drawing of the horoscope of "P. B. I. K. K." (that is, Prince Boris Ivanovich Koribut Kurakin), "in italiano" and "al stilo nuovo," from IRI RAN, Koll. 115. Op. 1. № 153. l. 7, is reproduced in Zitser, "The *Vita* of Prince Boris Ivanovich 'Korybut'-Kurakin," 174.

16. See Kurakin's "Zametki o respublike Venetskoi," in *Arkhiv,* 3:194, 200; *Arkhiv,* 4:115–16; and the discussion in Bushkovitch, *Peter the Great,* 437–39, 441–42.

17. The patronymic "Korybutowicz" served to demonstrate that a particular *szlachta* family descended from Lithuanian royalty. Kurakin may also have hoped to evoke the memory of a more recent bearer of this name, Michał Wiśniowiecki (1640–1673), the nobleman who ascended to the throne of the Polish-Lithuanian Commonwealth in 1669 as King Michał Korybut Wisniowiecki. After his death, Russian and Polish diplomats briefly considered marrying off Wisniowiecki's widow to Tsarevich Fëdor Alekseevich, thereby transferring the Polish crown to Muscovy. See Bushkovitch, *Peter the Great,* 70–71, 439n37.

18. See "Rodoslovnaia rospis' kniazei Golitsynykh i Kurakinykh," in *Rod kniazei Golitsynykh,* comp. N. N. Golitsyn (St. Petersburg: Tip. I. N. Skorokhodova, 1892), 1:28–36, signed by Kurakin's father on March 11, 1682; and Prince S. D. Golitsyn's letter to Prince B. I. Kurakin (May 11, 1722) "about our [common princely] family" (*vedenie o familii nashei*), based on "Russian chronicles as well as those translated from the Polish" (*letopistsy nashi russkie i perevedennye s pol' skogo*), in *Arkhiv,* 2:441–42.

19. Kurakin's emphasis in entry for the thirty-second year (from July 20, 1707, to July 20, 1708).

20. Kurakin appears to have borrowed the name from his former instructor, Francesco Damiani, conte de Vergada (Franjo Damjanić Vrgadski), an Italophile Dalmatian nobleman who taught Kurakin naval science, while also trying to instill in him the notion that "[t]he houses of illustrious heroes renowned for their magnanimity and greatness are illuminated not only by the splendor of their birth [*della nascita*], but are also immortalized by virtue of their education [*la virtù delle lettere*], which leaves an eternal memory to posterity." See *Arkhiv,* 4:78–79.

21. Entry for the twenty-ninth year.

22. The opening entry reads, "*1705—1—Iggulia: Giornal che io il primo volte scomencavo scriver del tutti cosi in mio vito, quanto cosa sara è ancoro tutto mio viagge per mundo*" (*Arkhiv,* 1:101). This "obscure phrase," written "in broken Italian" means, roughly, "Journal that I for the first time began to write of all the things in my life, how many things will happen and also

all my voyages around the world." See Sara Dickinson, "The Russian Tour of Europe before Fonvizin: Travel Writing as Literary Endeavor in Eighteenth-Century Russia," *The Slavic and East European Journal* 45, no. 1 (Spring 2001): 1–29, quotation on 6.

23. V. V. Vinogradov, *Ocherki po istorii russkogo literaturnogo iazyka XVII–XIX vv.* (Moscow, 1938 [Leyden: E. I. Brill, 1949]), 58; translated by Lawrence L. Thomas as *The History of the Russian Literary Language From the Seventeenth Century to the Nineteenth* (Madison: University of Wisconsin Press, 1969), 35.

24. Kurakin was not good at disguising his desire for a new "ministerial" position. It was apparent to both the astrologer who told the prince's fortune in 1707 and to the tsar, who publicly berated the prince for "seeking the chance to become a foreign ambassador" instead of "serving in the military"—a dressing down that may explain why Kurakin was the only guards officer to be passed over for promotion after the Russian victory at Poltava in June 1709. See "Latitudiny planet (Goroskop B. I. Kurakina)," *Arkhiv*, 3:147; and *Vita* entry for the thirty-fourth year (July 20, 1709, to July 20, 1710).

25. These documents constituted an important part of the Kurakin family archive. For the history of the family archive, see M. I. Semevskii, introduction to *Arkhiv*, 1:xv–xix; Semevskii, "Selo Nadezhdino i arkhiv kn. F. A. Kurakina v 1888 i 1890 gg.," *Russkaia starina* 68 (1890): 229–38; V. N. Smol'ianinov, "Istoricheskii arkhiv kniazia F. A. Kurakina, v sele Nadezhdine, Saratovskoi gub. (Iz gazety "Saratovskii listok" 169: 10 [avgust+ 1888])," *Russkaia starina* 59 (1888), 683–87; Semevskii, *Vosemnadtsatyi vek* 1 (1904), iii–xxxi; P. A. Druzhinin, "Sud'ba arkhiva kniazia A. B Kurakina," in *Neizvestnye pis'ma russkiskh pisatelei kniaziu Aleksandru Borisovichu Kurakinu (1752–1818)* (Moscow: "Truten'," 2002), 77–91; and B. R. Logashova, *Moskva. Dom natsional'nostei.* Izd. 3-e, dop. i pererab. (Moscow: GU MDN, 2008), 185–87, 196–99, 213.

Ivan Fedorov, *Empress Catherine II visits M.V. Lomonosov* (1884).

# 6

# Mikhail Lomonosov

## (1711–1765)

### MICHAEL D. GORDIN

As the old saying goes, comparisons are odious. To make sense of Mikhail Vasil'evich Lomonosov, historians have frequently resorted to comparisons more or less apt (usually less). Almost all of the comparisons emphasize his ventures in natural philosophy—the set of doctrines and practices concerning the study of nature that would, in the nineteenth century, acquire the moniker "science." Russian historians tended to see him as akin to Antoine Lavoisier (1743–94), the French chemist and member of the Parisian Académie des Sciences credited with the discovery of oxygen and the law of the conservation of matter: matter is neither created nor destroyed, but only changes form. This comparison bolsters (by suggestion) a claim for Lomonosov's priority for the conservation law, and also emphasizes the Russian's position as a member of the St. Petersburg Academy of Sciences—and hence his analogous location in a complicated absolutist patronage network. Western historians have likened Lomonosov to Benjamin Franklin (1706–90), emphasizing both men's research on electricity, folksy self-presentations, and positions as outsiders on the European stage of Enlightenment natural philosophy.[1]

Both comparisons leave something rather important out of the story: Lomonosov's pivotal role in the development of Russian verse through his promotion of iambic metrical schemes. For Lomonosov was not just a natural philosopher or a courtier—he was also arguably the greatest poet in eighteenth-century Russia (and certainly the greatest Russian poet in the first half of that century). The best comparison, then, if one must be made, might be to Francis Bacon (1561–1626), the man who served as lord chancellor for King James I of England, formulated the foundations of the experimental method in natural philosophy in works such as *The Advancement of Learning* and *The New Atlantis* (an important early scientific utopia), and pioneered the modern literary genre of the essay—reforming English prose in the process. Bacon encapsulates some of the same vigor, diversity, and eclecticism of Lomonosov. He also lived a century and a half earlier than Lavoisier and Franklin—or Lomonosov.

That chronological gap is the most important point—indeed, the only really significant point—of the Lomonosov-Bacon comparison. When analyzing a Russian life, the Westerner's tendency is to juxtapose rough contemporaries: Leo Tolstoy and Emile Zola, Lev Landau and Richard Feynman, Joseph Stalin and Adolf Hitler. This predilection for making parallels between Russian and European (or North American) developments works surprisingly well for nineteenth- and twentieth-century figures; for earlier periods, it breaks down. By the late eighteenth century, one is able to find good analogs of Russian figures in the contemporaneous West; in the seventeenth century, this is impossible (most of the best analogs, one finds, lived roughly two centuries earlier, spawning the classic argument that Russia leapt from the medieval period to the Enlightenment in the early eighteenth century, skipping the Renaissance).[2] One of the great lessons of Lomonosov's life is that he bridged the gap between radical incommensurability and direct comparison—that he himself is symptomatic of the "time lag" of early-eighteenth-century Russia, and instrumental in erasing the cultural division of Russia from Central and Western Europe.

Lomonosov's life was a highly unusual one, straddling not just different domains of learning and living in his adult years, but migrating across social classes (or estates) and proto-national boundaries over the course of his maturation.[3] He was born in the village of Mishaninsk on November 8, 1711, near the White Sea. His father, Vasilii Dorofeevich, was a reasonably well off owner of merchant and fishing vessels, which he used in the summer to accumulate wares which were then transported over the ice to Moscow in the winter (when transport was generally much easier in Imperial Russia). The young Lomonosov thus hailed from a community that had contented itself with its nearly self-sufficient trade networks for generations and was somewhat removed from the pro- and anti-Westernizing influences from Moscow; nonetheless, he was jolted by the Petrine reforms.

What little we know about Lomonosov's early studies (admittedly drawn heavily from his own testimony, a significant means of personal mythmaking) reveals an education largely Muscovite in its orientation. Upon first learning to read—in itself not common, even among merchants, above a very rudimentary level—he had access only to Old Church Slavonic texts from the nearby monastery, and so his reading was predominantly theological. When he was about fourteen, he obtained copies of two standard textbooks of the age that could be seen as prefiguring his later development: Meletii Smotritskii's *Grammatika* and Leontii Magnitskii's *Arifmetika*, the latter being the first mathematical textbook in the Russian language. (Both works were much broader in content than their titles suggest.)

Lomonosov was nothing if not impatient, and the routine life of a northern merchant was not to his taste. At age nineteen, on December 7, 1730, he left his village by trading convoy for Moscow. He was legally a peasant, and thus proscribed from matriculating even at such meager educational institutions as then existed in the old capital. Lomonosov adopted his usual solution to such difficulties: he exaggerated, and then he lied. He applied to the Slavo-Greco-Latin Academy and represented himself as the son of a nobleman from Kholmogory (near his actual birthplace), was admitted, and rapidly advanced in his studies, acquiring excellent facility in Latin as well as the foundations of Slavic grammar, arithmetic, geography, history, and catechism. He read extensively in the Academy's library, and his performance was so striking that he was not expelled when his deception was uncovered in 1734—an early indication of Lomonosov's excellent luck. That luck continued. In 1735, the new president of the decade-old Imperial Academy of Sciences in St. Petersburg, Baron Johann-Albrecht Korf, wrote to the Moscow school asking for twenty of their best students to be sent to the university attached to the fledgling Academy.[4] This being the early eighteenth century, only twelve students of passing competence were found, and Lomonosov was the best of the lot. Thus, on January 1, 1736, Lomonosov began to study at the St. Petersburg Academy of Sciences.

This was an affiliation and an institution that would dominate the rest of his life. The first way it did so was by sending him away—to study chemistry and mining in Marburg, a significant university in the German states, in order that upon his return he might assist the Academy in its series of expeditions to explore the mineral wealth of the empire. The key to the riches of Asiatic Russia lay with the Germans. Lomonosov was sent in autumn 1736, along with Gustav Reiser and Dmitrii Vinogradov, to study science and philosophy with Christian Wolff (1679–1754), Gottfried Wilhelm Leibniz's disciple and the most significant influence—after that deceased savant—on the philosophical orientation of the Petersburg Academy. Later, the Russians were dispatched to Freiberg to learn *Bergkunde* (mining arts) at the feet of Johann Friedrich Henkel. The Russian students got on well with Wolff; less so with Henkel. The feelings were mutual; Wolff was particularly impressed with Lomonosov: "Mr. Lomonosov apparently has the brightest head among them [the Russian students]; with good diligence he could learn a great deal, having shown great eagerness and desire to learn."[5] That eagerness lasted; the industrious diligence did not. Throughout their stay, the Russians—gorging on newfound freedom—gambled and cavorted, racking up huge debts that were further complicated by the irregularity with which their stipend payments arrived from home. With the collapse of Lomonosov's funding, he and Henkel bickered continuously, and in May 1740 the Russian left Freiberg and wandered through the German and Dutch states looking for a Russian ambassador so he could acquire enough funds to return to Russia. He failed and returned to Marburg, where, on June 6, 1740, he married Elizabeth Zilch, daughter of a onetime city councilor. He was finally able to contact St. Petersburg and received an official recall. The prodigal northerner arrived at his new home on June 8, 1741—but without his wife, as the marriage was kept secret for some years (she was only able to join him in the summer of 1744).

This German episode is important for several reasons, beyond what it reveals about Lomonosov's impulsive, obstinate, and rather lively character. First, one notes that the directorship of the St. Petersburg Academy in its early years considered their domestic intellectual resources thoroughly inadequate without significant scholarly assistance from abroad. This pattern of sending talented Russian scientists to German universities to complete their education would be repeated many times until the latter half of the nineteenth century.[6] The trip abroad was clearly important for Lomonosov, who used it to learn not just the doctrines of natural philosophy but also the practices of experimentation, the manners of disputation (somewhat rougher and more passionate than present-day readers might imagine), and additional foreign languages (there remains some dispute among scholars about which languages Lomonosov actually knew, based on the materials used in his library—estimates range as high as thirty, but many of these are dialects of Russian or other Slavic languages. It was clear, however, that he could read Latin, French, German, English, Italian, Dutch, and Greek, as well as some Scandinavian tongues).[7] Classic nationalist interpretations of Lomonosov, which laud him as a homegrown native genius, cannot hold if so much of his early formation was credited—both by himself and his contemporaries—to his time abroad. Finally, *where* and *what* he studied is important. By the middle of the eighteenth century, Wolff's brand of metaphysical idealism was both controversial and on its way to becoming outdated. Lomonosov's clear affinity for this philosophical orientation, as well as his cameralist training in mining chemistry, would shape many of his choices as an academician and public figure in mid-century St. Petersburg.[8]

Lomonosov's position at the Academy—he was made adjunct in physical science upon his return—seems secure in retrospect, but was constantly buffeted by the vertiginous politics of the post-Petrine court. He managed to keep his head down (but not too far down; he was briefly arrested and imprisoned in 1743) during the squabbles around Johann Daniel Schumacher's management of the Academy, and experienced a very productive decade in the 1740s, becoming in 1745 academician and professor of chemistry—and the first ethnically Russian member of the Academy of Sciences. (The Academy was originally—and necessarily—staffed by foreign scholars, but Russian membership grew throughout the eighteenth century. Lomonosov was a crucial trailblazer, but he was not unique.)[9] Although he retained his chemistry post until his death, he also undertook significant research in geography, mineralogy, astronomy, and meteorology, yet none of this formed the basis for a lasting scholarly reputation in the European Enlightenment outside Russia.[10] In 1748, Lomonosov had a chemical laboratory, the first in Russia, erected to his specifications; it was supposed to be devoted to pure and applied chemistry, but was mostly dedicated to the promotion of Lomonosov and his career.

Lomonosov engaged in two major spheres of political wrangling for the rest of his life: at the Academy and at court. These two dovetailed in interesting ways. He spent much of his effort in the laboratory producing colored glasses, which he used to create mosaics. He received permission in 1753 to manufacture these glasses, and built a factory staffed by peasants at Ust Ruditskii. From 1755 until his death he spent a great deal of time operating this factory. Glass was both his ticket out of the hotbed of Academy politics (by pulling him away from the capital) and a tool to gain him more favor at the court (since he produced mosaics to curry favor with powerful patrons).

No patron in the reign of Elizaveta Petrovna (1741–61) was more powerful than her lover Ivan Ivanovich Shuvalov (1727–97). Shuvalov was fascinated by

Lomonosov, as were many contemporaries at court: the academician was a witty conversationalist, an avid worker, and a truly stunning poet. It is his poetry, in fact, that was responsible for most of his reputation in Imperial Russia; at least until chemist Boris N. Menshutkin (1874–1938) unearthed his scientific writings and republicized them at the dawn of the twentieth century. Lomonosov's services to the Russian language in general, both in terms of reviving Slavonic roots and purging the language of some foreign importations, had by then long been recognized. In 1755 Lomonosov had produced the first grammar of the modern Russian language, which later went through eleven editions and was not outdone until the nineteenth century. His poetry, much more than the grammar, became canonical for Russian readers, even if it was later eclipsed by that of the titanic Alexander Pushkin (1799–1837). If Pushkin erected the edifice of modern Russian poetry in the first third of the nineteenth century, he built on the foundation laid by Lomonosov a century earlier.

This is no exaggeration. Lomonosov was instrumental, from his very first poetic effort in late 1739 (or early 1740) commemorating a Russian victory over the Turks outside the city of Khotin (a vaunting of imperial expansion appended to his criticism of the 1735 treatise on Russian versification penned by his rival and future fellow academician V. K. Trediakovskii). Lomonosov pioneered and championed the introduction of syllabo-tonic verse into Russian, as opposed to the older traditions modeled on Greek and Latin verse, which he deemed unworkable because they depended on the differing lengths of vowels, which Russian does not have. Instead, Lomonosov wrote primarily in heroic couplets and overwhelmingly in iambs (the same foot Shakespeare used, consisting of an unstressed syllable followed by a stress, as in the name "Michelle"), usually in four beats per line (iambic tetrameter).[11] Ninety-eight percent of Lomonosov's poetic output is in iambs, and it became the overwhelming favorite for Russian poets for the rest of the century. Even here, though, one should temper one's enthusiasm for his "universal genius," for his innovations in poetry, like his innovations in natural philosophy, were heavily derived from contemporary German efforts.[12] His poetry thus represented a characteristic of many Russian cultural forms (including science, art music, or the novel): the importation of a European mode and its adaptation and assimilation so that it acquired all the characteristics of being distinctly "Russian."

Much of Lomonosov's poetry was written to glorify some patron (such as Shuvalov) or the Russian autocrat. No matter whom he was praising, however, Lomonosov held Peter the Great in the highest of esteem, and used him as a model for proper governance. Although he has sometimes been dismissed as a casual panegyrist, Lomonosov's thoughts and images were always subtle and flexible. Consider his major poem, modestly titled "A Letter on the Utility of Glass," written in 1752 and addressed to Shuvalov. The poem, echoing the great "scientific" poems of Lucretius (*De rerum natura*) and Alexander Pope ("Essay on Man"), started with images of the simplicity of glass, comparing it to minerals from the ground, and then expanding on glass as a container for items of value, the source of mosaics, and then the lenses of instruments:

But in these enlightened days we see invention clearly.
Poets, to adorn their own verses,
Described punishment for imaginary sins.
We here receive the flame of solar Glass
And thus luxuriously imitate Prometheus.
Cursing the baseness of that absurd nonsense,
We smoke tobacco using sinless heavenly fire;
And only barely do we consider, regretfully,
Whether science has cast Prometheus down to destruction?
Would not the ignorance of savage tribes, becoming angry at him,
Form an incorrect impulse, not knowing of the inventions?
Would they not observe stars then through Telescopes
That the labor of happy Europe has now erected?
Had he not with Glass been able to bring from the heavens
And to inflict destruction on himself from the Barbarians
That betrayed him to punishment, having passed over a wizard?
How many such examples we have,
That envy, having concealed itself beneath the robes of holiness,
And the jealousy of rudeness with it, setting snares for truth,
Since antiquity has battled many times,
How much knowledge has died irreversibly![13]

We have moved from humble glass to the glories of Prometheus—an epochal transformer through transgression like Peter the Great (and, dare we imagine, Lomonosov himself?)—and then quickly on to a discussion of the Copernican model of the universe, of all things, couched in language saturated with themes of jealousy and envy, high and low. The "Letter" encapsulates a natural-philosophical, poetic, and political agenda in a patronage tribute to Shuvalov.[14]

The natural-philosophical agenda was both the most explicit in the poem, and arguably the most important to Lomonosov himself. Yet while it was clearly central to him, it was pursued in a fashion somewhat outdated with respect to his contemporaries in the West, and as a result has been less widely recognized—and, even worse, when it has been analyzed, it has been granted substantially greater perspicacity than it merits. Aside from his practical interests in areas such as glassmaking, which occupied a greater share of his time as he aged, Lomonosov also conducted a broad range of studies—some experimental, some theoretical—in various phenomena in the fields we would now call physics and chemistry (the boundary lines of the various disciplines have always been in flux, but were significantly more so in the eighteenth century). To the extent that there was a single unifying idea behind his diverse interests, it was the notion that all matter consisted of tiny corpuscles, and all forces were communicated through these corpuscles. This was not a precursor of today's atomism, but instead a more thoroughgoing notion of corpuscularism akin to that of René Descartes of the seventeenth century compared to the rigorous Newtonianism or Leibnizianism of Lomonosov's peers. Nevertheless, his research was well received, especially his most renowned paper, "Meditations on the Cause of Heat and Cold," read before the St. Petersburg Academy in 1745.[15] This was a quite sophisticated analysis of heat as nothing more than a species of motion, an understanding validated by the kinetic theory of heat in the mid-nineteenth century, but dating back at least to Francis Bacon a century before Lomonosov.

The second reason Lomonosov's work seemed somewhat out of pace with contemporary natural philosophy stems from *how* he delivered his theories. They were, almost without exception, delivered as orations to the public, in Russian, before the Petersburg Academy, part of the annual ritual decreed in Peter the Great's original plan. Although they were translated into Latin in the publications of the Academy, they were presented in a popularized format and directed to an audience of the Petersburg elite, *not* principally to fellow academicians or researchers. This specifically local coloration to Lomonosov's life and work provides the most consistent unifying feature of his many varied activities. He rose from extremely humble origins to be Shuvalov's client, the capital's most renowned poet, and the first Russian-born academician. He achieved all of these by focusing on local patronage networks, and it was to those networks that he remained faithful. His international reputation was, thus, rather slight compared to his huge profile in Russia, but the local profile was all that really mattered for his purposes. It was not until Russian scientists at the turn of the twentieth century retrieved Lomonosov's original manuscripts and papers (not his orations) out of the archives and published them that a revaluation of the significance of Lomonosov in natural philosophy emerged.

Lomonosov's final years were studded with the same combination of diverse research, poetic writings, Academic strife, and courtly gambits—although the scholarship was now more scattered and the politicking far less successful. In 1757, Lomonosov achieved a lifelong ambition and became a member of the Academy's chancellery, but this drew him away from active work in his laboratory and his factory. Then in 1760 he was placed in charge of the teaching functions of the Academy, a task both time consuming and unsuccessful (the pedagogical aspects of the Academy languished until being completely overhauled by the Academy's only female director, Ekaterina Dashkova, in the 1770s).[16] He never prepared the enormous treatise on a system of natural philosophy that he had planned—the very project itself had a scale of ambition characteristic of Wolff and his legacy—partly because he was ill, partly because of turmoil at the Academy, and partly because he had to pay ever more deference at court once his empress was gone and Shuvalov no longer a magic cure-all. This renewed effort of civility and courtliness was required to alleviate the debts accumulating at Ust Ruditskii. He died on April 4, 1765, early in the reign of Catherine the Great. It was during her reign that the St. Petersburg Academy of Sciences became one of the leading institutions of Europe, that Russian poetry (in Lomonosov's favored meter) began to flourish, and the empress lavished ever greater patronage on artists and Enlightenment *philosophes,* both foreign and domestic.[17] These were a patron and an age after his own heart, but he died before he could really enjoy them.

NOTES

1. W. Chapin Huntington, "Michael Lomonosov and Benjamin Franklin: Two Self-Made Men of the Eighteenth Century," *Russian Review* 18 (1959): 294–306.

2. Marc Raeff, "Seventeenth-Century Europe in Eighteenth-Century Russia?" *Slavic Review* 41 (1982): 611–19; and "On the Heterogeneity of the Eighteenth Century in Russia," in *Russia and the World of the Eighteenth Century,* ed. R. P. Bartlett, A. G. Cross, and Karen Rasmussen (Columbus, Ohio: Slavic, 1986): 666–80.

3. The following biographical details are drawn from A. V. Topicheva, N. A. Figurovskii, and V. L. Chenakala, eds., *Letopis' zhizni i deiatel'nosti M. V. Lomonosova* (Moscow: Izd. AN SSSR, 1961); Boris N. Menshutkin, *Russia's Lomonosov: Chemist, Courtier, Physicist, Poet,* tr. Jeannette Eyre Thal and Edward J. Webster (Princeton, N.J.: Princeton University Press, 1952); A. Morozov, *Lomonosov* (Moscow: Molodaia Gvardiia, 1965); B. M. Kedrov, "Lomonosov, Mikhail Vasilievich," *Complete Dictionary of Scientific Biography* (Detroit: Charles Scribner's Sons, 2007): 8:467–72; and Henry M. Leicester, "Mikhail Vasil'evich Lomonosov, 1711–1765," in *Great Chemists,* ed. Eduard Farber (New York: Interscience Publishers, 1961): 201–10.

4. On the establishment of the early Academy and the woes of its ancillary university, see Michael D. Gordin, "The Importation of Being Earnest: The Early St. Petersburg Academy of Sciences," *Isis* 91 (2000): 1–31.

5. Christian Wolff to Baron Korf, August 3 (17), 1738, reproduced as No. 31 in G. E. Pavlova, ed., *M. V. Lomonosov v vospominaniiakh i kharakteristikakh sovremennikov* (Moscow: Izd. AN SSSR, 1962), 96.

6. Michael D. Gordin, "The Heidelberg Circle: German Inflections on the Professionalization of Russian Chemistry in the 1860s," in "Intelligentsia Science," ed. Michael D. Gordin, Karl Hall, and Alexei B. Kojevnikov, special issue of *Osiris* 23 (2008): 23–49.

7. Iu. M. Lotman, "K voprosu o tom, kakimi iazykami vladel M. V. Lomonosov," *XVIII vek* 3 (1958): 460–62.

8. L. V. Pumpianskii, "Lomonosov i nemetskaia shkola razuma," *XVIII vek* 14 (1983): 3–44.

9. Ludmilla Schulze, "The Russification of the St. Petersburg Academy of Sciences and Arts in the Eighteenth Century," *British Journal for the History of Science* 18 (1985): 305–35. Schulze notes that foreign members were, however, paid more (315).

10. Although much of Lomonosov's work was neglected in the eighteenth century by his European contemporaries, twentieth-century scientists often pointed to his prescience. See, for example, A. S. Morris, "Mikhail Lomonosov and the Study of Landforms," *Transactions of the Institute of British Geographers* 41 (1967): 59–64; and L. A. Goldenberg and A. V. Postnikov, "Development of Mapping Methods in Russia in the Eighteenth Century," *Imago Mundi* 37 (1985): 63–80.

11. The typical Shakespearean line contains one more iamb—hence, iambic pentameter.

12. On Lomonosov's versification, see John Bucsela, "The Birth of Russian Syllabo-Tonic Versification," *Slavic and East European Journal* 9 (1965): 281–94; and idem, "Lomonosov's Literary Debut," *Slavic and East European Journal* 11 (1967): 405–22.

13. Lomonosov, "Pis'mo o pol'ze stekla," in M. V. Lomonosov, *Izbrannye proizvedeniia* (Moscow: Nauka, 1986), 2:239–40. Translation mine.

14. See the elegant interpretation of this poem in Kirill Ospovat, "Lomonosov i 'Pis'mo o pol'ze stekla': Poeziia i nauka pri dvore Elizavety Petrovny," *Novoe Literaturnoe Obozrenie* 87 (2007): 148–83.

15. On Lomonsov's corpuscular doctrines, see the translated documents and the analysis in Henry M. Leicester, ed. and trans., *Mikhail Vasil'evich Lomonosov on the Corpuscular Theory* (Cambridge, Mass.: Harvard University Press, 1970).

16. For a survey of Dashkova's tenure at the Academy, see Michael D. Gordin, "Arduous and Delicate Task: Ekaterina Dashkova, the Academy of Sciences, and the Taming of Natural

Philosophy," in *The Princess and the Patriot: Ekaterina Dashkova, Benjamin Franklin, and the Age of Enlightenment*, ed. Sue Ann Prince (Philadelphia: American Philosophical Society, 2006), 3–22.

17. On the growing importance of the Academy in this period, see J. Scott Carver, "A Reconsideration of Eighteenth-Century Russia's Contributions to European Science," *Canadian-American Slavic Studies* 14 (1980): 389–405.

Mikhail Shebanov, *Portrait of Catherine II* (after 1787). Hillwood Estate, Museum, and Gardens Archive, Washington, D.C. Reprinted with permission.

# 7

# Catherine the Great

## *(1729–1796)*

### HILDE HOOGENBOOM

As Empress Catherine the Great forged her own Russian identity, so did Russia. During Catherine's reign from 1762 to 1796, Russia discovered itself not only as European, but as a multinational and multiconfessional empire, and as Russian. A German, Catherine, with her legendary practicality, Russified herself, and at the same time promoted herself as a European ruler and Russia as a European nation. Yet she also inherited a vast Eurasian empire that doubled its population under her rule; until 1991, Russians and Russian Orthodox believers would make up less than fifty percent of its inhabitants. By the end of the eighteenth century, these tensions between Russia as a nation and as a diverse empire would come under pressure from new nationalist ideals.

After she arrived in Russia on February 9, 1744, at age fourteen from a small German state, Princess Sophie Auguste Frederike von Anhalt-Zerbst converted from Lutheranism to Russian Orthodoxy on June 28, became Grand Duchess Ekaterina Alekseevna, and began to learn Russian; over a year later, on August 21, 1745, she married the heir to the throne. She was crowned Empress Catherine II on September 22, 1762, after she took power in a coup d'état on June 28 against her husband, Peter III (b. 1728, r. 1761–62)—the nephew of Empress Elizabeth I (b. 1709, r. 1741–61)—who was murdered. Peter III was half German, the son of Elizabeth's sister Anna and Charles Frederick, the Duke of Holstein-Gottorp, and showed his devotion to King Frederick II (the Great) of Prussia (b. 1712, r. 1740–86) during his short rule when he ended the Seven Years' War (1756–63) with Prussia by returning land Russia had won. He then changed the color of the uniforms of the elite Russian guard units from their traditional green to Prussian blue. During her coup, Catherine used Peter's Prussophilia against him and wore a green guard's uniform to show her Russian colors. After the coup, her equestrian portrait as Russian ruler in the uniform of the Semenovskii Regiment by the Danish court painter Vigilius Eriksen (1722–83) made this point as well. Catherine had many copies made of this portrait, as well as of her coronation portrait by Eriksen, which were sent to the courts of Prussia, England, and Denmark. In the 1760s, he also made a portrait of Catherine dressed in national costume—with a *kokoshnik,* a traditional Russian headdress, as a *matushka,* or little mother—of which copies were made. Thus Catherine used different portraits of herself as a military leader, as empress, and as mother to her people, to represent herself variously as a Russian sovereign nationally and internationally.

Throughout her reign, in contrast to Peter III, Catherine was careful not to be too German, and the fact that we associate Catherine with French, and the French enlightenment and culture, is a testament to how well she succeeded in controlling her image. A typically polyglot European aristocrat, Catherine learned French from an early age that she might aspire to a royal marriage, which facilitated her assimilation into the Francophone Russian court and nobility. But her first language was German—and like French, she learned Russian; her papers are mainly in French and Russian, which she used for official business, with some letters in German. Nineteenth-century critics complained that she knew no language well and made mistakes in all three languages. In fact, she knew all three languages fluently, and her spelling mistakes were ordinary in the eighteenth century, when languages were not yet standardized. In the nineteenth century, "good" French became a status symbol and was synonymous with an elite education; Catherine's critics anachronistically applied this new standard to her writings. In an era when rulers were an international elite, Catherine was able to make herself at home in Russia by becoming Russian through religion and language, and by her always ardent defense of Russia against European criticisms that the nation and its people were primitive, and she was an Asiatic despot.

Catherine shared the enlightenment ideal of human beings as similar in possessing reason and thus being educable, yet she also followed the widely accepted ideas of Baron de Montesquieu, who argues in *Spirit of the Laws* (1748) that peoples develop differently and organically according to a country's climate and geography. Throughout her reign, Catherine defended Russia and Russians against criticisms by Montesquieu, Rousseau, Voltaire, the historian Claude-Carloman de Rulhière, and others by arguing that they did not know anything about Russia, which was true. But Russians also knew their empire poorly. After the publication of *Voyage in Siberia* by Chappe d'Auteroche in 1768, which similarly criticized Russia, Catherine ordered the Academy of Sciences to make expeditions, reports, illustrations, and maps in a survey of Russia. Catherine's "Academy Expedition" recalled Peter the Great's "Great Northern Expedition" of Siberia in the first half of the eighteenth century, which established Siberia as Asian and Russia as European, not only in surveys and on maps, but through the activity of participating in European explorations and mapmaking.[1] Peter had founded the Academy of Sciences in 1724 and staffed it with German scientists. Surveys brought back accounts of geography, resources, flora, fauna, and of different peoples and languages, and the Russian Empire gained the distinction of not only being the largest, but also of having the most diverse population. Moreover, many of the scientists and explorers who would survey and write about the Russia Empire were foreign, as were many officers in Russia's military, yet they were all Russian subjects in that they served the Russian state. By the early nineteenth century, this educated international elite, like the rulers they served, would be newly defined and restricted by their national origins, and would learn to compensate for their cosmopolitan origins by going national.

Catherine promoted ethnic and religious tolerance because she subscribed to theories that advocated population growth for the success of Russia's military and economy, which she believed to depend on agriculture and thus to require adequate population density. Her ideas on the economy were part of the debates about the economic importance of agriculture versus industrialization that were taking place across Europe and in America. On October 14, 1762, a month after her coronation, Catherine instituted a settlement program with financial incentives and the promise of religious freedom to encourage immigration. On July 22, 1763, she named Count Grigory Orlov (1734–83)—her favorite (1760–72) and father of her second son, Aleksei Grigorevich Bobrinsky (1762–1813)—president of the new Chancery of Guardianship for Foreigners, with an initial annual budget of 200,000 rubles. Orlov kept his post for ten years, even when he was no longer her favorite, and the program cost the state 5.5 million rubles by 1770. Nearly 30,000 Germans came to farm the Volga area with offers of subsidies. Ottoman Christians were invited with the promise of religious freedom. Catherine lifted the double tax Peter the Great had levied on Old Believers and encouraged them to return from the north with freedom to settle where they wished.[2]

Catherine tried to work with local traditions, privileges, and laws while promoting uniform Russian laws through a process she called "Russification." S. I. Ozhegov defines *obruset'* as "to become Russian in language and customs."[3] The writer, lexicographer, and ethnographer Vladimir Dal' (1801–72) includes the saying, "The Karelians and Mordva have gone native in Russia, but Yids take forever to Russify."[4] These definitions, similar to the first use of "Russify" in English at the end of the nineteenth century, indicate the linguistic and cultural roots of national identities that became part of debates about nationalism only in the nineteenth century.[5] But Catherine was mainly interested in policies that promoted political and legal structural integration with Russia of areas that had diverse ethnic groups and religions. For the most part, Catherine's policies left national and religious differences alone.

In February 1764, Catherine explained her principles of uniform governance for non-Russian provinces in her instructions (in Russian) to her new procurator-general, Prince Aleksandr Viazemsky (1727–96), who would be her most important administrator:

> Little Russia, Livonia, and Finland are provinces governed according to privileges that have been confirmed; to destroy them by revoking them all suddenly would be unseemly—but to call them foreign and to treat them as such would be more than a mistake, it can be called really stupid. These provinces, as well as Smolensk, should, by the simplest means, be brought to the point when they Russify and stop yearning like wolves for the woods. The approach to this is very simple if sensible people are appointed rulers of these provinces; when there is no longer a hetman in Little Russia we must strive to make the name and legacy of hetmans disappear and let no one be appointed to that post.[6]

By late February or early March 1764, Catherine had made life so difficult for hetman Kirill Razumovsky that he apparently asked to be relieved of his post. His position was abolished and Little Russia was put under the administration of Governor-General Peter Rumiantsev, whose secret instructions were to Russify Ukraine's governmental structures.[7] Always practical, Catherine did this despite her personal debt to Razumovsky, who had been Empress Elizabeth's morganatic husband, had helped lead Catherine's coup, and held positions in her new government.

The ethnic diversity of the Russian Empire was also on view in the Legislative Commission of 1767, which Catherine convened to aid in the creation of a new code of laws to succeed the Code of 1649, Russia's first legal codex. Catherine's innovative legislative exercise called for the election of representatives of three of the four estates (the nobility, merchants, and free peasants, but not the Church) and of areas with their own laws: the Baltic Provinces, Little Russia (including various Cossack hosts), and the non-Russian tribes. Tribesmen constituted the third largest group of representatives, nearly ten percent (54 out of approximately 570).[8] The semi-autonomous regions debated whether a Russian assembly could draft laws for them, but of even greater concern were the differences in social standing between delegates. Tensions over the legal rights that defined the estates (especially the rights of the nobility), rather than between ethnic groups, marked the deliberations, an indication that national differences had yet to become the divisive force they would be from the nineteenth century up to the present.[9]

From 1764 to 1787, Catherine made several well-publicized trips both to see her empire and to be seen by her new subjects; she spent three and a half years of her thirty-three-year reign traveling.[10] In the Baltic provinces, Little Russia (Ukraine), Belarus, and the Crimea, Catherine faced the problem of border areas that had different privileges and laws than the rest of Russia, especially regarding the nobility, serfs, judiciary, and taxation. In June 1764 she toured the Baltics for three weeks, visiting Reval in Estonia and Riga in Livonia, and going as far as Mitau in Courland, the only time she would ever leave the Russian Empire, before returning hastily to deal with the murder of Ivan VI. Although German was the lingua franca of the Baltics, official speeches were in Russian and Catherine went to Orthodox services.[11] In Livonia, in an experiment to improve the condition of serfs, agrarian reform was introduced in an area with extensive state lands, whereas nobles in the Landtag agreed to legal reforms for serfs, the Patent of April 12, 1765. But Catherine's Legislative Commission would make clear that the Russian nobility did not want to reform serfdom, but rather wished to increase their control over serfs; Catherine needed their support and shelved the subject. In 1767, before the opening of the Legislative Commission, she traveled down the Middle Volga, visiting Yaroslavl, Kostroma, Nizhnii Novgorod, Kazan', the ruins of Bolgary, and Simbirsk—areas that had been conquered by Ivan the Terrible two centuries earlier and would soon erupt in the Pugachev rebellion.

Not since the sixteenth century had Russia expanded on the scale it would under Catherine, nearly doubling its population from 23.2 to 41 million and increasing its territory by 11,000 square miles, to 305,794 square miles.[12] This process began two centuries earlier when Tsar Ivan the Terrible conquered the khanates of Kazan' and Astrakhan' in 1552. In 1721, Peter the Great looked to Europe and Rome, and away from the Byzantine Empire, when he claimed the title emperor and declared Russia to be a European empire. Catherine took up the military goals of her predecessors as she expanded Russia south toward ports on the Black Sea, west toward Poland, and northwest along ports on the Baltic Sea, and participated in the European wars between the great powers of England, France, Prussia, Austria, and the Ottoman Empire. She launched the First Turkish War (1768–74) and took Moldavia and Wallachia, which in the First Polish Partition (1772) she traded for parts of Belarus and Latvia. In 1783, Russia annexed the khanate of Crimea from Turkey, but it was again in play during the Second Turkish War (1787–92), as Russia moved southeast toward Constantinople (Istanbul) under Prince Grigory Potemkin's Greek project, which would have put Catherine's grandson Constantine on the throne of a Greek empire. The Treaty of Jassy (1792) recognized Russia's annexation of the Crimea, and led to the founding of Odessa, Russia's first port on the Black Sea since the twelfth century. Russia increased its land farther along the Black Sea, and in two more successive Polish Partitions (in 1793 and 1795), erased Poland from the map and took over Lithuania, Courland, and the remains of Belarus and Ukraine. When she died, Catherine was preparing to send armies to France together with Austria and Prussia in the First Coalition against Napoléon, and to Armenia and Georgia, where Russia had again established a protectorate.

In 1767, in a letter from Kazan' to France's greatest eighteenth-century public intellectual, Voltaire, Catherine contemplated the impossibility of bringing together Europe and Asia in her empire. Voltaire supported Catherine as a European sovereign, limited by natural rule of law, a position that Catherine promoted in her letters to him, and every letter in their famous correspondence begins with a short dance of mutual flattery. In this letter, she referred to a panegyric of herself, just published by Voltaire, *Lettres sur les panégyriques,* under the pseudonym Irénée Aléthès, professeur en droit dans le canton Suisse d'Uri. While traveling, she and her entourage translated Jean-François Marmontel's *Bélisaire* (1767), a history of the great Roman general (c. 500–65) who led the Byzantine army to conquer lands the Romans had lost, and which was dedicated to her; she translated chapter 9, "On the Ruler." Since 1765, she had been researching and writing her *Great Instruction,* a statement (in French) of her legislative principles that would confer legitimacy on her as an enlightened ruler when published in several languages in 1768. This letter expressed Catherine's awareness that the intellectual framework she brought to her job was only a first, limited step in dealing adequately with the diversity that the Russian Empire presented.

Kazan, May 29, 1767

I had threatened to send you a letter from some shack in Asia and I am keeping my word today.

It seems to me that the authors of the anecdote about Belisarius and of the letter about the panegyrics are close relatives of the Abbot Bazin [one of

Voltaire's pseudonyms], but wouldn't the gentleman prefer to publish all panegyrics to people after their death, for fear that sooner or later they prove unworthy, given the inconsequentiality and instability of human affairs. I do not know if after the revocation of the Edict of Nantes people took the panegyrics of Louis XIV seriously.[13] The refugees at least were not disposed to give them much weight.

I beg you sir to use your credit with the learned man of the Canton of Uri, that he not lose his time in composing a panegyric to me until my death. The laws about which so much has been said are after all not yet completed. And who can say if they are good. It is posterity and not us in truth who will be able to judge their goodness. Consider, I beg you, that they must serve both Asia and Europe. And what difference in climates, in people, in habits, and even in ideas. Here I am in Asia, I wanted to see this with my own eyes. There are in this city twenty different peoples who do not at all resemble each other. Yet a garment must be made that will fit them all. They may well find for themselves general principles, but what of the details? And such details! I would say that there is almost a world to create, to unite, to preserve. I wouldn't even finish and still there are too many details of all kinds. If all of this doesn't succeed, the scraps from my letters that I found cited in your latest publication will seem ostentatious (what do I know?) both to the impartial and to those jealous of me, and in any event my letters were only published out of respect and are not fit for print. It is true that it is very flattering and does me honor to see the sentiment with which the author of the letter on the panegyrics composed all this. But Belisarius says that just such a moment is dangerous for my kind. Being always right, Belisarius no doubt will not be wrong in this either. The translation of this latest book is finished and is going to be printed. To test this translation it was read by two people who did not know the original. One exclaimed that he would have had his eyes put out to be Belisarius. He would have been amply recompensed. The second says that he would be jealous of the other.[14] In closing, sir, receive this evidence of my recognition for all the marks of friendship that you have given me, but if possible, keep my scribbles out of print.

Catherine[15]

In this letter, Catherine raised the main problem that her empire presented, which was to devise a general pattern of administration that nevertheless would accommodate the particular details of many peoples. Throughout her reign she constantly studied how different countries arranged their administration of the various estates, geopolitical divisions, judiciary, and finances to devise plans that were suited to Russia and its diverse population and were effective. The many notes and drafts of plans in her own hand found in archives demonstrate the extent to which these projects consumed her time, intellect, imagination, and energy.

In her correspondence with Voltaire, which was widely read in France and published after he died in 1778, Catherine made sure she was seen to be studying governance, and presenting herself as an enlightened European ruler. During the first Russo-Turkish War from 1768 to 1774, Catherine wrote Voltaire more letters than at any other time, to promote her version of the war as a triumph for civilization against what she and Voltaire called Mustafa and the Muslim infidels. Catherine knew that many Europeans, including Voltaire, wondered if Russia could become a civilized European nation, and that they saw little difference between Turks and Russians; thus, her wars against the Ottoman Empire were an opportunity to represent herself and Russia as European and civilizing. At this time, Catherine even invited Voltaire and Diderot to come visit; Diderot did and was disappointed because Catherine was less receptive to his ideas in person. The Comte de Ségur recounted an anecdote from their meetings that underscores her practical concerns: "Monsieur Diderot . . . [i]n all your plans for reform you forget the difference between our two positions: you work only on paper, which tolerates everything; it is smooth, supple, and offers no resistance to either your imagination or your pen; whereas I, a poor Empress, work on human skin, which is much more irritable and ticklish."[16]

In response to the Pugachev Revolt of 1773–74, Catherine embarked on a decade of administrative reforms that fundamentally restructured local government to increase centralization and local control, especially in troubled areas. In 1780, Catherine traveled to the new western provinces after the first Polish Partition to inspect firsthand the results of her Gubernia Reform, enacted on November 7, 1775. She replaced Peter the Great's provinces with gubernias comprising uniform numbers of male inhabitants and further divided into *uezdy,* and designated and created capital cities and towns, which increased the urban population; these reforms lasted until 1917. Her judicial reforms, which created additional levels of courts to improve their efficiency, remained in place until Alexander II's great reforms of 1864. Catherine also instituted schools, hospitals, and poorhouses.

Catherine believed that education could shape and civilize Russians and tribesmen alike into citizens of her empire. In 1780, in the midst of these reforms, Catherine visited Narva, Pskov, Polotsk, Mogilev, Smolensk, and Novgorod along with experienced administrators, who made detailed reports at each stop. In Mogilev, Catherine met with Emperor Joseph II of the Austro-Hungarian and Holy Roman Empires. They shared strategic interests against the Ottoman Empire, and both sought to establish educational policy for a multinational empire. Catherine had set up the Commission on National Education in 1783, and was the first ruler to institute a plan for free general standardized education, for which she relied on a Serbian pedagogue, F. I. Jankovich de Mirjevo (1741–1814). He was a student of Johann Ignaz Felbiger (1724–88), who had shaped educational policies for Austro-Hungary and Prussia and was the author of the textbook Catherine chose, *The Duties of Man and Citizen* (1783), which was deliberately secular.

Reforms were instituted in the non-Russian borderlands in the mid-1780s, and included advice from the governors of Novgorod, Livland, and Finland, for Catherine recognized that the Baltic provinces had long had good local government. Nevertheless, following Catherine's policy of uniform laws and centralized administration, Estonians and Livonians were forced to bargain away some rights in exchange for others, and Ukrainians and Cossacks were handled similarly, despite protestations. Questions about noble status and rights were finally resolved by decrees that cut the nobility in Little Russia, inflated by many dubious claims, by over half, while in Livonia, the power of the nobility was diluted by adding the Landsassen, who under Russia's Charter to the Nobility (1785) were nobles through military and civil service, to a nobility based solely on birth. Reforms eliminated the Livonian Landtag (diet)—where the nobility debated laws, regulations, and taxes—based on the argument that they could now appeal directly to the governor, governor-general, and the empress, a change that increased the government's power over the nobility. In exchange, nobles were allowed to keep land that had accrued to them but belonged to the state. Little Russia's Cossacks were regularized in military units and treated like other recruits. The peasants and serfs were most affected by the poll tax (or head tax) and census, which in Little Russia forced the mobile peasantry to live where they had registered in order to pay tax. Although the Baltic provinces had almost no free serfs, free peasants were now forced to register, live, and pay tax in one place. The Church in Little Russia was put under government administration and stripped of its lands and peasants, who became state peasants, and in the Baltic provinces Russian Orthodoxy was given precedence over Lutheranism. Thus, Catherine streamlined various administrative structures in her quest to integrate and control old and newly acquired territories.

In 1787, she went on her last major journey, a six-month tour to Ukraine and Crimea, which culminated in month-long visit and tour of Crimea with her ally, Emperor Joseph II of Austria, whom she and Field Marshal Prince Grigory Potemkin (1739–91) endeavored to impress with Russia's military might and their joint conquest of the Crimea. The phrase "Potemkin villages" arose among the French diplomats and guests, a snide comment that suggested that all the accomplishments Potemkin put on display were an illusion to impress Catherine and her entourage. As part of this theater of empire, Catherine had her portrait painted by Potemkin's serf Shibanov in her traveling costume: a red caftan with the orders of St. Andrew, St. George, and St. Vladimir and a ruffle at her neck, and a fur cap with a tassel hanging down from the cloth top. She managed to appear both matronly and military; this was one of her favorite portraits and many copies were made as gifts.[17]

The Baltic provinces, Little Russia, and the Crimea each presented very different challenges for Catherine's reforms, but in the eighteenth century, it was the differences between social estates rather than between nationalities and religions that proved most challenging to reconcile in a society based on the legal rights of estates. Potemkin, viceroy for all of southern Russia and Catherine's primary military architect for her southern strategy (and mostly like her morganatic husband), was appointed governor-general of the newly created gubernii Azov and New Russia in 1775, and in 1785 of Yekaterinoslav and the district of Tauris (Crimea), and thus implemented Catherine's reforms in the Crimea. This led to an exodus of two thirds of the Crimean Tatars to Muslim lands by 1812, especially peasants, who fought attempts to take away their rights and sometimes succeeded. Potemkin diluted their religious presence by adding Greeks, Jews, and Armenians, as Potemkin and Catherine followed a policy of religious tolerance. Using recruiters in Europe, Potemkin sought to colonize the newly vacant lands of the Crimea through various schemes with Russians, Swedes, Corsicans, Germans, and even English convicts. To solve the problem of different systems of nobility, Tatar nobles were given Russian ranks and put in positions of authority.

Language is the primary distinguishing feature between peoples, and the differences among languages would become increasingly important in the nationalist debates of the nineteenth century. In the 1780s, when the British discovery of Sanskrit made comparative linguistics fashionable, Catherine established a research project to assemble a comparative dictionary of all languages, to demonstrate to Europeans not only the linguistic riches of the Russian Empire, but also the ancient roots of Russian. With a list of 285 words in two hundred languages, the Russian Empire contributed over sixty languages. This international project coincided with the establishment of the Russian Academy and its publication of the first dictionary of Russian, which emphasized the Church Slavonic and etymological roots of Russian rather than its vernacular use, and thus did not include many foreign loan words that were an important feature of Russian as it changed rapidly in the eighteenth century to adapt to the stream of European influences. Here it departed from its model, the dictionary produced by the French Academy in 1699, which followed the actual usage of contemporary French by educated society and writers. The tensions between Catherine's international scientific dictionary and the Russian Academy's national dictionary portended the new nationalist tensions of the nineteenth century, when the Russian Empire would become "Russia."

NOTES

1. Richard Wortman, "Texts of Exploration and Russia's European Identity," in *Russia Engages the World, 1453–1825,* ed. Cynthia Hyla Whittaker with Edward Kasinec and Robert H. Davis, Jr. (Cambridge, Mass.: Harvard University Press, 2003), 90–117.

2. The three main recent biographies of Catherine the Great in English are John T. Alexander, *Catherine the Great: Life and Legend* (New York: Oxford University Press, 1989), 80–81; Isabel de Madariaga, *Russia in the Age of Catherine the Great* (London: Phoenix Press, 2002), 361–69; and Simon Dixon, *Catherine the Great* (London: Profile Books, 2010), 145–46.

3. S. I. Ozhegov and N. Iu. Shvedova, *Tolkovyi slovar' russkogo iazyka* (Moscow: Russkii iazyk, 1989), 435.

4. V. I. Dal', *Tolkovyi slovar' zhivogo velikorusskogo iazyka* (Moscow: Gosudarstvennoe izdate'stvo inostrannykh i natsional'nyikh slovarei, 1955), 2:616.

5. Benedict Anderson, *Imagined Communities: Reflections on the Origin and Spread of Nationalism,* rev. ed. (New York: Verso, 2006).

6. Catherine's secret instructions to A. A. Viazemskii, *Sbornik Imperatorskogo russkogo istoricheskogo obshchestva* (St. Petersburg, 1871), 7:348.

7. Alexander, *Catherine the Great*, 87–88.

8. Madariaga, *Russia in the Age of Catherine the Great*, 150.

9. Alexander, *Catherine the Great*, 112–20; Anderson, *Imagined Communities*, 86–88.

10. Simon Dixon, *Catherine the Great* (New York: Longman, 2001), 42.

11. Madariaga, *Russia in the Age of Catherine the Great*, 62.

12. *Entsiklopedicheskii slovar'* (St. Petersburg: I. A. Efron, 1899; repr. Yaroslavl: Terra, 2001), 54:75, 55:473. In addition to 18 million Russians, there were approximately 7 million Ukrainians, 5 million Belarusians, and 2 million Poles. In addition, Finns, Tatars, Latvians, Jews, Lithuanians, and Estonians made up about a half million people, in addition to Chuvash, Moldavians, Germans, Swedes, Bashkirs, and others, including nomads. These peoples included Uniates, Catholics, Protestants, Muslims, Jews, Buddhists, and pagans. Catherine Evtuhov, David Goldfrank, Lindsey Hughes, and Richard Stites, *A History of Russia: Peoples, Legends, Events, Forces* (New York: Houghton Mifflin, 2004), 282. For an extensive description, see "Rossiia: Rossiia v etnograficheskom otnoshenii," *Entsiklopedicheskii slovar'*, 54:139–52.

13. In 1589, Henry IV issued the Edict of Nantes, giving Protestants equal rights in Catholic France to end the French Wars of Religion. The Revocation of the Edict of Nantes by Louis XIV in 1685 led to the exodus of Huguenots to neighboring Protestant lands. The daughter of a Huguenot refugee would be Catherine's French governess while growing up in Anhalt-Zerbst.

14. At the end of his life, Belisarius may have been blinded and forced to be a beggar by the Emperor Justinian I, a story Marmontel included and popularized.

15. Voltaire, *Voltaire's Correspondence*, ed. T. Besterman (Geneva: Institut et Musée Voltaire, 1961), 66:16–17.

16. Comte de Ségur, *Mémoires ou Souvenirs et anecdotes*, 2nd ed. (Paris, 1826), 3:42–43.

17. Several portraits of Catherine, including a copy of Shibanov's portrait, are on view at Hillwood Museum, Washington D.C., which has the largest collection of Russian art in the United States.

George Dawe, *Petr Ivanovich Bagration* (1822–23). Wikimedia Commons.

# 8

# Petr Ivanovich Bagration

## (1765–1812)

### SEAN POLLOCK

"When my father, King Iese, was in Persia for a time at the shah's court, I was left to live there in the capital of Isfahan . . . and I remained there with my mother, at the shah's court, where I was raised in their profane and abominable Mohammedan faith." So Prince Aleksandr Bagration stated in a 1759 petition addressed to Russia's Empress Elizabeth (r. 1741–62). Having escaped his enemies, "Christians in Georgia and impious barbarians in Persia," he requested "to be received into Your Imperial Majesty's eternal subjecthood and service and awarded a rank in accordance with that given to my kinsmen and nationals [in Russian service] . . . and a double grant in accordance with that given to foreigners as decreed by Your Imperial Majesty." Not only was Prince Aleksandr granted asylum in Russia, he was soon given command of the Georgian Hussar Regiment stationed in Kizliar, in northern Caucasia, and one of his sons was enrolled in the prestigious Noble Infantry Cadet Corps in the Russian capital of St. Petersburg. Following in his father's footsteps some years later, Prince Ivan Bagration settled with his family in Kizliar, where his son, Prince Petr Ivanovich Bagration, was raised before going on to become one of the most revered and remembered military commanders in Russian history.[1]

The Bagrations' immigration to Russia and Prince Petr's subsequent assimilation of Great Russian ways raise fundamental questions about the dynamics of Caucasia's borderlands, the nature of Russia's empire, and the experiences of its peoples. What forces drove the royal Bagrations to seek refuge in Russia? What did they hope to gain by becoming Russian subjects, and in what ways did they contribute to the life of the empire? What did the Russian government hope to gain by granting them asylum? Which state institutions were involved in integrating such immigrants into Russia's social fabric, and what ideological resources could be mobilized to accommodate them? To what extent did becoming a Russian subject entail acculturation—the creative and selective adoption of another group's beliefs and practices—or assimilation—the wholesale imitation of another group's cultural repertoire? How was it that Prince Petr Bagration, who was "by birth a Georgian" and presented "a purely

Georgian physiognomy," according to contemporaries, came to identify himself as a "pure Russian," and other Russian subjects, including fellow noblemen, as "foreigners?" Finally, what was the relationship between Russian empire building, which involved incorporating diverse territories and populations into the Russian body politic, and the development of Russian national consciousness, understood as an awareness of oneself as belonging to a distinct people or nation?

Formerly marginal to the study of Russian history, such questions are now central to efforts to understand the imperial dimensions of Russia's history and the experiences of non-Russians within its empire. While agreeing that difference—ethnic, confessional, cultural, and otherwise—has been a salient feature of Russian empire since at least the sixteenth century, historians are divided on the question of whether the dilemma of diversity was a source of weakness, strength, or both for Russia. Corollary to this question is another concerning the successes and longevity of the empire. It may seem foolish to approach such vast topics through the lens of an individual's life, but much as particulars are often characteristic when they relate to a distinguished individual, to paraphrase a renowned biographer,[2] so individual lives can be distinguishing when they relate to a great empire. By focusing on the story of Prince Petr Bagration's assimilation of Great Russian ways, it becomes possible to understand both how social solidarity could emerge amid national difference and how national difference in the dawning age of ethnocultural nationalism could set one Russian subject against another, thus highlighting the centripetal forces that help to explain social cohesion within the empire as well as the centrifugal forces simultaneously pulling at its social fabric.

The Bagrations' immigration to Russia and their settling in Kizliar highlight the ways the interests of Georgian elites and those of the tsarist state could overlap, as well as the avenues of integration and even assimilation open to those willing to advance Russia's imperial interests. Prince Petr's grandfather, Aleksandr, had sought refuge in Russia to escape his enemies in Georgia, where a rival line of royal Bagrations was in the process of consolidating its authority. When, in December 1766, Prince Petr went to Kizliar from Georgia, where he was probably born the previous year, Catherine II's government was in the process of recruiting foreigners to colonize Russia's southern borderlands.[3] Among the foreigners invited to settle in the vicinity of Kizliar were "people of any nation, Chechens, Kumyks, and other highland peoples and Nogai wishing to convert [to Eastern Orthodox Christianity]," as well as "people of Christian nations, Georgians, Armenians and others located beyond the borders of the Russian Empire."[4] Although Petr's father, Ivan, could not speak Russian, the government apparently decided that his proficiency in Ottoman Turkish, Persian, Armenian, and his native Georgian—in addition to his military experience—could be put to good use in and around Kizliar, where groups speaking those languages predominated. Unfortunately, little can be said with certainty about Petr's Kizliar years: he studied German and mathematics briefly at the garrison school for officers' children in 1782–83, he joined the Astrakhan' Infantry Regiment as a private supernumerary in May 1783, and he was literate in both Russian and Georgian. Violent conflict between tsarist troops and Caucasian highlanders was endemic at the time, and Prince Petr's regiment was often at the center of the action, although the prince himself was probably not directly involved in any of the fighting. Still, it may be that contact with non-Christian tribesmen served to heighten Bagration's awareness of himself as different from them, and more like Orthodox Russians, at least in terms of religion and language. A recent study of the tsarist army in this period argues that "the presence of Russian, primarily Orthodox Christian, soldiers in garrisons on the edges of empire where the local population was not only non-Russian but sometimes Muslim or pagan helped to forge a sense of identity in contrast to 'the other.'"[5] The sources are less than forthcoming concerning Bagration's "identity" as an adolescent, but it is not difficult to imagine that his service in the Imperial Army and his Orthodox Christian faith facilitated his assimilation of Great Russian ways.

To understand how Prince Petr came to view himself not only as a loyal Russian subject (*vernopoddannyi*), an ascribed category, but also as a "pure Russian" (*chistoi russkoi*), by which he meant something else, it is necessary to examine the ideological resources that were used to accommodate difference and shape ideas of Russianness in his day. Here ideology is understood as both a worldview and a context within which complex social interactions unfold. It comprises an interrelated set of symbols, assumptions, convictions, values, and beliefs; and offers individuals and groups ways of making sense of themselves and their surroundings, "defining enemies and allies, dangers and opportunities, us and them." National consciousness is a species of ideology, and the post-Petrine eighteenth century has been correctly characterized as a time of growing Russian national consciousness among Russia's governing and educated elites.[6] In debates over the presence of foreigners in government, the origins of the Russian state, the manners and morals of Russian subjects, the possibilities of a standardized and secular Russian language, the peculiar qualities of the Russian countryside and its "people" (*narod*), and the uses of history, Russia's writers evinced growing awareness of their society as distinct from other (particularly European) societies, and of themselves as Russians. This emerging national consciousness was expressed in a variety ways, sometimes as boastful pride in Russian conquests and its consequences, particularly rule over diverse peoples, and other times as concern about the perceived threat posed by foreigners to Great Russian traditions and culture—Orthodoxy and the Russian language in particular. These two ideological tendencies were obviously in tension with each other: the first accommodated individuals like Bagration, while the second potentially questioned the extent of his Russianness. A third tendency elided the question of national difference and focused instead on subjects' relation to sovereign and fatherland, informing an idea of civic nationhood that was largely an expression of state patriotism. These different ways of thinking about Russianness and otherness together constituted the ideological space in which Bagration became aware of himself as Russian. Prince Petr's sense of his own Russianness was a combination of the second and third tendencies and may have been typical of the majority of Russian soldiers in his day.

The language of civic nationhood informed the service ethos in the Imperial Army. Instruction in Russian military academies emphasized duty to sovereign and fatherland. So strong was the emphasis on inculcating in officers "love for the fatherland" that one German observer thought that it threatened family ties. Indeed, for Russia's officers in the early nineteenth century, the concept of fatherland (*otechestvo*) "began to vie with the established notion of personal loyalty to the autocrat." In 1812, one graduate of the Cadet Corps looked back nostalgically to his school days, "when each of us loved to contemplate how we might be useful to the Fatherland."[7] It was with such men that Bagration served. Still, the imperial Russian officer corps was a heterogeneous body that alone cannot account for Bagration's transformation from Georgian into Russian, particularly given that the prince himself did not graduate from a Russian military academy.

The cosmopolitan character of the Russian officer corps in Bagration's day should not be allowed to obscure the national character of the army as a whole. Leaving aside the officer corps and irregulars—sundry tribesmen and Cossacks who themselves could be assimilated through military service—most private soldiers in the army were ethnically Russian and practiced Orthodoxy.[8] In addition to distinguishing Russia's army from its western European counterparts, this relative homogeneity facilitated soldiers' transition to military life, promoted cohesion and esprit de corps, and may have translated into superior combat performance. Dead to his village, the peasant conscript became a member of the military estate and seemed to foreign observers to belong to "a nation apart," with the army becoming both "his fatherland and his family."[9] Bagration shared more in common with the Russian rank and file than he did with many officers. Most important, both he and they were Orthodox Christians. This fact distinguished them from both the soldiers of enemy armies and those imperial Russian officers of non-Orthodox faiths. For Bagration, as we shall see, confessional affiliation marked individuals as Russian or non-Russian. In addition, like most private soldiers, Bagration lacked the formal education that distinguished many of his fellow officers, a defect noted by contemporaries. According to one of them, Bagration knew only Russian—but not perfectly—never read books, and had "the tone and mannerisms of a soldier." His bravery in battle, "at once brilliant and cold-blooded," and his demonstrated concern for soldiers' well-being endeared Bagration to the rank and file. He was a soldier's soldier, "adored by all who served under his command."[10] If a yawning gulf generally divided the soldier's worldview from that of the officer, as has been argued, then Bagration was an exception to the rule.

As a commander, Bagration was shaped by two main experiences: his service under Alexander Suvorov (1730–1800) and extensive combat experience. "Prince Petr," as Suvorov affectionately called him, fought under the legendary general in Poland in 1794 and again in Italy and Switzerland during the War of the Second Coalition (1799–1802) against Revolutionary France in 1799. Suvorov urged soldiers "to love heartily our Sovereign Mother, for she is our first ruler on earth after God." He never tired of asserting his Russianness—"My ancestry and character together with my duty: God, Sovereign, Fatherland! I'm proud that I'm Russian"—and that which distinguished Russia's army from its European counterparts: "I am not a mercenary, I am a Russian."[11] Indeed, it has been argued that Suvorov epitomized a "Russian style" of military command. He emphasized training tailored to the characteristics of the Russian peasant conscript, the complementary nature of firepower and cold steel, and, most important, speed in attacking the enemy's main force.[12] As commander in chief of the combined Russian-Austrian forces during the Second Coalition, Suvorov instructed Bagration to train Austrian troops in the "secret of beating the enemy with cold steel"—that is, with bayonets—and to wean them from the habit of retreating.[13] Indeed, Suvorov equated retreat with treason, much as Bagration would in 1812.

Prince Bagration had fought with distinction in the Russian-Ottoman War of 1788–91, and against the Poles in 1794, but it was not until the War of the Second Coalition that he achieved renown beyond military circles. Educated Russian society began to celebrate Bagration as a national hero in the aftermath of the Austerlitz debacle of 1805. "They're talking everywhere about the feats of Bagration, who by his courage saved the rearguard and the entire army," the student and future critic Stepan Zhikharev enthused in December 1805. A few months later, Moscow's English Club hosted a dinner in honor of the "hero who had become so dear to the heart of every Russian." Bagration's "purely Georgian" features, his "big aquiline nose, arched eyebrows" and "darting eyes," were no obstacle to celebrating him in verse as "God of the army" (*Bog-rati-on*, a play on his surname), and vanquisher of Russia's enemies. An orchestra greeted his arrival at the club with "Thunder of Victory, Resound!" and toasts were raised to sovereign, fatherland, and Bagration.[14] Austerlitz and the subsequent Tilsit treaty, however, stung patriots like Bagration and his circle, which included the tsar's sister and brother, Grand Duchess Ekaterina Pavlovna and Grand Duke Konstantin Pavlovich, the future war minister Aleksei Arakcheev ("a Russian in every sense of the word," according to the famous military theorist Carl von Clausewitz, a member of the Russian general staff in 1812), and Fëdor Rostopchin, the military governor of Moscow in 1812. Bagration soon became the embodiment of anti-French sentiment in the army and the leader of a "Russian party" who resented the presence of generals with foreign-sounding names.[15]

Bagration expressed himself most fully as a "pure Russian," and other Russian subjects as in some sense non-Russian, in the course of the events surrounding Napoléon's invasion of Russia in 1812. What began as a difference of opinion on strategy and tactics between Russia's two leading military commanders was soon framed by Bagration and like-minded patriots as a struggle to defend Russia and Russians from "foreign" enemies, both external and internal. Emperor Alexander's decisions regarding strategy and command contributed to the sense of estrangement that Bagration felt from the outset of the war. Prior to the invasion there was little consensus, even among the tsar's advisers, regarding precisely how the war was to be waged. In the end, Alexander authorized a Fabian strategy aimed at drawing the enemy into Russia's interior and refusing battle until Napoléon's forces (450,000 men) were reduced to Russian numbers (200,000). Alexander appointed War Minister Michael Andreas Barclay de Tolly commander in chief of the First Army (130,000) and Bagration commander in chief of the Second Army (45,000). Barclay was the older of the two, but Bagration outranked him in terms of seniority. As war minister, however, Barclay was authorized to issue orders to all military personnel regardless of rank.

The two men were a study in contrasts. According to General Aleksei Ermolov, who claimed to know Bagration better than anyone else and served as Barclay's chief of staff during the 1812 campaign, their characters were "utterly different," even "contradictory."[16] They had fought together in the War of the Fourth Coalition (1806–1807), during which Bagration developed respect for his subordinate, and again during the Russo-Swedish War (1808–1809), after which Barclay was named commander in chief and governor-general for Finland, a move that flouted seniority and made the newly minted full general powerful enemies. The same may be said of his subsequent appointments as war minister in 1810 and commander in chief of the First Army in 1812. Barclay was a third-generation Russian subject from Livonia, where German language and culture and Lutheranism remained firmly established among his fellow aristocrats. In contrast, no one questioned Bagration's rise through the ranks; he had fought in almost every major campaign during his adult life (the exception being the Russian-Persian War of 1804–13, when he was engaged on other fronts). Unlike Barclay, he had no strong ties to his homeland and had given himself entirely over to military service, which became a kind of surrogate family for him, much as it was for the rank and file. Bagration was proud of his thirty years in military service and rarely missed an opportunity to emphasize his seniority in rank to "the minister," as the prince derisively referred to Barclay.

Given Russia's experiences in war and with Napoléon in particular, a defensive strategy was bound to be unpopular with both the soldiery and the public. Tsarist troops were used to fighting at the edges of Russia's empire or beyond its borders and tended to wage war on the offensive. Commanders and soldiers alike expected the coming war to be no different, and there was a burning desire to avenge the defeat at Austerlitz. In May 1812, Varvara Bakunina, a member of the St. Petersburg aristocracy, recorded what she believed to be the prevailing mood in the army:

> All the letters from the army are filled with a desire for war and good spirit; they persuade that even the soldiers are impatient to engage the enemy in order to avenge previous failures. The general desire of all is to march forward in order to forestall Napoléon in Prussia, but it seems that the tsar's close and trusted advisers are of the opposite opinion; in their profound wisdom, they have decided to fight a defensive war and to allow the enemy into our borders. Those who do not appreciate German tactics and judge according to reason are extremely disappointed by this and consider it the greatest evil.[17]

On the eve of the invasion it seemed to Major General Ermolov that all preparations had been designed for offensive warfare. Recalling Suvorov's prescriptions, Bagration himself voiced concern that retreat would leave a negative impression on the troops in addition to exhausting them in defensive maneuvers. "It would be far more useful," he suggested to the emperor, "to attack the enemy on his territory." Aware that Barclay, his closest adviser, the Prussian émigré Karl Maria von Phull, and their protégé, Baron Ludwig von Wolzogen, were counseling defensive operations, Bagration informed Alexander I that such men could not possibly fathom what was at stake for Russia: "I took an oath to serve you loyally, and we are yours. People of another faith (*inovertsy*) are not able to judge so zealously, for they risk nothing, while we—everything."[18] Thus, already prior to the invasion, Bagration had suggested that a defensive strategy would be a betrayal of Suvorov's legacy, and thus un-Russian, and that its proponents were demonstrably un-Russian, and that the otherness of Barclay and his German advisers made it impossible for them to serve as loyally as Orthodox Russian subjects. Subsequent events only pushed him further down the road of ethnocultural national paranoia.

Although it was part of the emperor's strategy, it was Barclay who ordered the retreat from Vil'na, and as a result his name came to be associated with national shame from the war's outset. Bagration had been conditioned to view retreat as a betrayal of Russia and even of Russianness. "They stretched my troops like a bow-string," he complained to Arakcheev, "and when the enemy walks in without firing a shot, they start retreating without [anybody] knowing why. You won't be able to prove to anyone in the army, in the whole country, that we haven't been betrayed." He viewed the retreat as a national disgrace: "Russians [*russkie*] ought not to flee. . . . We have become worse than the Prussians." The Russian way of waging war was to attack. Speaking "as one Russian to another [*kak russkoi russkomu*]," Bagration urged Arakcheev and anyone who would listen to order tsarist troops on the offensive. So distasteful was the current strategy to Bagration that he suggested he be relieved of command.[19]

Bagration spent the first ten days of the war force-marching his troops in blistering heat over difficult terrain, exactly what he had urged Alexander to avoid all costs. En route to Minsk, the commander stopped to prepare his men for battle. Not surprisingly, the prospect of fighting came as something of a relief to Bagration. "Finally we have encountered the enemy troops, and General Platov is attacking and driving them away." Taking a page from Suvorov's *Art of Victory,* Bagration ordered the troops to "attack bravely, quickly, paying no heed to the shooting"; the artillery to fire "accurately"; the irregulars to swarm the enemy's flank and rear; the cavalry to attack "quickly but also in good order"; and the infantry to "strike the enemy with bayonets until he is overrun." Written in his own hand, the order echoed the cadences of Suvorov's terse, aphoristic, exhorting style: "Attack the enemy! The bullet flies by. Approach him, he flees. Infantry, stab [with bayonet], cavalry, hack [with sword] and trample!" Bagration expressed confidence in the soldiers' readiness to fight bravely in defense of "our most gracious sovereign and our beloved fatherland," and to demonstrate "our filial love and invincible courage." Significantly, unit commanders were expected to emphasize the enemy's national otherness, that Napoléon's troops were "nothing more than riffraff from all corners of the earth [*svoloch' so vsego sveta*], while we are Russians and coreligionists [*russkie i edinovernye*]." What was at stake? In defeating the enemy "who dared to enter the Russian land [*russkuiu zemliu*]," Russian soldiers could expect to win "honor, glory, and the gratitude of the motherland" for themselves and "peace and utter bliss" for "our beloved fatherland."[20] The idea that Russian soldiers should defend their faith, their tsar, and their fatherland was echoed in the inaugural issue of the army newspaper, *The Russian*. How did the rank and file understand such exhortations? Bagration was revered by the soldiery and had good reason to believe his words would have the desired effect.

The presence of foreign troops on Russian soil offended the patriotic pride of officers like Bagration. Over the course of July, he continued to urge the emperor to order Barclay's army on the offensive. He believed this was the "saving and only" way to stop Napoléon's advance toward Smolensk and Russia's interior. Otherwise, "the tears of the beloved fatherland shall not wipe away the stain that will remain forever on the First Army." The more Bagration thought about Barclay's "protracted inaction," the more he began to question his comrade's loyalty and that of those around him. "I just cannot get along with the minister," he wrote to Arakcheev. "For God's sake, send me anywhere you desire, even to command a regiment in Moldavia or Caucasia. I cannot remain here; the entire headquarters is so filled with Germans that a Russian cannot breathe. . . . I truly had wanted to serve the sovereign and fatherland, but it turns out that I serve Barclay. I confess, I don't want to [serve under Barclay]."[21] This sentiment was apparently shared by many fellow officers who now openly scorned orders issued by General "All Bark and No Bite" (*Boltai da i Tol'ko*, a play on the minister's name). In letters to General Ermolov and Fëdor Rostopchin, the military governor of Moscow, Bagration characterized Barclay as an "idiot" and, stressing the minister's national otherness ("I obey, unfortunately, a Finn [*chukhontsu*]"), suggested that he was acting on Napoléon's orders.[22] Relations became so strained that the two commanders in chief attacked each other's character in the presence of others. Significantly, the verbal abuse was couched in national terms. "You're a German, you care nothing for Russians," Bagration exclaimed. "And you're an idiot, and you yourself don't know why you call yourself a native Russian," replied Barclay.[23]

When it became apparent that Napoléon was heading for Smolensk, Barclay and Bagration agreed on the need to defend "the first truly Russian city" encountered during the retreat.[24] But when French troops arrived and set fire to the town, reminding Napoléon of the eruption of Mount Vesuvius, Barclay ordered another retreat. Bagration and other senior officers were incensed; the grand duke allegedly said to his troops and the denizens of Smolensk, "What is to be done, friends! We're not to blame. . . . No Russian blood flows in him who commands us."[25] Again there was talk of treason. The destruction of Smolensk came as a shock to Russian patriots like Ermolov:

> The destruction of Smolensk acquainted me with an absolutely new feeling which wars endured outside the borders of the fatherland do not impart. I had not seen the devastation of my own land, the burning towns of my fatherland. For the first time in my life I heard the groans of my compatriots and saw the horror of their disastrous situation.[26]

Not surprisingly, many, like Rostopchin, blamed the loss of Smolensk on Barclay and attributed the nation's hatred of him to the perception that "he is not Russian [*on ne russkii*]."[27] Small wonder the army cheered when the tsar replaced Barclay with General Mikhail Kutuzov, who was viewed as "a true Russian," a disciple of Suvorov, and, at the very least, "better than a foreigner." The fact that Barclay was not a foreigner but a Russian subject who had served in the Imperial Army since his youth was not lost on Clausewitz. He understood, however, that this reality mattered less than the perception of Barclay's foreignness. But Clausewitz was wrong to think that Russians' suspicion of foreigners, which he considered "a trait of the Tartar [*sic*] character," was based solely on the sound of their names and preference for the German language.[28] There was also the matter of religion: for Bagration and likeminded Russians, Barclay's Lutheranism marked him as non-Russian.

It is worth noting that Bagration's view of his own Russianness and Barclay's foreignness left some observers nonplussed. Nicholas Grech, founding editor of the popular patriotic journal *Son of the Fatherland*, likened renouncing the participation of foreigners in the war effort to refusing a malaria patient quinine because it does not grow in Russia. "And in what way is the Livonian Barclay less Russian than the Georgian Bagration? You'll say that [Bagration] is Orthodox, but at issue is war, not the provenance of the Holy Spirit!" Unlike Bagration, Grech distinguished Germans from "those natives of our Baltic provinces: these are Russian subjects, Russian nobles who readily sacrifice their blood and lives for Russia."[29] Grech's vision of Russianness was a throwback to another age, that of Mikhail Lomonosov (1711–65) and other crafters of "Russian imperial nationhood,"[30] whereas that of Bagration reflected the dawning age of romantic nationalism.

Bagration's personal story parallels that of the Russian Empire in the late eighteenth and early nineteenth centuries. Russian territorial aggrandizement was one of the salient features of the period. Bagration took part in the colonization and conquest of Russia's borderlands, first as a foreign settler and later as a commander of Russian troops. He spent his entire adult life fighting Russia's enemies in Caucasia (although probably in a supporting role), Poland, the Balkans, and Finland, and he commanded troops in all of Russia's wars against Napoleonic France. As such, he deserves to be counted among Russia's greatest military commanders and empire builders. The business of building Russia's empire, however, in no way interfered with Bagration's emerging sense of himself as belonging to a Russian nation defined in religious, ethnic, and cultural terms, comprising the native Russian-speaking Orthodox Christian population of the Russian Empire. To Bagration's mind, Barclay's Lutheranism made him an *inoverets,* literally, a person of another faith, and his German language and culture made him a *chukhonets,* a term used by Bagration to underscore Barclay's Baltic provenance and national otherness; together, these attributes marked him as fundamentally non-Russian in a national sense. Such a vision of nationhood anticipated the "official nationalism" of Nicholas I and his successors, as well as the ethnocultural nationalism that gained prominence throughout Europe in second half of the nineteenth century and that developed into a chauvinistic nationalism of race and cultural exclusivity underwriting a new age of imperialism in the period between 1870 and 1918. By examining Bagration's life and thinking broadly about the history of Europe in the nineteenth century, it becomes possible to see the imperatives of empire and nation building as sometimes complementary processes.

Notes

1. The petitions are in *Dokumenty po vzaimootnosheniiam Gruzii s Severnym Kavkazom,* comp. V. N. Gamrekeli (Tbilisi: "Metsniereba," 1968), 143–45, 180–83.

2. James Boswell, *Life of Samuel Johnson, LL.D.,* 2nd ed. (Chicago: Encyclopaedia Britannica, 1990), 4.

3. The date and place of Petr Bagration's birth have yet to be fixed in the historiography; 1762, 1764, 1765, and 1769 have all been suggested, and many students of his life have claimed that he was born in Kizliar. Based on his father's 1767 petition, cited above, we know that the family did not arrive in Kizliar until December 1766. On this question, see Z. Tsintsadze, "'Neizvestnyi' Vam Kniaz' Bagration," *Voenno-istoricheskii zhurnal* 6 (1994): 89–90.

4. Senate report to Catherine II, October 9, 1762, in *Kabardino-russkie otnosheniia v XVI–XVIII vv.,* ed. T. Kh. Kumykov et al. (Moscow: Izdatel'stvo Akademii nauk SSSR, 1957), 2:219.

5. Janet Hartley, *Russia, 1762–1825: Military Power, the State, and the People* (Westport, Conn.: Praeger, 2008), 6.

6. See Jennifer W. See, "Ideology," in *Encyclopedia of American Foreign Policy,* ed. Richard Dean Burns, Alexander DeConde, Frederik Logevall, 2nd ed. (New York: Charles Scribner's Sons, 2002), 2:188; and Hans Rogger, *Russian National Consciousness in Eighteenth-Century Russia* (Cambridge, Mass.: Harvard University Press, 1960).

7. John L. H. Keep, *Soldiers of the Tsar: Army and Society in Russia, 1462–1874* (Oxford: Clarendon Press, 1985), 243, 244.

8. William C. Fuller, Jr., "The Imperial Army," in *Cambridge History of Russia,* vol. 2, *Imperial Russia, 1689–1917,* ed. Dominic Lieven (Cambridge: Cambridge University Press, 2006), 533. Some in Catherinian Russia viewed the national and social homogeneity of the Russian soldiery as an advantage: "The strength of the army consists in, most basic of all, the existence of a common language, religion, customs and blood," was the opinion of one military commission. Quoted in Christopher Duffy, *Russia's Military Way to the West: Origins and Nature of Russian Power, 1700–1800* (London: Routledge and Kegan Paul, 1981), 126.

9. Quoted in Keep, *Soldiers of the Tsar,* 218.

10. A. P. Ermolov, *Zapiski A. P. Ermolova 1798–1826* (Moscow: "Vysshaia shkola," 1991), 152; "Zapiski grafa Lanzherona: Voina s Turtsiei (1806–1812 gg.)," *Russkaia starina* 134 (June 1908): 672.

11. Suvorov's exhortation to "love heartily" quoted in Keep, *Soldiers of the Tsar,* 206. His "proud to be Russian" claim quoted in *A. V. Suvorov: Pis'ma,* ed. V. S. Lopatin (Moscow: "Nauka," 1986), 416; elsewhere Suvorov speaks of his "affinity for things national [*svoistvo moe k otechestvennomu*]" (ibid., 396).

12. William C. Fuller, *Strategy and Power in Russia, 1600–1914* (New York: Free Press, 1992), 157–66; Bruce W. Menning, "Train Hard, Fight Easy: The Legacy of A. V. Suvorov and His 'Art of Victory,'" *Air University Review* 38, no. 1 (1986): 79–88.

13. Suvorov to Bagration, May 30 (June 9), 1799, in *Suvorov: Pis'ma,* 340.

14. Zhikharev, *Zapiski sovremennika,* 135, 184, 196, 198.

15. Andrei Grigor'evich Tartakovskii, *Nerazgadannyi Barklai: Legendy i byl' 1812 goda* (Moscow: "Arkheograficheskii tsentr," 1996), 58–61; Carl von Clausewitz, *The Russian Campaign of 1812*, intro. Gérard Chaliand (New Brunswick, N.J., and London: Transaction Publishers, 2007), 5.

16. Ermolov, *Zapiski,* 149. Although he was clearly in Bagration's camp and biased against Barclay, Ermolov registers the winning and less attractive qualities of both men in *Zapiski,* 149–53.

17. Quoted in Tartakovskii, *Nerazgadannyi Barklai,* 63.

18. Bagration to Alexander I, June 6 (18), 1812, in *General Bagration: Sbornik dokumentov,* ed. S. N. Golubov and F. F. Kuznetsov (Leningrad: Gospolitizdat, 1945), 153; Bagration to Alexander I, June 8 (20), 1812, in *Otechestvennaia voina v pis'makh sovremennikov (1812–1815 gg.),* ed. N. Dubrovin (Moscow: Gos. publichnaia istorihceskaia biblioteka Rossii, 2006), 15.

19. Bagration to Arakcheev, June 26 (July 8), 1812, cited in Michael and Diana Josselson, *The Commander: A Life of Barclay de Tolly* (Oxford and New York: Oxford University Press, 1980), 102; Bagration to Arakcheev, June 1812, in Golubov and Kuznetsov, *General Bagration,* 190; Ermolov to Bagration, June 30 (July 12), 1812, in Golubov and Kuznetsov, *General Bagration,* 189.

20. The order, dated June 25 (July 7), 1812, is in Golubov and Kuznetsov, *General Bagration,* 179–81.

21. Bagration to Alexander I, June 30 (July 12) and July 3 (15), 1812, in Golubov and Kuznetsov, *General Bagration,* 188, 199; Bagration to Arakcheev, July 29 (August 10), 1812, in Golubov and Kuznetsov, *General Bagration,* 226.

22. Bagration to Ermolov, n.d., in *Prilozheniia k zapiskam A. P. Ermolova,* ed. N. P. Ermolov (Moscow: Katkov, 1865), 1:170; Bagration to Rostopchin, end of July, in Dubrovin, *Otechestvennaia voina v pis'makh,* 74, 75.

23. Quoted in S. Mel'gunov, *Dela i liudi Aleksandrovskogo vremeni* (Berlin: [Vataga], 1923), 125.

24. Alexander to Barclay, November 21 (OS), 1812, quoted in Josselson, *Commander,* 164.

25. Mel'gunov, *Dela i liudi,* 122. The conspiracy against Barclay was led by several generals including Bennigsen, Bagration, Ermolov, and others.

26. Ermolov, *Zapiski,* 168.

27. Rostopchin to Balashov, August 13 (25), 1812, in Dubrovin, *Otechestvennaia voina v pis'makh,* 94.

28. "Barclay was, in truth, no foreigner; he was the son of a Livonian clergyman, a native of that province; he had served from his youth in the Russian army, and there was nothing foreign in him but his name, and perhaps, also, his speech, for he spoke Russian ill, and was more accustomed, by preference, to the German language. This was sufficient, under present circumstances, be considered a foreigner" (Clausewitz, *Russian Campaign,* 80). On the "Tartar character," see Clausewitz, *Russian Campaign,* 81.

29. N. I. Grech, *Zapiksi o moei zhizni* (St. Petersburg: Izdanie A. S. Suvorina, 1886; repr. Moscow: Kniga, 1990), 211.

30. I borrow the phrase from Harsha Ram, "Russian Poetry and the Imperial Sublime," in *Russian Subjects: Empire, Nation, and the Culture of the Golden Age,* ed. Monika Greenleaf and Stephen Moeller-Sally (Evanston, Ill.: Northwestern University Press, 1998), 23.

Undated lithograph by Tiulev. The caption on the image reads, "The late Johannes Ambrosius Rosenstrauch, consistory councilor and pastor of the Evangelical-Lutheran congregation at Khar'kov. Proceeds to benefit the Pastor Rosenstrauch Memorial Foundation of the church school at Khar'kov." Courtesy of the Russian National Library, St. Petersburg.

# 9

# Johannes Ambrosius Rosenstrauch

## (1768–1835)

ALEXANDER M. MARTIN

There are two principal justifications for writing someone's biography.[1] Some people (such as Catherine the Great or Lomonosov) are significant for the individual roles they played in history. Others performed no great deeds, yet if we ask the right questions, they can tell us much about the world in which they lived. This approach—"microhistory"—is especially rewarding in the case of immigrants, religious converts, and others who experienced a change in their social position, for how they exchanged old identities for new ones illumines the wider process by which social identities are formed and maintained.

The life of Johannes Ambrosius Rosenstrauch—immigrant, stage actor, merchant, freemason, religious convert, writer, and pastor—is a case in point. Crisscrossing his native Germany, emigrating to St. Petersburg, making his fortune in Moscow, and finally settling on the Russian steppe frontier, he repeatedly refashioned himself socially, professionally, and spiritually. The only known likeness of him, a painting by Johann Baptist Lampi the Younger that belongs to the State Hermitage Museum in St. Petersburg and is entitled "Portrait of a Pastor," dates from the final stage of Rosenstrauch's journey. By then, as a man of the cloth, he had achieved sufficient public regard that after he died, his grateful congregants could sell an engraving made from Lampi's painting as a fundraiser. Look closely at that engraving: Does it not seem that alongside the demonstrative air of piety, the artist captured a hint of irony in Rosenstrauch's expression? There was more to this man, he seems to suggest, than meets the eye.

This chapter will explore three dimensions of Rosenstrauch's story that help illumine the wider society of his time. What was it that drove him to conceal his past whenever he remade his social identity? How was his personal spiritual odyssey connected to upper-class culture in Russia as a whole? And what can we learn about the culture of imperial Russia from the way it (mis)remembered Rosenstrauch's story?

## International Man of Mystery

Rosenstrauch is an elusive figure. This is part of what makes him interesting, since it illustrates how conditions in Russia allowed immigrants to escape their past and reinvent their identities, so I will begin by discussing the nature of his elusiveness before attempting to reconstruct the main facts of his biography.

I "discovered" Rosenstrauch in 2002, when archivists in Moscow drew my attention to a copybook containing an anonymous German merchant's account of his harrowing experiences during the Napoleonic invasion of Russia in 1812. Two years later, in a different archive at the opposite end of Moscow, I inadvertently came across an obscure document that was written in the same hand, repeated key details from the copybook, and was signed "Rosenstrauch."[2] Once I began watching for that name, I found references to him in a variety of texts from nineteenth century Russia and Germany. However, in most cases the authors knew only one side of his persona— that he had been, say, a freemason, or an actor, or a pastor. Few seemed to know his whole story.

Reconstructing Rosenstrauch's biography ought to be easy, for one should expect the surviving evidence to be plentiful. He wrote at length about his war experience, kept a diary (now apparently lost) for at least twenty-five years, and wrote many letters, proving that he lacked neither the skill nor the desire or opportunity to reflect on, and tell others about, his life. His son Wilhelm (1792–1870) lived in Moscow for over fifty years; for most of that time, he was a leading merchant, prominent citizen, and consul for the king of Prussia, so he, too, was evidently sociable, widely known, and well connected. Through their involvement in commerce, theater, freemasonry, the clergy, and the consular service, father and son knew others who likewise wrote letters, diaries, and memoirs; for example, Otto von Bismarck (the future "Iron Chancellor" of Germany) wrote a testimonial to Wilhelm's service as Prussian consul, and the prominent Russian intellectual Mikhail Pogodin wrote a lengthy obituary when Wilhelm died.[3] Yet what people knew remained fragmentary and misleading. No details were known about Rosenstrauch's life before he came to Russia, few who knew him as a pastor realized that he had earlier been an actor, and erroneous stories circulated that he had once been a theater director and later became a bishop. A paranoid German conspiracy theorist even alleged that Rosenstrauch had been the agent of an international plot by Jews and freemasons to overthrow the monarchs of Europe.[4] His son Wilhelm's admirers, meanwhile, apparently had no idea that Rosenstrauch was his father. Publishing first-person accounts of the heroic struggle against Napoléon was all the rage in mid-nineteenth-century Russia, yet Wilhelm evidently consigned his own father's memoir of the 1812 war to oblivion; by the first and only time it was discussed in print, in a scholarly journal article from 1896, Wilhelm had been dead for twenty-six years and it was no longer even known who the author of the memoir had been.[5]

To some extent, this opacity reflects the times. Among educated eighteenth-century Europeans, international travel was common, eased by porous borders and a shared Enlightenment culture. The era was in love with disguise and mysticism—masquerades, transvestite balls, and spiritualist séances were in fashion—and the telegraph, photography, and standardized passports had not yet been invented to make modern forms of identification possible. Hence, it was a golden age of adventurers who moved from country to country, perpetually shrouded in an aura of mystery. What was the true identity of the celebrated Italian alchemist Count Cagliostro? Was the famous French spy Chevalier d'Eon really a man or a woman? In a time uncertain about the identity even of major international celebrities, it seems less surprising that Rosenstrauch should have been able to keep silent about his own background. That he should have wanted to do so, however, reflects the issues in his past that drove him to emigrate to Russia in the first place.

The outlines of his biography seem to have been as follows.[6] He was born to a Catholic burgher family in the Prussian city of Breslau in 1768, and ran off as a youth to join the theater. We know nothing else of his origins, not even what his name was before he adopted the stage name "Rosenstrauch": in what seems to be the earliest account of him, a fellow freemason who knew him around 1800 recalled that "he never spoke about his background, nor did he reveal his true name."[7] By his mid-thirties he had spent his entire adult life as an actor with various German theater companies, was separated from his wife (who was also an actress), had at least four children, belonged to several Masonic lodges, had become a Protestant, and lost contact with his family of origin. These details are pieced together from scattered bits of evidence or inferred from the gaps and silences in the evidentiary record. Rosenstrauch himself spoke little about his past: after his death, one of his friends wrote that Rosenstrauch "always told me only individual fragments [of his life], but the linkages between even these episodes remained unknown to me."[8]

In 1804, he left for Russia and apparently never looked back. From this point on, the evidence becomes much more solid and consistent. At first, he pursued his acting career at the German theater of St. Petersburg, but in 1809 he quit to become a merchant of luxury goods, a business that he moved to Moscow in 1811. After surviving the devastation of Napoléon's invasion in 1812, he rebuilt his business and became a wealthy merchant, selling elegant fashion accessories and housewares in a store on Moscow's fanciest shopping street. In 1820, he moved to Odessa to be trained as a Lutheran minister, then served as pastor to the German community in the town of Khar'kov (today the Ukrainian city of Kharkiv) from 1822 until his death in 1835, and wrote edifying religious texts that were published in multiple editions and diverse languages. His son Wilhelm, meanwhile, carried on his father's business in Moscow and was one of the city's leading citizens until he died in 1870.

Both Rosenstrauch's career and his reluctance to reminisce reveal much about his times. Europeans, particularly Germans, lived in a society of corporations (for example, the clergy, nobility, artisan guilds, or merchant guilds) that were mostly hereditary and were jealous of their collective honor and privileges. For Rosenstrauch to leave the esteemed status of burgher to become an actor—a profession that society deemed just a notch above being a vagrant—must have been a slap in the face to his entire family. The resulting dishonor probably followed him wherever he went, and the frustrations were compounded by economic insecurity: like many circus performers today, actors were hired on a seasonal basis by theater companies that were continually on the move, and Rosenstrauch sometimes spoke of the aching hunger he and his children had endured.[9] If this interpretation is correct, and he kept mum about his past because he was haunted by bitter memories of exclusion, humiliation, and poverty, then we can infer that he emigrated with his children to Russia to escape these troubles.

Russia presented Rosenstrauch with new opportunities and challenges. His problem in Germany was, at bottom, the country's provincialism—it was a land of poor, clannish, intolerant small towns, where he could neither find secure employment as an actor nor leave the theater behind him and be readmitted to respectable society. In St. Petersburg, by contrast, both the German expatriate community and the Russian elite had money and were starved for European culture, so the city could support a permanent German theater. Moreover, a perennial skills deficit caused the Russian Empire to welcome all manner of un- or underemployed Westerners, provided they had academic degrees, military training, or other useful expertise, so a dubious personal history was readily forgotten or forgiven.

Rosenstrauch found a market for his services because he proved adept at providing the kind of Western culture that was in demand among the Russian upper classes. The Russian elite was attracted to elements of European life that promised to offset the harshness of Russian society: theaters staged plays that modeled virtuous behavior; freemasonry allowed men to pursue moral self-improvement and socialize without the usual obsessive regard for social rank; the spread of luxury goods encouraged the refinement of manners; and Western religion supplemented Russian Orthodoxy as a source of moral inspiration. Moreover, the probity, self-discipline, and civic spirit that were attributed to Germans appeared as salutary alternatives to Russian vices. Rosenstrauch gained respect among Russians precisely by acting as an agent of this kind of Westernization—as an actor, freemason, merchant of luxury goods, pastor, and religious writer.

Finding a niche in the social hierarchy, however, was more difficult. He was too much the foreigner and newcomer to be able (or willing) to assimilate into the Russian middle classes, and as a commoner he was excluded from the nobility. His only option was to join the German expatriate community, but there he encountered the same prejudice against actors as in Germany. This is probably why he left the stage in 1809 to become a merchant. However, shedding his past was not easy: even after he became a pastor, fellow German Lutheran pastors in Russia still scorned him as an "actor-turned-shopkeeper" who had no right to join their cliquish community, and his past helped prevent him from obtaining an appointment as pastor in the Moscow church where he had long been an active layman.[10]

To escape these debilitating prejudices, Rosenstrauch took advantage of the geographic mobility and selective amnesia that Russian conditions made possible. He did not move to Russia's Baltic Provinces (today's Latvia and Estonia), where the towns were ethnically German and local society resembled his German homeland. Instead, he ventured first to Moscow, deep in the Russian heartland, and then to the empire's frontier. Studying for the pastorate by taking an informal crash course in divinity in the multiethnic Black Sea boomtown of Odessa, and then ministering to German settlers in Khar'kov on the southern steppe, he was surrounded by transients, newcomers, and provincials; some of them admired his energy, humanitarianism, and austere piety, while others resented his fiery denunciations of gambling and drinking, but few, it seems, asked awkward questions about his past.[11]

One folder from a St. Petersburg archive illustrates Rosenstrauch's caginess about his past. It holds personnel files submitted to the ecclesiastical authorities by Rosenstrauch and sixty-five other Lutheran pastors in the Russian Empire. Half were ethnic Germans; the rest were Swedes, Finns, or Balts. Sixty-one reported having a university or other advanced education, and two mentioned studying on their own; only Rosenstrauch and two others were silent about their schooling as youths. Almost half had gone directly from school or university into the clergy. Rosenstrauch was one of eighteen who failed to account for what they did during some part of their adult lives, but while the most that others omitted was about twenty years, Rosenstrauch reported nothing about his life before he moved to Moscow at the age of forty-three.[12]

Russia was a land of opportunity, but building a future required—and permitted—suppressing his past. However, Rosenstrauch's variegated career should not be attributed only to his desire for affluence and respectability; he was also on a spiritual quest, a quest closely connected with wider forces shaping the culture of Russia's Westernized upper class.

## A Spiritual Odyssey

In 1821, Tsar Alexander I included the following note in a letter to his advisor, and fellow religious mystic, Prince Aleksandr Golitsyn: "I have marked in pencil and with a dog-ear one of Rosenstrauch's letters that deserves your attention. I agree completely with what he says."[13] It would be fascinating, of course, to know just what that letter contained. However, the very fact of his acquaintance with the tsar and Golitsyn suggests that Rosenstrauch was at least a bit player in a much larger story—that of Russia's encounter with Western, particularly German spirituality.

Germany occupied an important place in the spiritual life of upper-class Russians. Compared with its French and British counterparts, the eighteenth-century German Enlightenment seemed congenial to Russians because it stressed moral introspection and service to the community, not subversive political ideas or religious skepticism. Also in the eighteenth century, a desire among German Protestants for a warmer, more individualistic spirituality produced the movements of Pietism and the Awakening, comparable to Methodism and the Great Awakening in the Anglo-American world. Pietist and Awakened ways of living one's faith appealed to Russians who were too Westernized to feel fulfilled by traditional Orthodoxy but refused to convert to Catholicism and felt less attraction to the Protestantism emanating from the disconcertingly alien, liberal society of Great Britain. The German spirituality encouraged an introspective, cosmopolitan, ecumenical faith that promoted fellowship with other believers and devotion to the public good but did not conflict with obedience to the tsar and membership in the Orthodox Church.

Like so much else, Rosenstrauch's own religious development is shrouded in mystery. At least into his thirties he may have felt spiritually adrift. As a traveling actor, he was marginalized by respectable society and unable to join a stable religious congregation, yet the theater's Enlightenment culture and bohemian lifestyle fell short of his social and moral aspirations. This simmering personal crisis occurred amidst a wider societal upheaval as Germany faced repeated invasions by revolutionary France. Rosenstrauch was therefore on multiple simultaneous quests—for an improved social status, a comforting spirituality, and the fellowship of kindred spirits. Neither the traditional society of the ancien régime nor the Enlightenment values recently hijacked by the French Revolution provided a framework for attaining these goals. Instead, he pursued them by joining the freemasons (around 1800), moving to Russia (1804), leaving the theater (1809), and—at some unknown date—converting from Roman Catholicism to Protestantism.

What attracted him to the freemasons was most likely that their lodges cared more—at least in theory—about their members' spiritual growth than their class origins. Freemasonry held great significance for him and probably supported his deepening religious faith; he was initiated into advanced Masonic degrees, led a major St. Petersburg lodge, personally lobbied the tsar for permission to found another in Moscow, and remained an active mason until 1822, when he was already a pastor and the Russian government shut down all the lodges.[14]

In his attraction to a Masonically inflected spirituality, Rosenstrauch was in sympathy with influential portions of the Russian upper class. How he met the tsar and Golitsyn is unknown, but since many of the tsar's kin and officials were Germans, Protestants, freemasons, patrons of the St. Petersburg German theater, or some combination thereof, the opportunities for contact were numerous. Key figures among the Russian elite believed that by popularizing the progressive and cosmopolitan ethos of freemasonry as well as a politically conservative version of Pietism, they could reshape their culture's values in a way that allowed the upper class to continue to grow increasingly educated and Westernized without importing dangerous revolutionary attitudes from Western Europe. Tsar Alexander, who saw Russia's victory over Napoléon as a direct sign from God, promoted these ideas in various ways: for instance, he persuaded Europe's monarchs to form an ecumenical Christian "Holy Alliance"; he placed Prince Golitsyn in charge of a new government ministry that coordinated all educational institutions and religious denominations and was charged with infusing a Christian spirit into all areas of Russian upper-class culture; and he gave official patronage to a range of organizations that blended freemasonry with mystical or ecumenical Christianity.

Rosenstrauch was connected with these wider trends in Russian elite society in two ways. First, his experience of social and (in Russia) ethnic marginality inspired hopes and anxieties similar to those of upper-class Russians, whose status as over-privileged half-Europeans left them feeling isolated both at home and abroad. Second, because of the influence of German culture and spirituality in Russia, Germans like himself played an active role in shaping educated Russians' understanding of Western culture.

Rosenstrauch thus both mirrored and helped influence the spiritual outlook of the Russian upper class, a pattern that continued even as the mood shifted after the early 1820s. By that time, Tsar Alexander's efforts to reshape Russian and European culture had collapsed under the weight of repeated policy failures, political intrigues, and public opposition. In 1822, Alexander shut down the Masonic lodges, which he now viewed as incubators of subversion, and by 1824 Prince Golitsyn was forced from office in the face of a resurgent Russian Orthodoxy. Pietist attitudes survived among the Russian elite, but the culture of the next thirty years favored denominational orthodoxy in religion, deference to state authority in politics, and a deepening—though often Germanophile—Russian nationalism. Rosenstrauch moved in the same direction: in the reminiscences of his friends and the texts he wrote when he was a pastor in 1822–35, which form nearly the entirety of his known writings, he appears as a conventional Lutheran clergyman and member of an insular German expatriate community. In keeping with the changing times, it is this incarnation of his persona—not the earlier versions as actor or freemason—that lived on in Russian memory long after he died in 1835.

## THE TWO ROSENSTRAUCH NARRATIVES

The name Rosenstrauch appears with some frequency in Russian writings—letters, journalism, fiction, scholarship, and memoirs—from the 1840s onward, but the references are mostly cursory and devoid of context. "Rosenstrauch," it seems, did not evoke a fully developed individual, only a collection of vague clichés. Taken together, however, the clichés add up to two distinct narratives, each of which elaborated one facet of his life while ignoring the others. Both were cultivated by Rosenstrauch and his son Wilhelm, but they also reflect the evolving expectations Russians had toward Germans.

One narrative grew out of Rosenstrauch's pastorate, which became widely known through the literary legacy that he left behind: his eloquent letters and sermons, and the moving account he wrote of his effort to give spiritual comfort to people on their deathbeds. He had passionate admirers among his German Lutheran congregants, who knew almost nothing of his biography—aside from a vague sense that his life had been filled with sorrow and tribulations—but who posthumously published his writings, sold his image to raise money for the poor, and perpetuated his memory in their own memoirs. His works were subsequently collected and republished in book form in Germany in 1838–39, and then in a much expanded edition in 1845 and 1871.[15]

Rosenstrauch's pastoral image appealed to Russians as well because it matched their culture's needs at that point in history. As the nineteenth century progressed, educated Russians were caught on the horns of a dilemma: they favored Westernization but hated the ways it isolated them from the Russian masses, and while they resented their country's oppressive social order, they also took offense at the Russophobia that was increasingly prevalent in Western Europe. Rosenstrauch's image suggested that a reassuring middle ground existed. Germans were bona fide Westerners, but not the threatening, Russophobic kind. Far into the nineteenth century, foreigners commonly associated Germany with medieval castles, deep-thinking philosophers, and a dreamy spirituality, by contrast with more Russophobic Britain (land of squalid slums and heartless industrialists) or France (home of Napoleonic warmongers and revolutionary fanatics). A characteristic product of this romantic Germany seemed to be wise old men who lived apart from upper-class society and forthrightly denounced its evils: examples included the Pietist writer Johann Heinrich Jung-Stilling, who enjoyed cultlike status in the entourage of Tsar Alexander I, or the humanitarian Moscow prison doctor Friedrich Joseph Haas. Russian thinkers also increasingly admired Russians of the higher classes who reached out to the poor and fearlessly spoke truth to power, such as the writers Tolstoy and Dostoevsky or the *startsy* (elders) of the Orthodox clergy. Rosenstrauch was remembered as a man in that mold—a wise old European who was free of Russophobia, cared for the poor, showed true spiritual humility, and was uncorrupted by money or power.

The narrative of Rosenstrauch as pastor was periodically updated to reflect the evolving moods and concerns of educated Russian readers. The German edition of his writings was first translated into Russian in 1846. Although Rosenstrauch had been dead for only a decade, the translator knew virtually nothing about his life (for instance, she thought that he had been born in Russia). Lacking hard information about him as an individual, readers were free to imagine him as they wished. In 1846, Russia was ruled by Tsar Nicholas I (reigned 1825–55), whose conservative ideology commanded all citizens to honor God, obey the tsar, and accept their place in society Reflecting this system of values, a Russian newspaper's review of the translation described Rosenstrauch as a model subject of Nicholas's Russia: "a simple and magnificent man whose entire life was devoted to the strict and humble execution of the most sacred and noble obligations."[16] By the time the second Russian edition of his works appeared, in 1863, Russia was a far more turbulent place, rocked by radical social reforms, growing Russian Orthodox nationalism, armed revolt in Catholic Poland, and the beginnings of a homegrown revolutionary movement. Responding to these changed circumstances, Russia's premier conservative newspaper published a long review that presented his humane, tolerant piety as a model of Orthodox-Protestant harmony as well as an antidote to Catholic fanaticism and the irreligion of radical social critics.[17] By the 1870s and 1880s, educated Russians became intensely preoccupied with understanding the psychology of Russia's common people, especially the recently emancipated peasantry. Again, Rosenstrauch proved useful. In 1886 the writer and literary critic Nikolai Leskov cited him at length to support Tolstoy's observation that the poor faced death with more dignity than did the wealthy, thereby making the case that Tolstoy understood the soul of the common people better than did Dostoevsky.[18]

Like other Russians who mentioned Rosenstrauch's works, and who included such luminaries as the writers Vasilii Zhukovskii and Nikolai Gogol, Leskov seems to have thought he understood Rosenstrauch despite knowing virtually nothing of him as an individual. Public knowledge of Rosenstrauch's biography was limited to a single simplistic storyline in which he featured as a stereotyped character who seemed too familiar to educated Russians to require further investigation.

The other Rosenstrauch narrative draws on a different aspect of the German-Russian encounter. Russians by mid-century were increasingly concerned that their country was falling behind economically; that those who had power—tsars, serf owners, policemen, fathers—wielded it despotically over degraded subjects who cowered in fear and resentment; and that incautious reforms might trigger a catastrophic breakdown of society. German ways appeared as an antidote to these woes, for Germans were seen as forward-looking yet loyal to authority: they were practical, industrious, entrepreneurial, honest, and respectful both of the monarchy and of the lawful rights of others. The name Rosenstrauch forms part of this narrative as well. The family business in Moscow, founded by Rosenstrauch and carried on for a half-century by his son Wilhelm, was so well known and successful that it appeared repeatedly in works of fiction, including, for example, the novel *On the Eve* by Turgenev; both Rosenstrauchs, father and son, were dedicated philanthropists, supporters of education, and laymen active in their Moscow church; and Wilhelm served both the tsar and the people of Moscow as a member of a commission to help the poor, even while he promoted Russian-German commerce as consul for Prussia. The name Rosenstrauch thus offered evidence that Germans could help Russia gain the benefits of Western economic dynamism and civic energies while avoiding the terrible dislocations plaguing Western Europe in the nineteenth century.

## EPILOGUE

The Rosenstrauchs' relationship with Russia was a two-way street. Tsarist Russia welcomed German immigrants and allowed them to refashion their identities and achieve greater social mobility than in their homeland. Conversely, the Russians before the 1917 revolution read the immigrants' experience in light of stereotypes designed to help make sense of Russia itself. In this context, Rosenstrauch and his son Wilhelm embodied the stereotype of Germans as "good" Europeans who were Russophile and free from the selfish coldheartedness attributed to other Westerners. When the two world wars turned Russians' sympathy for the German nation to hatred, the name Rosenstrauch lost relevance and seemed to disappear from Russian culture. More recently however, as communism collapsed and Russia embarked on its difficult journey to rejoin Europe, Germany has reemerged as its principal Western partner and the Western country whose values seem least alien. It is therefore no surprise that the two Rosenstrauch narratives from the nineteenth century have also resurfaced—Rosenstrauch's book about his pastoral work was reissued in 1998, followed the next year by an admiring article on Wilhelm as an exemplary merchant and citizen[19]—for they embody dimensions of the Russian-German encounter that remain as relevant today as when Johannes Ambrosius Rosenstrauch first arrived on Russia's shores two centuries ago.

NOTES

1. I thank the American Councils for International Education (ACTR/ACCELS), the National Council for Eurasian and East European Research, and the Nanovic Institute for European Studies at the University of Notre Dame for providing the funding that made the research for this project possible.

2. "Geschichtliche Ereignisse in Moskau *im Jahre 1812,* zur Zeit, der Anwesenheit des Feindes in dieser Stadt," Otdel Pis'mennykh Istochnikov Gosudarstvennogo Istoricheskogo Muzeia (Division of Written Sources of the State Historical Museum), f. 402, d. 239; Tsentral'nyi Istoricheskii Arkhiv Moskvy (Central Historical Archive of Moscow), f. 20, op. 2, d. 2219, ll. 171–171 ob.

3. Geheimes Staatsarchiv Preußischer Kulturbesitz (Secret State Archive Prussian Cultural Heritage, Berlin), III HA, MdA, Abt. II, Nr. 442, fols. 82–83; M. Pogodin, "Nekrolog," *Moskovskiia Vedomosti,* June 5, 1870.

4. This last claim was advanced by Karl Didler in *Freimaurer-Denkschrift über die politische Wirksamkeit des Freimaurer-Bundes als der unter verschiedenen Namen und Formen unter uns im Finstern schleichenden Propaganda zum Sturz der legitimen Throne und des positiven Christenthums* (Berlin: als Geheimschrift gedruckt., 1864), 13.

5. M. Korelin, "Novyia dannyia o sostoianii Moskvy v 1812 godu," *Russkaia mysl'* 10 (1896): 57–73.

6. On Rosenstrauch's biography, see also Alexander M. Martin, "Middle-Class Masculinity in an Immigrant Diaspora: War, Revolution, and Russia's Ethnic Germans," in *Gender, War, and Politics: Transatlantic Perspectives, 1775–1830,* ed. Karen Hagemann et al. (Basingstoke, UK: Palgrave Macmillan, 2010), 147–66.

7. "Johann Ambrosius Rosenstauch," *Die Bauhütte: Organ des Verein's deutscher Freimaurer,* June 21, 1862, 198 (reprint of an 1837 article, apparently by Christian Nettelbladt).

8. Heinrich Blumenthal, "Johannes Ambrosius Rosenstrauch," *Dorpatische Evangelische Blätter,* July 19, 1836, cols. 253–60, quotation on 253.

9. Johann Philipp Simon, *Russisches Leben in geschichtlicher, kirchlicher, gesellschaftlicher und staatlicher Beziehung* (Düsseldorf: Buchdruckerei von Hermann Voß, 1854), 316–17; "Interesting Account of a Lutheran Pastor," *The Church of England Magazine,* May 25, 1844, 339.

10. K. Limmer, *Meine Verfolgung in Rußland. Eine aktenmäßige Darstellung der Jesuitischen Umtriebe des D. Ignatius Feßler und seiner Verbündeten in jenen Gegenden* (Leipzig: Carl Heinrich Reclam, 1823), 176; A. W. Fechner, *Chronik der Evangelischen Gemeinden in Moskau* (Moscow: J. Deubner, 1876), 2:116–21.

11. Simon, *Russisches Leben,* 307–309.

12. Rossiiskii Gosudarstvennyi Istoricheskii Arkhiv (Russian State Historical Archive), f. 828, op. 1 dop., d. 37.

13. Nikolai Mikhailovich, *Imperator Aleksandr I. Opyt istoricheskago izsledovaniia* (St. Petersburg: Ekspeditsiia zagotovleniia Gosudarstvennykh bumag, 1912), 1:557.

14. On Rosenstrauch's masonic career, see A. I. Serkov, *Russkoe masonstvo 1731–2000: Entsiklopedicheskii slovar'* (Moscow: ROSSPEN, 2001), 708.

15. Johann Christian Friedrich Burk, *Evangelische Pastoral-Theologie in Beispielen* (Stuttgart: J. F. Steinkopf, 1838–39), 1:20–21, 2:399–459; *Mittheilungen aus dem Nachlasse von Johannes Ambrosius Rosenstrauch, früherem Consistorialrath und Prediger in Charkow* (Leipzig: Karl Tauchnitz, 1845; repr. Dresden: Ramming, 1871).

16. The translation appeared as *Iogann-Amvrosii Rozenshtraukh, liuteranskii pastor v Khar'kove*, trans. A. Ishimova (St. Petersburg: V tipografii Imperatorskoi Akademii Nauk, 1947), 8; the review appeared in *Biblioteka dlia chteniia*, 81 (1847), section "Literaturnaia letopis'," 42.

17. *Severnaia pchela*, March 30, 1863.

18. N. S. Leskov, *Sobranie sochinenii* (Moscow: Gosudarstvennoe izdatel'stvo khudozhestvennoi literatury, 1958), 11:140–45.

19. I. A. Rozenshtraukh, *U odra umiraiushchikh* (St. Petersburg: "Bibliia dlia vsekh," 1998); "Dobrosovestnyi obyvatel': Obshchestvennyi deiatel' Vasilii Ivanovich Rozenshtraukh (1793–1870)," in *Moskovskie obyvateli*, ed. M. I. Vostryshev (Moscow: Molodaia Gvardiia, 1999), 117–18.

Mosaic of Imam Shamil in modern-day Gunib. Photograph by Rebecca Gould.

# 10

# Imam Shamil

## (1797–1871)

REBECCA GOULD

When the Georgian modernist poet Titsian Tabidze decided to commemorate his recent excursion to the mountain village Gunib, the site of Imam Shamil's surrender to the Russian general Bariatinskii in 1859, it was not necessary to provide much context for his Georgian readers. Written in 1928, the poem was never published in his lifetime, and only made it into his collected works in 1966. Titsian was well aware of his poem's unpublishability under the conditions of Stalinist rule. The most articulate text produced by a Georgian about the Russian conquest of the north Caucasus, a conquest facilitated by Georgian generals in the Tsarist army, thereby escaped censorship. Thanks to this evasion, the words that have been preserved have not lost their resonance:

> I crossed Daghestan. I saw Gunib.
> I, an infidel, now a shahid.
> My sword is an arrow; it will not bend
> Though it may kill me. [ . . . ]
> I see the ghost of a nest, ravaged by eagles.
> My eyes recall my shame.
> How did they embalm these cliffs?
> Why did they exterminate this sky?
> Georgia, this mountain's grief belongs to you.
> Our bones rot beside our swords and bayonets,
> I pity my gangrened Georgian flesh.
> Those who gave their lives are safe in paradise.
> As for you who remain behind,
> My Georgian brothers, memory has no mercy.
> Tonight, the wind shudders.
> Shamil prays for his men.
> You sold us into slavery, you spoiled the battle.
> The night won't weep for cowards under a foreign sky.
> I never pulled the fatal trigger.

I never donned the fighter's armor.
But this battle moves even me to ecstasy.
I don't want to be a poet drunk on blood.
Let this day be my penitence.
Let my poems wash away your treachery.[1]


It is not known whether Soviet Georgian authorities were directly acquainted with Titsian's evocation of Imam Shamil's defeat. Certainly the Russian authorities were not, as the poem was never translated into Russian. Nor has the text been rendered into Russian in the eighty years since it was written. But it seems unlikely that Titsian's execution nine years later, while the poet was imprisoned on the charge of espionage and after he had undergone torture intended to extract a confession, was entirely unconnected to his authorship of this poem. Arguably his masterpiece, "Gunib" was never translated by Boris Pasternak, translator of Titsian's finest poems into Russian, and Nobel laureate for his own poetry and prose. Pasternak is largely responsible for Titsian's fame as the second-greatest modernist poet in Georgian among readers of Russian, but he remained ignorant of this particular masterpiece.

Not by coincidence, Titsian Tabidze was working on a novel about Imam Shamil when the NKVD (Stalin and Beria's secret police) arrived in his Tbilisi apartment to take him away to jail. Titsian's compatriot Grigol Robakidze did escape Soviet Russia before the purge. From his Geneva home, Robakidze wrote the story Titsian never wrote, or at least never published: "Imam Shamil" in his 1932 collection *Caucasian Novellas*.[2] Significantly, Robakidze wrote his account in German rather than Georgian or Russian, as if to suggest that the European Shamil was more likely to pique his readers' interest than the Shamil known to Robakidze in his own language.

Imam Shamil, who led the peoples of Chechnya and Daghestan in their resistance to the twenty-five-year Russian conquest of the northeast Caucasus (1834–59), has never lost his hold in the imaginative historiography of Russian colonialism. Born in 1797 to an Avar family in the village of Gimri in mountainous Daghestan, Shamil's original name was 'Ali. During a childhood illness, 'Ali was rechristened Shamūēl, a name meaning "that which repels sickness." Shamūēl was modified to Shamil, the name by which he is known today in both Arabic and European sources.

From birth, Shamil was a weak child, but after the name change, he grew to be strong, courageous, and widely esteemed for his eloquence and learning. By the age of twenty, Shamil had mastered all the traditional subjects taught in the *madrasas* of the north Caucasus: Arabic grammar and rhetoric, *hadith* (stories and sayings of the Prophet), and Islamic jurisprudence (*fiqh*) and theology (*kalam*). This training was to prove useful in later years when it became necessary to establish a state in the Caucasus based on Islamic principles.

Shamil received his initial training in guerrilla warfare while fighting under Ghazi Muhammad, the first spiritual leader of the Daghestani Muslim forces. Ghazi Muhammad was the head of the same Sufi brotherhood that had reclaimed Daghestan from the Qajar Persians in 1813, and who, using the Sufi term for "dis-

ciple," called themselves Murids. The leaders of this organization had been inspired
by the Naqshbandiyya Sufis who had been traveling to Daghestan via Shirvan since
the 1810s (the history of Sufism in the Caucasus begins in the eleventh century, but
the wide reach of this new Sufism was driven in part by colonial incursions). Ghazi
Muhammad was killed by the Russians in 1832, after which leadership of the Murid
brotherhood passed to Hamza Bek, himself killed two years later by his own followers. This left the path open to Imam Shamil, who was chosen in 1834 by the remaining members of the Murid brotherhood and the Avar ʿulama (elders) to lead a united
Daghestan and Chechnya against the Tsarist army and to serve simultaneously as
head of the northeast Caucasian Islamic state.

Thus Imam Shamil became the third imam of the Caucasus, succeeding Ghazi
Muhammad and Hamza. Muhammad b. al-Qarahi (d. 1882), Shamil's secretary and
biographer, described the imam's rise to power in eulogistic terms that underscore the
Murid movement's global outlook. Al-Qarahi wrote how the "able scholar Shamil"
was "famed in the east and the west for his jihad so that the people of Mecca and
Medina, the scholars of Balkh and Bukhara, and pious people from all over the world
. . . prayed for his victory, success, and prosperity."[3]

Shamil was far more than a military leader; he was also builder of a new state. In
addition to adapting shariʿa to his local environment, Shamil formulated a set of or-
dinances for situations shariʿa did not address. This second set of regulations resulted
in a body of law called *nizam,* modeled on the legal system prevalent in the Ottoman
Empire at the time, *kanun.*[4] Finally, Shamil was the leading diplomat for the state he
built. In his official correspondence, he applied the term *amir al-muʾminin* to himself, alongside titles such *qazi* (judge in Islamic law).[5] The first title is both the most
controversial and revealing, for *amir al-muʾminin* ("Commander of the Faithful"),
generally reserved for the Caliph, who ruled from Baghdad until 1258. The title was
assumed by the Ottoman sultans in subsequent centuries, but in the colonial period
few Islamic rulers were daring enough to call themselves *amir al-muʾminin.*

That Shamil arrogated this title to himself reflects his formidable political ambitions. But when it came to dealing with Russian authorities, Shamil, ever the consummate statesman, uses self-deprecating terms such as "the slave of god" (*al-ʿabd al-faq-
ir*) in lieu of Imam and *amir al-muʾminin.*[6] Even when he was not directly addressing
Ottoman rulers, Shamil evinced a respect for Ottoman sovereignty that appeared to
exceed his regard for the Tsar. He once told Ilya Orbeliani, a Georgian officer whom
he had taken captive, "There is only one God in heaven and one *padishah* on earth,
the Ottoman *hünkar* [ruler]."[7] By reserving the title *amir al-muʾminin* for himself,
Shamil managed to retain at least certain aspects of sovereignty for himself.

It would be impossible to recount here all the legends recorded about the great
imam. Most sources for the historiography of Shamil and his state are in Arabic, and
include both contemporary chronicles and letters and decrees composed by Shamil
himself. The most important such source is the official biography by Shamil's son-
in-law, al-Qarahi. In addition to being a record of Shamil's life, this text is a detailed
firsthand account of the events of the Caucasian war. A second class of sources

comprises largely Russian memoirs by officers in the Tsarist army and travelers to the Caucasus, as well as accounts by Russians who became acquainted with Shamil in exile, such as Maria Nikolaevna Chichagova, wife of a Tsarist official charged with monitoring Shamil in his captivity, and author of *Shamil in the Caucasus and Russia* (*Shamil' na Kavkaze i v Rossii*). The most notable officers' memoirs are Runovskii's *Notes on Shamil* (*Zapiski o Shamile*) and Zissermann's *Twenty Five Years in the Caucasus* (*Dvadtsat'piat' let na Kavkaze*). A third class of sources comprises the numerous European accounts of Imam Shamil by the now-forgotten Friedrich Wagner and John Baddeley. With varying degrees of credibility, these works fashion Shamil alternately as a fanatic, a tyrant, and an enlightened, truth-seeking, idealist reformer. As indicated in Charles King's contribution to this volume, the European engagement with Shamil penetrated even into the American public sphere during the nineteenth century.

Arabic sources generally present Shamil as a devout and well-informed follower of the Naqshbandiyya Sufism, and a reformer opposed to the non-Islamic customs (*adat*) which still held sway over the Daghestani and Chechen mountaineers in the mid-nineteenth century. Shamil's scholarship in the domain of religious studies was so notable that as we have seen above, al-Qarahi underscored Shamil's preeminence in this field but had little to say about the intellectual attainments of the previous imams, Hamza and Ghazi Muhammad. Scholarship was the foundation on which Shamil mounted his critique of both the Russian infidels (*kaffur*) and the ignorant (*jahili*) not-fully Islamicized and excessively quietistic mountaineers of Daghestan and, especially, Chechnya.

The conflict between Islamic law (shari'a) and *adat* in Shamil's political praxis appears with particular clarity in a story concerning his treatment of his mother, Bahou Messadou. By 1843, the Caucasian War had already become too brutal for most peace-loving residents of the Caucasus to endure. The mountaineers wanted an end to the shedding of blood and the slaughtering of their neighbors. Like the majority of Chechens and Daghestanis, particularly those who resided on the plains, Bahou wished for an end to the war. She met with her son and informed him of her desires. Shamil then went to the mosque to pray.

Three days later, Shamil emerged from the mosque and announced that Allah had issued the following order: one hundred lashes to the person who advised Imam Shamil to surrender to the Russians. According to this judgment, the person most deserving of punishment was, as Shamil himself knew, his mother Bahou. A crowd assembled and his mother was brought before him, her limbs tied together to prevent her escape. Shamil lifted his whip. He delivered five strokes, after which his mother lost consciousness. Although the instruction from God had stipulated one hundred strokes, Shamil could not bear to see his mother suffer any more. He fell to the ground and instructed his assistants to whip him instead of his mother. The assistants hesitated to punish their master, but Shamil would not permit an abrogation of the sacred commandment. He threatened that anyone who refused to whip him would be executed. By his own command, Shamil suffered the ninety-five remaining lashes of the whip. When the punishment was fully administered, the imam staggered to his feet, covered in blood, and instructed his attendants to report the incident to the community. This punishment was staged to persuade the war-weary that the fight must persist until the end.

In his youth, Shamil studied with Muhammad al-Yaraghi (also known as Mulla Magomet), the most influential leader of Sufism in Daghestan. Unlike the political theory Shamil and his scholars developed to uphold his state, Yaraghi's teaching did not include the call to *jihad,* or *gazawat,* as holy war in defense of Islam is generally termed in Daghestani contexts. The politicization of Sufism that we see in the campaigns of Shamil may have been a response to political exigency more than an expression of religious faith.

Many Sufistic movements in the north Caucasus, such as that led by Kunta Haji of the Qadiri order, were emphatically nonviolent and even quietistic to the point of enjoining a complete isolation from political events. Northeast Caucasian Sufism is often divided into two major groups: those that, like Imam Shamil, actively resisted Russian incursions, and those that opted for surrender in the interests of peace. These divisions make it all the more ironic that Imam Shamil became a poster child for political amelioration after he surrendered, while the 1864 repression of Kunta Hajji's quietist followers who belonged to the Qadiri order contributed to the popularity of the more militant Naqshbandiyyas.

It is not hard to understand why Shamil appealed to so many people in so many different ways. To those disgusted by corruption among the Islamic clerics, Shamil was at the vanguard of a reform movement that promised to cleanse Daghestan and Chechnya of religious impurities. To those grief-stricken by the bloodshed of war, Shamil offered a beam of light for Caucasian autonomy and ultimately for peace. To Russian idealists such as Tolstoy and the bestselling children's writer Lydia Charskaia, Shamil was a symbol of courage, the like of which was not to be found among the Russians, even though both writers were critical in their own ways of the Avar warrior.

Everyone who lives in the contemporary Caucasus confronts the historical memory of a man who forestalled the incorporation of the north Caucasus into the Russian Empire by the world's largest army for a quarter of a century. One interesting twist in the Shamil legacy has been the aspersion cast on him in local mountaineer sources as a result of his surrender at Gunib. Particularly in recent Chechen accounts—such as the historical trilogy by Chechnya's most famous contemporary writer, Abuzar Aidamirov (d. 2005), which opens with Shamil's imamate—Imam Shamil is portrayed as a traitor to the cause of north Caucasian freedom.[8] During the recent Chechen wars, the Chechen bard Timur Mucuraev committed many Chechen legends to poetry. One of his most famous songs based on Chechen oral memory is called "Imam Shamil." In this poem, we learn that Shamil was responsible for the defeat of the north Caucasus. Shamil decided to accept captivity, whereas his more steadfast Chechen colleague, Baisangur, was prepared to battle the Tsar's army until his death. When Shamil surrendered to Bariatinskii at Gunib, the precipice

Titsian later memorialized in his poem, Baisangur refused to give in. Rather than allow Chechnya to become part of Russia, he left for the mountains, taking many armed Chechens with him. Anticolonial guerrilla warriors, such as the Chechen Sheikh Mansur, preceded him, and anticolonial warriors, such as Baisangur and the abrek Zelimkhan of Kharachoi, followed.[9] This legacy of Chechen military zealousness contrasts interestingly with the pleadings of those Chechens from the plains who asked Bahou Messadou to persuade her son to make peace with the Russians. Tolstoy's portrayal of Shamil in *Hadji Murat* (1912) is another example of the Chechen-Avar split in Shamil's legacy.

Nearly all the lives that have shaped north Caucasian history ended in execution or surrender. Shamil was the luckiest among this group: he lived out his final days in pleasant exile in Kaluga, a mere one hundred twenty miles from Moscow, under the watchful gaze of the provincial administrator Chichagov and his wife. Disturbed by the cold climate of Kaluga, Shamil later moved to Kyiv, where he requested permission to perform the haj for the second time in his life. During his sojourn in Mecca, Shamil met the equally famous Sufi leader of the Algerian anticolonial resistance, 'Abd al-Qadir al-Jaza'iri (1808–83), whom many scholars regard as Shamil's Algerian counterpart.[10] Shamil also traveled to Damascus, where he visited the grave of Ibn al-'Arabi, and to Baghdad, where he visited the grave of 'Abd al-Qadir al-Jilani, both major figures in classical Sufism. Shamil died in Medina in 1871. He is buried in the cemetery Jannat al-Baqi, not far from the graves of Fatima, the daughter of Muhammad the prophet, and four of the earliest Shi'a imams.

The images Shamil's memory has produced express distinct and often conflicting cultural and political priorities. There are many Shamils: the Shamil of the Daghestanis, the Shamil of the Chechens, the Shamil of poets and of war chroniclers. There is a Shamil viewed through the lens of the Tsar, and another generated by popular memory. There is a Shamil who sternly gazes on a gambling house in modern-day Gunib (fig. 10), and a Shamil whose exploits Modest Mussorgsky set to music in a *Marsh Shamilia* (1859) set to a Georgian text.[11] Most recently, Shamil the philosopher has engaged in a debate with the fourth-century church historian Socrates Scholasticus about the meaning of prayer.[12] To the Soviet authorities, who published the appropriately titled *Shamil: A Supporter of Sultanate Turkey and of the English Colonizers* (1953), Shamil was a counterrevolutionary bandit and spy for foreign powers.[13] Each Shamil contradicts the one that came before.

In certain respects, the Soviets were right to be wary of the inflammatory implications of Shamil's deeds. The third imam did seek help from foreign powers. He wrote to Queen Victoria, complaining that "every year we must defend ourselves against the invader's fresh armies" and asking the queen to come to his aid.[14] He also wrote to the Ottoman Sultan Abdülmecid (r. 1839–61), pleading for support from the Ottoman Empire in his battle with the Tsarist army, and boasted that "cannons, gunpowder, and Congreve rockets" were now being produced within the bounds of his Imamate.[15] But Shamil's greatest hopes were directed further south: toward the Egyptian Pasha Muhammad 'Ali and his son Ibrahim, who in 1839 won a stunning defeat against the Ottomans at the battle of Nezib, and thereby demonstrated the superiority of Egyptian military power to Ottoman forces. In a letter circulated across Shamil's imamate, Ibrahim promised "all the Chechen and Daghestani *ulama* and elders" that they would "together conquer the provinces of Daghestan, recover Astrakhan', Derbend, and Azoz, and drive out the unbelievers from the land of Islam."[16] Our only source for this document is a Russian translation published in the nineteenth century. Whether it did not fact originate with the son of the Egyptian pasha, or whether its origin should be traced to local Daghestani actors, Imam Shamil made the most of his public alignment with a ruling family whom a French consul in Tbilisi recognized as the regime's most respect by the mountaineers of the Caucasus. The consulate's observation that "Muhammad Ali stands much higher than the [Ottoman] Sultan, because he conquered an entire realm from him, became the supreme ruler of the Muslims, and subdued the infidel English [*Ingliz*] and French [*Ifrang*] nations" went well heeded by our master statesman.[17]

Shamil never lost his grip on the Soviet imagination, as we see from the writings of Titsian Tabidze and another Georgian writer, Mikheil Javakhishvili, who devoted a special section in his longest novel, *Arsena of Marabdeli* (1935), to a theory that Shamil was the bastard child of the Georgian officer Grigol Orbeliani. Not coincidentally, it was to Orbeliani that Titsian addressed the following line from "Gunib": "You sold us into slavery, you spoiled the battle. / The night won't weep for cowards under a foreign sky." The passage concerned with Shamil's genealogy was censored from later Soviet editions of Javakhishvili's novel; as a result, the Georgian claim to genealogical affiliation with Imam Shamil has remained unknown not only to foreign scholars, but to many scholars from the Caucasus as well.

More than his deeds, Shamil's most lasting legacy is his imaginative afterlife in the memory of the peoples of the Caucasus and Russia. Shamil's legacy is evident today in the names of the streets bisecting central Maxachkala, Daghestan's capital; in the city's bookstores, filled with memoirs, novels and poems about the Imam; in the names of Daghestani philanthropical projects and publishing houses; and in the practice of calling Muslim boys from the Caucasus region Shamil. Why does the third imam refuse to die?

Perhaps the best way of illuminating the contemporary relationship to Shamil would be to share a conversation I had with a half-Russian and half-Daghestani (Lezgin) woman in northern Azerbaijan's former colonial outpost Zaqatala, on the border with Daghestan. It was a July morning, and the sun was already blistering overhead. I asked for directions to the nearest hotel, and she replied, "Come inside and drink some tea with me. I have lived in this town all my life. I have pictures to show you, and I can tell you the history of everything here." I followed the old woman past the wrought iron gates opening onto her garden. A peach tree was in bloom, and white blossoms covered the ground like petrified snow.

My host extended her hand to greet me after she closed the gate. "My name is Svetlana." It was a Russian name, pronounced with an accent as fluent as that of any native speaker. Clearly Russian was her first language. I thought that maybe she was a *pensionerka* who had wound up by some fluke of circumstance stranded on the Azeri-Daghestan border. But it turned out that her ethnic origins were as mixed as that of all the locals. "My father was Lezgin," Svetlana explained. "He met my mother, a Russian Cossack, in Krasnodar. They came together to Zakatala and they liked it so much that they decided stay here forever."

The first thing Svetlana showed me was a tattered copy of a newspaper published fourteen years before in Russia: the August 12, 1992, edition of *Literaturnaia Gazeta*. The headline of the article she wanted me to read was "WE WILL NOT MAKE WAR ON OUR TERRITORY." The cover story to which the headline referred was an interview with Jawhar Dudaev, independent Chechnya's first president, fated to die from a targeted Russian missile in 1995. The message was obvious: Russia's literary elite was embracing the first president of the self-proclaimed Republic of Ichkeria, just as he was embracing the Russians. Even more surprising was that fourteen years after its original publication, this text had been preserved—a sacred scroll on the decaying wooden dining table in the garden of a provincial Azeri home. I asked Svetlana why she had kept this article for so long, and why she was showing it to me now.

"Dudaev was here for the unveiling of the monument," she said reverently.

"Which monument?" I asked, confused. No history or guidebook mentioned anything about a monument relevant to Dudaev. The streets of Azerbaijan's backwater towns were still filled with Soviet war heroes, with women who had been the first in their family to ride tractors, and who had ripped off their veils to signal their embrace of Bolshevik power. I had yet to see a monument to Chechen or Daghestani heroes in the Azeri mountains, or any other acknowledgement of the long history of resistance to foreign rule that characterized this region.

"The monument to Shamil, of course," she said.

I asked her what monument to Shamil she was talking about. I had seen no such thing, and I had been in Zakatala for over a week.

"It's in the park. Haven't you seen it?"

I had been to the park many times. It was, after all, the central site in downtown Zakatala, and the most logical place for a monument. There was in fact a monument in the middle of the park. It wasn't to Shamil, however, but rather to Heidar Aliev, Azerbaijan's recently deceased president. In the 1990s Aliev led his country from the chaos of the Nagorno-Karabakh conflict to fragile stability. Aliev was a former communist leader who had been transformed by the media into the saint of Azeri nationalism. In 2003, Heidar Aliev's son Ilham "won" the Azeri presidential elections with a landslide victory of 76.84 percent, thereby repeating a pattern common to post-Soviet and postcolonial states such as Egypt, whereby sons follow their fathers by right of lineage rather than political acumen.

As we basked silently in the aura of Azerbaijan's illustrious president, Svetlana suddenly remembered that the Shamil monument had been relocated to the edge of the town, near the border with a village called Jar, populated by Avars rather than Azeris, and far from Zaqatala's central spaces. Shamil was himself an ethnic Avar, so the replacement of the monument was no coincidence. We decided to take an excursion to the monument, as Svetlana had not been there since the replacement of Shamil by Aliev. Although both monuments were only a kilometer away, I insisted on taking a taxi because the blistering sun had sapped my energy. I did not understand why Svetlana insisted on walking instead of taking a taxi until we reached the park and I opened my wallet to pay the driver. Svetlana thrust forward a five-manat bill— the equivalent of five dollars—probably her pension for an entire week. She protested that she had to pay because I was her guest, but I finally prevailed on the driver to accept my money instead of hers.

Svetlana wanted to visit the park before going to the Shamil monument. We passed the regal black gates opening onto the idyllic "Heidar Aliev Park." While the gates were still overhead, Svetlana pulled from her purse a packet of Soviet-era post-cards. On the front side of every card was a severed head, the image of a war hero. On the back was an explanation of why every Soviet-citizen was duty-bound to honor the image on the obverse. One of the postcards matched the severed head that stood in the corner of park, and we headed straight for the corresponding image. The statue, of gleaming white limestone, was covered with graffiti and surrounded by refuse. Svetlana read to me from the back of the postcard: "In 1908, Zakatala was stormed by a group of Russians who called themselves Potemkinites. They were rebelling against the Tsar."

We finally reached the center of the park, where the Aliev monument stood. Then I recalled how an Avar bus driver had recently told me that the monument to Shamil had been replaced by Aliev's bust. How could I have forgotten what he said? "Cretins," the Avar spat into the earth as he recalled the removal of Shamil's monu-ment to the edge of the town. "Traitors."

Svetlana froze reverently. "Let us stand silently and pray," she said finally, and closed her eyes. She rocked back and forth on her heels in a kind of trance. "Aliev was a great man," she finally said with a sigh, and moved away.

"This is the first time I have ever been here," Svetlana said reverently when we reached Shamil's bust, fronting a Sunni mosque attended by Jar's Avar population. It was on the Jar-Zakatala border. "All these years I have lived in Zakatala," Svetlana sighed, "and I have never once visited this holy site." Then she kneeled down, scooped up a handful of earth, and pressed it to her chest.

Thus Shamil is remembered in the act of his forgetting. He is remembered even as the most troubling aspects of his legacy are consigned to oblivion by statist his-toriography. Shamil's humanity is in the process of being replaced by a mythical war hero. There is no telling what this means for the future of the Caucasus. As the present changes, so does the past, and so does the need to remember it. No figure is more central to this act of memory than Imam Shamil. Shamil's many afterlives encapsulate two centuries of colonialism and anticolonial resistance from Chechen, Daghestani, Georgian, and Russian perspectives. Ultimately, it is not Shamil the guerrilla warrior who has determined the course taken by Caucasian history, but the uses to which his legacy has been put by local memories, many of which have yet to be recorded.[18]

NOTES

With the exceptions of the *hamza* (') and *'ayn* ('), diacritics have been removed from Arabic-based words. I wish to thank Dana Sherry for her comments on an earlier version of this chapter.

1. Georgian text and English translation by Rebecca Gould in *Metamorphosis: A Journal of Literary Translation* 17 (1): 70–71.

2. Grigol Robakhidze, *Kaukasische Novellen,* ed. Käthe Rosenberg (Leipzig: Insel-Bücherei, 1932; reprinted Munich: n.p., 1979).

3. Muhammad Tāhir Qarāhī, *Bariqat al-suyuf al-Daghistaniyah fi b'ad al-ghazawat al-Shamiliyah* [Shining of Daghestani Swords in Certain Campaigns of Shamil], ed. A. M. Barabanov and I. G. Krachkovskii (Moscow: Akademii Nauk, 1946), 8.

4. For Imam Shamil's nizam in Russian translation, see "Nizam Shamilia," *SSKG* 3 (1870): 1–18.

5. *Araboiazychnye dokumenty epokhi Shamilia,* ed. R. SH. Sharafutdinova (Moscow: Izd-vo atelskaia firma "Vostochnaia literatura" RAN, 2001), letters 84 and 65.

6. *Araboiazychnye dokumenty,* letter 63.

7. V. G. Gadzhiev and Kh. Kh. Ramazanov, eds., *Dvizhenie gortsev severo-vostochnago Kavkaza v 20–50kh gg XIX veka. Sbornik dokumentov* (Maxachkala, Daghestan: Dagestanskoe knizhnoe izdatel'stvo, 1959), 422.

8. Abuzar Aidamirov, *Darts: Roman, "Ekha bu'isanash" trilogin kkoalgha kniga* (Grozny: GUP, 2006). The first volume of Aidamirov's trilogy has been translated into Russian as *Dolgie nochi* (Moscow: Agraf, 1996).

9. Rebecca Gould, "Transgressive Sanctity: The Abrek in Chechen Culture," *Kritika: Explorations in Russian and Eurasian History* 8, no. 2 (2007): 271–306.

10. For example, Boualem Bessaïh, *De l'emir Abdelkader à l'imam Chamyl: Le héros des Tchétchènes et du Caucase* (Alger: Dahlab, 1997; repr. Alger: Casbah, 2009); Michael Kemper, "The Changing Images of Jihad Leaders: Shamil and Abd al-Qadir in Daghestani and Algerian Historical Writing," *Nova Religio: The Journal of Alternative and Emergent Religions* 11 (2007): 28–58.

11. Thomas M. Barrett, "The Remaking of the Lion of Dagestan: Shamil in Captivity," *Russian Review* 53 (1994): 363.

12. R. G. Abdulatipov, *Dialog o molitve: Sokrat i Shamil'* (Moscow: AVIR VVTS, 2001).

13. Sh. V. Tsagareishvili, *Shamil'—stavlennik sultanskoi Turtsii i Angliyskikh koloniztorov. Sbornik dokumental'nykh materialov* (Tbilisi: Gosizdat Gruzinskoi SSR, 1953).

14. Quoted in Leslie Blanch, *The Sabers of Paradise* (London: John Murray, 1960), 255. This authenticity of this letter has been questioned by Moshe Gammer in "The Imam and the Lord: An Unpublished Letter from Shamil to the British Ambassador in Constantinople," *Israel Oriental Studies* 13 (1993): 110. Gammer's article also adds another valuable letter to the extant archive.

15. Tsagareishvili, *Shamil',* 367.

16. A. Iurov and N. V., "1840, 1841 i 1842-i gody na Kavaze," *Kavkazskii Sbornik* 10 (1886): 400–401.

17. Gadzhiev and Ramazanov, *Dvizhenie gortsev,* 421.

18. For the best account of the many lives of Imam Shamil, see, in addition to the works cited above, Moshe Gammer's "Nationalism and History: Rewriting the Chechen National Past," in *Secession, History and the Social Sciences,* ed. Bruno Coppieters and Michel Huysseune (Brussels: Brussels University Press, 2002), 117–40; and *Muslim Resistance to the Tsar: Shamil and the Conquest of Chechnia and Daghestan* (London: Taylor & Francis, 2003). Anna Zelkina's work studies the social history of Chechnya during Shamil's time: *In Quest for God and Freedom: The Sufi Response to the Russian Advance in the North Caucasus* (New York: New

York University Press, 2000); and "Islam and Society in Chechnia: From the Late Eighteenth to the Mid-nineteenth Century," *Journal of Islamic Studies* 7, no. 2 (1996): 240–64. Both authors should be read alongside the writings of Alexander Knysh, who criticizes certain tendencies in the Romanticist approach to Shamil. See his "Sufism as an Explanatory Paradigm: The Issue of the Motivations of Sufi Movements in Russian and Western Historiography," in *Die Welt des Islams* 42, no. 2 (2002): 139–73.

The performer known as Zalumma Agra, c. 1860, from a contemporary photograph. Author's collection.

# 11

# Zalumma Agra, the "Star of the East"

## *(fl. 1860s)*

CHARLES KING

Zalumma Agra was the victim of circumstance, but she was also the beneficiary of incredible good fortune. From her native Circassia, in the beech- and oak-covered hills northeast of the Black Sea, she ended up a slave in the Ottoman Empire. Formerly a subject of the Russian tsar, she came to live in the harem of a senior Ottoman official as part servant, part concubine. She might have been acquired in the thriving open-air market in the center of Constantinople, which had been closed only a short time when Mark Twain visited in 1867. Girls like Zalumma could be had for the equivalent of twenty or thirty dollars, he said, and the still-brisk trade in people, even if conducted in private, was pursued with a shameless savvy that only Americans could beat. "Best brands Circassians, crop of 1850, £200; 1852, £250; 1854, £300" was Twain's fantasy of an American version of the "white slave" trade around the Black Sea. "Best brands Georgian, none in market; second quality, 1851, £180."[1]

By the time of Twain's visit, Zalumma was already gone. An American traveler had rescued her—that is, purchased her—three years earlier. She accompanied him back to the United States, where she was taught English, converted from her own uncertain version of Islam to Christianity, and dressed in the fashionable bustles and corsets of a New York lady. She was also given a job. For a small fee, she would tell visitors about her life in the Caucasus Mountains and beyond: the idyllic upland village, the voyage aboard a lateen-rigged Turkish ship, the depravities of the harem, and her miraculous deliverance to Manhattan. Paying customers might walk away with a booklet about Zalumma's life or even a photographic portrait, her wild hair still incorrigible despite her newly acquired manners. If they turned around at the exit, they would see the sign advertising her employer: the American Museum, Phineas T. Barnum, proprietor.

Almost everything about Zalumma Agra was a fake, courtesy of P. T. Barnum himself. He detailed her story in his notoriously unreliable memoirs, and photos of Zalumma—and her many imitators—are today easily obtainable from collectors of circus memorabilia, along with the old souvenir brochures doled out to gullible guests.[2] Her real name and identity were lost to Barnum's energetic showmanship, but she almost certainly had no connection to Russia or the Caucasus; she may simply have been an Irish immigrant from the Lower East Side drafted for the role of the "Star of the East." She developed the trademark feature that other "Circassian beauties," as they were known, would incorporate into their own acts: the intentionally frizzed hair that surrounded her head like a somber and savage halo. By the beginning of the twentieth century, no small-time museum or traveling midway was complete without someone like her.

But the important thing about Zalumma's manufactured life is how much of it was actually true. There was a real place called Circassia, located exactly where Barnum claimed. For centuries women were transported from there to the Ottoman Empire, where they became the wives and concubines of Ottoman grandees. And Russia's long-running war against Caucasus highlanders, from the late 1810s through the mid-1860s, was fought in part in the lush landscape portrayed in fantastic detail by Barnum's writers. Zalumma was even described as "a niece of the Prophet Schemyl"—a phrase that means little to most Americans today but that referenced the real-life Shamil, leader of Muslim guerrillas in the northeastern Caucasus. A century and a half ago, all these themes must have resonated to such a degree that Americans were willing to pay twenty-five cents—the going rate—to hear more about them from Zalumma herself. Just as our great-great-grandchildren will wonder why we were so exercised about forgotten places called Bosnia and Kosovo, the Circassian beauties—and Circassia as a place—were famous in ways that are hard to credit today.

In the nineteenth century, Russians, Americans, and Europeans shared the form and substance of lowbrow, sensational entertainment that was developing apace in all three places. Wild West shows toured the Russian Empire. Trick riders from Russia toured America. The beauty of Circassian women was extolled by European and Russian poets alike. Zalumma's story was so believable and her popularity so widespread precisely because there was a pre-existing cultural mold into which she slipped, frizzy hair and all. It was the common product of English travelers, German ethnographers, and Russian writers and imperial officials, and at its core was the familiar exoticism of the Caucasus.

\*   \*   \*

Today, a political dividing line runs along the Caucasus mountain chain, the range of green uplands and snow-covered peaks that stretches across the land bridge between the Black and Caspian seas. To the south are the three independent countries of Armenia, Azerbaijan, and Georgia. To the north is an array of small republics and regions that form part of the Russian Federation. The entire area is dizzyingly complicated in ethnic, linguistic, and religious terms. People self-identity as Muslim or Russian Orthodox, Apostolic Christian or Jewish, or none of the above. They place themselves in ethnic categories that include Georgian, Chechen, Circassian,

Armenian, Azerbaijani, Ossetian, Avar, Lezgin, and scores of others, few of which have any linguistic connections.

But beneath this political, demographic, and cultural complexity, there has long been a certain unity to the Caucasus. Diverse ethnic groups share legends, folk cuisines, costumes, songs, and dance forms—along with the habit of insistently denying that they do. Outsiders, too, have often seen the Caucasus as a single place and, in the process, managed to invent a way of thinking about its landscape and people that has remained remarkably durable for centuries.

The earliest observers of the Caucasus, Greek and Roman writers such as Herodotus and Strabo, often treated the region as the distant edge of the world. It was located far beyond the major cities of the Mediterranean, even though the ancient peoples of the Caucasus were engaging in trade with their southern neighbors from perhaps the early first millennium BC. Its peoples spoke languages foreign to Greek and Latin ears, and the variety of peoples and cultural habits shocked many early visitors. But the region was not always treated as the locus of barbarism and oddity. When Italian and other European merchants began engaging in long-distance trade with China in the early modern period, they came in direct contact with the various political powers that governed both sides of the Caucasus mountains: the kings and princes of Georgia, the princely castes of lowland Circassia, and eventually the Mongol-Tatar khans who swept into the region from the east.

Their opinions, however, were often full of the prejudices of self-assured cultures regarding unfamiliar ones and of those that valued sedentary civilizations over nomadic ways. The Roman Catholic priest Giuseppe Zampi left one of the earliest detailed records of travel to Georgia, from the 1630s. He was entertained at the illustrious court of several wealthy notables, including the princes of Mingrelia, Imeretia, Guria, and Kakheti, but his views were clear. "They know nothing of Faith or Religion," he wrote, "and the greater part regard the afterlife as a fable and a human invention"—despite the fact that all his interlocutors had been part of a self-consciously Christian civilization for more than a millennium.[3]

Depending on the period, European travelers either echoed Zampi's views or presented more sympathetic portraits of the cultures of the Caucasus. But by the eighteenth and nineteenth centuries, the region had become a stock feature of Western literature and art. It featured in plays and musical entertainments about the exotic East. Poets such as Lord Byron saw it as the raw material for orientalizing and often erotic fantasy. Painters and lithographers featured images of lithe, porcelain-skinned Circassian women bathing à la turque beneath the watchful eye of a black agha. But it took geopolitical change for the Caucasus to enter fully into the imagination of Europeans, usually through the prism provided by the region's northern neighbor, the Russian Empire.

Russia's active engagement with the Caucasus went back to the sixteenth century, when Muscovite princes sent emissaries to the rulers of Georgia and established dynastic marriages with the princes of Kabarda, who controlled part of the expansive plain on the mountains' northern slope. Communities of Cossacks, who would eventually form the vanguard of Russia's military presence in the region, were living there long before the empire discovered their usefulness. But it was only under Peter the Great and Catherine the Great, in the late seventeenth and late eighteenth centuries, that these diplomatic forays were wed to a vision of the Caucasus as essential to Russian security and national flourishing. In the transition from principality to empire, Russia's rulers came to see the Caucasus, both north and south of the mountains, as a matter of manifest destiny—a Christian and Orthodox empire reaching down to champion fellow Christians, protect loyal Muslims, and subdue the rebellious regardless of their religious persuasion. But the path to empire was not straight. Peter's early forays around the Sea of Azov and on the western shore of the Caspian Sea yielded temporary control of major fortresses and towns, yet these were rather quickly abandoned. The other imperial powers with interests in the region—the Ottomans in the west and the Persians in the east—found ways of frustrating Russian encroachments, while never quite succeeding at making local Caucasus rulers into fully loyal subjects.

In two wars under Catherine the Great, the Russian empire managed to take control of the northern coast of the Black Sea, remove the khan of the Crimean Tatars as an Ottoman vassal, and create a key strategic relationship that would eventually cement Russia's role in the Caucasus. The king of Kartli-Kakheti in eastern Georgia, seeking protection against the Persians as well as the depredations of highland raiders, requested Russia's assistance as a protector power, a position that Catherine was happy to provide. The empress did not always live up to her end of the bargain; Tiflis (present-day Tbilisi) was sacked by Persian forces in 1795. But by 1801 that relationship had been transformed into one not of protection but of full absorption of the eastern Georgian lands into the Russian Empire—a move that also required the Russians to unseat disgruntled Georgian royals and buy off the Georgian nobility by introducing them into the elaborate imperial system of ranks, titles, and privileges.

For the next six decades, the Russian Empire worked to bring both the northern and southern slopes of the Caucasus into the domain of the tsar. Sometimes that process involved co-opting local political and religious elites, both Christian and Muslim. Paying off supporters, gathering taxes, creating schools, and reforming legal codes are the unexciting parts of imperial management, but these were the linchpins of Russia's "conquest of the Caucasus" over the course of the nineteenth century. However, it was the gorier and more glorious bits that got most of the attention, both at the time and from later historians.

Over a half century of periodic international conflicts, seasonal military campaigns, and what would now be called counterinsurgency, the Russian army sought to bring two outlying regions of the Caucasus into the ambit of the tsar—and both of them were located on the near side of the mountain chain, not the distant south. In the northeast, a series of military-religious leaders had long fought against Russian attempts to extend tsarist control beyond the course of the Terek River. By the 1830s a figure emerged who would become the legendary exemplar of Caucasus resistance: Imam Shamil. Until the end of the 1850s, Shamil led one of the largest—and certainly the most notorious—native uprisings against tsarist power. By turns described as ingenious, cruel, sympathetic, and pious, Shamil wove together revivalist Islam, opposition to traditional secular authorities in the Daghestani highlands, and resistance to Russian imperial governance. He is now celebrated across the region as the quintessential highland fighter, and the creator of a proto-state—or imamate—in the north Caucasus. Eventually driven into the mountains and rapidly losing followers once his fate seemed sealed, he surrendered to imperial troops in 1859 and was sent into exile in central Russia.

Despite tsarist censorship and the absence of real war reporting at the time, the northeastern theater was common knowledge in both Russia and abroad, in large part because of the personality of Shamil. The imam kept up a lively written correspondence with his own subordinates, Russian officials, and the Ottoman sultan. His sensational kidnapping of two Georgian princesses in the 1850s made him infamous across Europe (and also ensured that no European power would back him in his fight against the Russians). His twelve years of internal exile and public appearances after 1859—in which he became a Russian version of Sitting Bull, the worthy enemy now bowing honorably to a superior power—meant that many Russians were at last able to see him in the flesh. But it was in the northwest, along the Kuban River and the hills and plains of historic Circassia, that tsarist troops would fight their longest war of conquest.

The Circassians (or Adyga, the local self-designation) had no ethnic or linguistic relationship to the Chechens and Daghestanis who formed the bulk of Shamil's loyalists. In fact, the imam's great failing was his inability to merge the struggles in the northeastern and northwestern Caucasus, and thereby present the tsar with a united front of Muslim highlanders. The Circassians' cause was always more complex than in the east. There was never a single political or religious figure to unite them, and particular clans or lineage groups might cooperate with the Russians in some seasons and turn back to raiding Russian settlements across the Kuban in others. Some linguistically Circassian groups—such as the Kabardians—remained solidly royal to the imperial state, even producing some of the region's best local administrators. Others resisted Russian rule and sought the protection of Great Britain, whose subjects had been crisscrossing the region as spies and casual travelers for decades.

The Circassian resistance ended five years after Shamil's surrender, when in 1864 a massive Russian campaign swept along the Black Sea coast and emptied one Circassian village after another. Circassians were either removed north of the Kuban River or were forced into exile in the Ottoman Empire, a fellow Muslim state that opened its doors to fleeing coreligionists. Precise figures for the number expelled are impossible to reconstruct, but Ottoman officials and European consuls reported boatload after boatload of Muslims arriving in Ottoman ports in the 1860s—tired, hungry, and dying. The exile not only changed the demographic structure of the northwestern Caucasus, but it also produced a substantial ethnic Circassian diaspora that ultimately spread all the way from Jordan to New Jersey. All of these events were covered at the time in the major European newspapers, with detailed accounts by correspondents in Constantinople and beyond, just as the fight against Shamil and his followers in the northeast had produced a wealth of real information and fantastic biographies of the bandit-hero.[4]

Running parallel to the military and political reshaping of the Caucasus was an active cultural construction of the zone and its many peoples. Alexander Pushkin, Mikhail Lermontov, and Leo Tolstoy are the most famous creators of the literary Caucasus, and the work of each author—from Pushkin's poem "Captive of the Caucasus" to Lermontov's *Hero of Our Time* to Tolstoy's *Hadji Murat*—sculpted the Russian cultural edifice of highland heroes and wartime cruelties. What most literate Russians knew of the ethnic makeup of the region they gleaned from Pushkin, who accompanied "Captive of the Caucasus" with footnotes on highland mores and traditions. What they knew of Shamil and his sometime nemesis, the traitorous Hadji Murat, came from Tolstoy—who like Lermontov, had spent time as an army officer in the endless highland wars (Pushkin's sole engagement, by contrast, involved taking the waters in a north Caucasus spa town and then traveling once through Georgia into eastern Turkey). In all of these works, the Circassians featured so prominently that the term in Russian and other languages—*cherkes, circassien,* Circassian (based originally on a Turkic label for the Adyga)—became the standard way of referring to all Caucasus highlanders in the nineteenth century, including unrelated peoples whom we would now label Chechens, Avars, Lezgins, and others.

But even these works rested on other, older sources. From the time of Catherine the Great, Russian explorers traveled across the Caucasus to record the riches that the empire was in the process of acquiring there. A string of German academics commissioned by the Imperial Academy in St. Petersburg produced hefty and learned tomes that delineated the region's peoples and cultures just like they recorded its flora and fauna. Works such as Johann Anton Güldenstädt's *Travels in Russia and the Caucasus Mountains* (1787–91) and Julius von Klaproth's *Travels in the Caucasus and Georgia* (1812–14) bequeathed to the empire its standard understanding of who lived in the Caucasus, what these people were to be called, and what imperial officials were likely to expect in dealing with them. For example, we now call Circassians by that label rather than Adyga—the name they call themselves—all because early Russian informants probably gathered their nomenclature from neighboring peoples who used a variant of that term.

Average Russians had little direct exposure to this academic work, of course, but as the nineteenth century progressed they had other sources beyond the literature of Pushkin or Tolstoy. Plenty of Russians directly experienced the Caucasus, as well-bred officers seeking to augment their fame with a tour on the burning frontier, or average peasants dragooned into a lifetime of military service far from their homes and families. Occasional memoirs appeared as Russia's publishing industry and reading public began to develop. Popularizers also emerged—people who took the arcane information provided by academics and ethnographers and translated it for a less specialized audience. One of the most important, Semyon Bronevskii, met Pushkin before the poet had written "Captive of the Caucasus" and may well have provided some of the material that gave a hint of verisimilitude to Pushkin's narrative poem.[5]

Tsarist officials helped cement the way in which the Caucasus was perceived and administered. Censuses created linguistic and religious categories and eliminated others. Some political elites—the Georgians, for example—were merged into the structure of the Russian nobility, retaining some of the great family names and princely titles of the past. Others—the shamkhal of Tarki, the khan of Avaristan, the sultan of Ilisu—eventually disappeared, their lands and titles now alien and forgotten. The empire did not always impose itself on the societies of the Caucasus. In some eras, its officials learned to work with and through indigenous forms of law and religion, even preserving ways of life that might otherwise have been lost. But the choices of military commanders in the field, frontier administrators in the regional seat in Tiflis, and ministries in St. Petersburg all helped shape what the Caucasus would become. Much later, the Soviet system would depend on many of the same categories and tactics that had been pillars of tsarist rule.

*  *  *

All of this leads back to the crowds gathering in Lower Manhattan outside Barnum's American Museum and the strange career of Zalumma Agra. The exotic only makes sense if it plays off something familiar, and in Zalumma's case the character she created rested on two centuries of active cultural construction—the conquest of the Caucasus not just in a military sense but also through the articulation and diffusion of common images, beliefs, and prejudices about the region. At the same time that American visitors were paying to hear Zalumma's stories, Russians were experiencing much the same thing. Shamil was now living in gilded captivity in Kaluga, and was carted out every now and then to provide a celebrity presence at the opening of a sugar factory or flourmill. Military parades featured highland regiments clothed in the *cherkeska* and *papakha,* the long tunic and fuzzy hat common throughout the Caucasus. Russian spectators could thrill at the reenactment of major Caucasus battles, in which valiant Russian soldiers, clad in their gray greatcoats and forage caps, squared off against bearded Circassian highlanders, whooping and waving their deadly long muskets.

Zalumma was an American creation, but she was born of Russia's long-term engagement with its own Caucasus frontier—the "wild south" where, just as in the American West, many of the traits now thought to be typically Russian were originally forged. Georgian habits of toasting and speechifying, the buttery sweetness of Armenian brandy, the silky curls of an astrakhan hat, and the legendary beauty of mountains like Elbrus and Kazbek became part of the way in which Russians—and later Soviets—imagined themselves. But there was also a dark side to these inventions. If Zalumma was the approachable enchantress, her opposite was the devious, fearsome, reckless, and often Muslim man of the Caucasus—the great resistor of Russian power and a persistent worry to the Soviet Union and post-Soviet Russia. Terror, not just exoticism, was also one of the products of the imaginary Caucasus, and it has proved to be an even more durable symbol than Zalumma Agra.

The horrors of the 1990s and early 2000s—two wars in Chechnya, suicide bombers who bring down Russian airplanes, brutal civil wars in Georgia and Azerbaijan, and the brief but worrying Russia-Georgia conflict of 2008—all reinforced the vision of the Caucasus as volatile and prone to violence. But even that view depends on the same kinds of cultural templates that produced the likes of Zalumma Agra. It privileges some aspects of the region's history over others and remains silent on the everyday and boring ways in which, over the centuries, people have built a durable civilization by and through, not in spite of, the region's striking diversity. This may be the real lesson of Zalumma's fabricated past: in creating the imaginary Caucasus through literature, politics, and popular culture, Russians and Americans have never been very far apart.[6]

NOTES

1. Mark Twain, *The Innocents Abroad,* in *The Complete Travel Books of Mark Twain* (Garden City, N.Y.: Doubleday, 1966–67), 1:242.

2. Phineas T. Barnum, *Struggles and Triumphs: Or, Forty Years' Recollections* (Hartford, Conn.: J. B. Burr, 1869; repr. New York: Arno Press, 1970), 578–81; *Biographical Sketch of the Circassian Girl, Zalumma Agra; Or, Star of the East* (New York: Barnum and Van Amburgh Museum and Menagerie Co., 1868).

3. Giuseppe Maria Zampi, *Relation de la Colchide et de la Mingrellie,* in *Receuil de voyages au nord, contenant divers memoires très-utiles au commerce et à la navigation* (Amsterdam: Jean Frederic Bernard, 1725), 7:199.

4. There is a large and increasingly sophisticated literature on Russia's Caucasus experience and on local politics and society. For a small sample, in addition to the foundational work of Ronald G. Suny on Georgia and Armenia, see Thomas M. Barrett, *At the Edge of Empire: The Terek Cossacks and the North Caucasus Frontier, 1700–1860* (Boulder, Colo.: Westview Press, 1999); Stephen F. Jones, *Socialism in Georgian Colors: The European Road to Social Democracy, 1883–1917* (Cambridge, Mass.: Harvard University Press, 2005); Michael Kemper, *Herrschaft, Recht und Islam in Daghestan: Von den Khanaten und Gemeindebünden zum Gihad-Staat* (Wiesbaden, Germany: Reichert, 2005); Georgi Derluguian, *Bourdieu's Secret Admirer in the Caucasus* (Chicago: University of Chicago Press, 2005); Michael Khodarkovsky, *Bitter Choices: Loyalty and Betrayal in the Russian Conquest of the North Caucasus* (Ithaca, N.Y.: Cornell University Press, 2011); V. O. Bobrovnikov, *Musul'mane severnogo Kavkaza: obychai, pravo, nasilie* (Moscow: Vostochnaia literatura, 2002); Victor A. Shnirelman, *Voiny pamiati: Mify, identichnost' i politika v Zakavkaz'e* (Moscow: Akademkniga, 2003); and idem, *Byt' Alanami: Intellektualy i politika na Severnom Kavkaze v 20 veke* (Moscow: Novoe literaturnoe obozrenie, 2006).

5. See Semyon Bronevskii, *Noveishiia geograficheskiia i istoricheskiia izvestiia o Kavkaze, sobrannyia i popolnennyia Semenom Bronevskim,* 2 vols. (Moscow: Tipografiia S. Selivanovskago, 1823); and Charles King, *The Ghost of Freedom: A History of the Caucasus* (Oxford: Oxford University Press, 2008), especially ch. 3.

6. For important work on these themes, see Susan Layton, *Russian Literature and Empire: Conquest of the Caucasus from Pushkin to Tolstoy* (Cambridge: Cambridge University Press, 1994); Thomas M. Barrett, "The Remaking of the Lion of Dagestan: Shamil in Captivity," *Russian*

*Review* 53, no. 3 (July 1994): 353–66, and "Southern Living (in Captivity): The Caucasus in Russian Popular Culture," *Journal of Popular Culture* 31, no. 4 (Spring 1998): 75–93; Austin Jersild, *Orientalism and Empire: The North Caucasus Mountain Peoples and the Georgian Frontier, 1845–1917* (Montreal: McGill–Queen's University Press, 2002); Harsha Ram, *The Imperial Sublime: A Russian Poetics of Empire* (Madison: University of Wisconsin Press, 2003); and Bruce Grant, *The Captive and the Gift: Cultural Histories of Sovereignty in Russia and the Caucasus* (Ithaca, N.Y.: Cornell University Press, 2009).

Walenty Wańkowicz, *Portrait of Adam Mickiewicz* (1827–28). Wikimedia Commons.

# 12

# Adam Mickiewicz

## *(1798–1855)*

THEODORE R. WEEKS

For the Russian Empire in the nineteenth century (to 1914), the single most problematic nationality—aside, possibly, from the Jews—were the Poles. The life of Adam Mickiewicz, the Polish national poet, reflects the complicated relations between these two closely related Slavic nations, Poles and Russians. The Poles were unique among European non-Russians in that they possessed a well-developed high culture (unlike, for instance, peasant peoples like Ukrainians or Latvians), a noble landowning class, and an accurate historical memory of past greatness. Both the life and the works of Adam Mickiewicz demonstrate the uncomfortable and problematic position of Poles under tsarist rule.

It is a rare Pole who does not know the first lines of *Pan Tadeusz,* Mickiewicz's most famous work: "Lithuania! My homeland! You are like health—Your worth is only truly appreciated by he who has lost you." Lithuania? For the Polish national poet? Mickiewicz's famous lines made perfect sense to Poles of the nineteenth century who saw "Litwa" ("Lithuania") not as a national-linguistic marker but as a region of the Polish-Lithuanian Commonwealth. Of this state—the second-largest in Europe during the sixteenth and seventeenth centuries—Nobel Prize–winning Polish poet Czeslaw Milosz remarked that although the Polish-Lithuanian Commonwealth has long since disappeared from maps, for centuries it existed like other more familiar multiethnic units such as Savoy, Transylvania, or Languedoc.

Mickiewicz was born not quite a decade after the start of the French Revolution that would make nationality and nationalism key elements of the European (and later world) political order. But during the first half of the nineteenth century—Mickiewicz's lifetime—nationality in Eastern Europe remained rather fluid and far less important than social class and religion. Thus it is misleading but not wrong for tourist authorities in today's Vilnius (the capital of Lithuania, but for Mickiewicz a Polish-Jewish city he knew as Wilno) to speak of the "Lithuanian poet Adomas Mickevičius." The statement is leading, because Mickiewicz did not speak Lithuanian and wrote his famous works in Polish, but not wrong; Mickiewicz himself did speak of "Litwa" and set his most famous works in that part of—for him—Poland. Perhaps unique among national poets, Mickiewicz never visited either of the two contenders for the title of Poland's cultural-spiritual capital (there being no Polish state, there could be no political capital), Warsaw or Kraków. Mickiewicz never lived in a region with a homogenous ethnic Polish population, and after leaving Wilno for the Russian interior late in 1824, never returned to his hometown and only once spent time in a Polish-speaking area, when he visited Poznania (ruled from Berlin) in 1831–32.

Mickiewicz's life parallels in remarkable fashion many important events in the history of the Russian Empire. He was born just three years after his birthplace, Nowogródek (now in Belarus), was incorporated into the Russian Empire in the third and final partition of Poland in 1795. As a teenager he experienced the Napoleonic invasion welcomed by many Poles and cursed by the Russians. He was in Moscow when the Decembrists launched their ill-fated rebellion against Tsar Nicholas I in 1825; he was acquainted with several of the conspirators and might well have shared their fate of Siberian exile had he been in St. Petersburg at the time. And he died on November 26, 1855, in the midst of the Crimean War that would force Russia to embark on the major state restructuring we know as the "Great Reforms." The arch-reactionary tsar Nicholas I had died nine months earlier, in February. Mickiewicz's life reflects both the specific fate of the Poles, a proud historic nation without a state, and the complicated position of artists and thinkers under tsarist rule.

Adam Bernard Mickiewicz was born on Christmas Eve (NS) 1798 on a modest noble estate outside Nowogródek. In this region, social class generally overlapped with ethnicity. Typically, landowners—like Mickiewicz's family—spoke Polish, the language of high culture there. Peasants spoke Belarusian or, slightly further west, Lithuanian. The towns had a very large Jewish population that generally led their lives quite separate from their Christian neighbors, except for commercial transactions. In everyday life Jews spoke Yiddish, although nearly every male could at least make out prayers in Hebrew. Russians were not yet present in this region in large numbers, but in larger towns like Wilno or Minsk one could come across Russian administrators and soldiers. On the whole, however, the courts, schools, and administration continued to use Polish. Various religions were practiced. The majority of the population was Catholic but to the east the peasant population (people we would call Belarusians) mainly followed the Orthodox Christian religion, like the Russians. Synagogues and Jewish prayer houses were an inevitable site in any town, and one could even find mosques where the descendants of Tatars invited centuries before continued to follow their forefathers' faith.

Mickiewicz's family was not rich, but they were prosperous enough to want their son to obtain an education. Adam's first lessons were given him by his mother and tutors at home, which was typical for that time period. His grades in school were good, but hardly brilliant. His teachers were both laymen and priests, and among the subjects he studied were Latin, geometry, history, natural history (for us, "science"), and Polish literature. As a thirteen-year-old boy he experienced the march of French troops through Nowogródek, led by Polish prince Joseph Poniatowski and the king of Westphalia, Jérôme Bonaparte (Napoléon's younger brother). According to a Mickiewicz family tradition, Napoléon's brother spent the night at their estate, but historians find this unlikely. Many Poles hoped that Napoléon would help restore the Polish state, but their hopes were dashed when the Grande Armée in which thousands of Poles served was unsuccessful at forcing Tsar Alexander I to surrender.

At the age of seventeen, Mickiewicz left home to attend university in the large town of Wilno, some hundred miles from Nowogródek. In 1815, Wilno had a population of about 30,000—making it the largest and most important city in the region. Jews and Poles together made up around 80–90 percent of the city's population, with somewhat more Jews than Poles. Belarusians, Russians, and Lithuanians along with a few exotic individuals (such as Armenians and Frenchmen) made up the remaining 10–20 percent. The city's high culture, including its university and a number of publishing houses, remained Polish even after twenty years of Russian rule. The university had been founded as a Jesuit academy in the sixteenth century (Wilno had been a famous center of the counterreformation), but it only received the official status of university in 1803 from Tsar Alexander I. When Mickiewicz was a student at the University of Wilno, it was the largest university in the Russian Empire, with a student body of around five hundred students in 1816 and over one thousand ten years later. Mickiewicz was lucky to have a number of excellent professors, including the young Joachim Lelewel (1786–1861), later to gain renown as one of the most important Polish historians of the era.

When Adam arrived in Wilno in mid-September 1815 he had never spent any significant amount of time away from home. But he rapidly found friends among his fellow students and with them founded the Philomath (lovers of knowledge) Society in October 1817. The Philomaths gathered to read each other's poems and other literary works, or simply to socialize. They were, after all, young men—nearly all were either teenagers or in their early twenties. At the same time, they also declared serious aims for their society: the cultivation of knowledge, creation of literary works, and the encouragement of patriotism. This last element of the Philomath—and later Philoret (lovers of virtue)—program was to get Mickiewicz and his friends into serious trouble later on. How were Poles to be patriotic, after all, when they lived under Russian rule? Still, it seems unlikely that Mickiewicz and his friends were particularly concerned about this apparent contradiction. In the immediate aftermath of the Napoleonic Wars, Poles enjoyed a good deal of cultural and political autonomy in the Russian Empire; it appeared possible to be at once a loyal subject of the tsar and a good Pole. Members of the Philomath and Philoret societies were more interested in cultural and moral issues than in politics, and, in any case, it was clear that there was no place in Russia for open political dissidence in the last reactionary years of Tsar Alexander I's reign.

After getting his degree in 1819, Mickiewicz moved to nearby Kowno (now Kaunas) to take up a teaching job at a classical high school (*gymnasium*). As one could have predicted, after four years among brilliant company in Wilno, Mickiewicz felt bored and frustrated grading student papers in a charmless provincial town. He continued to write poetry—his reputation as a poet was already growing, at least in Wilno and among the Polish-speaking Lithuanian intelligentsia—and fled the nearly one hundred miles from Kowno to Wilno whenever he had a vacation.

Beginning in May 1823, a series of unlikely events led to the government's uncovering of the "secret societies" (Philorets and Philomaths) that Mickiewicz had belonged during his student years in Wilno. By early November Mickiewicz and several of his friends had been arrested and were incarcerated in the Basilian Monastery in Wilno. The arrest of these hardly revolutionary young men for their participation in secret societies that mainly advocated the spreading of Enlightenment is an indication of the Russian government's paranoia during the last years of Alexander I's reign. The government's uneasiness was considerably exacerbated by the Polish patriotism that was expressed among these student groups: Alexander had granted the Poles a constitution and their own parliament (the Sejm) in Warsaw, but this self-rule did not extend to the Lithuanian and Belarusian provinces where Mickiewicz had been born and attended university. The Russian government feared Polish nationalism as a destabilizing factor in the so-called western provinces (western, that is, from the Russian point of view) where Polish landowners dominated and Russian culture was weak.

Mickiewicz spent six months imprisoned in the Basilian Monastery in Wilno, although the prison regimen was not especially strict (the prisoners gathered nightly in Mickiewicz's cell, and received meals and books from well-wishers). In April he signed a confession admitting that he had belonged to the secret societies under investigation and was released from prison, his former history professor Joachim Lelewel having guaranteed that Mickiewicz would not leave Wilno. One hundred sixty-six names were mentioned in the report on secret societies at Wilno University, Mickiewicz and his two brothers among them. Mickiewicz was condemned to exile in the Russian interior. His punishment was considerably less harsh than that meted out to some of his friends who were exiled to Siberia or forcibly recruited into the army. In November 1824, Mickiewicz left Wilno for St. Petersburg. He would never see his beloved "Lithuania" again.

Mickiewicz's years in Russia were astonishingly important and fruitful ones for his life and his poetic works. The conditions of his exile were, to put it mildly, hardly inhumane. He was officially employed in various government offices, but, in fact, the young poet had plenty of time to write, travel, and socialize. During the nearly five years he spent in Russia, Mickiewicz became well acquainted with the cream of the Russian literary intelligentsia, including the Russian national poet, Alexander Pushkin, a fact made much of during the years of communist rule in Poland. Mickiewicz also met several of the future Decembrists while in St. Petersburg; he was in Moscow when the revolt broke out. Mickiewicz published several important works during his Russian stay, including his *Sonnets* and *Konrad Wallenrod*. These works were published in Moscow and St. Petersburg, where the censorship of Polish works was much less severe than in Warsaw (or Wilno), and a number of Russian translations of Mickiewicz's work also appeared during these years.

In late May 1829 Mickiewicz was allowed to leave Russia "for health reasons"; he never returned to the empire. Late the following year Poles in the Russian Empire rose up against what they saw as the unreasonable and illegal actions of Tsar Nicholas I against the Polish constitution and Polish autonomy. Mickiewicz traveled to the Prussian province of Poznania hoping to cross into Russia, but he was unable to join the rebels. The crushing of the November 1830 insurrection by Russian troops and the subsequent abolition of the Polish constitution and Sejm certainly added to Mickiewicz's already acute distaste for Russian and tsarist rule. This loathing would find particular expression in his *Books of the Polish Pilgrimage* (written 1832–33), in which Catherine the Great, who presided over the Russian partition of Poland, is described as "the most dissolute of women who like a shameless Venus called herself a pure virgin."

Mickiewicz spent most of the 1830s and 1840s in Paris, where from late 1840 he lectured at the prestigious Collège de France on Slavic literature: the first such lectures at a major university in Western Europe. Mickiewicz's lectures covered an amazing amount of ground, starting with the Slavic migrations in the sixth century and ending with contemporary literature in Russian, Polish, Czech, and other Slavic languages. The lectures were not strictly limited to Slavic languages; Mickiewicz dedicated one (course 3, lecture 15) to the Lithuanians, discussing their language ("the Lithuanian language is the oldest one spoken on the European continent"), mythology, customs, and religion. As one might expect, Mickiewicz's lectures portray Peter the Great as despotic and cruel, but he also admired the Russian tsar's energy and intelligence. Mickiewicz condemned the despotism of the Russian tsars, but presented Russian literature as full of lyrical beauty. Mickiewicz's lectures reflected the Russian intelligentsia's own self image as the conscience of the nation, opposed to the tyranny of the tsarist state.

Unfortunately for Mickiewicz, his lectures' emphasis on freedom—always associated with the Polish nation in his works—aroused the suspicions of the French authorities and he was obliged to suspend his courses in 1844 (he took them up again after the revolutions of 1848, but was again forced to resign in 1852). When uprisings swept Europe in 1848, Mickiewicz thought that the hour had come for the liberation of the Polish nation and even organized a Polish legion to fight for that goal. Unfortunately, the "Springtime of Nations," as the 1848–49 events are known in Central Europe, did not reach the Russian Empire and no Polish state reappeared (that would have to wait until after a much greater cataclysm, World War I). Still, Mickiewicz did not lose hope. In 1854, when tensions between Russia and the Ottoman Empire erupted in war, and France and Britain sent troops to fight against the Russians in the Crimean War, Mickiewicz rushed to Istanbul to set up a Polish legion to liberate his countrymen from Russian rule. Despite Russian defeats, no Polish liberation resulted, and Mickiewicz died of disease in the Ottoman capital in November 1855.

Mickiewicz's poetic works, like the events of his life, also reflect the position of Poles under Russian rule. As we have seen, several of his early works were published in Russia; his *Sonnets* (Moscow, 1826), for example, were inspired in part by a trip to the Crimea and the exotic sights and people he observed there. But four works in particular—one published in Russia, another in part written there, and two from the early 1830s—reveal Mickiewicz's vision of what it meant to be a Pole in the Russian Empire. These are *Konrad Wallenrod* (1828), *Dziady* ("Forefathers' Eve," 1820s–32), *Books of the Polish Nation and Polish Pilgrimage* (1833), and *Pan Tadeusz* (1833–34). After publishing the epic poem *Pan Tadeusz*, Mickiewicz ceased to write poetry, although he would live over twenty years longer.

    *Konrad Wallenrod,* published in St. Petersburg in 1828, is perhaps the most disturbing of all of these works. This historical tale in verse set in the fourteenth century recounts the life of a pagan Lithuanian prince captured as a boy by the Teutonic Knights and brought up as a Christian among the Germans. Despite the kind treatment he received from the Germans, Konrad remains inwardly a pagan Lithuanian (with the very un-Lithuanian name "Alf"), although his brave deeds as a Teutonic knight ultimately win him the position of the grand master of the Teutonic Order. Once in that position, Konrad unleashes his plan of revenge against the Germans, leading them in suicidal battle against the Lithuanians. On one level, of course, Konrad/Alf commits the worst kind of treachery against the Teutonic Order. On another, however, he remains faithful to his original identity as Lithuanian and pagan, waiting patiently his entire life to exact the most painful revenge from the Germans who had defeated his people. The parallel between Konrad and Poles under Russian rule was only too clear—although apparently not to the Russian censors, who allegedly demanded that just one line be cut: "The only weapon of a slave is treason."

    Nikolai Novosil´tsev, the Russian official who presided over the investigation and punishment of Mickiewicz and the Filomaths at Wilno University, wrote a special memorandum to the tsar in which he discussed *Konrad Wallenrod* and its "immorality." Interestingly, Novosil´tsev began this document by arguing that Polish patriotism "within the proper limits" could be reconciled with loyalty to the tsar. But Mickiewicz's work, Novosil´tsev argued, showed that excessive patriotism could have very harmful effects, as it "touches on the strongest feelings of the heart and teaches the most cunning treason, presenting it as the noble striving of a magnanimous patriotism." Novosil´tsev's strong condemnation of *Konrad Wallenrod* prevented the work from being republished in Russia, but had no negative consequences for the poet himself.

    Already before his departure for St. Petersburg, during his years teaching in Kowno (Kaunas), Mickiewicz had begun work on the "*poema*" *Dziady* ("Forefathers' Eve," referring to an old ceremony in Lithuania that commemorated one's forefathers). Poema in Polish (as in Russian) refers not to lyric verse, but an epic in poetic form (usually rhymed). But *Dziady* is a much more confusing mishmash of dramatic, poetic, and narrative elements. To further complicate matters, the work is divided into parts 2, 4, and 3—in that order—with no part 1, and several other poems that do not specifically fit into any part. Whether Mickiewicz planned to add a part 1 or was just playing with the reader—not impossible for a romantic writer—we do not know. For our purposes, part 3 of *Dziady,* written just after the failed Polish insurrection of 1830–31, is most pertinent: here we find in dramatic form a retelling of the events of 1823–24: the investigation into secret student societies at Wilno university, Mickiewicz's arrest (the poet does not appear here, but several of his friends do, as does "Pan Senator," Novosil'tsev), and his journey to Russia. The work is by turns amusing and biting, poetic and dramatic, and includes actual historical persons as well as devils and angels (literally) among its dramatis personae. Mickiewicz satirizes not only the Russian authorities (Novosil'tsev) but also ineffectual salon intelligentsia in Warsaw who claim to be concerned with the national cause but do little to support it. The work ends with a number of poems describing Mickiewicz's voyage to Russia, sights of the Russian capital (including the monument to Peter the Great immortalized in Pushkin's *poema* "Bronze Horseman"), and finally "Do przyjaciół Moskali"—"To my Muscovite friends" in which he both remembers and in a sense settles accounts with his Russian friends (the word "Moskal" in Polish is negative and by combining it with the word "friend" Mickiewicz achieves an ironic effect).

*Dziady* is foremost a work of poetry and emotion, but its third part clearly reflects the spiritual anguish of the poet—and many other Poles—at his nation's subjugation to Russian rule. The idea of Poland as a savior of nations and a symbol of freedom appears here and would be developed even more specifically in *The Book of Polish Nation and Pilgrimage.* Here the veiled criticism of Russian tyranny (as in *Konrad Wallenrod*) was out in the open; the printing of *Dziady* was forbidden by Russian censorship, although many copies were smuggled in at some risk. The play has become a Polish standard from the nineteenth century to the present, with ever-changing interpretations of the figures, language, and action. Perhaps the most famous staging of *Dziady* occurred in Warsaw in 1968, when the overly enthusiastic applause was taken (correctly) as an anti-Soviet demonstration, leading the communist authorities to shut the play down. In the end, however, *Dziady* is less anti-Russian than deeply Polish, identifying the Polish nation with freedom and justice.

Mickiewicz took this patriotic line much farther in *The Books of the Polish Nation and the Polish Pilgrimage,* written 1832–35. This prose work combines political and religious topics, mysticism, and of course a great deal of Polish patriotism. For the present-day reader this work—unlike *Dziady* or *Pan Tadeusz*—may seem confusing, bizarre, and even exasperating. We are no longer accustomed to sweeping generalizations about nationalities, and when Mickiewicz compares Poland to Christ (through its suffering the Polish nation will not just redeem itself but provide freedom for other nations as well) we may be tempted to shake our heads and roll our eyes. Even upon the book's first publication in late 1832, it was criticized by the Catholic Church as blasphemous and by Polish democratic émigrés as murky and mystical. In fact, it is all of these things at once. But it is also a magnificent manifesto of the ideals of early liberal nationalism that identified freedom with the cultural-moral development of one's nation. Nationalism at this stage saw the enemy not in other nations (positive mentions of Jews and Lithuanians, for example, abound in Mickiewicz's work) but in political tyranny, exemplified in Mickiewicz's case by tsarist autocracy. Mickiewicz's *Books of the Polish Nation* not only inspired Polish patriots at a dark time in their history—just after the crushing of the 1830–31 rebellion—but exemplified a nationalism that celebrated national-ethnic difference and the freedom of any nation, large or small, to nurture and develop its own culture.

Mickiewicz's masterpiece, it seems fair to say, is the epic poem *Pan Tadeusz,* written 1833–34. For the non-Polish speaker, possibly the best introduction to the work is Andrzej Wajda's lush 1999 film of the same title. Unfortunately English translations— at least so far—fail to capture the magnificent language of the Polish original. The work's title refers to its main hero, "Master Tadeusz," a young nobleman coming of age in Lithuania (again, in the historical not ethnographic, sense). The action takes place in 1811–12, after Napoléon has defeated Russia (Treaty of Tilsit, 1807) but just before the actual French invasion of Russia (the story ends with the newly married Tadeusz going off to war against the Russians). If *Dziady* (part 3) recounts Mickiewicz's life in 1823–24, *Pan Tadeusz* reflects on Mickiewicz's youth; Tadeusz would have been just a few years older than the poet himself (Mickiewicz turned fourteen in 1812; Tadeusz marries at the end of the *poema*). Mickiewicz also expressed his homesickness both for the friends and fatherland he had left behind—with little hope of ever seeing again—and for a more hopeful period in Polish history when the resurrection of the Polish state seemed to be on the horizon. The work's subtitle—"The Last Foray in Lithuania, a Story of the Gentry from the Years 1811 and 1812"—suggests that the events described here belong to a world that no longer exists. Even while gently mocking the endless legal squabbles between the two main families, the Soplica and the Horeszko clans (the feud is, we hope, ended by Tadeusz's marriage to Zosia of the Horeszko family), Mickiewicz portrays their life and values as a kind of lost idyll. Mickiewicz himself described *Pan Tadeusz* as a "rural poem" and it is full of memorable descriptions both of the Lithuanian countryside and of the traditions still followed there. It is a work of nostalgia and the mourning of a lost homeland that in a sense is the flipside of Mickiewicz's more mystical patriotism in *Books of the Polish Nation.* In *Pan Tadeusz* we see the beauty of traditional Polish life (to be sure, almost exclusively of the gentry class) in Lithuania, a culture that has been swept away by political events (such as Napoléon's defeat and the failure of the 1830–31 insurrection) but also simply by the passage of time. In *Books of the Polish Nation* Mickiewicz presents Poland as a Christ figure and beacon of freedom for all nations; in *Pan Tadeusz* the poet's narrower homeland within Poland—Lithuania—is presented as warm, safe, and loving.

Mickiewicz is remembered as the Polish national poet, but he was also deeply affected by the fact that he was born and spent the first half of his life in the Russian Empire. At that point the memory of the Polish state destroyed by Prussia, Austria, and Russia in the partitions was fresh, and Mickiewicz gave voice to the anguish felt by Polish patriots at their present situation under foreign rule. But Mickiewicz's work also reflects the complexity of national identity at this point, as indicated in the first line from *Pan Tadeusz:* "Lithuania, my homeland! . . . Your worth is only truly appreciated by he who has lost you." Lithuania, a multiethnic province of Poland where the nobility was of Polish culture, the towns inhabited mainly by Jews, and the peasantry was Lithuanian or Belarusian, was Mickiewicz's birthplace and homeland. After the ravages of the twentieth century, that place no longer exists. Thus, the literary works of Adam Mickiewicz not only reflect the realities of Polish statelessness under Russian rule but also portray a world where different ethnic groups lived peacefully side by side—a world swept away by the political and ethno-national conflicts of the twentieth century.[1]

NOTES

1. The literature on Mickiewicz in Polish is enormous but unfortunately very little has been published on the poet in English. The best introduction is Anita Debska, *Country of the Mind: An Introduction to the Poetry of Adam Mickiewicz* (Warsaw: Burchard Edition, 2000), which contains a useful short bibliography of both secondary literature and translations of Mickiewicz's works. See also Roman Koropeckyj, *Adam Mickiewicz: The Life of a Romantic* (Ithaca, N.Y.: Cornell University Press, 2008).

Innokentii, Archbishop of Kherson. Originally published in *Sochineniia Innokentiia, Arkhiepiskopa Khersonskago i Tavricheskago,* vol. 1 (Moscow: Sviato-troitska Sergieiva Lavra, 1907).

# 13

# Archbishop Innokentii

## (BORISOV, 1800–1857)

MARA KOZELSKY

Few places in the empire rivaled the diversity of New Russia, a vast territory lining the northern Black Sea littoral conquered from the Ottomans in the eighteenth century. From the era of Catherine II (1762–96), the empire promoted cultural autonomy and religious toleration among subject populations, yet recognized Orthodoxy as the state religion. These policies left a legacy of mixed rights and privileges that divided populations for decades. Rather than assimilating immigrants into the empire, imperial policies often reinforced or created new boundaries around native identities. Of Crimea, for example, one French visitor commented that "sometimes, just to cross the street, you believe you are passing from Europe to Asia." Unlike the Americas, Europe and Asia, where "diverse peoples exist, but they mix in the same quarter, and strive . . . to assimilate," he noted that in Crimea "there is nothing similar; at the minimum is one race, who lives in the village inhabited only by its own, or within a separate quarter in the village that becomes two in which the religion, the manners, the dress, the houses are all very different from one to the other."[1] He was most struck by the isolation of these groups from each other, noting that peoples of Crimea—Tatars, Jews, Eastern Europeans, Greeks, Germans, Roma, and Russians—lived in their own colonies, divided largely by their confession.

Many Russian officials shared the Frenchman's assessment. On the eve of the Crimean War (1853–56), these men worried about managing the non-Russian peoples of the Black Sea region. In the province of Kherson, the Odessa city council complained about the city's mixed population and "ceaseless relations" with "all the European ports which were boiling with spiritual turmoil."[2] Local authorities in the neighboring province of Tauride felt similarly. "Runaways from landlords, those associated with war businesses, foreign immigrants, and even criminals" chiefly populated Tauride. It was not surprising, they complained, that "such a riff-raff of peoples, not having any links between them, preserve their former habits and faiths. The immigrants here of various sides and sects, although brought together as neighbors, cannot acquire any ties or any similar mentality."[3] War sharply focused the concerns of imperial bureaucrats, who questioned the loyalties of non-Russian populations.

Archbishop Innokentii (1800–57) arrived in New Russia in 1848, just as national tensions in the Black Sea region intensified. Innokentii rose to prominence with his controversial book *The Last Days of the Earthly Life of Jesus Christ.* In this book, Innokentii synthesized the gospels to provide a harmonious narrative of Jesus' last three years. He wrote at a time when the Russian Orthodox Church experimented with providing the first major translation of the New Testament in Russian for a general readership. He used contemporary literary devices to capture readers' imaginations, and tapped into recent archaeological discoveries and histories of the ancients to fill New Testament gaps. But Innokentii went too far. Although readers snapped up the journal in which the book originally appeared in serialized form, many church officials were horrified, fearing that the work was overly literary, if not fictive. Church censors yanked the manuscript from future publication and critics branded Innokentii a neolog, a derogatory term applied to those who interpreted the Bible logically as opposed to literally.

Official censure did not discourage Innokentii, who believed his calling was to make the Russian Orthodox Church meaningful in everyday life. He continued to interpret Jesus' life through other outlets, especially sermons. When Innokentii graduated with his doctoral degree in 1829, wary church hierarchs exiled him from the imperial hub in the north to the periphery in Kyiv. Once considered the center of Slavic Christianity, Kyiv had long been eclipsed in Church circles by the more powerful cities of Moscow and St. Petersburg.

Distance from the center ironically provided freedom, and Innokentii turned his new post at the Kyivan Spiritual Academy into a platform for his novel approach to Orthodoxy. He transformed the curriculum by introducing critical analysis into biblical scholarship. He also advanced the study of homiletics and practical theology. In fewer than ten years, Innokentii made Kyiv a rival institution to the traditionally more powerful and conservative academies in Moscow and St. Petersburg. "In seminary circles," wrote one of his students, "Innokentii was the subject of lively conversation, frequently and hotly contested. . . . [P]eers from the Moscow school continuously opposed him during any discussion about his rectorship or preaching."[4] His own reputation as a preacher grew as well, leading a contemporary to remark that audiences awaited the publication of Innokentii's sermons with "impatience and greed," which "were read and reread by all people from all estates, from high and low. . . . Innokentii's name resounded in all of the immeasurable borders of Russia."[5]

After his successes at the Kyivan Spiritual Academy, the pendulum of opinion swung in Innokentii's favor. The Church promoted him through a series of increasingly prestigious administrative posts in the 1840s—first bishop of Kharkov in present-day eastern Ukraine, then bishop of Vologda in Russia's north and, finally, archbishop of Kherson and Tauride in the Black Sea region. The appointment to the distant Kherson-Tauride diocese was not intended as exile. Instead, it represented the

Church's increasing interest in expanding into New Russia, for by now, Innokentii was a highly influential Church hierarch and a member of the Holy Synod. His new post contained Odessa, Russia's most active southern port, which had its own stock exchange; and the city of Nikolaev, the original home of the Black Sea fleet. The see also included Crimea, famous today as the location of the Yalta Conference as well as Sevastopol, the city of five bays, now the shared home of the Black Sea fleet controversially divided by Russia and Ukraine.

Despite the increasing importance of this region to the empire—Odessa paralleled Chicago in terms of boomtown growth, and Crimea possessed strategic potential matched by few places in the empire—the Church's presence remained relatively insignificant. As Innokentii prepared for his new appointment, he received a letter from a prominent Odessan of Romanian heritage, Alexandru Sturdza, describing local religious affairs. Sturdza wrote that "conversions of the Old Believers and the sectarians are significant. The question of converting Crimean Tatars remains hitherto untouched, nothing has been done." Sturdza advocated that the seminary in Odessa teach *Kirimtatar* (Crimean Tatar) for "the door of faith remains closed without the key of language."[6] Like his Russian counterparts, Sturdza believed that Orthodoxy was a key component of Russian identity and that Crimea's majority Muslim population represented a weak link.

New Russia's governor general for three decades, Prince Mikhail Vorontsov (1823–55) strenuously resisted Church efforts to expand into Crimea. When Archbishop Innokentii attempted to establish an independent bishopric for Tauride, Vorontsov blocked his efforts, citing "the government's eternal devotion to the system of religious toleration."[7] Vorontsov believed that a strong Church might endanger the stability of Crimea and that any perceived threat to Islam could potentially lead to Tatar insurgency. For him, maintaining Islam in Crimea was a practical matter of preserving social order.

Although Innokentii and Vorontsov enjoyed a cordial relationship, often dining together and discussing their mutual interest in philosophy, they disagreed over the role of religion in the empire. Innokentii argued that Tatar rights were incongruous with their status as a conquered group, that they "received from [the Russian Empire] such distinctions and advantages, that not one Russian in our region has; they do not pay any taxes; they are not obligated to military conscription; they are not subject to landlord rights, in the same measure as our poor serfs and others."[8] Innokentii did not exaggerate the difference in rights between Tatars and Russian serfs. In November 1827, Nicholas I signed the "Conditions for the Tatar Population and Landowners in the Tauride Province," which permitted Tatars to own movable and immovable property, to sell land, and to transfer to another estate or to government lands after fulfilling agreed upon labor obligations. Tatars also could bring complaints against landlord abuses to court, which serfs could not. As one historian has noted, Tatars had more rights than government peasants, demonstrating "the extent to which different religious and national groups in the Russian empire composed different estates with different juridical statuses."[9] To be sure, however, Tatars' status looked far better on paper than in reality, as savvy Russian nobility slowly eroded Tatar claims to the land during the nineteenth century.

Kherson-Tauride's new archbishop despaired over the restrictions placed upon the church. The problem, as Innokentii stated in a letter to Grand Duke Konstantin, was the "unfortunate religious character of the region." The Orthodox populations were surrounded by "non-orthodox believers and foreigners" inside regional borders and were subject to the "continuously pernicious influence of the sea." He cast his diocese in the bleakest of terms, writing, "I wish I could say something to you that is happy about the spirit of our Kherson-Tauride flock, but the hours of happiness still have not arrived for us. [The diocese] requires detailed and tireless work to cultivate a removal of thorns and weeds; to sow and water with both hands."[10] A consummate gardener—a man known for his passion for roses and commitment to the Southern Agricultural Society—such metaphors well illustrated his approach. Nurturing the region's Orthodox populations, many of whom were not ethnically Russian, became the center of his platform.

In particular, Innokentii hoped that Greeks, Armenians, and Bulgarians could be united with Russians to form a single, cohesive laity. Balkan Christians settled the Black Sea region for centuries, and arrived in even greater numbers after Russian conquest. Greek merchants were so influential in Odessa that the stock exchange conducted business in their language and Greek sailors outnumbered Russians in the early years of the Black Sea fleet. Similarly, Greeks and Bulgarians composed a highly visible proportion of Crimean Orthodox believers, and conducted church services in their own languages. Innokentii embraced the non-Russian Orthodox Christians in his diocese—especially the Greeks, whom he viewed as "the godfathers of the font of holy Christening," and emphasized that supporting the "various spiritual needs of the people of Greece" was a crucial part of his mission.[11]

One of Innokentii's most imaginative and enduring initiatives involved creating Russian Athos, a pan-Orthodox holy place in Crimea based on Mount Athos in Greece. An active, energetic man even as his health began to fail, Innokentii spent weeks touring Crimea, visiting newly established Bulgarian colonies and ancient Greek churches that dated to the peninsula's Byzantine era. He walked the spine of Crimean mountains and gathered folk traditions of saints and holy places. He was convinced that Crimea was as holy as Mount Athos, writing, "If Mount Athos has abundant holy monuments and memories, so does Russian Athos." Innokentii amassed an impressive array of evidence that he culled from Tradition, saints' lives, and historical documents. One tradition held that Andrew the Apostle visited Crimea en route to his mission field in Scythia. Two Roman popes, Clement and Martin, were exiled to the peninsula, where they lived in the Inkerman caves. Cyril and Methodius stopped in the ancient city of Chersonesos, as did Prince Vladimir, the man credited with converting all of Rus'. "How many examples of faith and good deeds!" Innokentii rejoiced to the Holy Synod, in a petition that promoted his plan. Even the Tatars of Crimea, who were at one time Christian "express their memory of their former beliefs in their occasional pilgrimages to places sanctified by Christianity."[12]

Indeed, Crimean Tatars, like Bosnian Muslims and a few Caucasian tribes, converted to Islam from Christianity. Over the centuries, Tatars living along the coast had syncretized Orthodox traditions, many of which had deeper pagan roots. A Ukrainian pilgrim visiting the church of St. Anastasia happened upon a Tatar kneeling in prayer. As he prayed, the man "drew water from the well, repeating the following blessing: 'Allah ekber' (God is Great)."[13] Other Tatars regularly visited the St. George monastery in Balaklava, where they "observed the fasts, and brought fruit and fish" to the monks.[14] Another site located at the natural springs named after the third-century saints Cosmas and Damian and called Savluk-Su in *Kirimtatar* attracted both Tatars and Christians on the saints' feast day. Innokentii hoped that restoring ancient Crimean churches and reopening long abandoned Greek monasteries might attract Tatars by their own initiative.

During the five years leading to the Crimean War, Innokentii spent his time preparing the Russian Athos monastic community. He planned to either build or renovate a chain of monasteries and invited monks with experience on Moun Athos, especially those who could speak Greek. Before the war, the church opened three new communities in the old Tatar capital of Bakhchisarai, the ancient Greek city of Chersonesos and the cave-city complex of Inkerman. Pleased with his success, he wrote a colleague in the church,

> Our Crimea, thanks to God, is beginning to thaw the ice of Islam. The new Bakhchisarai skete apparently is attracting the friendly attention of the Tatars. A week does not go by in which some Tatar family asks to enter the cave church: upon entering, they fall on their knees in front of the icon and pray with tears. All of this encourages us in the work of our new holy place.[15]

Innokentii integrated separate spaces for Tatar worship in some sites, such as erecting bathhouses for Tatars at the springs of Cosmas and Damian, and several Tatars responded positively to the renovation of certain Christian churches. Unfortunately, however, the companionable relationship between the church and Tatars failed in the face of war, a war that pitted Christians against Muslims.

From the era of Catherine II, Russians questioned their obligation to Eastern Christians living in the Ottoman Empire. Catherine dreamed of liberating Orthodox Christians from Ottoman rule and placing her grandson on the throne of Constantinople. A pragmatic political disposition checked her ambitions. Similarly Alexander I vacillated between his commitment to European alliances and pressures to support Christians on the Balkan Peninsula living under Ottoman rule. In contrast to his predecessors, Nicholas I could not resist the pull of faith. Believing that Russia should liberate the Eastern Christians, he went to war not once but twice. In 1828, Nicholas I sent Russian troops to support the Greeks in their struggle for liberation and in 1853 he sent troops across borders in defense of Bulgarians. When the Crimean War subsequently erupted, many Russians applauded.

Innokentii, like most of his peers in the church, perceived the Crimean War as a crusade, a holy mission ordained by God and Russia's destiny. A pan-Orthodox perspective, characterized by a unified Orthodox world led by Russians, permeated Innokentii's sermons and writings about the war until its end. His unswerving, confident presumption that Russia would succeed in this task was gradually replaced by foreboding pessimism as the war progressed. Yet, even at the war's beginning, the archbishop did not anticipate an easy victory. Rather, he compared the predicament on the Balkan Peninsula to a menacing storm that finally settles "to allow nothing other than a rain of blood, with lightning and thunder of destruction."[16]

As his metaphor portended, the declaration of war opened a long struggle with tremendous loss of life on all sides. The conflict dramatically exposed the weaknesses of outmoded military traditions, while ushering in new technologies and methods of killing, from the telegraph to the trench. Although this war ultimately preserved the delicate balance of the Ottoman Empire, it produced major changes in Europe. It ended the Holy Alliance, catalyzed a unified Germany, and freed the serfs in Russia. The introduction of wartime correspondence and photography also forever changed the culture of war with exposés that revealed the dark underside of war to a distant yet powerful public opinion. Nowhere, however, experienced the same level of change as Crimea, the primary theater of violence.

From the first bombardment of Odessa in April 1854, until the last stage of the siege of Sevastopol in September 1855, the Black Sea region and the peninsula in particular was almost unrecognizable. Enemy troops covered the full shoreline of Crimea, from the western gate of Evpatoria through the Kerch Strait in the east. Russia lost tens of thousands of soldiers to fighting and disease, with figures as high as one thousand per day in the summer of 1855. Vast series of barracks dotted the once bucolic countryside; public buildings became hospitals, private homes became officers' quarters, and roads became trenches. Crimea became the focus of the empire and Sevastopol emerged as the mythical "city of Russian glory."[17]

Anyone who had the means fled the violence. But not Innokentii. Amid exploding bombs and thundering shells during the most dreadful battle of the Crimean War, Archbishop Innokentii addressed Sevastopol's soldiers, urging, "There is a time to make observations and to act, a time to pray, and if necessary, to die, as is befitting Christians and true sons of the fatherland!" His words conveyed an epic struggle, one religion meeting another in war: "the details of this affair will be illuminated in time; but the essence is now already visible: it completes the fall of Islam! It is a decisive uprising against the humiliation and slavery of the Orthodox East! It is a severe denunciation and bloody lesson to the nonbelievers deeply rooted in the arrogant West!"[18] A long-time advocate of Balkan independence from the Ottoman Empire, Innokentii became one of the chief publicists of the war.

Innokentii died in 1857, one year after the conclusion of the Crimean War, before realizing his dream of consolidating Christianity in Crimea. The war ended badly for Russia, and destroyed Crimea in the process. Innokentii also failed to establish a separate bishop for the province of Tauride, a cornerstone of his program. Still, he did lay the groundwork for both projects. His successor achieved the division of the diocese into more manageable units by 1860, and the Russian Athos community grew by leaps and bounds. On the eve of the 1917 Revolution, Crimea had a large network of active monasteries and sketes housing several hundred men and women. By the end of the Crimean War, observers noted that the Black Sea region in general had become "more and more Russian and more and more Orthodox," a comment that reflected the *perception* of Crimea's Christian identity as much as actual growth of Christian institutions.[19]

Innokentii's legacy is a powerful one. His collected writings fill eleven volumes. Church historians regard him as a father of Russian moral theology and homiletics today. *Last Days of the Earthly Life of our Lord Jesus Christ* has gone through more than twenty editions since the fall of the Soviet Union, and has taught Russians and Ukrainians schooled in atheism about the feats of Jesus. He strengthened the Kyivan Spiritual Academy, making it competitive with Moscow and St. Petersburg, and he brought the church into Crimea, transforming a Muslim region into a Christian one. Furthermore, due to his refusal to leave soldiers in their hour of spiritual need during the Crimean War, Innokentii acquired the epithet "great patriot of the fatherland," a descriptor first coined by the conservative nationalist, Mikhail Pogodin. For these reasons and others, the Church canonized Innokentii in 1997.

It is interesting to speculate what Innokentii would think about his accomplishments today had he survived to witness the region's tragic developments. Immediately after the Crimean War, two hundred thousand Crimean Tatars left Russia for the Ottoman Empire. Why and how they left is a subject that needs further study. It is, however, apparent that the war produced new tensions as the Russian government began to suspect the Crimean Tatars as a potentially traitorous group, and considered their deportation to the interior. Nearly one hundred years later, Stalin did just that. Tens of thousands of Tatars died during the 1944 deportation. Survivors and their children have only recently begun the slow return to Crimea after the collapse of the Soviet Union. Whether or not the Stalinist deportation is connected to the persecution of the Tatars under the imperial government, Tatar decline was evident during the Crimean War. One Englishman stationed in Crimea in 1855 observed, "The Tatars are a rapidly diminishing race; and failing numbers is accompanied with declining moral energy. . . . It is painful to reflect, that the present war must be an additional disaster to them."[20] This man blamed their predicament not so much upon the malicious premeditation of government, but upon a generic process of imperial expansion that might oppress any conquered people through loss of lands, decreased political autonomy, and greed of local agents.

In light of the voluminous holy war rhetoric and the reclamation of ancient Christian sites, however, questions about the role of religion remain. At least one man, himself a bishop of Crimea, Germogen (Dobronravov, 1882–85), connected the expansion of the church to the Tatars' postwar plight. "In general before the Crimean War," he wrote, "the Christian population grew slowly and from year to year, new churches increased by one, by two, and sometimes by three . . . but after the Crimean War, when 85,000 [sic] Tatars left Crimea for Turkey and especially after the foundation of an independent Tauride diocese, the number of churches and parishes significantly increased."[21] Does Innokentii, literally a saint, and in life a man who gave selflessly to a variety of causes, who drew inspiration from Tatar religious practices and preserved space for Tatar worship, share even a small part of responsibility for the dislocation of the Tatars? Or were his actions the product of a deeply flawed and contradictory policy of toleration? Perhaps, as some scholars have postulated, the problem is religion itself. The Chosen can exist only at the expense of the Forsaken, and humanity inevitably, fatally errs in the hubristic divination of the will of God.

NOTES

1. Victor Amanton, *Notices sur les diverses populations du gouvernement de la Tauride et spécialement de la Crimée: Mœurs et usages des Tatars de la Crimée* (Besançon, 1854), 3–4.

2. Rossiiskii Gosudarstvenyi Istoricheskii Arkhiv (hereafter cited as RGIA), f. 797, op. 19, d. 42668, l. 3 (about founding a religious procession in Odessa).

3. Metropolitan Filaret, "Zamechanie Preosviashchennago Filareta na donesenie Tavricheskoi Palatyi Gosudarstvennykh imushchestv o prichenakh slabago vlianiia dukhovenstva Tavricheskoi eparkhii . . . ," *Mneniia otzyvi i pis'ma Filareta, Mitropolita Moskovskogo i Kolomenskago, po raznym voprosam za 1821–1867* (Moscow, 1905), letter dated March 7, 1840.

4. "Innokentii, Arkhiepiskop Khersonskii i Tavricheskii," *Russkaia Starina* 21 (1878): 562.

5. Makarii, Bishop of Tambov, "Biograficheskiia zapiski o Vysokopreosviashchennago Innokentii," 19–39, *Venok na mogilu Vysokopreosviashchennago Innokentiia, arkhiepiskopa Tavricheskago* (Moscow, 1864), 27.

6. A. S. Sturdza to Innokentii, Odessa, April 5, 1848, Rossiiskii Natsional'naia Biblioteka (hereafter cited as RNB), f. 313, d. 42, l. 31 (Documents from the correspondence of Archbishop Innokentii of Kherson, 1841, 1847–50); reprinted in *Pis'ma A. S. Sturdza k Innokentiu, Arkhiepiskopu Khersonskomu i Tavricheskomu* (Odessa, 1894), 20.

7. RNB, f. 313, d. 37, l. 120, Prince Vorontsov to Innokentii, August 10, 1852.

8. Archbishop Innokentii to the Grand Duke Konstantin Nikolaevich, Odessa, June 20, 1852, *Russkaia Starina* 25 (1879): 368–69.

9. E. I. Druzhinina, *Iuzhnaia Ukraina v period Krizisa Feodalizma, 1825–1860* (Moscow, 1981), 17.

10. Archbishop Innokentii to Grand Duke Konstantin Nikolaevich, Odessa, February 27, 1852, *Russkaia Starina* 25 (1879): 192–93.

11. Archbishop Innokentii to K. V. Nesselrode, May 1851, in *Innokentii, arkhiepiskop Khersono-Tavricheskii k stoletiiu dnia ego rozhdeniia*, ed. Sv. S. Petrovskii (Odessa, 1901), 20.

12. Archbishop Innokentii, "Zapiski o vostanovlenii drevnikh sviatykh mest' po goram krymskim/Arkhivnye dokumenty, otnosiashchiesia k istoriiu Khersonesskago Monasteryia," *Izvestiia Tavricheskoi uchenoi arkhivnoi komissii* (*ITUAK*) 5 (1888): 94; ibid., 88.

13. Artemii Tereshchenko, "Ocherki Novorossikago Kraia: Nekotoria mestnostaia Iuzhnago Kryma," *Zhurnal ministerstva narodnogo prosveshcheniia* 84, no. 2 (1854): 76.

14. Leontii Cherniavskii, "Feleton: Balaklavskii Georgievskii Monastyr'," *Odesskii vestnik* 75 (1850).

15. Archbishop Innokentii to Archbishop Gavriil, December 19, 1850, "Pis'ma Arkhiepiskopa Khersonskago i Tavricheskago Innokentiia k Gavriilu, arkhiepiskopu Riazanskomu, 1829–1857," *Zapiski Odesskago Obshchestva Istoriia i Drevnostei* 14 (1886): 764.

16. Innokentii, "Rech' po prochtenii vysochaishago manifesta o voine s turtsieiu," *Sochineniia* 8 (St. Petersburg, 1874): 8.

17. Serhii Plokhy, "The City of Glory: Sevastopol in Russian Historical Mythology," *Journal of Contemporary History* 35, no. 3 (July 2000): 369–83.

18. Archbishop Innokentii (Borisov), "Slovo pri poseshchenii pastvy," June 16, 1855, *Sochineniia Innokentiia* 2 (St. Petersburg, 1901–1908): 262–63, 264–65.

19. Aleksandr Ivanov, "Vospominaniia o Vysokopreosviashchennom Innokentii, arkhiepiskop Khersonskom i Tavricheskom," *Tavricheskie eparkhial'nye vedomosti* 23 (1900): 15–16.

20. Thomas Milner, *The Crimea, Its Ancient and Modern History: The Khans, The Sultans, and the Czars; With Notices of Its Scenery and Population* (London: Longman, 1855), 367.

21. Germogen, Bishop of Pskov, *Tavricheskaia eparkhiia* (St. Petersburg, 1886), 92–94.

Monument to Nikolai Gogol, Villa Borghese, Rome, Italy. Photo by Emilia Orlandi (February 2005). Wikimedia Commons.

# 14

## Nikolai Vasilievich Gogol

### *(1809–1852)*

EDYTA BOJANOWSKA

On the face of it, the biography of Nikolai Gogol seems an Imperial Russian success story: a model of metropolitan openness to peripheral diversity. A twenty-year-old Ukrainian youth of humble means moves to St. Petersburg and launches his career as a writer in Russian, soon to earn recognition as a founding father of Russian prose and as the author of a beloved national icon: the image of Russia as a rushing carriage, about to overtake all nations. The Ukrainian subject matter of Gogol's first volumes of stories—*Evenings on a Farm near Dikanka* (1831–32) and *Mirgorod* (1835)—in no way diminishes the warm welcome with which the Russian audience greets the new talent from Ukraine. Gogol soon befriends key figures in the cultural life of the capital, among them the Russian poets Zhukovskii and Pushkin, who encourage and support his work. Sumptuous grants from the empress and the tsar follow. The period's most important arbiter of literary value, Vissarion Belinskii, lavishes accolades on the young Ukrainian, pronouncing him the head of the new nationally conscious realist movement in Russian literature. Gogol moves to Russian themes, and after his masterful comedy *The Government Inspector* (1836), he writes what will become a foundational text in the history of the Russian novel, *Dead Souls* (1842). Gogol's ascendancy in Russian culture would seem to offer proof of the powerful appeal that the imperial, metropolitan culture held to provincials and of this culture's receptivity to an art of non-Russian ethnic provenance.

While the large brushstrokes of this picture are basically correct, the story of Gogol in its detail offers a less happy image of cultural diversity and openness in the Russia of Nicholas I. The complicating factor proved to be the rise of ethnic and linguistic Russian nationalism, which displaced the earlier, more inclusive celebration of Russian uniqueness as rooted in the culturally and ethnically heterogeneous empire. This new, russocentric nationalism set the criteria and the price for admission into the theater of imperial culture. Gogol's ascendancy to Russian cultural icon was therefore far from painless and easy. Tensions and problems accompanied both the Russian reading public's reconciliation with Gogol's Ukrainian identity and Gogol's own efforts to cater to his readers' vociferous demand for an uplifting national image of Russia. To the extent that Gogol is an imperial success story, he became one against considerable odds.

What were the adjustments that Gogol felt he had to make in order to be accepted as a Russian writer? From the start, these involved his ethnic and cultural background, which was quite typical of early nineteenth-century Ukrainian gentry. Gogol's mother came from Polish-Ukrainian nobility and his parents used the Polish "Ianovskii" (Polish transcription: Janowski) as part of the family name. The family estate in Vasilevka, in the Poltava region, was known among locals by the ancestral name Ianovshchyna. Gogol's mother called him Nikola, which is a mixture of the Russian Nikolai and the Ukrainian Mykola. The family was trilingual, although they used Polish mostly for reading. Gogol's father subscribed both to *The Ukrainian Herald* and the *Polish Monitor,* wrote letters to his wife in Ukrainianized Russian, and penned comedies in folksy, idiomatic Ukrainian. Research has cast doubt on this fact, but as far as Gogol knew, his paternal ancestor Ostap Hohol received nobility from the Polish king for his services in the Polish-Lithuanian Commonwealth's war against Muscovy. The future Russian bard grew up hearing his family refer to the Russians as *moskali,* an ethnonym with a derogatory connotation similar to the colonial name for the English—the redcoats.

Upon moving to St. Petersburg, Gogol's Ukrainianness and its Polish admixtures became an aspect of his identity that he felt compelled to manage very carefully. His experiments with his family name exemplify this well. Up to his early months in St. Petersburg, Gogol typically signed his letters Gogol-Ianovskii; in a few childhood letters he even skipped the Ukrainian "Gogol" in favor of the Polish "Ianovskii." After the Polish November Uprising against Russia (1830–31), however, he dropped completely "Ianovskii" and settled on "Gogol" (the last letter signed "Gogol-Ianovskii" comes from September 29, 1830). He admonished his mother to address her letters to him as to "Gogol," since Poles had become "suspect" in St. Petersburg. Even earlier, when signing an early journal publication, Gogol tried to Russify the Polish-sounding "Ianovskii" by shortening it to "Ianov," to achieve the Russian -ov ending. The Polish Uprising created a climate in which Ukrainians were under pressure to dissociate themselves from the insubordinate Poles and to affirm their happy belonging to the fraternal East Slavic, Orthodox Russian empire. Tsarist authorities at the time encouraged limited Ukrainian particularism as a way to counter irredentist Polish nationalism. In the area of culture, this coincided with the craze for Ukrainian folklorism in the capital, whose wave elevated the author of *Evenings on a Farm near Dikanka* to instant celebrity status.

In fact, Gogol calculatingly devised *Evenings* to appeal to this fashion—genuinely inspired and gratifying though his work on it was. The collection appeared under a fictitious folksy Ukrainian pen name, Rudy Panko, and depicted historic and contemporary Ukraine with inimitable humor, originality, and a national inflection that was in high demand among audiences and critics. In fact, the stories' first reviewers treated Gogol as a Ukrainian writer and an important manifestation of Ukrainian national spirit—despite his use of the Russian language, however Ukrainianized (each volume included a glossary of Ukrainian words). In the early 1830s, many thought that the spirit of a work rather than its language determined its belonging to a national tradition. Indeed, the work offered Ukrainian *narodnost'* not only in the sense of folklorism but also of nationalism. However, it did so in a way that did not threaten Russian sensibilities. Gogol's simpleminded rustic narrators created an image of a Little Russian—as Ukrainians were then called—that did not challenge the sense of metropolitan, Great Russian superiority. Gogol also used a Panko-like persona in ingratiating letters to Pushkin.

Gogol's upbringing and his Russificatory education in the Nizhyn Lycée, which trained young Ukrainian noblemen for careers in imperial administration, fostered his identity as a citizen of the Russian Empire who happened to live in Ukraine. The experience of St. Petersburg, ironically, turned him into a self-conscious Ukrainian. In addition to writing fiction on Ukrainian themes, Gogol delved into serious research of Ukraine's history and ethnography, avidly collecting Ukrainian folk songs and antiquities. After a series of low-level jobs in government administration, theater, and tutoring, Gogol settled around 1834 on the calling of a historian. He decided to move to Ukraine and to obtain the post of professor of universal history at the newly created Kyiv University. He hoped by this to continue his historic and ethnographic research on Ukraine in the company of his colleague and friend, the famous Ukrainian ethnographer Maksymovych. He mobilized all his connections to obtain the post. He even appealed through friends to the minister of education, Sergei Uvarov, and published various pro-governmental articles in the Ministry's journal. When he failed to secure the post and was offered instead a position in Russian history, Gogol rejected it, claiming that the subject was more boring than botany. The episode with the Kyiv professorship was a crucial fork in Gogol's life. It demonstrates the strength of Gogol's early commitment to Ukraine, which he developed while in St. Petersburg, a city he came to despise as the inorganic, soulless center of a dehumanizing bureaucratic machine, a place bereft of any imprint of nationality—a sinister symptom of Russia's pervasive dilemma of identity.

The failure of his plans to move to Kyiv coincided with Gogol's reappraisal of the value of his literary efforts. A steady flow of critical acclaim and inspired beginnings of his work on the novel *Dead Souls* finally convinced Gogol to embrace his calling as a writer. This decision proved crucial for Gogol's national self-fashioning. Due to the underprivileged position of Ukrainian literature within the institutions of the Russian Empire, Gogol's ambition could be satisfied only within the field of Russian letters. Since Gogol believed that the principal form of a writer's social utility lay in making manifest a country's national character, becoming a Russian writer meant becoming a Russian nationalist. Ambitious new artistic ventures led Gogol more decisively toward Russian themes—a transition in which he was publicly encouraged by his reviewers, such as Vissarion Belinskii and Stepan Shevyrev, an important Slavophile-leaning literary theoretician of the government's Official Nationality policy. While Gogol was inimitable as a Ukrainian humorist, they held, only Russia could provide Gogol with a thematic matrix worthy of his talent. The same critics were responsible, around 1835, for the reengineering of Gogol's status from a Ukrainian to a Russian writer. What earned Gogol this "promotion," however, is less his use of the Russian language or his themes than his classification as a phenomenon of high culture. As Oleh Ilnytskyj reminds us, many of Gogol's less-talented Ukrainian peers who also wrote in Russian were never granted this honor.[1]

Gogol's authorial traumas and the Russian readers' unease with Gogol's works begin at this juncture. As readers were quick to note, the tenor of Gogol's Russian works differed sharply from that of his Ukrainian ones. Biting satire replaced benevolent chuckle. A depressing analysis of contemporary problems replaced playful folkloric stylization and heroic historicity. Cruel stabs at the Russian national ego in no way resembled the author's loving affirmation of Ukraine's national wholeness. The Russian reception of Gogol's *The Government Inspector* (1836) and *Dead Souls* (1842) features a persistent strain of dissatisfaction with the national content of Gogol's work, which even his admirers found somewhat troubling. The critics who were sympathetic to Gogol—nearly all were his personal friends—hoped that Gogol would offer a brighter national image in his future works. However, when the writer proved unable to cater to this expectation, many of his staunchest supporters lost patience. The pivotal moment was the publication of his *Selected Passages from Correspondence with Friends* (1847): a collection of epistolary essays which, though steeped in patriotic zeal, eschewed any feel-good nationalism.

The negative strain in Gogol's reception is now largely forgotten, but at the time reached in fact the greater part of the reading public, as indicated by the various journals' subscription statistics. In responding to *The Government Inspector* and *Dead Souls,* many readers took Gogol's satirical vistas of Russia as a malevolent Ukrainian's calumny against the Russian nation. Gogol was widely accused of national slander, a malicious distortion of what Russia is truly like. The critic Sękowski charged Gogol with "systematically demean[ing] the Russian people."[2] Despite his earlier assumption into a pantheon of Russian writers, the conservative press now downgraded Gogol back to the status of a Ukrainian writer. The most widely read journals of the time, *The Library for Reading* and *The Northern Bee,* asserted that the action of *The Government Inspector* must be taking place in Ukraine or Belorussia, since the stupidity and abuses portrayed in the comedy could never exist in Great Russian provinces. Gogol's professions of love for Russia—in *Dead Souls*'s lyrical digressions, *Selected Passages,* or other texts—were seen as two-faced Little Russian trickery. His depressing—despite its humor—vision of Russia was branded as the insidious work of a Ukrainian fifth column in Russian culture. Some privately expressed a wish to see the author marched in chains to Siberia.[3]

Against the backdrop of Gogol's newer works on Russian themes, the Ukrainian ones that launched his fame suddenly became an uncomfortable point of reference for his readers, and for their author—a serious liability. He even contemplated excluding *Evenings on a Farm* from his *Collected Works* of 1842. Surprised by this stormy political reception, Gogol attempted to neutralize the politics of his works and to make them less noxious to Russian national pride in a sizeable corpus of explanatory and supplementary texts both to his famous comedy and to the novel. Troubled by his audience's displeasure with his Russian masterpieces' imperfect nationalism, Gogol ultimately rejected these works himself. He promised his readers a corrected, more uplifting version of Russia in the future volumes of his novelistic trilogy, of which *Dead Souls,* he claimed, was merely the first. The national inferno of the existing volume would be redeemed by the coming apotheosis of the Russian nation. However, despite a decade of painstaking research and multiple drafts, he proved unable to produce further volumes. He burned the manuscript of volume 2 a few days before his death, apparently unhappy with the outcome. During his life critics deemed Gogol's divination of Russia's national essence imperfect or incomplete—looking forward to the next volumes' correctives. After his death they enshrined an interpretation of the extant works that explained away Gogol's uncomplimentary national vision. The key to *Dead Souls,* according to this view, lies in the few lyrical digressions that seem to idolize Russia; these digressions' profound and multiple ironies can be brushed aside. Although even today this approach to Gogol remains canonical, a look at the fervid national debate that surrounded Gogol's works at the time of their publication was in fact truer to the spirit of these works. This debate was also symptomatic of a deep-rooted anxiety about Russian identity, so inextricably bound up with national and imperial questions alike.

Gogol's nationalist philosophy was steeped in organicist Herderian notions, whereby a nation's spirit revealed itself through history and culture, especially folk culture. This philosophy suited well Gogol's conception of Ukraine but adhered less well to his vision of Russia, which he saw as a nation in the process of becoming, still reeling after the ruptures of Peter I's cultural revolution. Time and again, his sense of duty toward the Russian nation led him to diagnoses of social problems and ambitious, often singularly unrealistic, programs of reform (as in *Selected Passages*). These were meant to point Russia in a worthy direction as it strove to develop a national self. In straining to inject positive values into his image of Russianness, Gogol also kept reaching for Ukrainian particulars, cross-dressing his Ukrainians as Russian nationalists. The principal example of this is the eponymous hero of *Taras Bulba,* an epic tale from the history of Cossack Ukraine (the work in fact exists in a Ukrainophile 1835 and a Russified 1842 version). Yet his Russian audience craved both more idealized and more strictly "Russian" national images, something that Gogol never managed to deliver.

Gogol's identity, to the extent that we can speculate about this complex matter, involved a combination of facets that proved troubling from the imperial Russian viewpoint. Gogol's Russianness seems a consciously adopted aspect of his public persona rather than an innermost feeling. His civic commitment to Russia's future national greatness coincided with a sense of ethnic and cultural belonging to Ukraine. Much as he tried, Gogol could not make himself any more Russian than that. Although this combination of commitments was earlier acceptable from the imperial Russian viewpoint, from the 1840s onward, rising ethnolinguistic Russian nationalism demanded a stricter acculturation to the Russian core.

Exasperation on the part of Gogol's Russian colleagues and friends with the resilience of his Ukrainian interests and cultural identity crops up at many junctures in his life. Their image of Gogol was that of a Ukrainian chrysalis transformed into a Russian butterfly. Signs of reversion appeared troubling to them. For Belinskii, Gogol became a truly Russian, hence great, writer once he renounced the topic of Ukraine and moved to Russian themes. Ivan Aksakov also praised this transition for establishing the properly subordinate relation of Ukrainianness to Russianness. Gogol's return to Ukrainian themes, such as his work, in the years 1839–41, on a tragedy from the history of the Zaporozhian Sich that he claimed would be his best work, were greeted with dismayed incomprehension: why would Gogol trifle away his time on passé Ukrainiana at the expense of his much-advertised panorama of Russia, *Dead Souls*? Zhukovskii seems to have made a point of falling asleep during Gogol's reading of this tragedy, which led Gogol to burn it. Sergei Aksakov's description of Gogol's 1850 birthday party, during which Gogol's beloved Ukrainian folk songs were sung (Gogol himself throughout his life amassed a collection of 750 folk songs, mostly Ukrainian), captures well that displays of Ukrainian narodnost' at mid-century, two decades after their enthusiastic reception in *Evenings,* repulsed Gogol's Russian supporters as indecent grotesquerie:

> Three *khokhly* [a dismissive Russian ethnonym for Ukrainians] were just charming— sang even without accompaniment—and Gogol read to me some interminable historical songs [*dumy*] of some *khokhlatskii* Homer. Gogol recited and the remaining *khokhly* gesticulated and whooped. Khomyakov and Sofia witnessed this, though the presence of the latter visibly bothered Gogol, but as soon as she left, the former grimaces and twisty hand movements resumed. Khomyakov, Solovyev, and I feasted our eyes on this display of nationality, but without much sympathy. One could sense disdain in Solovyev's smile, in Khomyakov's laughter—good-natured mockery. And I simply felt absurd and funny looking at them, as if at Chuvash or Cheremis natives . . . and nothing more.[4]

It appears that some of Gogol's chauvinistic friends forgave his embarrassing Ukrainian "id" thanks only to the "superego" of his artistic talent that could be useful for Russia. The comparison of Ukrainians to Russia's Asiatic, "savage" tribes of the Chuvash and Cheremis betrays a palpable colonialist sense of metropolitan superiority.

Gogol read this message clearly in published polemics about his works and no doubt sensed it in personal contacts. But even earlier, toward the end of his St. Petersburg years, Ukrainianness became for Gogol ever more an inner refuge rather than a part of his public persona, an aspect of his selfhood that he felt compelled to conceal or mitigate. A passion for Ukrainian folk songs soon became something he reserved for private occasions. There are good reasons to read Poprishchin's anguished search for a workable identity—in the story "The Diary of a Madman"—as a metaphor of Gogol's own identity dilemmas in his St. Petersburg period. In fact, an analysis of all of Gogol's writings, correspondence, fragments, and discarded drafts, yields a record of startling evasion, dissimulation, and disguise. "A sly Little Russian" (*khitryi maloros*)—a Great Russian stereotype of Ukrainians—is a persona that Gogol in fact played to the hilt when navigating the perilous sea of Imperial Russian culture. He did so especially when attempting to smuggle ideas and images that jarred with the triumphalist rhetoric of Official Nationality—since 1835 an official ideology of the imperial government. These ideas and images included the ever more unwelcome expressions of his Ukrainian sympathies. Such "slyness" required a pretense of sim-pleminded naïveté so as to lull the vigilance of those in power or evade punishment when caught. This was Gogol's chief mode of defense—although well intentioned, I simply knew no better—and it stood him in good stead in his authorial odyssey within Imperial Russian culture.

But the historical record, not to mention a more careful reading of his works, allows us to see behind this expedient mask. Could Gogol's ideological floundering have been more resolute and willful than he made it appear to his Russian readers, critics, and friends? A number of "anomalous," from the perspective of the writer's ca-nonical biography, texts and sets of biographical data offer reasons to think this pos-sible. These involve, again, delicate questions of Ukraine's and Poland's status within the Russian Empire. Unsurprisingly, much of this evidence comes from the time that Gogol spent in Western Europe as an expatriate. In fact, he spent half of his adult life (twelve years, excluding two winters) in Western Europe—mainly Italy, but also Germany and France. His warm encomiums for his beloved Italy find no equivalents in Gogol's correspondence about Russia, to which he steadfastly refused to return, despite his friends' promptings. It is in Western Europe that Gogol wrote *Dead Souls* and befriended many Poles, including the Lithuanian-born poet Adam Mickiewicz and the Ukrainian-born Bohdan Zaleski. Most of them were political exiles from tsarist Poland who fled to the West after the defeat of the November Uprising of 1831. The extant record shows that Gogol gladly joined them in criticizing Russia, sharing both racy anecdotes and serious ideas. He sought and read Mickiewicz's anti-Russian works. For a while, he lived in one Polish anti-tsarist conspirator's home in Rome. He encouraged Countess Rostopchina to publish, in 1846, a verse allegory that un-der the guise of a forced marriage presented Russia's annexation of Poland as essen-tially a rape. What gives one pause is that these contacts and actions continued until very late, 1845 or 1846—well into Gogol's public campaign to establish himself as a straight-laced Russian nationalist.

Another example of such an "anomalous" text is Gogol's unpublished fragment titled "Mazepa's Meditations," which questions Russia's imperial right to Ukraine. This idea does not mesh easily with the ideology of Gogol's published historical fic-tion, in which Cossacks pose for Russian nationalists, Poles are the treacherous en-emy, and Ukraine is happily poised to join the Imperial Russian fold. Gogol privately experimented with ideas that challenge or invert this model. "Mazepa's Meditations" presents the Ukrainian hetman who tried to secede from Russia in a most favor-able light, as a prudent statesman and devoted patriot. The Poles appear as Ukraine's friends and kinsmen rather than foes, and the Russians as a nation of slaves, inured to tyranny by their autocrat. Gogol's unpublished historical notes on the Kyivan period, to offer another example of Gogol's unorthodox thinking about Ukrainian history, show Gogol engaged in a project that contradicts the official imperial historiographer, Nikolai Karamzin. Gogol tries in these notes to include the Kyivan period within a narrative of Ukrainian national history, rather than Russian, in which Karamzin had earlier famously sealed it.

Discussions of Gogol's national identity unfailingly cite Gogol's comments to Alexandra Smirnova, his lifelong friend, who asked him point blank if he considered himself Russian or Ukrainian.[5] Three months later, Gogol answered,

> I'll tell you that I myself don't know what soul I have: Ukrainian (*khokhlatskaia*) or Russian. I only know that I would grant primacy neither to a Little Russian over a Russian nor to a Russian over a Little Russian. Both natures are generously endowed by God, and as if on purpose, each of them in its own way includes in itself that which the other lacks—a clear sign that they are meant to complement each other. Moreover, the very stories of their past life are dissimilar, so that the different strengths of their characters could develop and, having then united, could become something more prefect in humanity. (December 24, 1844)[6]

This is as harmonious an image of a hyphenated identity as can be. It gives no inkling of any trauma or dilemma on Gogol's part. It exudes balance and calm, as if Gogol truly were at peace with his Ukrainian-Russian identity. It celebrates the fortuitous union of the two national characters within the imperial framework.

But to foreclose all inquiry into Gogol's identity dilemma with this glib statement is to miss its meaning. To truly understand this epistolary exchange, we must look to its genesis and context. The question Smirnova posed to Gogol arose at a gathering in aristocratic Russian society, at which Gogol was accused of insufficient love for Russia and excessive devotion to Ukraine. On November 3, 1844, Smirnova followed up with details (again, the term for "Ukrainian" in these remarks is the derogatory *khokhol*):

> Tolstoy [the American] remarked that you portrayed all Russians in a negative light, just as you gave all your Little Russians something that inspires sympathy . . . that even their funny sides have something naively pleasant about them. [He said] that none of your Ukrainians is as vile as Nozdrev, that Korobochka [characters in *Dead Souls*] is not disgusting only because she is Ukrainian. He, Tolstoy, thinks that your lack of brotherly feeling [*nebratstvo*] involuntarily revealed itself when you said of two conversing muzhiks "two Russian muzhiks" . . . Tiutchev . . . also observed that Muscovites would never say "two Russian muzhiks." They both said that your whole Ukrainian soul revealed itself in *Taras Bulba,* where with such love you presented Taras, Andrii, and Ostap.[7]

In 1844, two years after the appearance of *Dead Souls,* Gogol's Russianness was for many still in question.

Gogol's accusers capture the mid-century shift of the national-imperial paradigm that I mentioned earlier, whereby peripheral identities could no longer easily coexist with imperial ones. After Russian nationalism gained confidence, it began to champion the primacy of the Russian ethnic and cultural component within the imperial culture. Gogol's Russian public, through the question relayed to him by Smirnova, asked the writer to choose his one and only national allegiance, finding the combination incompatible. In this context, Gogol's refusal to choose—"I myself don't know what soul I have"—shows the writer pushing back. Given his very public

1840s posturing as a heartfelt Russian nationalist, and his perfect understanding of the answer that his Russian readers desired, Gogol's unwillingness to renounce his Ukrainianness shows the remarkable strength of this part of his identity and the value that he attached to it.

Gogol's initial reply to Smirnova's question, from October 24, 1844, is similarly instructive. The question irritated Gogol: "You say, 'Reach the depth of your soul and ask yourself, are you really a Russian, or are you a Ukrainian?' But tell me, am I a saint? Can I really see all my loathsome faults?"[8] In this initial reply, Gogol's binationalism, rather than doubling his advantages, seems to have multiplied his "faults." A hysterical tirade follows, in which Gogol chastises Smirnova for failing to reform him, gripes about those who accuse him of "two-facedness," complaints of the insults he has suffered, and speculates about unnamed people who wish to do him harm. In closing, he expresses a desire to become a better person. Far from calm and rational, this impulsive outburst reveals Gogol's anguish and deep-seated insecurity about his national identity. Far from a harmonious union, Gogol's Ukrainian-Russian identity emerges in this letter as an accursed affliction. Interestingly, the anguish stems less from Gogol's own inner dilemma, if he had one, but from his understanding that something else was expected of him. His Russian audience, both in print and in public, communicated clearly its discomfort with dual national commitments and demanded an unequivocal and unitary allegiance.

It took Gogol two months to collect himself and to produce the eventual balmy reply about a harmonious union of Ukrainianness and Russianness. This final, now widely known pronouncement was Gogol's carefully calibrated answer geared for the consumption of aristocratic Russian society, in which Smirnova served as Gogol's emissary. To the extent that this reply reflects Gogol's genuine national self-diagnosis—if it does—its ideologically charged circumstances illuminate the stakes involved and show that Gogol's admission to Russian culture had a price that he found dear.

NOTES

1. Oleh Il'nyts'kyj, "Hohol' i postkolonial'nyi kontekst," *Krytyka* 29 [4.3] (2000): 11.

2. O. I. Senkovskii, review of N. Gogol, *Pokhozhdeniia Chichikova, ili Mertvye dushi, Syn otechestva* 6 (1842): 26.

3. For a detailed discussion of Gogol's contemporary reception, see Edyta Bojanowska, *Nikolai Gogol: Between Ukrainian and Russian Nationalism* (Cambridge, Mass.: Harvard University Press, 2007).

4. Sergei Aksakov, letter to Ivan Aksakov of March 20, 1850, quoted in *N. V. Gogol': Materialy i issledovaniia*, ed. V. Gippius (Moscow: Izd. Ak. nauk SSSR, 1936), 1:217.

5. A. O. Smirnova, letter to Gogol, September 26, 1844, in *Russkaia starina* 59 (1888): 59.

6. Nikolai Gogol, *Polnoe sobranie sochinenii* (Moscow: Izd. Ak. nauk SSSR, 1937–52), 12:419.

7. A. O. Smirnova, letter to Gogol, November 3, 1844, in *Perepiska N. V. Gogolia* (Moscow: Khudozh. literatura, 1988), 2:124.

8. Gogol, *Polnoe sobranie sochinenii* 12:357.

Ilya Repin, *Portrait of the Composer Anton Rubinstein* (1887). Oil on canvas, 110 × 85 cm. The State Russian Museum, St. Petersburg. Wikimedia Commons.

# 15

*~✶~*

# Anton Rubinstein

*(1829–1894)*

RICHARD STITES

Anton Grigorevich Rubinstein (Rubinshtein), although born at the edge of the Russian Empire, a member of a despised people, nonetheless became a central figure in the life of what is, alongside literature, Russia's first great cultural contribution to the world in the nineteenth century—classical music. Not a great composer, his music falls out the canonical progression that begins with the compositions of Mikhail Glinka (1804–57). Rather he became a world-renowned concert pianist, an aggressive promoter of European art music in Russia, and the founder—against tough odds—of the first Russian conservatory. Rubinstein in many ways always remained a bridge between Russia and Europe, even down to his Jewish roots on both sides. His mother hailed from Silesia, an eastern wing of the Kingdom of Prussia. His father, Russified and a convert to Orthodoxy, came from a town in a corner of Podolia near Bessarabia, recently acquired from the Ottoman Turks—a true borderland where dwelled Ukrainians, Romanians, Russians, Jews, Tatars, Turks, and Greeks. Characteristically, the "western" bride and the "eastern" groom met in Odessa, one of the great crossroads of Europe.

Anton's father, Grigory, did not flee the Jewish Pale to escape pogroms—the hideous massacres that had been the scourge of Jewry in the seventeenth and eighteenth centuries and which would explode again in the 1880s. What he gained on that day in 1831 when sixty members of the Rubinstein clan assembled in a church in its ancestral town of Berdichev to be baptized was what all Jews gained upon admission into the Orthodox faith. This included exemption from the 1827 laws on double taxation of Jews and avoidance of the cantonal system which swept Jewish children into the alien realm of the Russian army with all its hazards, brutality, and discrimination—the main scourge of Jewish life under Tsar Nicholas I. Converts also gained the right to make their exit from the Pale, which one scholar has called a huge pressure cooker, and move into the Russian interior, a new world where mere conversion to Orthodoxy could be turned into a life of Russification. Three years after the baptism, Grigory followed one of those thousands of "pathways of empire" that took his family from the ethnic vinaigrette of southern Podolia, to the merchant quarter on the south bank of the Moscow River.

The location of Rubinstein's home and the small factory he owned in the Zamoskvorechie district, at the heart of the Moscow merchantry, helped open to the family a wide diversity of social contacts that lubricated the road to assimilation. This became possible due to two of the father's assets: personal wealth, which he used to entertain guests lavishly; and a jovial and good-natured personality which attracted to his home not only Russian merchants, but petty nobles, students, and members of the budding intelligentsia. The lively domestic milieu served as a training ground for the kind of social skills needed when Anton began his climb toward—but never quite into—the upper reaches of the beau monde.

The boy's musical training came from his mother, a talented pianist in the strict German style. Throughout Europe in this era, piano lessons had become de rigueur for families of the middle class and upward, but more often for girls than boys. Anton's innate talent and his mother's stringent practice regime steered him from the role of a sociable domestic piano player into that of a major concert artist. Happily, the path to this prominence was well prepared. After the specter of the Napoleonic invasion of 1812 had faded, European artists whose countrymen had marched with the Grande Armée—Frenchmen, Poles, Italians, and others—swarmed into St. Petersburg and Moscow and even provincial towns to join the international concert circuit. Liszt, Berlioz, the Schumanns, and countless divas and ballerinas accustomed the Russian public to foreign, semi-foreign, and exotic star power. Child prodigies of whatever origin became the rage in the reign of Tsar Nicholas I. Since many of them, as well as foreign virtuosi, were Jewish, another door was opened to talented young artists of Jewish background at the very moment when other teenaged unconverted Jews were bent under the stick of regimental life as cantonists. Thus the arts, like the professions and high finance and big industry later, provided a narrow road to success for selected Jews or ex-Jews of the Russian Empire.

One such Wunderkind of the 1830s, Yuliya Grünberg, had had the noted French émigré Alexandre Villoing as her piano teacher. Rubinstein's mother engaged him for her son. After a few years under Villoing, the diminutive curly-haired child made his debut at an outdoor concert and then appeared at Moscow University to rave reviews. One triumph led to another. Rubinstein was able to tour Europe in concert and to be greeted politely by those two daunting but muted antisemites, Chopin and Liszt. Upon returning to Russia on the death of his father, Rubinstein found that his European fame had augmented his repute at home. The St. Petersburg Philharmonia, founded in 1803 and by then the foremost concert venue in the empire, invited Rubinstein to play there. The emperor, apprised of the youngster's renown, invited—meaning commanded—him to play for the royal family in the eleven-hundred-room Winter Palace. With his mother, the boy traveled to Berlin for advanced study under Professor Siegfried Dehn, Glinka's former teacher. While there he also gave over two hundred recitals. In standard histories of Russia's paranoid censorship practices in 1848–49, as revolution raged all over Europe, the story is often told that border guards not only searched for subversive literature but even examined the notes of musical scores for revolutionary codes. In fact, Rubinstein's experience at the frontier was the case in point. Unscathed, although nearly arrested, he made his way home and then onto the concert circuit through Russia.

Two events in the early 1850s launched Rubinstein in a new direction, but one still deeply connected to his musical life. In the stringently hierarchical social system of estates and in-between categories of nobles, clergy, merchants, state peasants, and serfs—no designation existed for composers or performing artists, unless they were employed by the state. Rubinstein learned of this in a very personal way in 1850 when he took confession at Kazan' Cathedral in St. Petersburg. By custom, after the verbal confession, Orthodox believers had to register the fact with their name along with estate or class status. Rubinstein inscribed himself as "artiste" or performer. But since he was attached to no school, theater, or government body, the deacon kept asking him what he was—that is, how he fit into the Procrustean bed of Russia's social and juridical system, which had no category of independent performer. Thus challenged, the pianist renowned all over Europe had to identify himself as "merchant's son." Russian society's obsession with rank and ascription angered Rubinstein because it assigned no particular value or even identity to a famous and hardworking musical artist. Rubinstein was a proud man and the incident, as he later wrote, led him to fight for a legitimate official designation for people like himself. He sought elevation to the status and title of free artist for the independent professional musician, a title equivalent to the free artist of the Academy of Arts, with its concomitant status.

But such a title would require the existence of a musical institution analogous to the Academy of Arts, a government-run school founded during the reign of Empress Elizabeth—in other words, an academy of music or conservatory. Concert music simply lacked the status held by the visual and plastic arts in early-nineteenth-century Russia. Orchestras in the capitals were staffed largely by "Germans" (foreign or native to Russia and the Baltic provinces); and small ensembles by noble amateurs who were forbidden to play to a general public. Provincial bands, manned by serf musicians, catered to private audiences. Rubinstein recognized that professionalizing and fully Russifying musical life in his country would require rigorous training in a conservatory. Ultimately, the full flowering of Russian musical talent could also be attained only after the emancipation of the serfs. Rubinstein, in a second transforming event, found a high-ranking patron who shared his views.

Born Princess Charlotte Marie of Würtemburg, Grand Duchess Elena Pavlovna was the wife of the tsar's younger brother, Mikhail Pavlovich. Ironically, this new figure in Rubinstein's life was a German—but one who took a strong interest in the life of her adopted country, although not in the fanatical and mystical manner of a later and all-too-famous German bride of a Romanov tsar. Like other royal consorts, she nurtured the fine arts—particularly classical music performance, which she hosted in the lavish Mikhailovsky Palace (now the Russian Museum, on the Square of the Arts). Members of the imperial family, courtiers, and, indeed, all nobles were prohibited from performing in public to a paying audience. Such activity was considered "work," was tainted by the market, and would require highborn persons to entertain commoners and thus be subject to their approval or critique. The ban applied even more stringently to acting. The restriction did not inhibit the elite from entertaining one another, for example, in amateur theatricals or musical evenings. When royal talent was in short supply, the host would employ "stiffeners," or trained commoners, as accompanists or chamber music players sitting side by side with princes and dukes. Elena Pavlovna's Thursday evening musical salon, which she dubbed "morganatic" because of its social mix, became one of the most noted, among many, in the capital.

The young virtuoso Rubinstein—a talented and polished veteran of Europe's finest concert venues—caught the attention of the grand duchess in 1852 and was appointed a court pianist or accompanist, a post previously held by renowned European artists. While in her service in the 1850s, Rubinstein composed one of the most celebrated small-form piano pieces in the musical literature, "Melody in F" (simply "Melodiya" in Russian), a delightful, quasi-Mendelssohnian work that has charmed piano pupils and teachers for a century and a half. Rubinstein dedicated the piece to Elena Pavlovna. His growing stature got him modestly paid assignments at various palaces and mansions in and near the capital. For a twenty-three-year-old converted Jewish son of a Moscow merchant, this was a spectacular achievement in status. But Rubinstein, proud beyond measure, remained unsatisfied. He saw himself as little more than a palace servant and nicknamed himself the "musical furnace attendant" of the imperial clan. To supplement the meager "tips" from royalty, he gave lessons and concerts. For the latter, he was required by custom to sell tickets to the upper classes in order to fill the seats. His betters indeed treated this mere musician as a commoner whom they addressed as they did their butlers, with the slightly demeaning form of you (*ty*).

Rubinstein escaped his thankless toils by way of a European tour in the mid-1850s. While there, he wrote an article on Russian composers for a Viennese musical journal that bluntly held up the Russian musical world to criticism. This brought a hurricane of negative response in Russia. The aging Glinka wrote to a friend that "the Jew [*zhid*] Rubinstein has undertaken to acquaint Germany with our music and has written an article in which he flings mud at us all, touching rather arrogantly my old lady, *A Life for the Tsar*." Behind Rubinstein's comments on particular Russian musical forms lay his loathing of amateurism and absence of a professional musical infrastructure in Russia—in contrast to Western Europe. As early as 1853, he had called for a conservatory of music, and he was not alone on this matter. But the Vienna article made him enemies in high places and the conservatory project bore no fruit for the time being.

Rubinstein eventually learned the politics of reform from above. If any progress toward a conservatory could be made, it would have to have the blessing of highly placed figures. Once again, Elena Pavlovna appeared in his life. She was wintering in Nice in 1856–57 and invited Rubinstein, then on tour, to visit and play for her Riviera entourage. In conversation, Rubinstein was apparently successful in winning her allegiance for a conservatory. Back in St. Petersburg, the ambitious and energetic pianist-composer, a prophet returning from the wilderness and still an outsider snubbed for his Vienna article, launched a campaign of lobbying for the creation of the title of free artist for trained musicians at the very moment when preparations were underway for the emancipation of half the population of Russia. He organized his own musical salon in his home where his colleagues hatched their plans. The first step was the creation of the Russian Musical Society, which, in the words of its charter, intended "to effect the spread of musical education in Russia, facilitate the development of all branches of musical art, and encourage talented Russian composers, performers, and music teachers." The Society, primarily a concert organization, was also a proto-conservatory which aspired to emulate the Academy of Arts and the Theater School, but with a national outreach all over the country. By October 1861, the St. Petersburg Conservatory was chartered.

Coinciding with the freeing of half the population, the new school reflected the spirit of the times by admitting young men and women of every class or estate, rich and poor, and all ethnic groups, including Jewish pupils who thus collected their ticket out of the Jewish Pale of Settlement—yet one more rivulet in the broadening stream of Jewish emancipation and assimilation. Another dream of Rubinstein's came true when graduates were granted the title free artist. The world significance of Rubinstein's conservatory and that opened in Moscow in 1866 by his brother Nikolai can be detected in the eminence of their graduates. A mere handful of these from the late nineteenth and early twentieth centuries include Balanchine and Diaghilev; Tchaikovsky, Shostakovich, and Prokofiev; the Russian-born American violinists Jascha Heifetz and Nathan Milstein; and countless European violinists who came to study with the Hungarian-born professor Leopold Auer. Rubinstein's determination to Russify the musical profession ironically meant laying the strict foundations of German musical pedagogy, but also internationalizing the reputation of Russian musicianship.

Throughout Rubinstein's struggle, one can hardly have missed the enormous role played by Western Europe and its cultural institutions. The status of the budding virtuoso, built on the earlier presence of visiting Europeans playing for the Russian elite, endowed him with the needed prestigious credentials. His story fitted in nicely with what Richard Wortman has described as the European symbolic and cultural side of Russian monarchy. But as the second half of the century dawned, distant cousins of the Slavophile sensibility—minus its program—began to assert themselves in the idiom of a Russian high-cultural nationalism. Rubinstein, with his perpetual lack of tact, unwittingly fed its chill wind in another of his brutally frank assaults on the Russian ways of musical life. In January 1861, on the eve of his victory in the campaign for a conservatory, he published an article in the journal *The Age* on his pet peeve: amateurism in music. Poor training, social snobbery, laziness, and hobbyism—and the low status of good musicians—kept the need for serious music education in abeyance. Here and in other writings, Rubinstein asserted the virtues of professionalism: a lifetime of dedication, endless practice, focus, suffering and sacrifice; even a desire—horribile dictu—for personal success, fame, and money; as well as a willingness to face critics. Russia needed a marketplace of competition, an updraft of talent from every class and element, and a rigorous training system that would eventually replace foreigners with competent Russian musicians. Rubinstein did not hesitate to unveil the dirty word "ambition."

Such notions clearly implied a breach of class taboos, the slamming of informal salon music making, and urging nobles to give up a life of ease in favor of sweating at the keyboard—for a fee!—as if noble status was not a sufficient social achievement in itself. Rubinstein's arguments offended the amateur set, doubly so since their author was an arrivé of humble origins. And his bluntly expressed opinions also riled up Russian musical figures, particularly Aleksandr Serov and a circle of budding composers, later to be dubbed "The Mighty Handful" or "The Five"—Mily Balakirev, César Cui, Modest Mussorgsky, Aleksandr Borodin, and Nikolai Rimsky-Korsakov. Some of them saw too much formal training, especially along Western lines, as cramping and alien to "spontaneous" play and composition and an arrant insult to the alleged authentic Russian style of creativity. A kind of pedagogical war broke out when Balakirev, spurning the conservatory, opened a Free School of Music where the regimen was more relaxed and the level of training more modest than that of the conservatory. Both Balakirev and the eminent spokesman for The Five, Vladimir Stasov, despised the idea of a conservatory as a reactionary and antiquated device that stifled pure creativity.

The pedagogical conflict soon descended into an often nasty exchange about national authenticity in music, a debate fueled by personal feuds. Rubinstein the man and the musician had very strong opinions and was not shy in voicing them in acid tones. His enemies responded to his views with personal barbs in print, and sometimes with racist slurs in private. To them he looked like another Stolz, who tried to outshine all the lazy Russian Oblomovs. Rubinstein's own work habits and his demands for the same in others rattled those who preferred the "lyrical disorder" of the allegedly more relaxed Russian manner. Modest Mussorgsky gave him the insulting name "Tupinstein," called his conservatory the "German Musical Ministry," and saw in his notions of professionalism nothing more than a race after fame and money. Balakirev, an extreme Russian chauvinist, disliked Jews, Germans, Poles, and Catholics. He looked upon Rubinstein as a "musical Baltic German general."

Rubinstein, in his early career, had encountered few open references to his Jewish origin. He recited and listened to mild "Jewish" jokes from colleagues. But from the 1860s, the very decade in which Tsar Alexander II had included an easing up on Jewish restrictions among his many reforms, signs of antisemitism emerged in the musical wars. To his bitterest foes among and around The Five, Rubinstein had many strikes against him: his name, his European connections, his music, his pedagogical program, and his Jewish background. Composer Alexander Serov, although not a member of The Five and its circle, spoke of the Musical Society as the "Jew Musikverein" and the conservatory as the "Piano Synagogue." Stasov privately referred to Rubinstein in correspondence as a Jew (he used both *evrei* and the more demeaning *zhid*), ignoring the fact that the composer had long lost his Jewish identity. For the reading public, Stasov employed more restraint. In a published article of 1861, he wrote, "Mr. Rubinstein is a foreigner, with nothing in common either with our national character or our art." Rubinstein's alleged "foreignness"—European tutelage and musical contacts—outweighed his specific Jewishness for the critic whose hostility would have been the same had Rubinstein been an ethnic German. In any case, the antisemitic elements in the conflict paled beside that of Richard Wagner's assault on Mendelssohn and Meyerbeer a decade earlier in his diatribe *Jewishness in Music.*

Stasov also overstepped the bounds of logic and common sense by claiming that the particular Russianness in the musical compositions of The Five resulted not only from their genuine Russian ethnicity but from their provincial origins as well. As it happens, by family origin, Balakirev was descended from Tatars, as, in part, was Borodin. Cui had French and Lithuanian roots. As to provincial upbringing, Borodin was born in St. Petersburg, whereas Tchaikovsky, the supposed practitioner of Western or un-Russian music, was in a sense the most provincial of them all—born in distant and isolated Votkinsk, in the Perm province.

The musical schism of the 1860s, despite its sometimes absurd rhetorical posturing, probably enriched rather than hindered musical advancement in Russia. Each side redoubled its efforts to outdo the other. Prior to 1861, most would-be composers who aspired to further heights had to pass through the hands of foreigners in Russia or abroad. With the growth of aspiring amateur composers and non-serf musicians came a demand for homegrown Russian education. Both the conservatories and the Free School in their different ways helped fill this need. Eventually some of the early rancor dissolved and many ties were established between the two currents and their members.

Anton Rubinstein's stormy relations with musical "nationalists" carried over to his position as director of the conservatory. Internal politics led him to resign and move to Europe in 1887. When he returned he upgraded discipline and rigor in the curriculum. His second exodus was due to a much darker political issue. During the 1890s, when the reactionary policies of Tsar Alexander III and his ministers were in full swing, the government set racial quotas for Jews applying for admission to higher education. When it began to do so for the conservatory, Rubinstein resigned in protest and left for Europe once more. He returned briefly in 1894 and died there soon after. After the Bolshevik Revolution of 1917, all institutions bearing the designation "Imperial" were renamed. The St. Petersburg and Moscow conservatories would, by ordinary rules of historical courtesy and accuracy, have been named after the Rubinstein brothers. Instead they were, and remain, named after Rimsky-Korsakov and Tchaikovsky, respectively. Anton Rubinstein lived on as a highly respected cultural figure throughout the Soviet period, in the affectionate memory of Soviet musicians and the intelligentsia, in Ilya Repin's magnificent portrait of him that still hangs in the Russian Museum, and—a comic grace note—in a Leningrad-Petersburg street that eventually became home to jazz and rock clubs in the late twentieth century.

In looking back on the spectacular but stormy career of Anton Rubinstein, it might be clarifying to see him not just as a famous musical pioneer, but also as one embodiment of the "man of empire." Some of these men—and women as well—performed that role in the confinement of a borderland or ethnic enclave. Others did so by transporting themselves to one of the capitals. Starting at least in the Muscovy period, such people often brought with them not only colorful costumes to adorn state balls, but a certain style or mentality which, when joined up to Russian behavioral norms, enriched them. Only a racist would deny that Rubinstein was anything less than a genuine Russian. But he was also the son of Jewish parents who gave him both an expansive personality and a sense of discipline and rigor. Interestingly, the great pianist made his mark on Russian life not only at the dawn of a limited emancipation of Jews into some peaceful precincts of Russian life—law, business, and medicine—but also at the moment when young Jews entered the radical community of the 1860. Non-Jewish conspirators and populists often looked on their Jewish comrades as a kind of energy-giving yeast that raised the bread of revolutionary organization. In quite another realm of imperial life, Rubinstein added a quotient of yeast to Russian culture.

Frontispiece to Aleksandr Borodin's published score for the Opera *Prince Igor* (1890).

# 16

# Aleksandr Borodin

## (1833–1887)

DAVID SCHIMMELPENNINCK VAN DER OYE

No musical composition is more closely associated in the West with the tsarist East than Aleksandr Borodin's *In the Steppes of Central Asia.*[1] A track on virtually every bargain basement collection of Russian classical hits, the orchestral sketch was commissioned to honor the twenty-fifth anniversary of Emperor Alexander II's reign, in 1880. The celebration's grandiose plans featured a conversation between "the Genius of Russia" and "History," to be illustrated by various orchestral tableaux vivants highlighting the monarch's achievements. In addition to Borodin's contribution, other pieces included "Slava" (Glory), a chorus by Nikolai Rimsky-Korsakov, and a march by Modest Mussorgsky commemorating the capture of the Ottoman stronghold of Kars in 1877. The the projected performance never took place, as its promoters mysteriously disappeared. Nevertheless, *In the Steppes of Central Asia* quickly acquired great popularity both at home and abroad.[2]

Borodin's sketch combined Russian and Eastern tunes to convey melodically the ethnic harmony of Alexander's newly conquered realms in Turkestan, as he explained in his notes to accompany the score:

> The unfamiliar strains of a peaceful Russian song first waft over the uniform, sandy Central Asian steppes. We hear the sound of approaching camels' and horses' hooves, we hear the doleful strains of an Oriental tune. A native caravan passes over the boundless desert, guarded by Russian troops. It continues its long journey confidently and without fear under the protection of Russian arms. Farther and farther away the caravan recedes into the distance. The pacific singing of the Russians and the natives blends into a single harmony, whose refrain is long heard over the steppe until it, too, vanishes into the distance.[3]

On one level, Borodin's melodic symbiosis of Russian and Asian is typical of European propaganda during the high age of imperialism, which sought to portray colonial subjects as the happy subjects of white rule. The musicologist Richard Taruskin suggested that the composer's opera *Prince Igor* should be heard in the same way: "Prince Igor made overt the pervasive subtext to 19th-century Russian essays in Orientalism: The racially-justified endorsement of Russia's militaristic expansion to the east." According to Taruskin, Borodin's composition adhered entirely to the schema popularized by the late literary scholar Edward Said in his profoundly influential *Orientalism,* and, subsequently, in *Culture and Imperialism.* Although the latter focuses on novels, there is a chapter about opera. Giuseppe Verdi's *Aïda,* Said points out, "as a visual, musical, and theatrical spectacle . . . confirms the Orient as an essentially exotic, distant and antique place in which Europeans can mount certain shows of force."[4]

But a closer look at Borodin's masterpiece suggests that it is not quite in the same league as some other cultural artifacts of European colonialism. Although it was conceived at a time of rapid expansion into Central Asia, the opera's portrayal of the Eastern Other actually reflects its composer's ambiguous attitude towards his own continental identity. In this way, *Prince Igor* anticipated the fascination with Russia's Oriental self of such fin-de-siècle Asianists as the newspaper publisher Prince Esper Ukhtomskii, not to mention the twentieth century's Eurasianists and their disciples, such as Lev Gumilev.[5]

*     *     *

Aleksandr Porfir'evich Borodin was born in St. Petersburg in 1833 as the illegitimate son of a Georgian prince of Tatar ancestry, Luka Stepanovich Gedeanov, and his much younger Russian mistress, Avdot'ia Konstantinovna Antonova. Both European and Asian blood, therefore, coursed through his veins. Borodin's dual ancestry was evident at first glance. The critic Vladimir Stasov, who knew him well, remarked, "all . . . were struck by his characteristically Oriental appearance." In a playful nod to his Eastern roots, Borodin occasionally appeared at costume balls dressed in Chinese robes. Mixed blood was no disgrace in the multinational empire of the Romanovs. Some of its most venerable noble houses proudly bore an Eastern provenance, such as the Iusupovs, Dashkovs, Kochubeis, and the Ushakovs. Many of these were descended from aristocratic Tatars who had entered into Muscovite service during the lengthy struggles with the Mongol Golden Horde and its successors. In the medieval Russian mind, race mattered less than caste, and some lineages even took to fabricating spurious Tatar noble ancestry.[6]

To deal with the awkward question of Aleksandr's birth out of wedlock, Prince Gedeanov arranged for the boy to be baptized as the son of one his serfs, Porfiry Borodin (Gedeanov eventully freed Aleksandr Porfir'evich from serfdom and he was subsequently registered as a merchant of the third guild). The prince also dutifully provided for a financially secure upbringing and eventually married Avdotia off to a retired medical officer. According to aristocratic custom, the boy was educated at home, in his mother's comfortable house in the capital. There she indulged him in his two passions—music and chemistry. He proved unusually gifted in both early on. By the age of nine, Aleksandr composed his first polka, and four years later he wrote a concerto and a string trio, both of which were subsequently published. Meanwhile, the lad was allowed to concoct dangerous pyrotechnics and carry out chemistry experiments at home, fill-ing the apartment with a seemingly unending variety of noxious odors.

When the time came for Aleksandr to pursue higher education, his mother was reluctant to send him to university. St. Petersburg's campus already had the repu-tation of being a hotbed of student unrest, and she therefore enrolled him in the Military Medical Academy on the advice of a family friend. Borodin excelled in every subject, and graduated in 1855 with the highest distinction, *cum eximia laude* (with exceeding praise). He was particularly close to his chemistry professor, who began grooming him as his successor. Although Borodin went on to earn a medical doctor-ate, his heart lay not in being a physician. Instead, he eagerly took up his mentor's advice to join him as an assistant professor at the Medical Academy in 1862, after a three-year study trip to the West. Respected by his colleagues and well liked by stu-dents, in a little over two years Borodin won promotion to the chemistry chair, a post he would hold until his death.

Borodin did not abandon his other love in medical school. The first surviving works, some chamber partitas and songs, date from his undergraduate days. One day during his internship at a military hospital, he met a refined young subaltern in the elite Preobrazhenskii Guards Regiment, Modest Mussorgsky, and the two immedi-ately hit it off as they chatted about music. A few years later, when Borodin again saw the officer, Mussorgsky played some of his own compositions, including an "Oriental" trio. Borodin recalled,

> I was flabbergasted by these fantastic musical elements, which were totally new to me. I can't say that I especially liked them at first; their novelty rather puzzled me. But after listening a little, I began to develop a taste for them.[7]

For the time being, Borodin's musical outlook remained distinctly Occidental. Describing himself as "an avid Mendelssohnian," after the early Romantic composer Felix Mendelssohn, during his stay in Heidelberg in the early 1860s he frequently played chamber pieces with his friends. It was also in the German university town that he met his future wife, Ekaterina Protopopova, a talented pianist who had trav-eled there from Moscow in search of a treatment for her consumption. Their romance blossomed quickly, as she introduced him to the delights of Frédéric Chopin and Franz Liszt and they became acquainted with Richard Wagner's operas.

\* \* \*

Borodin came of age at a time when Russian music was finding its own path. The pio-neer was Mikhail Glinka. As the first composer to establish a distinct national idiom, Glinka was to Russian music what Alexander Pushkin was to his nation's literature. Active at a time when the autocracy favored Italian opera, Glinka rejected the cosmo-politanism of St. Petersburg's musical establishment to advocate a style based on na-tive themes and motifs. As he supposedly put it, "The common people compose; we only arrange." Glinka took the capital by storm in 1836 with his first opera, *Zhizn' za tsaria* (A life for the tsar), a patriotic adventure set in the Polish War during the early seventeenth century's Time of Troubles. His *Ruslan i Ludmilla* (Ruslan and Ludmilla), which followed six years later, was less successful but ultimately more influential. Like Pushkin's epic fairy tale of 1820, to which the libretto was set, the opera incorporated Russian folk elements with orientalisms. The latter included a Persian chorus as well as a set of Turkish, Arabic, and Caucasian dances. But, as Glinka argued, these were not necessarily alien: "There is no doubt that our Russian song is a child of the North, but the people of the East have also given it something."[8]

Some musicologists have suggested that Russians exaggerate the originality of Mikhail Glinka's achievement by pointing out that he was hardly the first to blend native melodies into his compositions.[9] Furthermore, his folkloric interests were entirely in keeping with European Romanticism. Nevertheless, he did have some influential disciples who carried on his legacy. Among them was a talented young pianist, Mily Balakirev. Like Glinka, Balakirev hailed from the provinces, and he had similarly been trained outside of the academy. Although the latter's creative achievements were relatively modest, he championed Glinka's nationalist orientation to a group of composers who in the nineteenth century's second half collectively oversaw the full flowering of what came to be known as the Russian School. Nicknamed *Moguchaia Kuchka* (The Mighty Handful)—and, more simply, The Five—they included some of the greatest names in Russian music: Nikolai Rimsky-Korsakov, Modest Mussorgsky, and Aleksandr Borodin. (The fifth, and least known today, was César Cui.)

Like the painter Vasilii Vereshchagin, The Five subscribed to the realist aesthetics of the 1860s. Balakirev had even contemplated honoring the age's cultural oracle, Nikolai Chernyshevsky, with an opera of his novelistic manifesto *What Is to Be Done?* In his survey of art during the nineteenth century's middle decades, the critic Vladimir Stasov, a friend and tireless advocate of The Five, explained the Russian School's approach to music.[10] Most important, its members refused to submit to the dictates of the European tradition. Largely self-taught, Balakirev and his circle opposed the St. Petersburg Conservatory, which saw itself as the bearer of Western musical culture. Hand in hand with this aversion to the academy was the Russian School's "aspiration for the national essence" (*stremlenie k national'nosti*). This did not mean strict isolationism; The Five closely followed European developments, traveled abroad, and were friendly with foreign composers. And, of course, nationalism was characteristic of Western trends at the time. Meanwhile, in keeping with Chernyshevsky's teachings, The Five also rejected abstraction in favor of programmatic works—in other words, music meant to convey an idea or tell a story.

According to Stasov, another important characteristic of the Russian School was "the Oriental element." Mily Balakirev, who shared Stasov's beliefs about the Asian origins of *byliny,* traveled to the Caucasus several times during the 1860s to collect folk tunes among its diverse peoples. Several of Balakirev's compositions of the time have a distinctly Eastern flavor, including his Oriental fantasy for piano *Islamey* (1869) and the symphonic poem *Tamara* (1867–82), which was based on Mikhail Lermontov's poem about a legendary Georgian siren.

Rimsky-Korsakov recalled that Balakirev spent many evenings with his fellow *kuchkists* playing the melodies he transcribed during his rambles in Russia's Oriental highlands.[11] They likewise developed a fascination for Asian music, as such works as Korsakov's *Sheherazade, Antar,* and *Le coq d'or* (the golden cockerel), Mussorgsky's "Shamil's March," not to mention Borodin's *In the Steppes of Central Asia,* attest. The musicologist Marina Frolova-Walker suggests that The Five shared Glinka's attitudes about the East:

> Balakirev did not see the Oriental style as a means for representing a separate, alien people, and Other, in current parlance, but as an essential component of musical Russianness. The use of the newly constructed Oriental style was thus for Balakirev (and for the rest of the Kuchka in their earlier years) the easiest way to assert a distinct, non-European identity.[12]

Among the Kuchkists no one understood this better than Aleksandr Porfir'evich Borodin. Borodin had fallen under the spell of the charismatic musical guru shortly after taking up his teaching post back at the Military Medical Academy in 1862. His relationship with the domineering Balakirev eventually soured somewhat, but their years together strongly shaped the young professor's tastes. According to Stasov, who knew him well, Borodin "was soon transformed into a composer, whose abilities were most strongly characterized by the Russian, and inseparably linked with it, Oriental element."[13]

Aleksandr Borodin's orchestral debut was his First Symphony, which premiered at the Russian Musical Society in early January 1869 under Balakirev's baton. Although there were some negative reviews, the response was generally quite favorable. Emboldened by his success, Borodin told his friends that he now wanted to write an opera, preferably on a Russian subject. One person who was in a good position to provide some ideas was Stasov, who held a post at St. Petersburg's Public Library. In April 1869, after a lengthy conversation, Stasov sent Borodin a detailed plan for an opera based on the twelfth-century *Igor Tale* (*Slovo o polku Igoreve*).

The *Igor Tale* was a medieval epic that described the ill-fated expedition of a twelfth-century prince against the Polovtsians, a nomadic people on the steppes north of the Black Sea. In many ways, it is the Russian equivalent of the *Chanson de Roland,* a verse about the dangerous struggle of Christendom against the heathen Other. The main difference between the *Chanson de Roland* and the *Igor Tale,* other than the fact that the *Igor Tale* was written in Slavonic and takes place not in the Pyrenées but somewhere in what is now Ukraine, is that, unlike Roland, Igor lives. In fact, the prince is captured by the Polovtsians and held in their camp until he finally manages to escape. Russians traditionally see the *Igor Tale* just like Frenchmen do the *Chanson de Roland,* as a tale of patriotism against a perfidious, heathen Other.

At first, the suggestion appealed to Borodin immensely. "I don't know how to thank you," he wrote Stasov. "*I just adore the subject.* But do I have the strength for it? I don't know. If you are afraid of wolves, don't go into the forest. I'll give it a try."[14] With Stasov's help, he devoured almost every relevant work in the Public Library's holdings—including medieval chronicles; other epics, such as the *Zadonshchina;* Nikolai

Karamzin and Sergei Solov'ev's histories; as well as various Turkic songs. Borodin also traveled to Ukraine with his wife that summer to get a better idea of the terrain where Prince Igor's adventures took place, and he learned about the appearance of twelfth-century ladies by studying the frescoes in Kyiv's ancient St. Sophia Cathedral. By September he had already begun composing, but it was slow going. Early in 1870, the composer grew discouraged and abandoned the new undertaking for four years.

When Borodin took up his project again in 1874, he worked on the second act, which introduces the Polovtsians, Prince Igor's nomadic foe. Curious about their music, he turned to the ethnographer Vladimir Mainov, who wrote a colleague in Budapest, Pál Hunfalvy. During the Mongol onslaught in the thirteenth century, some Polovtsians had migrated west, and their descendants still lived around northern Hungary's Matra Mountains. Hunfalvy, who had a strong interest in folklore, had published some of their songs. However, as he pointed out in his reply, by now these erstwhile Polovtsians were almost completely Magyarized. In relaying Hunfalvy's letter, Maikov suggested that Borodin might have more luck by studying the "guttural and jarring sounds" of more pristine, ethnically related Turkic nationalities like the Chuvash, Baskhirs, and Kirgiz. Nevertheless, Mainov forwarded a list of Hungarian folk songs, which included a "special collection of Polovtsian melodies."[15] Although there is no direct evidence that Borodin used any of the latter for the opera, his most authoritative Soviet biographer makes a convincing case for their influence on the Polovtsian Dances. Other sections of the second act draw on more distant exotic sources, including a French edition of Algerian and Tunisian songs the composer had bought in Paris, and even a "chanson nègre" by the American Louis Moreau Gottschalk.[16]

Borodin's musical depiction of the Polovtsians abounds in Orientalist clichés. Their maidens, who appear as the second act begins, are sultry indeed. The opening solo underscores their strident sexuality with its sensuously sinuous melismas (a single syllable sung over several notes) and "iconically erotic" syncopation and descending chromatic line, which, Taruskin suggests, "completes the picture of the seductive East."[17] When the Royal Opera staged *Prince Igor* at London's Covent Garden in 1990, nude bathers gently carried out their ablutions to the melody to further heighten its carnality. As for the men, the strident gyrations in the famous Polovtsian Dances and the jarring Polovtsian March that introduces the third act effectively convey their barbarous savagery. And their leader, Khan Konchak, who is characteristically sung by a bass, lavishes his prisoners with Eastern hospitality.

For all of these genuflections to European conventions about the Asian Other, there are also some striking dissonances. Although the Polovtsians are a formidable foe, Borodin presents them in a remarkably favorable light. Their warriors cause much misery and grief when they raid the Kyivan lands. But war is war. Back in their camp, they are honorable men. The only bad Polovtsian is the secretly baptized Ovlur, who is wicked precisely because he betrays his kinfolk by converting to the enemy's faith.

The contrast with Borodin's portrayal of the Christian Rus' is striking. In the prologue, the boyars and people all join in Prince Igor's capital, Putivl, to wish their leader victory as he sets off against the Polovtsians "for the Faith, for Rus', for the

People."[18] But their show of unity was highly deceptive. As soon as Igor has set off, his brother-in-law, Prince Galitskii, tries to usurp power and begins an orgy of drink and rape. Skula and Eroshka, two Russian fiddlers introduced in the opera as a comic element, desert Igor's army in the prologue, and in act 4 hypocritically save their skins by announcing Igor's return from captivity.

One of the opera's most sympathetic characters is the Polovtsian leader, Khan Konchak. Although he is a formidable warrior, the khan is respectful and solicitous of Prince Igor, whom he holds in captivity. When in a lengthy duet in act 2 Igor rejects Konchak's offer of an alliance, the khan good-naturedly laughs it off, praises his involuntary guest's spirit, and calls in the dancing girls. In a curious reversal of stereotypical gender roles, here Konchak, the Oriental, is the suitor and Igor, the Occidental, is the reluctant maiden. Later on, when Igor's son, Vladimir, tries but fails to escape from Polovtsian captivity, Konchak magnanimously spares his life.

This sympathetic portrayal marked a distinct departure from Stasov's plan, not to mention the original *Igor Tale*. Unusually for a composer, Borodin wrote the opera's libretto himself and, in doing so, made some important changes. If Stasov emphasized the conflict between the Rus' and their alien foes, Borodin toned them down. Thus he deleted a violent fit of rage by the khan and instead stressed his chivalry. Stasov's scenario had also included a group of foreign merchants in Putivl, who join Prince Galitskii's reign of debauchery after Igor leaves, but in Borodin's libretto the usurpers are all native Russians. And Borodin ends his opera differently. According to Stasov, the formulaic ending nuptials had Prince Igor's son return home with the khan's daughter, where the two were joined in a Christian ceremony and presumably lived happily ever after, as Konchakova was fully assimilated into the Rus'. By contrast, Borodin's Vladimir Igor'evich doesn't escape from the Polovtsian camp, and settles down as Konchak's son-in-law.[19]

Toward the conclusion of their duet Konchak offers Igor his freedom if the prince pledges never again to take up arms against the Polovtsians. When Igor obstinately refuses, Konchak responds, "I am like that myself!" It is an interesting remark. In a letter to Stasov about the opera, Borodin wrote, "I cannot escape dualism—not in the form of a dualistic theory in chemistry, nor in biology, philosophy and psychology, or in the Austro-Hungarian monarchy!" The composer's motif of the sun is another example. The symbol of regal power for Louis XIV, France's seventeenth-century *roi soleil*, in the opera it is a metaphor both for the authority of the Christian Prince Igor and the pagan Khan Konchak. The people of Putivl open the prologue by singing to their prince: "All hail the sun in its beauty." Toward the end of act 2, as the Polovtsians dance for Konchak, they salute the khan in a very similar vein: "He is like the sun at midday."[20]

The khan's assertion, "I am like that myself!" underscores one of the Borodin's central messages. If the twelfth-century *Igor Tale* presented the Polovtsians as the Other, in the opera they are binary selves. One Soviet musicologist pointed out that, in *Prince Igor*, Borodin "repeatedly stresses this . . . synthesis of Oriental and Russian."[21] Like its composer, who had both European and Asian blood, *Prince Igor*'s West and East are two sides of the same coin. His Asia is not a Saidian Other, but the Christian

Rus' alter ego. Together they created Russia; both Prince Igor and Khan Konchak are the empire's ancestors. "Nowhere [in the sources] was there any mention of a decisive victory over the Polovtsians," Borodin reminds us.[22] The composer clearly was no musical Skobelev, wielding bass clef and quarter time instead of shashka and knout to subjugate the Orient. As he saw it, Russia did not vanquish the Orient, but joined with it, much as the Christian Prince Vladimir Igorevich was united to the pagan khan's daughter Konchakova in marriage.

\* \* \*

Aleksandr Borodin did not live to complete his opera. With many distractions, both as professor and as an activist for women's higher education, he could only rarely snatch quiet moments to compose. As Borodin joked in a letter, "In winter I can write music only when sickness keeps me from going to work. For this reason, my musical friends, contrary to general custom, always wish me ill rather than good health."[23] By the time a heart attack suddenly claimed his life in 1887, eighteen years after he had first begun, *Prince Igor* remained unfinished. Fortunately, Nikolai Rimsky-Korsakov and a younger composer, Aleksandr Glazunov, recognized its value and picked up where he left off.

The opera's premiere was on October 23, 1890, at St. Petersburg's Mariinsky Theatre. Reflecting Emperor Alexander III's preference for Petr Il'ich Tchaikovsky's more Western style, the Mariinsky's director had hesitated staging it, and there would be fewer than fifty performances before 1917. At the same time, according to the journalist Aleksei Suvorin, *Prince Igor* met with an enthusiastic reception from the audience. Although some grumbled that the Polovtsians were portrayed more positively than the Rus', most contemporaries saw the piece as a patriotic work that celebrated the Orthodox Slav's struggle against the heathen foe.[24]

Borodin had remarked about his composition that it was "essentially a national opera," written for Russians who wanted to see "the origins of our nationality brought back to life on stage."[25] His vision of Russia's past, however, was not hostile to its Asian roots. Albeit with entirely commercial motives, the enterprising impresario Sergei Diaghilev conveyed this well when he began producing some of the more spectacular Polovtsian dances and songs from *Prince Igor* for Parisian audiences in 1907, thereby launching the fashion abroad for the highly orientalist *style russe*.

NOTES

1. I am very grateful for funding from the Social Sciences and Humanities Research Council of Canada, a Brock University Chancellor's Chair for Research Excellence, and the National Humanities Center, which helped support my research on this subject. This chapter benefited enormously from comments and *kritika* by Ralph Locke, Richard Stites, Bernice Glatzer Rosenthal, Anne Schwartz, and Elizabeth Valkenier. A version of this chapter subsequently appeared in my *Russian Orientalism: Asia in the Russian Mind from Peter the Great to*

*the Emigration* (New Haven, Conn.: Yale University Press, 2010), and is reprinted here with kind permission of the publisher.

2. Nikolai Rimsky-Korsakov, *My Musical Life,* trans. Judah A. Joffe (New York: Tudor Publishing, 1935), 181–82.

3. A. Borodin, *"V Srednei Azii." Muzikal'naia kartinka dlia orchestra* (Leipzig: M. P. Beliaev, 1890), 3.

4. Taruskin's argument appears in Stanley Sadie, ed., *The New Grove Dictionary of Opera,* s.v. "Prince Igor" (New York: Grove's Dictionaries of Music, 1992); Edward A. Said, *Orientalism* (New York: Vintage, 1979); Said, *Culture and Imperialism* (New York: Knopf, 1993). The quotation is from Said, *Culture,* 112.

5. On Asianism, see David Schimmelpenninck van der Oye, *Toward the Rising Sun* (DeKalb: Northern Illinois University Press, 2001), 42–60.

6. Stasov's views appear in V. A. Stasov, "Aleksandr Porfir'evich Borodin," *Izbrannye sochineniia* (Moscow: Iskusstvo, 1952), 3:329; for more on Russian families fashioning Tatar ancestors, see Boris Unbegaun, *Russian Surnames* (Oxford: Oxford University Press, 1972), 23–25; N. A. Baskakov, *Russkie familii tiurkskogo proiskhozdeniia* (Moscow: Nauka, 1979).

7. S. A. Dianin, *Borodin* (Moscow: Gos. Muzykal'noe Izdatel'stvo, 1955), 38–39.

8. Glinka's quotation on the common people appears in Edgar Istel and Theodore Baker, "Rimsky-Korsakov, the Oriental Wizard," *The Musical Quarterly* 15, no. 3 (July 1929): 393; his words on the Russian song are in Vladimir Vasil'evich Stasov, "Dvadtsat'-piat' let russkogo iskusstva" in Stasov, *Izbrannye sochineniia* (Moscow: Iskusstvo, 1952), 2:528.

9. Richard Taruskin, *Defining Russia Musically* (Princeton, N.J.: Princeton University Press, 1997), 38–44.

10. Stasov, "Dvadtsat'-piat'," 523–28.

11. Rimsky-Korsakov, *My Musical Life,* 58.

12. Marina Frolova-Walker, *Russian Music and Nationalism* (New Haven, Conn.: Yale University Press, 2007), 153.

13. The definitive biography, *Borodin,* was written by his adopted daughter's son, S. A. Dianin. See also Stasov, "Aleksandr Porfir'evich Borodin," 329–65; André Lischke, *Alexandre Borodine* (Paris: Bleu nuit, 2004). A more impressionistic life is Nina Berberova's *Borodin,* trans. Luba Jurgeson (Paris: Actes Sud, 1989). The quotation is from Stasov, "Aleksandr Porfir'evich Borodin," 347.

14. Italics in the original. A. P. Borodin, *Pis'ma A. P. Borodina* (Moscow: Gosudarstvennoe Izdatel'stvo Muzykal'nyi Sektor, 1927), 1:142.

15. S. A. Dianin, *Borodin,* 194–95, 329.

16. Serge Dianin, *Borodin,* trans. Robert Lord (London: Oxford University Press, 1963), 305–21. This English edition includes an extensive analysis of the composer's principal works. For a more recent discussion of the second act's sources, see Marek Bobéth, *Borodin* (Munich-Salzburg: Musikverlag Emil Katzbichler, 1982), 47–51.

17. Taruskin, *Defining Russia Musically,* 165.

18. A. P. Borodin, *Kniaz' Igor* (N.p.: Edition M. P. Belaieff, n.d.), 11.

19. Firoozeh Kharzai, "Orientalism in Borodin's *Prince Igor*" (unpublished paper), www .anotherbirth.net/orientalism.htm. The text of Stasov's scenario is reproduced in S. A. Dianin, *Borodin,* 70–75.

20. Borodin, *Igor,* 195, 2, 203. The letter to Stasov appears in Borodin, *Pis'ma,* 3:69.

21. G. N. Khubov, *A. P. Borodin* (Moscow: Gosudarstvennoe muzykal'noe izdatel'stvo, 1933), 73.

22. Serge Dianin, *Borodin,* 325n1.

23. Borodin, *Pis'ma,* 2:108.

24. Harlow Robinson, "'If You're Afraid of Wolves, Don't Go into the Forest': On the History of Borodin's *Prince Igor,*" *The Opera Quarterly* 7, no. 4 (Winter 1990–91), 9–11. For these contemporary reactions, see A. S. Suvorin, "'Igor' Opera Borodina," *Novoe Vremia,* October 24, 1890, 2; A. S. Suvorin, "Malenkiia Pis'ma," *Novoe Vremia,* October 30, 1890, 2.

25. Quoted in Alfred Habets, *Alexandre Borodine* (Paris: Librarie Fischbacher, 1893), 63.

Main Mosque in Ufa. Photograph by Sergei Prokudin-Gorskii (1910). Selim-Girei Tevkelev was buried on the grounds in 1885. A predecessor had built the mosque and the adjoining residence in 1830 as the seat of the Orenburg mufti. Library of Congress Prints and Photographs. Public domain. See www.loc.gov/pictures/item/prk2000000797/.

# 17

# Kutlu-Mukhammad Batyr-Gireevich Tevkelev

## (1850–?) AND FAMILY

CHARLES STEINWEDEL

In August 1916, two State Duma deputies, Alexander Kerensky and Kutlu-Mukhammad Batyr-Gireevich Tevkelev, traveled to Turkestan to investigate the causes of an uprising against conscription into labor battalions among the region's native peoples.[1] Both men had connections to central Asia. Kerensky had spent part of his youth in Tashkent where his father served as a school administrator. Tevkelev's great great grandfather, also Kutlu-Mukhammad Tevkelev (1674/75–1766), had traveled to central Asia two centuries before as a translator for Peter the Great. This Tevkelev took the name Aleksei Ivanovich in 1734, served as second in command of Ivan Kirilov's Orenburg Expedition, and became notorious in Bashkiria for his vigorous use of lethal force to suppress the Bashkir uprising of 1735–39. The Tevkelev family's five-generation journey from one Kutlu-Mukhammad considered a tsarist "executioner (*palach*)"[2] to another who was an elected leader of the Muslim fraction in the State Duma tells much about the changing possibilities for elite Muslims in the Russian Empire from the seventeenth century until its collapse in 1917.

The origins of the Tevkelev family are not well known, but lay among Tatar princely families (*murzy*) of the middle Volga region. As the Muscovite state expanded eastward, some Muslims whose lands lay in its path chose to change sovereigns from the heirs of Chinggis Khan to the Muscovite tsar.[3] Tevkelevs had served as translators for Moscow as early as the late seventeenth century. As tsarist forces moved still farther east, some of these new subjects used their linguistic skills and credibility as Muslims to serve as intermediaries between the tsar and Muslim populations. Kutlu-Mukhammad first served under Peter the Great during the Pruth campaign against the Turks in 1711. During Peter's reign (1682–1725) eastward momentum picked up, as did the possible rewards for being part of it. Ever envious of European powers, Peter sought to go overland to build an empire in Asia that would cut Russia into the Asian trade that had become a source of British, French, and Dutch power in the seventeenth and early eighteenth centuries. As part of this effort, Peter told Kutlu-Mukhammad that he would be well rewarded for getting Kazakhs to swear allegiance to the tsar and thus bring the tsar's influence closer to sources of wealth in the East.[4] Peter died before this happened, but not by much. Had he lived another decade, he would have seen Kutlu-Mukhammad convince some Kazakh leaders from the Small and Middle Hordes to become subjects of the tsar. Kutlu-Mukhammad's proposal to further Russia's eastward expansion by creating a fortress to help administer Kazakhs was picked up by another protégé of Peter's, Ivan Kirilov. Kirilov set out in 1734 to build what became not a fortress but the city of Orenburg. In order to take a responsible position in the Orenburg Expedition, though, Kutlu-Mukhammad faced a consequence of Russian policy toward the East. Already in 1680, a decree ordered that servitors convert to Russian Orthodoxy or lose their serfs.[5] Peter and his successor, Anna, intensified pressure on Muslim elites. Peter considered Russia a European country and sought to minimize the influence of Islam. Kutlu-Mukhammad took the name Aleksei Ivanovich. Evidence of Kutlu-Mukhammad's formal conversion to Russian Orthodoxy is lacking, but by taking the name of Peter the Great's father, the "most pious" Tsar Aleksei, Tevkelev certainly sought to project an outward appearance of having done so. In 1734, at about the same time he took his new name, he received his promotion to colonel and second in command of the Orenburg Expedition. His harsh suppression of Bashkir resistance to the Orenburg Expedition and work as a diplomat eventually did earn him the reward promised by Peter. In the eighteenth century, Kutlu-Mukhammad and his family acquired 216,905 *desiatinas* of land, making them some of the wealthiest landowners in the region. Kutlu-Mukhammad became Russia's first Muslim General in 1755 and eventually became a sort of co-governor of Orenburg in the late 1750s.[6] He served in the Ministry of Foreign Affairs in St. Petersburg from 1759 until his death in 1766 at more than ninety years of age.

The next two generations of Tevkelevs pursued military careers with less distinction. During the Pugachev Rebellion of 1773, the Governor of Kazan' called on Kutlu-Mukhammad's son Iusuf/Osip to repeat his father's success in suppressing Muslim rebels. The rebels killed Iusuf/Osip instead.[7] Catherine the Great's 1784 decree permitting Muslim nobles to enter the noble estate did change the family's status. In 1789, Iusuf/Osip's widow, Daria, presented materials to the Ufa Noble Assembly demonstrating the family's noble origins. Catherine made it possible to be openly Muslim and officially a noble.

The next Tevkelev to gain prominence in the empire, Selim-Girei (1805–85) initially followed his father's path into the military. He fought the Turks in 1828–29 and helped suppress the Polish Uprising of 1830. His sister brought the family closer to Russian life by eloping with a Russian Orthodox man, an event recounted by Sergei Aksakov in his classic *Family Chronicle*.[8] Selim-Girei took the family in a different direction—toward the open embrace of Islam. Selim-Girei had a Russian Orthodox name, Aleksandr Petrovich, but ceased using it. He married the eldest daughter of Khan Dzhangir of the Kazakh Inner Horde, making his descendents Chinggisids. Selim-Girei's brother, Batyr-Girei, married his daughter to Dzhangir's son, cementing the families' alliance.[9]

Selim-Girei's turn toward Islam became more intense after he retired from the military. In 1852, he made the pilgrimage to Mecca. When the Orenburg mufti, the head of the Orenburg Muslim Ecclesiastical Assembly, died in 1862, Orenburg governor-general Bezak thought of Tevkelev for the post. Bezak rejected candidates for mufti who lacked a "general education" without which they could "hardly surpass a literal interpretation of the Koran" in order to become "transmitters (*provodniks*) of the idea of a rapprochement (*sblizhenie*) of the Muslim population with the Russians." Tevkelev, on the other hand, enjoyed high status in Russian-speaking society, having served as marshal of the nobility in Bugul'minsk county of Samara province. Finally, and perhaps most important, Tevkelev would be an effective executor of state policy who could overcome the "harmful influence of the mullahs." In 1865, Selim-Girei became Orenburg mufti, the official religious leader of Muslims in the empire's East.[10]

As mufti, Selim-Girei sought to balance enforcing imperial policies with promoting Islam and the interests of Muslims. He issued a fatwa calling on Muslims to learn Russian. When imams in Ufa and Perm provinces aided Bashkirs resisting new military service obligations in 1874, Tevkelev proved as effective at ending the small-scale rebellion as his great grandfather Kutlu-Mukhammad had at ending a large-scale one—although by firing, suspending, or exhorting imams rather than through violence. Yet he sought to promote Islamic practice and warned Orenburg Governor-General Kryzhanovski of the dangers of inflaming Russian Orthodox-Muslim tensions. His loyalty to the emperor was rarely questioned—and never successfully. When Selim-Girei was aging and ill, he sought to retire. When he heard rumors that his replacement might be someone he considered unsatisfactory, he wrote to his superiors, "I, as a Russian nobleman [*kak russkii dvorianin*], for the common good, eagerly agree to continue service."[11] In the nineteenth century, it was still possible to be perceived as a loyal servant of the emperor and an advocate for the interests of the people Selim-Girei administered.

Selim-Girei left no direct descendents. Instead he left two thousand desiatinas of land to endow an orphanage and almshouse. Selim-Girei's nephew Kutlu-Mukhammad followed the family tradition of a military career by starting in the prestigious Corps of Pages, the elite officer training school in St. Petersburg. He rose to the rank of colonel and fought in the Russo-Turkish War of 1877–78. Upon his retirement in 1885, however, he left the military and bureaucracy behind. He returned to his estate in Belebei County in Ufa Province and began to devote his energies to a wide range of social and civic activism. Belebei's overwhelmingly (80 percent) Muslim population and reputation as a backwater certainly helped him transition into local office. Tevkelev's wealth, family connections, and elite education did the rest. Belebei simply did not see many Corps of Pages graduates. By May 1886, Tevkelev was elected marshal of the nobility in Belebei.

By 1887, Kutlu-Mukhammad's tenure as Marshal had raised eyebrows. As marshal of the nobility, Tevekelev headed the county's School Council, which had as its duties opening schools and finding resources for them, inspecting schools, and removing unreliable teachers. Tevkelev's election allowed a Muslim to have supervisory duties for Russian Orthodox education. The Ministers of Education and Internal Affairs raised this concern with Ufa governor Poltoratskii, suggesting that perhaps Tevekelev should not be permitted to be marshal of the nobility. Poltoratskii defended Tevkelev by stating that Tevkelev had done nothing to cause the governor to suspect that he pursued "any tribal or religious goals . . . to the detriment of the interests of Orthodoxy and the Russian population." There was no cause to remove Tevkelev from his position. Tevkelev retained his post, but authorities in St. Petersburg promulgated a law which shifted the marshal of the nobility's educational responsibility to a Ministry of Education official in the event the chairmanship fell to a non-Christian.[12] This was early evidence of a turn against Muslim participation in civic life that would become more apparent in the 1890s and especially after the turn of the century. Perhaps as a result of the evident suspicion, Tevkelev resigned the post of marshal of the nobility after only a year and a half in office. He ran again in 1894, however, and held the post for most of the Romanov dynasty's remaining years.

As part of the first generation of Tevkelevs to come of age in the post–Great Reform era, Tevkelev began to turn some of his energy toward service neither to bureaucracy nor to estate bodies but to the zemstvo and the vision of public service it offered. Muslims had been well represented in the Belebei County zemstvo, where two Muslims served a total of three terms as county Zemstvo Chairman. Tevekelev entered zemstvo service in the 1880s, when over half of the county's zemstvo deputies were Muslim. Tevekelev remained in zemstvo service when political winds turned against Muslim involvement in the zemstvo. The zemstvo counterreform of 1892 did not specifically limit Muslim participation. Representatives from the peasant estate, however, were now selected by the governor rather than elected by their peers. The local administration used this fact, it seems, to reduce Muslim participation substantially. Muslim representation was at a low point in the entire history of Ufa self-administration in the period from 1890 to 1905, decreasing in the provincial zemstvo assembly to only 3 percent in 1903, and to less than 20 percent in the assembly of overwhelmingly Muslim Belebei County.[13]

Tevkelev, with his wealth and status, remained immune from such challenges. He clearly enjoyed the respect of fellow deputies—he often outpolled Russian Orthodox deputies to serve on various commissions and committees, despite the presence of only a few Muslim deputies at the provincial level. He lent his name and time to numerous organizations in a manner typical of leading zemstvo activists, but his chairmanships included both Muslim organizations, such as the Committee for Elderly Muslim Men and Boys, and those not specifically Muslim, such as the Council of the Ufa Cooperative Society.[14]

For all the respect given Tevkelev, he neither sought the most visible zemstvo posts on the county zemstvo board, nor acquired a high profile through frequent interventions regarding the most controversial zemstvo affairs. He typically took positions that required a mastery of money rather than polemical speeches. He served as the zemstvo representative to the government's Peasant Bank and from the noble estate to the Noble Bank. He routinely served on the zemstvo's audit committee and on the committee that had the crucial task of assigning the zemstvo's tax burden. The one major exception to Tevkelev's reluctance to speak out regarded Muslim education. Beginning in about 1898, a group of left-leaning provincial zemstvo deputies identified the spread of education as the "most immediate" task of the zemstvo.[15] The group included mostly non-Muslims, but also Tevkelev and the provincial zemstvo's other Muslim deputy. In 1898 and 1902, Tevkelev moved that the provincial assembly petition the Ministry of Education for the establishment of a Tatar Teachers' School in Ufa modeled on one in Kazan'.[16] The zemstvo supported the petition, but the Ministry turned it down.[17] The collaboration of Tevkelev with progressive non-Muslims prefigured the closer collaboration across the confessional divide that occurred in 1905 and after.

Tevkelev's prominence as a nobleman, a Muslim, and a member of the left-leaning block in the zemstvo enmeshed him deeply in the turbulent politics of 1905, even if he did not stand at the forefront of political activism. Ufa's provincial zemstvo was among the most leftist in the empire. Most zemstvo leaders embraced the challenge to central authority in 1905 and the promises of the October Manifesto. At the same time, local political society fractured as some officials in the provincial administration opposed the zemstvo activists and even the provincial governor, Tsekhanovetskii, for being neither sufficiently supportive of tsarist authority nor sufficiently harsh in their suppression of rebellion. Muslim marshals of the nobility such as Tevkelev and Sultanov, the son of the current mufti, were not alone in supporting the governor and rejecting efforts to get him replaced. Being associated with opponents of autocracy had additional implications if one were Muslim, however. Those on the right accused Tevkelev and Sultanov of trying to "form a Muslim state out of Ufa province and [the provinces] around it."[18] Priests in Belebei County blamed Tevkelev for apostasies among the "benighted masses of Tatars" because Tevkelev had supposedly announced a more expansive view of new policies of religious toleration than existed in law.[19] Churchmen's suspicions of Muslim activism dating back decades combined with a more general hostility toward Muslim political participation.

In the wake of 1905, such suspicions grew in part due to the mobilization of Muslims that the new political context made possible. Mosque construction and the number of men taking the examination for position of mullah increased. Greater press freedom brought about the growth of a Tatar-language Muslim press. An October 1906 decree restored the ability of Muslims in the zemstvo's peasant curia to elect zemstvo deputies once again. 1906 also saw the creation of the first all-imperial legislative body, the State Duma. Muslims mobilized with zeal to participate in both the zemstvo and the Duma. On the local level, Muslim deputies of the provincial zemstvo grew from about 6 percent in 1906 to approximately 15 percent in 1909.[20] Muslims made up nearly half of the deputies elected to the Belebei zemstvo in 1909. Muslim turnout for elections to the First State Duma in early 1906 was equally enthusiastic. When the provincial electoral assembly met in March 1906, Muslims had an absolute majority (74–70) among electors. As the vote totals became clear, Muslim expectations for the elections rose. Earlier Muslim leaders had discussed the need to have two of the province's ten seats reserved for Muslims or to have proportional representation from Muslim and non-Muslim communities. Now, though, some Muslim leaders argued that Muslims should hold all ten of Ufa's places in the Duma. Since Muslims would be less likely to be elected from other provinces with smaller, scattered Muslim populations, some believed it necessary to have a large delegation from Ufa. Other members of the Muslim leadership, including Tevkelev, rejected such a move because they wanted to maintain alliances they had developed with leftist Russians. In the end, Tevkelev helped negotiate an agreement that six Muslim and four Russian deputies would represent the province, and that the Muslims could approve or veto the Russians selected.[21] Tevkelev himself became a Duma deputy and was reelected for each of the four Duma convocations before 1917.

Tevkelev thus became one of 25 Muslim Duma deputies (of 499) who eventually filled the Tauride Palace in St. Petersburg. Tevkelev let others do most of the talking, much as he had in the Ufa provincial zemstvo. He made no major interventions in the First Duma. The emperor disbanded the First Duma for being too radical. The second, however, had even more Muslims—36 out of 518—than the first. With seven Muslim deputies, Ufa province had the largest provincial Muslim representation in the body. Tevkelev did not speak in the Second Duma, either. On June 3, 1907, the government dissolved the Second Duma, and the Tsar issued new electoral rules for the next Duma. The new system increased representation of the nobility and reduced that of peasants. Limiting non-Russian representation was also a major objective. According to the decree announcing the new electoral rules, the State Duma was "created for the strengthening of the Russian [*Rossiiskogo*] state," so the Duma must also be "Russian [*russkoi*] in spirit." The empire's other ethnic groups (*narodnosti*) must have their needs representatived in the Duma, but "they must not be present in numbers which give them the opportunity to be arbiters of purely Russian questions."[22] The new electoral system had an immediate effect on the size of the Muslim contingent, which fell from 37 to 10.[23] Most of the decrease resulted from the greater voice given to noble electors, among which there numbered few Muslims, and a decrease in rural electors, among whom Muslims had greater representation. As a result of the relatively large number of Muslim nobles in Ufa province, 40 percent of Muslim Duma deputies from the entire empire came from that one province.

Much as the 1907 Duma electoral rules were intended to reduce Muslim participation in that body, so the Ufa governor began to make the province's zemstvos more reliably "Russian" institutions. In 1909, Ufa governor Kliucharev eliminated those who promoted Muslim interests from the Belebei zemstvo leadership, regardless of whether they themselves were Muslim. He explained to the Minister of Internal Affairs that Muslims had united with leftist Russians to form a "Kadet-Muslim bloc" in Belebei. In order not to be cut off from this bloc, Kliucharev argued, Russians were "required to concede much to the Muslims in their purely national demands." Muslims in the zemstvo appeared intent on forcing Russian monarchists out of public positions and realizing "Tatar-national demands at public expense." Kliucharev denied confirmation to four people elected to the Belebei zemstvo board: a Muslim and three Russian Orthodox whom the governor accused of having sympathies toward Muslims.[24] In 1912, Governor Kliucharev's replacement, Peter Bashilov, reduced the power of Muslims in the Ufa zemstvos even further. Two Muslim noble families, the Teregulovs and Enikeevs, had held land in common since the eighteenth century. Individually their holdings were not large but together 149 heads of household of the two families controlled more than 7,300 desiatinas of land. As many as one hundred participated in the first *curiia* for zemstvo elections, and they usually sympathized with the zemstvo's left.[25] In the first zemstvo elections in 1912, the local administration allowed the two families to participate in elections in the first, the landowner's, curiia. Eleven of eighteen deputies elected from the curiia were Muslim. Belebei zemstvo board chairman Vasilii I. Bunin petitioned the Senate, arguing that the Teregulovs and Enikeevs did not have proper documentation to participate in the first curiia's deliberations. The Senate agreed with Bunin's petition, denied the two families the right to participate in the first curiia's elections, and annulled the elections that had taken place. Without the participation of the Teregulovs and Enikeevs in the first curiia for the second set of elections, Tevkelev was the lone Muslim nobleman and the lone liberal elected. He resigned as a zemstvo deputy in protest.

As state actions caused the ranks of Muslim activists in elective office to dwindle, Tevkelev took on a somewhat greater role in the Duma. He became chairman of the Duma's Muslim fraction. His voice was heard in Duma session for the first time in June 1908, when he spoke against the Ministry of Internal Affairs's budget, which allocated only one five-hundredth of its budget for Muslim confessional institutions despite the substantial proportion of the empire's population that practiced Islam. Tevkelev spoke the following year in favor of a legislative project that would have fleshed out promises of religious toleration by making movement from one confession to another easier. He made two short interventions in 1910 to convey the Muslim fraction's opposition to the Ministry of Internal Affairs's closing of Muslim schools and its rejection of the government's proposed land laws in Turkestan before the overall administration of the area had been reformed. This was the sum of his interventions in Duma debates for the five years the Third Duma met.

The Muslim contingent in the Fourth Duma, elected in 1912, was even smaller—only six deputies—than it had been in the third. Tevkelev at first declined the post of chairman of the Muslim fraction, then reluctantly took it once again when his replacement, Gais Enikeev, became too busy with work on Duma commissions. Although Tevkelev remained in the Duma to its very end, the government's successful efforts to limit non–Russian Orthodox representation made a legislative strategy for realizing Muslim interests seem improbable. Tevkelev and the five other Muslim Duma deputies continued to speak in favor of greater fairness in the distribution of state resources to the Muslims and an end to state harassment, but their collective voice was much diminished. The position of a Muslim legislator also became more difficult during the Fourth Duma. The Ministry of Internal Affairs created publications such as *V mire musul'manstva,* which contained criticism of the Muslim Duma delegation. Tevekelev and another deputy were criticized for being late to a Duma session declaring the body's support for the war until a victorious conclusion.[26] They managed to get statements declaring Muslim support for the cause into the Duma's record only in January 1915. Tevkelev's trip to Tashkent with Kerensky marked the last major endeavor a Tevkelev would undertake for the tsarist state and its institutions.

In response to frustrations within the Duma, Tevkelev turned toward activism outside of the Duma's walls. He joined members of the Muslim fraction to publish a newspaper, *Milliat,* and called a Muslim congress to address efforts to reform Muslim confessional institutions. He worked to develop the Muslim political party, "Ittifak al-Muslimin," a project that was disrupted by the outbreak of World War I. Other extraparliamentary initiatives yielded greater success. Tevkelev and the Muslim fraction called a congress of Muslim philanthropic societies that resulted in the "Temporary Muslim Committee for the Rendering of Assistance to Warriors and their Families." Realizing that the Muslim fraction's small numbers left them in need for more day-to-day support, Tevkelev called on Muslim populations in major cities to send additional people to work with the Muslim fraction. This action caused one person mobilized to St. Petersburg, future Bashkir revolutionary Zaki Validi Togan, to consider Tevkelev "self-critical" and "brave."[27]

After the February Revolution, Tevkelev was chosen a member of the "Temporary Central Bureau of Muslims of Russia," but he disappeared from events soon afterward. Undoubtedly, his advanced age of sixty-seven years in 1917 had something to do with this. Building a new regime in Russia would be a task for younger men and women, and ones with less aristocratic roots. It is fitting, too, that a family so closely associated with the making of the empire disappeared about the time of the empire's demise. The empire had grown powerful and expanded due in large part to its ability to draw into the tsar's service Muslims such as the Tevkelevs. Some two centuries of service left the Tevkelevs with social status and wealth. After 1905, however, state officials gradually worked to squeeze out the last of the Tevkelevs. In the eighteenth century, one Kutlu-Mukhammad Tevkelev had sided with the imperial state against the interests of most Muslims in Bashkiria. In the early twentieth century, another Kutlu-Mukhammad Tevkelev sided with the people. He had been left with little choice.

Notes

1. Daniel Brower, *Turkestan and the Fate of the Russian Empire* (London: Routledge Curzon, 2003), 168–69; Richard Abraham, *Alexander Kerensky: First Love of the Revolution,* (New York: Columbia University Press, 1987), 9–12, 107–109.

2. Bulat S. Davletbaev, *Bol'shaia Oka: Istoriia sela,* (Ufa: RIO Ministerstva pechati i sredstv massovoi informatsii, 1992), 17.

3. I. V. Erofeeva, "Sluzhebnye i issledovatel'skie materialy rossiiskogo diplomata A. I. Tevkeleva po istorii i etnografii Kazakhskoi stepi," in *Istoriia kazakhstana v russkikh istochnikakh XVI–XX vekov,* comp. Erofeeva (Almaty: Daik-Press, 2005), 3:6.

4. Ia. V. Khanykov, "Raznyia bumagi general maiora Tevkeleeva ob orenburgskom krae i o Kirgiz-Kaisatskikh ordakh, 1762 god," *Vremennik Imperatorskogo moskovskogo obshchestva istorii i drevnostei Rossiiskikh* 13 (1852): 15.

5. *Pol'noe sobranie zakonov Rossiiskoi imperii* (hereafter cited as *PSZRI*), series I, vol. 2, no. 823 (St. Petersburg, 1830), 867.

6. Dmitrii Iu. Arapov, "Pervyi russkii general-musul'manin Kutlu-Mukhammad Tevkelev," *Sbornik russkogo istoricheskogo obshchestva* 5, no. 153 (2002): 36.

7. Sergei A. Golubtsov, ed., *Pugachevshchina* (Moscow: Gosudarstvennoe Izdatel'stvo, 1931), 3:231.

8. Sergei T. Aksakov, *The Family Chronicle*, trans. M. C. Beverly (New York: E. P. Dutton, 1961), 216–19.

9. Erofeeva, "Sluzhebnye i issledovatel'skie materialy," 46–47.

10. Rossiiskii gosudarstvennyi istoricheskii arkhiv (hereafter cited as RGIA), f. 821, op. 8, d. 601, ll. 73, 85–85ob, 86. Quotations from Bezak, l. 73.

11. RGIA, f. 821, op. 8, d. 754, l. 114.

12. RGIA, f. 1287, op. 27, d. 1497, ll. 4–5ob., 20 i ob.

13. Before the 1890 statutes, as many as 18 percent of the provincial assembly and 65 percent of the Belebei assembly were Muslim.

14. Larissa Iamaeva, *Musul'manskie deputaty Gosudarstvennoi dumy Rossii, 1906–1917* (Ufa: Kitap, 1998), 304.

15. *Protokoly XXIV Ufimskogo Gubernskogo Zemskogo Sobraniia 1898 goda* (Ufa, 1899): 145.

16. Ibid., December 10, 1898, 63.

17. The provincial zemstvo also allocated five hundred rubles a year for the translation and publication of brochures in Tatar (Ibid., 134).

18. Soiuz Russkago Naroda, *Gosudarstvennaia izmena* (St. Petersburg, 1906), 26, 79.

19. Nikolai Egorov, "Otkliki iz eparkhii. Kak inye ponimaiut zakon 17 April 1905," *Ufimskie Eparkhial'nye Vedomosti*7 (April 1, 1906): 483–86.

20. Statisticheskii otdel Ufimskoi Gubernskoi Upravy, *Istoriko-statisticheskiia tablitsy deiatel'nosti Ufimskikh zemstv. K sorokoletiiu sushchestvovaniia zemstv Ufimskoi gubernii, 1875–1914*, ed. M. P. Krasil'nikov (Ufa: Pechat', 1915), 226–28.

21. Ivan Zhukovskii, "Moim izbirateliam," *Ufimskoi zemskoi gazety*, May 5, 1906, 3–5.

22. *PSZRI*, series III, vol. 27, no. 29,240 (June 3, 1907): 320, 324.

23. Regarding the change in the Duma's electoral law on June 3, 1907, and its effect on Muslim representation, see Rustem Tsiunchuk, "Peoples, Regions, and Electoral Politics: The State Dumas and the Constitution of New National Elites," in *Russian Empire: Space, People, Power, 1700–1930*, ed. Jane Burbank, Mark von Hagen, and Anatolyi Remnev (Bloomington: Indiana University Press, 2007), especially 380–89.

24. RGIA, f. 1288, op. 2, 1909 razdel, d. 25b: 3ob, 7, 8ob-10, letter from acting governor Tolstoy to the MVD Main Administration on Affairs of the Local Economy, December 1, 1909.

25. Individual members of the two families held between 35 and 154 desiatinas each. *Ufimskie Gubernskie vedomosti*, prilozhenie k no. 60 (1912), 16–19. RGIA, f. 1288, op. 2, 1909 Razdel, d. 46, 35–38ob, svod svedenii o khode vyborov zemskikh glasnykh na trekhletie s 1912 po 13 gubernii.

26. Iamaeva, *Musul'manskie deputaty*, 205.

27. Zaki Validi Togan, *Vospominaniia*, trans. G. Shafikov and A. Iuldashbaev (Ufa: Kitap, 1994), 162.

M. Zhukovskii, *Doctor Petr Badmaev* (1880). Wikimedia Commons.

# 18

# Petr Badmaev

## *(1851–1920)*

DAVID MCDONALD

As much as any other figure of his time, Petr Aleksandrovich Badmaev embodied the conflicting notes of ambition, ambivalence, optimism, and suspicion that marked Russia's career as an imperial power in East Asia during the last decades of Romanov rule. Historians know him best as the author of an elaborate 1893 memorandum advocating Russia's historic mission to extend the "white tsar's" sway over eastern China and Tibet. Contemporary observers and posterity alike also regarded him as a symbol of the autocracy's decadence or disarray during its final years under Nicholas II, one of those shadowy figures like his sometime associate Rasputin who played an unsavory role "behind the scenes of tsarism."[1] While these perspectives certainly offer useful approaches to understanding Badmaev as a "personality of empire," they also downplay or submerge two other salient facts—his visible exoticness as a Buriat who made his livelihood in the imperial metropolis, and the degree to which his improbable career, and historical notoriety, themselves resulted from the same forces that propelled Russia into East Asia during the years after 1855.

Even before Badmaev came to the attention of official St. Petersburg in the 1890s, his biography could have served as a success story for Russian rule in Asia. He had entered the world in 1852 as Zhamsaran Badmaev, the youngest son of a modest Buriat cowherd living in the hill country southeast of Lake Baikal. However humble his origins, Badmaev came from a family driven by strong ambition. Two of his older brothers, Sultim and Ampil, had made their way to St. Petersburg by the 1860s, studying and teaching Asian languages at St. Petersburg University and, notably, converting to Christianity. Sultim also profited from his childhood training in Tibetan medicine at the lamaist Buddhist monastery in Aga, opening a clinic offering remedies consisting of the herbs, powders, and other applications prescribed by this "ancient" healing art.

Young Zhamsaran emulated his brothers' ambition and wanderlust. Rather than attend a state-sponsored primary school for Buriat children, he enrolled in the early 1860s in the Irkutsk *gimnaziia* as a "pensioner of His Majesty" Alexander II, thanks to an appeal by Ampil. According to family tradition, Zhamsaran had gained his parents' permission for this unusual educational choice, persuading them that he wished to serve the "white tsar."

Following his graduation, Badmaev joined his brothers in St. Petersburg, where he studied in the university's Oriental Department (*Vostochnyi fakul'tet*). Like Sultim and Ampil, Zhamsaran also accepted Christianity, taking the baptismal name Petr Aleksandrovich: his patronymic honored his godfather, Grand Duke Aleksandr Aleksandrovich, the future Alexander III. Although none of the available records suggest why a grand duke would assume this role, it seems plausible that the education and conversion of a Buriat from farthest Siberia exemplified to Alexander a model for the civilization of the empire's non-Christian *inorodtsy,* the Russian version of the "civilizing mission" proclaimed by European imperialists at the time.

In 1876, Badmaev entered imperial service in the Asiatic Department of the Ministry of Foreign Affairs, where he made a "commonplace" (*zauriadnyi*) career unmarked by advancement or special recognition. His most recent biographer sees this record as a sign of Badmaev's thoroughgoing mediocrity, but other explanations merit consideration. Likely employed for his linguistic skills, Badmaev occupied a doubly marginal status in the ministry, as in imperial society: he was visibly Asian in a bureaucracy that was almost exclusively European; as important, he lacked the connections and social antecedents of most ministry officials, who sprang overwhelmingly from the landowning gentry or capital-city aristocracy.[2]

If Badmaev achieved little distinction in his official career, he certainly did in his career as a doctor. After his arrival in St. Petersburg, Badmaev had assisted at his brother's Tibetan medicine dispensary. When Sultim died in 1873, Badmaev, despite his lack of formal training, took over the "practice," and went on to enjoy great success in the years that followed. By early 1893, he claimed to have seen "227,506 visitors" seeking "medical assistance" between 1875 and 1892. Moreover, he estimated that he consulted with approximately 17,000–20,000 patients annually, including referrals by local physicians.[3] Interestingly, whether due to his godfather's favor or his contacts with prominent figures in "authority [*vlasti*], learning, literature, and the press," Badmaev rose from the ninth to the sixth steps in the Table of Ranks in just over three years before he formally left the foreign ministry in 1894.

Badmaev's careers as an official and as a "Tibetan doctor" owed much to the shifting cultural and political contexts of late-nineteenth-century Europe and St. Petersburg alike. The Far East had emerged as a new zone of imperial contestation among the European powers, with China's evident weakening following the Opium Wars and Taiping Rebellion, as well as the emergence of a dynamic Meiji empire in Japan. If the exploits of Przhevalskii and Cherniaev thrilled Russian readers after the miseries of the Crimean War, the education and careers of the brothers Badmaev attested to the growth of an intellectual infrastructure in response to the increasing strategic significance of the Far East as an area of Russian interest, particularly as apprehensions grew in ruling circles over the possibilities of Chinese encroachment into the neighboring Russian territory.[4] By early 1893, the newly appointed Minister of Finances, S. Iu. Witte, had persuaded Alexander III of the necessity of constructing a rail line across Siberia to the Pacific; among the many boons he promised from this colossal project, Witte included the prospect of a "peaceful penetration" into China by fostering trade to increase the Middle Kingdom's dependence on Russian influence.

Similarly, increasing European involvement in East Asia brought in its train a parallel fascination with Asian culture as imbued with an ancient wisdom lost or corrupted in a modern materialistic Europe, itself a small part of a larger spiritualist movement that swept belle époque society. This view found particularly trenchant expression in Madame E. P. Blavatskaia's Theosophy, a quasi-religion that claimed to incorporate authentic Asian spirituality. Equally notably, the future Nicholas II had spent more than a year on an Asian version of the traditional "grand tour," visiting India, Japan, Thailand, and other destinations under the tutelage of Prince E. E. Ukhtomskii, a newspaper publisher and leading Easternizer (*vostochnik*), espousing Russia's historical destiny in Asia. This quickening interest in Asia helps explain the notable success of the Tibetan medical practice Badmaev inherited from his brother.

Borne on these currents, on February 13, 1893, Badmaev submitted to his godfather, Alexander III, an expansive memorandum that initiated the next phase of his own career and of Russia's own entanglement in East Asia. The length and detail of this document and the recommendations it offered suggest that Badmaev had long reflected on the grand possibilities that the new rail route opened for Russia. As such his proposal represented an interesting pastiche of prevalent views of Asia and its relationship with Russia, combining the spiritual perspective espoused by Easternizers like Ukhtomskii with the attractions of "peaceful penetration" that Witte had promised in his advocacy of the trans-Siberian route. Badmaev argued that the newly undertaken construction of the great rail route would bring Russia into closer contact with the "life and interests of the East." He urged a careful consideration of Russia's future role in Asia, bearing in mind "our historical calling, since the name of the white tsar is used in the East with reverence [*obaianie*]";[5] elsewhere in this memorandum, he suggested that Buddhist populations in East Asia saw in the "white tsar" the embodiment of the "tara" from religious prophecy. The vista and policies he laid before his imperial master rivaled in their comprehensiveness and ambition Witte's own depiction of the transformation that the Siberian route would bring to Russia's economy and international stature.

Badmaev proposed the construction of a branch from the trunk line southward to the central Chinese provincial capital of Lanzhou, 1500 versts south of the Russian frontier. This route would bring a series of notable benefits to the Russian Empire. Lanzhou's proximity to silk- and tea-producing areas would afford Russia an advantage in export trade, while yielding access to a lucrative Chinese market. More importantly, this branch line and a Russian presence in the Chinese heartland would help focus and rally simmering discontent among the Chinese, Mongolian, and Tibetan inhabitants of the area. Badmaev argued that the days of the reigning Qing dynasty were numbered: to pre-empt the possibility of anarchy or a European intervention, the Russian government should itself take steps to secure the allegiance of these populations, cementing an age-old historical relationship with Asia that reached back to Mongol times.[6]

This memorandum arrived on Alexander III's desk with a cover letter from Witte, who had learned of Badmaev's aspirations from their mutual acquaintance Ukhtomskii. Witte heartily endorsed the memorandum's proposals, most notably the use of private initiative to construct the spur line from Lanzhou to the Trans-Siberian Railway. Doing so would supply the Russian route with valuable trade that could help cover the great expense of this endeavor; indeed, Badmaev had offered the prospect of virtually monopolizing China's export traffic. Witte also underscored Badmaev's depiction of Russia as a mediator between Asia and Europe. Most of all, he emphasized Badmaev's authority on the matter, referring to his "Buriat descent" (*proiskhozhdenie*), which rendered him "closely acquainted" with affairs among "the peoples of the Mongol-Tibetan-Chinese East."[7]

Alexander III reacted to the memorandum with deep ambiguity. In a note written upon the text, he declared, "All this is so new, unusual and fantastic, that it is difficult to believe in the possibility of success."[8] Nonetheless, he agreed that the state should support Badmaev's initiation of the project with a two-million-ruble loan at highly favorable rates. Badmaev used this money to establish the "Badmaev & Co. Trading House," which would serve as the organizational base of operations that would include trading and the establishment of links with the indigenous populations of Mongolia, eastern China, and, it was hoped, Tibet. In February 1894, he arrived in Chita to oversee matters in person. Very quickly, the company began to purchase homes and set up shops in the region, as well as establishing a hotel in Chita and publishing a newspaper in Russian and Buriat.

The years 1893–97 marked a brief high-water mark in Badmaev's career as empire builder. Notwithstanding the premature death in late 1894 of Alexander III, his erstwhile patron and godfather, Badmaev enjoyed the "confidence" (*doverie*) of the new ruler, Nicholas II, thanks in large measure to the initial support of Ukhtomskii. In a series of letters and reports to the new emperor, Badmaev documented an impressive variety of activities: the purchase or rental of properties across eastern Siberia and Mongolia, ostensibly for the conduct of trade; two trips to China, with sojourns in Beijing to speak with "Mongol princes"; the dispatch of emissaries across Mongolia, northern China, and the borderlands of Tibet, to cultivate links and gather intelligence from inhabitants; and his reception of various religious and other luminaries at his own headquarters.

Often, these reports also offered Badmaev's advice on various matters of policy. Following the Japanese Empire's victory in the Sino-Japanese War of 1894–95, he strongly urged Nicholas and the Russian government to ensure that Japan did not acquire any territory on the Asian mainland; similarly, through dispatches from his local agents, he alleged Japanese efforts to infiltrate local courts in Mongolia and Tibet. At other times, he proffered advice and criticism of Russian policy or its representatives in eastern Siberia or China.

These reports also noted the steadily increasing resistance Badmaev encountered from imperial officials in St. Petersburg and eastern Siberia, which combined to bring an end to his empire building in the Far East. Witte, who had originally conveyed Badmaev's 1893 memorandum to Alexander III, quickly turned on the Buriat when he received orders to provide Badmaev with yet another two-million-ruble loan. The minister of finance doggedly resisted disbursing the funds until ordered to by Alexander III, after numerous entreaties from Badmaev. During his time in the Far East, Badmaev's "private" activities ran afoul of imperial authorities in the Trans-Baikal region and Russian representatives in Mongolia and China. He bemused the former in his repeated claims to intimacy with Nicholas II, a relationship he trumpeted to great effect among his fellow Buriats, as well. Later, in 1900–1901, he spearheaded Buriat opposition to government plans to restrict Buriat autonomy. Meanwhile, for their part, various ministry agents stationed in Mongolia and China chronicled Badmaev's unilateral meddling in Chinese and Mongolian politics, often at cross-purposes with Russian policy.

Throughout this period, Badmaev petitioned Nicholas II repeatedly, seeking new loans—with limited success, given Witte's resistance—and support for his policies. Thus, in February 1895, he proposed a thoroughgoing reorganization of administrative responsibilities in eastern Siberia, placing these territories in the charge of two quasi-governors-general, who would rank equally with ministers, while exercising full authority over all policy spheres in their territories and overseeing Russian diplomatic agents in China and Japan.[9] In a letter that he copied to Nicholas in late 1896, Badmaev reproached Witte for his recalcitrance, accusing him of abusing his influence over the tsar and warning that the ruler would find others to do his will. In the meantime, he continued to seek Nicholas's financial support, in letters that alternated reports on his activities and plans with pleas for another two million rubles.[10]

Badmaev's efforts proved unavailing. By 1898, Witte had successfully dissuaded Nicholas from providing any further financial support to Badmaev's plans; several years later, the latter filed for bankruptcy, leaving little demonstrable benefit from the considerable expenditures he had made on behalf of the "white tsar."

Although he never again achieved the political prominence and entrée to the emperor that he had enjoyed for those six years, Badmaev did not fade into obscurity. Instead he sought repeatedly to regain his lost influence, while continuing to advance the cause of Russia's role in Asia. Also, as the autocracy found itself under mounting threat from military defeat and revolution, he sought to ingratiate himself with Nicholas II and his family as the Asiatic counterpart to the other purportedly authentic Russians who wandered in and out of the imperial retinue during the dynasty's final years.[11]

During his time in Chita, Badmaev had begun recruiting young Buriat boys for enrollment in a school he had established in 1894 in St. Petersburg. He sought through this endeavor to create a cadre of young, educated servants of the Russian Empire who could study and strengthen cultural contacts with Mongolia and Tibet.[12] He also provided support for such Buriat youth as G. C. Tsybikov—one of the first outsiders to explore Tibet—to attend St. Petersburg University.[13] Interestingly, his Buriat charges and their families bridled at the school's instruction in Orthodoxy and Badmaev's attempts to baptize students, apparently without their parents' consent.

In addition, he helped broker contact—through Tsybikov and others—between the Russian government and yet another prominent Buriat, Agvan Dorzhiev, a Buddhist monk and intimate of the thirteenth Dalai Lama. Dorzhiev visited Russia on numerous occasions, beginning in 1896, and fled with the Dalai Lama to Urga [Ulaanbataar] when the British troops on the Younghusband "expedition" invaded Tibet.[14] Badmaev helped Dorzhiev and fellow Buddhists in the Russian capital build a temple in St. Petersburg, despite considerable opposition from the Orthodox Church: it opened in 1913.[15]

Badmaev continued to advertise his own vision of Russia's destiny as the leading power in Asia. In 1900, he published an expanded version of his 1893 memorandum, now under the title *Russia and China*—which he reissued in 1905, following the debacle of the Russo-Japanese War. He also contributed articles to conservative newspapers and labored over the translation of the *Zhud Shi* [*sic*], the foundational text of Tibetan medicine. Indeed, his Tibetan medical clinic continued to provide a thriving livelihood—to his numerous properties in St. Petersburg, he added after 1900 a chauffeur-driven automobile and a "wonderfully furnished" sanatorium in a prestigious suburb, where he "healed the aristocratic elite with Tibetan grasses."[16]

Yet these years also saw the emergence of an underside of European and Russian views of Asia and Asians, especially with regard to Badmaev and his ambitions. Alongside the undoubted interest in Asia that marked the late nineteenth century, there also arose a decidedly more fearful view, rooted in biological theories of race and a turn in some circles to historical philosophies stressing the decline or endangerment of western civilization—in Russia, these would crystallize into a chiliastic Eurasianism in the years following the maelstrom of war and revolution that engulfed the empire after 1914. Such notions as the Yellow Peril, or such literary figures as Dr. Fu Manchu—who made his first appearance in 1912—drew attention to the threat emanating from an awakening Asia that threatened to overwhelm the West with sensuality and numberless hordes. In Russia, these apprehensions found expression most notably in the poem "Pan-Mongolism," written in 1894 by religious philosopher Vladimir Solov'ev, who warned of a providentially inspired overthrow of Russia and Europe by a new yellow horde.[17]

These views certainly framed contemporaries' characterizations of Badmaev. The poet Alexander Blok, later author of "The Scythians," referred to him as a "wise and cunning Asiatic." Writing of the "Buriat doctor Badmaev," Witte observed, "[He] belongs among the most typical Asiatics [*aziatsy*]; he is undoubtedly highly intelligent; as concerns his treatments, he possesses a large proportion of charlatanism." For his part, V. V. Shul'gin recalled Badmaev as "the Tibetan magician [*kudesnik*]," much as the early Soviet historian V. P. Semennikov underlined his exoticism as the "Tibetan doctor Badmaev" in the subtitle of his own book.[18]

In the years after 1900, Badmaev also began to encounter controversy, even as his medical practice and financial stature grew. St. Petersburg physicians began to publish articles questioning his qualifications as well as the scientific bases of Tibetan medicine or his translation of the *Zhud Shi*—Badmaev defended himself energetically against all of these charges. Nonetheless, repeated calls to close his clinic brought no result, a sign of the protection he enjoyed either from Court or from high official-dom in St. Petersburg.

The period from 1912 until Nicholas II's abdication in 1917 saw the final phase of Badmaev's career, one in which he became enmeshed in the sorts of intrigue that came increasingly to symbolize for many the irredeemable decadence of the autocracy. In 1912, Badmaev took part in the events that led to Rasputin's expulsion from St. Petersburg. By 1916, however, Badmaev and the same Rasputin—restored to his former favor at court, particularly with the departure of Nicholas II for the front in mid-1915—collaborated in an effort to save the empire and dynasty from the strains of war and revolution. Indeed, throughout the war, Badmaev undertook a concerted campaign to regain the intimacy with power that he had enjoyed all too briefly in the mid-1890s.[19] He peppered Nicholas, Alexandra, the dowager empress, and other courtiers with letters offering in turn his advice on matters of state and protestations of his undying loyalty for monarchy and autocracy in face of the growing socialist threat.[20] With Rasputin's aid, Badmaev sought to place his patients and associates in high state positions; thus, he succeeded in gaining the appointment of A. D. Protopopov as minister of internal affairs in September 1916.[21] These communications also included complimentary copies of such publications as *Wisdom in the Russian People,* which he sent to the members of the imperial family in January 1917. This latter opus foresaw Russia's salvation and future glory in the development of agriculture and, as he wrote to the Empress Alexandra Fëdorovna, in the "spread of private dairy farming [*molochnoe khoziaistvo*]" through the aid of women from all parts of society.[22]

In February 1917, even as the empire and dynasty slid toward the revolution that engulfed them, Badmaev sought one last time to revive the imperial dream he had first articulated in 1893, requesting from Nicholas II financial and institutional support for a project to link the port of Murmansk and a new installation he named "Port Romanov" with the Trans-Siberian trunk. To Badmaev, this project promised Russia's ultimate preeminence in both Europe and Asia, since the former would depend on Russia as a conduit for Asian goods, while the latter would come equally to rely on Russian support for its own economic development. Obviously this dream went unfulfilled.

According to family records and reminiscences, the last three years of Badmaev's life—from the February Revolution in 1917 until his death in the summer of 1920—proved a difficult denouement amid the fall of the autocracy and the privations brought on by successive revolutions and civil war. These years saw him continuing to ply his specialty in increasingly difficult conditions punctuated by a series of arrests beginning in the fall of 1917, when the provisional government sent him and several other former courtiers to Helsinki for questioning aboard the erstwhile imperial yacht *Polar Star,* before permitting him to return to Petrograd.[23] The succeeding Bolshevik government requisitioned his suburban home and much of his apartment in Petrograd. Badmaev's unrepentant monarchism led as well to detention by the

Cheka on several occasions, but he enjoyed the protection of former patients in the new bureaucracy, who always managed to gain his release.[24] An interesting glimpse into this stage of his life comes from a statement he addressed to a Cheka officer named "Com[rade] Medved'" in August 1919.[25] Badmaev twice referred to himself as an "old man of 109 years of age" and a "doctor of Tibetan-Mongolian medicine." Moreover, as he told his investigators, "I am international by my profession. I cured persons of all nations, all classes and persons of extreme parties—terrorists and monarchists. A mass of proletarians were cured by me, as well as wealthy and aristocratic [*znatnyi*] classes." He died a year later, on July 29, 1920, after yet another brief imprisonment.[26]

For the most part, historians have followed Badmaev's contemporaries in their depictions. An investigative commission for the provisional government identified him as a significant member among the "dark forces" that surrounded Nicholas's throne, a perspective reinforced by his first Soviet chronicler, V. P. Semennikov, whose publication of the Badmaev "archive" began with the war years before turning back to the Asian "adventure" of the 1890s. His most recent biographer sees in him a symptom of the "serious illness of autocratic power in Russia,"[27] a view also encountered in Western historiography: both literatures associate him with the succession of favorites and hangers-on who appeared with alarming frequency at the imperial court—Rasputin, Iliodor, Monsieur Philippe, or "Bezobrazov & Co.," to name only a few. To greater or lesser degree, these accounts emphasize his opportunism, his sham practice of Tibetan medicine, and—implicitly or explicitly—his exoticness as an "Asiatic" or "Tibetan doctor."

Photographs of Badmaev, read against the background of his career and aspirations, suggest a more complex characterization, bound up with Russia's experience as an Asian empire. One in particular, taken in 1914, shows him as a prosperous and unmistakably "Asiatic" figure, standing against a painted background of columns against an indistinct trompe l'oeil landscape depicting a garden scene. His face appears distinguished, framed by high cheekbones, what contemporaries would have regarded as Mongolian eyes, and a carefully tended long goatee. Badmaev radiates success, wearing a well-tailored suit of rich wool cloth and well-polished shoes. In hands folded across an ample stomach that reinforces the impression of prosperity, Badmaev holds a hat that could be Russian or Asian.

This portrait blends conventional symbols of accomplishment—one thinks here of his automobile or the suburban "clinic" at Poklonnaia Gora—with the Asian exoticism that struck his contemporaries, suggesting yet another entrée into this figure as a "personality of empire." In the course of a career that took him from Buriatiia to the elite circles of imperial St. Petersburg, Badmaev had refashioned himself into an imperial subject, able to accommodate pride in his Buriat antecedents with dedication to Russia's own imperial mission in Asia.

Certainly, opportunism played no small part in his actions. Yet, arguably, Badmaev's self-refashioning as a Christian Buriat and intimate of the "white tsar" served as the template for his vision of Russia's imperial destiny in Asia—his choice of dress and his modes of consumption and display might have suggested to his Petersburg contemporaries the possibilities of the civilizing mission he had pursued so ardently at court. Indeed, his attempt to bring his co-nationals to St. Petersburg for education and ultimate entry into state service recapitulated the trajectory followed by his and his brothers' lives in the mid-nineteenth century, including conversion to Christianity. Devotion to Orthodoxy ran like a red thread throughout all his historical and political writings. At the same time, echoing much of the mysticism of the time and the Orientalism of such figures as Ukhtomskii or Blok, he plumbed his own background and knowledge of Buriat lore to give his proposals and analyses an air of authenticity that persuaded such acquaintances as Witte or Nicholas II, however briefly.

Ultimately, Badmaev's career demonstrated the increasingly intimate association between the two strands of "empire" that became intertwined in the Russia of Nicholas II. One of these involved the growing fascination with Asia that pervaded Russia and Europe in tandem with the possibilities presented by China's apparent decline. For his part, Badmaev combined views associated with a Witte or Ukhtomski with his own visible authenticity to promote his vision for Russia's aims in the Far East. The immediate outcome of this activity came in 1905, when the Russo-Japanese War put an end to Russia's Chinese dreams and revolution nearly overthrew the Romanov dynasty. This latter event and its consequences brought into play the second aspect of Russia as an empire—the nature of autocratic power and its holder, Nicholas II. In this new context, the ruler's propensity to rely on favorites rather than his own officials came to symbolize the decadence of autocracy as a social and political order. If Rasputin served as the most evocative symptom of this illness, Badmaev the "Tibetan doctor" also figured in these perceptions as a particularly baleful and exotic "dark force" in a milieu that had already begun to see the world in often mystical, racialized, and apocalyptic terms.

## NOTES

1. This phrase comes from the title of the best-known work on Badmaev, V. P. Semennikov, *Za kulisami tsarisma arkhiv tibetskogo vracha Badmaeva* (Leningrad: Gosudarstvennoe izdatel'stvo, 1925). More recently, Badmaev's grandson, Russian journalist Boris Gusev, has sought to rehabilitate his ancestor's reputation. Cf. Gusev, "Moi ded Zhamsaran Badmaev: iz semeinoi khroniki," *Novyi mir* 11 (1989): 199–226; *Doktor Badmaev: Tibetskaia meditsina, Tsarskii dvor, Sovetskaia vlast'* (Moscow: Russkaia kniga, 1995); and *Petr Badmaev: Krestnik imperatora, tselitel', diplomat* (Moscow: Olma-Press, 2000). Most of the biographical details in this sketch come from I. V. Lukoianov, "Vostochnoe politika Rossii i P. A. Badmaev," *Voprosy istorii*, April 2001, 111–26. Curiously, virtually alone among historians interested in this figure, Lukoianov turned to holdings in the Russian State Historical Archive [RGIA] and the State Archive of the Russian Federation [GARF], which contain official state documents concerning Badmaev's career, including his personnel file compiled during his service in the Ministry

of Foreign Affairs. For an interesting recent treatment that stresses the orientalist context of Badmaev's times, see Marlène Laruelle, "'The White Tsar': Romantic Imperialism in Russia's Legitimizing of Conquering the Far East," *Acta Slavica Iaponica* 25 (2008): 113–34.

2. See, for example, D. A. Abrikosov, *Sud'ba russkogo diplomata* (Moscow: Russkii put', 2008), 83, 84.

3. Semennikov, *Za kulisami,* 76–77.

4. S. C. M. Paine, *Imperial Rivals: China, Russia, and Their Disputed Frontier* (Armonk, N.Y.: M. E. Sharpe, 1996), chapters 5 and 6.; Andrew Malozemoff, *Russian Far Eastern Policy, 1881–1904: With Special Emphasis on the Causes of the Russo-Japanese War* (Berkeley: University of California Press, 1958), 20–27.

5. Semennikov, *Za kulisami,* 49–75.

6. Ibid., 73–74.

7. Ibid., 77.

8. Ibid., editor's note, 81.

9. See the conclusions of a memorandum he wrote in February 1895, in the wake of the Sino-Japanese War: *Za kulisami,* 94. Interestingly, in August 1903, Nicholas implemented a very similar delegation of powers for Russian policy in the Far East to Admiral E. I. Alekseev, thus eliminating Witte's already wavering role in the empire's actions in Manchuria and East Asia. Cf. McDonald, *United Government,* 62–64.

10. *Za kulisami,* 102–103, 106–10.

11. On the prevalence and roles of these figures at the imperial court, see Robert D. Warth, *Nicholas II: The Life and Reign of Russia's Last Monarch* (Westport, Conn.: Praeger, 1997), ch. 9.

12. Semennikov, *Za kulisami*; D. Schorkowitz, *Staat und Nationalitaten in Russland: Der Integrationsprozesz der Burjaten und Kalmucken, 1822–1925* (Stuttgart: Franz Steiner Verlag, 2001), 260–61.

13. Schorkowitz, *Staat und Nationalitaten in Russland,* 260–61.

14. Schimmelpenninck van der Oye, "Russian Intelligence and the Younghusband Expedition to Tibet," in *Intelligence and Statecraft: The Use and Limits of Intelligence in International Society,* ed. P. Jackson and J. Siegel (Westport, Conn.: Praeger, 2005), 121–25; Schorkowitz, *Staat und Nationalitaten in Russland,* 283.

15. Laruelle, "The White Tsar," 118–19.

16. V. V. Shul'gin, *Gody. Dni. 1920 god* (Moscow: Novosti, 1990), 311, 312.

17. For an insightful genealogy of shifting Russian discourses about China and Asia, see S. S. Kim, "Between Spiritual Self and Other: Vladimir Solov'ev and the Question of East Asia," *Slavic Review* 2 (2008): 321–41. See also Schimmelpenninck van der Oye, *Toward the Rising Sun: Russian Ideologies of Empire and the Path to War with Japan* (DeKalb: Northern Illinois University Press, 2001); and Milan Hauner, *What Is Asia To Us? Russia's Asian Heartland Yesterday and Today* (London: Routledge, 1992).

18. For these references, see David Schimmelpenninck van der Oye, "Tournament of Shadows: Russia's Great Game in Tibet," in *The History of Tibet,* vol. 3, *The Modern Period: 1895–1959, the Encounter with Modernity,* ed. Alex MacKay (London: Routledge, 1993), 49; S. Iu. Vitte and B. V. Anan'ich, *Iz arkhiva S. Iu. Vitte: Vospominaniia. Tom I Rasskazy v steno-graficheskoi zapisi* (St. Petersburg, 2003), 433; V. V. Shul'gin, *Gody. Dni. 1920 god* (Moscow: Novosti, 1990), 311, 312; and Semennikov, *Za kulisami.*

19. Alexandra referred to him occasionally in her wartime correspondence with Nicholas. See, for example, M. N. Pokrovskii, ed., *Perepiska Nikolaia i Aleksandra Romanovykh,* vol. 5, *1916–1917 g. g.,* (Moscow-L: Gosudarstvennoe izdatel'stvo, 1927), 74, 95.

20. Letters in Semennikov, *Za kulisami,* 19–47.

21. Ibid., x–xi; Lukoianov, "Vostochnoe politika Rossii," 120. Alexandra wrote Nicholas in October 1916 that Protopopov had not dismissed his assistant P. G. Kurlov, whom Rasputin

disliked; apparently, Kurlov was "an intimate friend" of Badmaev, who had in turn cured Protopopov, thus earning the latter's gratitude. Pokrovskii, *Perepiska,* 5:95.

22. Semennikov, *Za kulisami,* 38.

23. Gusev, *Doktor Badmaev,* 57–60; "Moi ded," 215.

24. Apparently a couple named Ivanov—both holding positions in the new Soviet government in Petrograd—acted repeatedly as Badmaev's protector. See, for example, Gusev, *Doktor Badmaev,* 62; and "Moi ded," 216–17.

25. G. V. Arkhangel'skii, "Petr Badmaev—Znakhar', predprinimatel' i politik," *Voprosy istorii,* February 1998, 83; Gusev, *Doktor Badmaev,* 65–66; *Petr Badmaev,* 90–91. In *Doktor Badmaev,* Gusev includes a photocopy of the apparent original in a pictorial insert after 128.

26. Gusev, *Doktor Badmaev,* 75–76.

27. Ibid., 123.

Ekaterina Sabashnikova-Baranovskaia posed between her two brothers and two unknown individuals. Chernigovskii province, 1890s. *Zapiski Mikhaila Vasil'evicha Sabashnikova* (Moscow: Izd-vo im. Sabashnikovykh, 1995).

# 19

# Ekaterina Sabashnikova-Baranovskaia

## *(1859–?)*

### BARBARA ALPERN ENGEL

At my father's death I was left an orphan, and in charge of a large family and a substantial and dispersed estate. When I married Aleksandr Baranovskii, who was twice my age, I naturally expected to find my husband a support for my orphaned family. So in the first year of marriage I presented my husband with the right to conduct the affairs of my sisters and brothers, over which my uncle, my father's brother, stood guardian. The guardian died a year after my marriage. . . . My husband then proposed that his brother Egor take the guardian's place. None of my siblings wanted that, and not knowing Egor at all, instinctively neither did I. But my husband was so insistent and my resistance elicited such dissatisfaction from him that eventually I gave in. His brother moved into our home, assumed control over our affairs, and ruled over everything despotically. . . .

My husband demanded that I bring the children to his brother Egor's estate and said that if I failed to do so voluntarily, he would take them by force. He took the children and brought them to his brother's house, leaving them in the company of alien, non-Russian people in Mogilev.

Thus began the appeal of Ekaterina Baranovskaia (née Sabashnikova), to Tsar Alexander III (1881–94), requesting the right to live separately from her husband, Aleksandr, and, most importantly, to gain custody of their five children. Ekaterina Sabashnikova was the eldest child of a wealthy and cultivated merchant family. Ten years before this appeal, when Ekaterina was twenty-one years old, she had accepted the marriage proposal of Aleksandr Baranovskii, nineteen years her senior, nobly born and of Polish background, with a family estate in Mogilev gubernia. The age, estate (*soslovie*), and cultural differences between them proved no obstacle to marriage or to early years of wedded bliss: "I'm so happy that I am ashamed of my happiness and ask myself—why am I so happy? What have I done to deserve it?" Ekaterina wrote a friend in 1881, a year after the couple's wedding.[1] But after a decade of marriage and the birth of five children, and after the Baranovskiis' relationship had deteriorated beyond repair for other reasons, the cultural differences, at least, came to matter a lot.

They provided an important, perhaps even crucial component of Ekaterina's effort to escape the relationship and helped to shape the outcome.

Submitted in spring 1890, Ekaterina Baranovskaia's appeal to the tsar was far from unique. Between 1884 and 1914, tens of thousands of unhappily married women addressed petitions to the tsar seeking relief from Russia's patriarchal family laws. Governed by the church, which regarded marriage as a sacrament and permitted divorce only under exceptional circumstances, and then only grudgingly, Russian family law subjected a wife almost completely to her husband. It also required couples to cohabit, and strictly forbade any act that led to the separation of spouses. Under the law, a wife required her husband's permission before she could take a job, enroll in school, or acquire the separate internal passport she needed to reside more than roughly twenty miles from her husband's ascribed place of residence. Ekaterina's petition was forwarded to the Imperial Chancellery for Receipt of Petitions (hereafter the chancellery), a branch of the imperial bureaucracy that served as a kind of final court of appeals for unhappy wives. It, like the marriage itself, offers evidence of the cultural mixing that was commonplace in Russia: several of its leading figures—including two of its heads, Otto Rikhter and Baron Alexander Budberg—were Baltic Germans. Acting in the name of the tsar, the chancellery held the power to supersede the law forbidding spousal separation and to grant a woman a passport of her own—and if officials deemed appropriate, custody of the children as well.[2]

If Ekaterina Baranovskaia's appeal was merely one of tens of thousands of appeals from unhappily married women seeking separation, the issues it involved were nevertheless far from typical. Most appeals emphasized the husband's excessive drinking, domestic violence, adultery, or failure to support his wife, none of which figured in Ekaterina's complaint. Hers stressed very different issues: the couple's clashes over control of the vast Sabashnikov fortune and the cultural distinctions that had mattered so little at first. The case was atypical in other ways as well. The couple was unusually well connected: one of Russia's highest officials, the formidable Konstantin Pobedonostsev, head of the Holy Synod, sought to influence the outcome, and eventually Tsar Alexander III himself became involved. Most such disputes were resolved within a year; that of the Baranovskiis dragged on for almost four years and involved multiple petitions and letters and heaps of supporting evidence. The copious documentation, amounting to roughly one thousand pages, is still preserved in the chancellery's archive.

The initial source of the Baranovskiis' conflict was finances, just as Baranovskaia's petition indicated. Ekaterina Sabashnikova had been an unusually energetic young woman with a practical turn of mind, who, as the eldest child in the family, held herself responsible for the fate of the Sabashnikov family fortunes. Although she was only twenty years old when her widowed father died in 1879, she did her best to take his place in addition to managing the household and raising her younger siblings, responsibilities more typical for an eldest daughter. "Valuing her remarkable intellect, persistence, and businesslike approach [*delovitost'*]," the guardian of the family's financial affairs consulted her on all major decisions, remembered her younger brother Mikhail. Sabashnikova took over her father's study, where she was often seen hard at work.[3] But after her marriage to Baranovskii in 1880, she surrendered to her husband her role as co-manager, and following the death of the guardian, appointed Aleksandr's older brother Egor guardian over the family's gold mines at her husband's request, while installing her husband as manager of a sugar refining factory in which the Sabashnikov family held controlling shares. As the detailed documentary record in the case files demonstrates, the Baranovskii brothers' management was disastrous for the Sabashnikov family fortunes, resulting in the loss of thousands of rubles and leaving their financial affairs in a muddle. Eventually, the other partners forced the brothers out of their positions.

It was conflicts over property that led to the initial breach in the marriage. The Baranovskii brothers wanted to gain complete control of the Sabashnikov family fortunes, taking advantage of a contradiction in Russian law. On the one hand, and by contrast with much of Europe at this time, in Russia married women retained their legal right to own and manage their own property and to pursue property claims in court, even against their own husbands. But on the other hand, Russian law granted husbands virtually unlimited power over their wives. Family law required wives to render "unconditional obedience" to husbands and offered no legal remedy to wives whose husbands mistreated them or otherwise abused their authority.[4] Aleksandr Baranovskii's legal authority, from which the law offered no escape, enabled him to exert enormous pressure on his wife, Ekaterina, designed to force her to sign over to him her rights to the Sabashnikov properties.

But the couple's growing tensions over control of the property either quickly overflowed into other realms, or ignited already smoldering differences over other matters. One of their disputes involved childrearing, and was likely linked to their different social backgrounds. Ekaterina wanted to educate the children at home, as merchants often did, and keep them in her care until they were old enough to pursue more advanced education. Aleksandr wanted his sons to follow in his footsteps: to leave home at a tender age to attend a preparatory school, and then enroll in the Imperial School of Jurisprudence, an elite institution that admitted only sons of the nobility and that Baranovskii himself had attended. The school not only prepared noble sons for civil service, but also fostered the kind of personal connections that ensured a successful career. That social differences had begun to matter is suggested by Ekaterina's brother, who recalled that Aleksandr blamed the couple's marital difficulties on his wife's merchant origins, which purportedly prevented her from "rising to the needs of a noble husband."[5] To place the children in a setting he deemed more appropriate and to intensify the pressures on his wife, Aleksandr had moved the children from the couple's home in Moscow to his family estate in Mogilev province shortly before Ekaterina Baranovskaia petitioned.

It was their cultural differences, however, that Ekaterina emphasized in her petition, as embodied in the estate in Mogilev province, once part of Poland, and the purportedly Polish Catholic Baranovskii family who resided there. Ekaterina adopted this line, at least in part, for strategic reasons. Bereft of her children and lacking legal recourse to protect herself against her husband's efforts to gain control of her property, Ekaterina had little choice but to take what her brother Mikhail called the "desperate step" of petitioning the tsar, and little hope of succeeding in her appeal not only for the right to live apart from him, but also for custody of the five children. The excellent personal connections that Aleksandr enjoyed in St. Petersburg, where the chancellery was housed, were likely to influence the outcome in his favor. More importantly, during the reign of Tsar Alexander III (1881–94), the chancellery was highly reluctant to approve women's appeals for separation. An exemplary family man, Tsar Alexander III regarded himself as the guardian of the sanctity and steadfastness of the family principle, and under his leadership chancellery officials exercised great caution in interfering with the marital bond.

Under these circumstances, it was imperative for Ekaterina to use the cultural materials available to her to present herself in the most favorable terms possible as well as to undermine her husband's case. To make a compelling case, she evoked gendered expectations concerning childrearing as well as anxieties about the ethnic Other that continued to characterize state policy despite, or perhaps also because of, the commonality of cultural mixing. Although the Russian state was formally committed to ethnic and religious diversity, it also granted preeminence to Russians and to the Russian Orthodox Church, especially during the reign of Tsar Alexander III.

This was reflected in the laws governing marriage as well as in other policies. In the late nineteenth century, and long after marriage had become a civil matter in most other European states, the Russian state remained committed to a religious form of marriage. In order to accommodate the religious diversity of its multinational empire, it left religious rites in the hands of each confession but gave absolute preeminence to the Russian Orthodox faith when one of the parties was Russian Orthodox. Thus, Russian law required couples that intermarried to legalize their union according to the rites of Russian Orthodoxy and children born of the marriage to be baptized and raised in the Orthodox confession.[6] In addition, during the reign of Tsar Alexander III, tolerance for national differences declined, while Russification intensified, bringing the imposition of Russian language and institutions on non-Russian peoples, including those who inhabited the western provinces won from Poland in the late eighteenth century, from which the Baranovskiis derived and where their estates were located. The state was already suspicious of the loyalty of Poles as a result of a series of uprisings, the most recent in 1863, in which Poles sought freedom from Russian rule.

It was to these state concerns that Ekaterina Baranovskaia appealed in her efforts to gain custody. The Sabashnikovs were ethnically Russian and of the Russian Orthodox faith; the Baranovskiis were not only of Polish background, but also of the Roman Catholic faith, or so Ekaterina Baranovskaia alleged. Invoking the nationalist, Orthodox and Russocentric discourse that characterized the reign of Tsar Alexander III, her petitions drew attention to her in-laws' "alien" and "non-Russian" ways. The Baranovskiis "are Roman Catholic and one sister is even a Roman Catholic nun," she asserted. "That is the milieu in which my children now find themselves.

Remaining longer in that milieu will harm them," Ekaterina declared in her initial petition, which followed her husband's removal of the children to the Mogilev estate. "Polish Catholics are currently teaching the children Russian subjects," she contended in her subsequent appeal.[7]

Ekaterina linked the government's interests and her own in another way as well. The tsarist government expressed a strong interest in the proper moral education of the young. Russian law made no distinction between the responsibility of fathers and mothers to their children, and explicitly linked parents' fulfillment of their duties towards their children to the concerns of the state itself: "Parents must give all their attention to the moral education of their children and strive by means of domestic upbringing [*vospitanie*] to school their morals and further the well-being [*sodeistvovat' vidam*] of the state," reads article 173 of the law governing parent-child relations.[8]

In her appeal, Baranovskaia emphasized her own exemplary qualities as a mother, describing the enormous sacrifices she was prepared to make for the sake of her children's welfare. This included enduring systematic mistreatment. "Despite my most sincere efforts," she wrote to the chancellery in August 1891, soon after the couple's attempt at reconciliation, brokered by the chancellery, had collapsed, "I have become fully convinced that it is impossible for the children to continue living with my husband without harm to their moral and physical health." She then provided an account of the couple's failed reconciliation. At Aleksandr Baranovskii's insistence, the couple had settled on his estate in Mogilev guberniia, to which he had earlier removed the children against his wife's wishes. There, in an effort to force her to surrender her property, he isolated her from all support, forbidding her to entertain friends or family or to bring along her own servants. He then humiliated her by depriving her of all authority over the household and treating her "like a servant" while subjecting her to psychological pressures that included insisting in the presence of their ailing child that she surrender her property.[9] Before fleeing and petitioning the chancellery, she had endured this situation for close to six months, attempting to maintain the façade of her marriage for the children's sake. A file hundreds of pages long, stuffed with letters she wrote to friends and family during those trying months, bears out her claims: it offers a portrait of a woman willing to put up with a lot for the sake of her children, but eventually pressed beyond her endurance.

Although both these arguments influenced officials' judgment, buttressed as they were by the testimony of all but two witnesses in the case, the argument concerning Polish influence was probably decisive. One of the dissenters was the governor of Mogilev, who upheld Aleksandr's allegations that the breakdown of the marriage was entirely the fault of the neurotic and stubborn Ekaterina, and denied any Polish influence on the children. His insistence that the children were being raised "in a pure Russian spirit," which was ignored by officials, suggests the power of Baranovskaia's claim to the contrary.[10] The efforts made by Konstantin Pobedonostsev, the powerful procurator of the Holy Synod, on Aleksandr's behalf were equally fruitless. In the end, the chancellery not only approved the requested separation but also awarded sole custody of the children to Ekaterina. In so doing, they contravened yet another of Russia's laws, that which recognized the authority of both parents over their children, but gave preference to the father as head of the household. The mother, and only the mother, resolved officials, should be given "the sacred responsibility of raising the children."

Despite officials' own mixed cultural backgrounds, the Baranovskiis' ethnicity and religious faith figured prominently in the decision. Officials echoed Ekaterina Baranovskaia's allegation concerning the "alienness" of the Baranovskii milieu and Aleksandr's insistence that his Catholic sister, rather than their own mother, raise the children. "Polish Catholics" taught the children "Russian subjects," the chancellery's decision observed. Polish preferences had reigned in other realms as well according to officials: having assumed control of a Sabashnikov family sugar concern, Egor Baranovskii purportedly had fired all the Russians in the administration and replaced them with Poles.[11]

But if concerns about the primacy of Russianness and Orthodoxy were decisive in the outcome of the case, as they surely were, also important was Ekaterina's successful portrayal of herself as a self-sacrificing Russian mother. The chancellery's decision dwelled at length on Ekaterina Baranovskaia's moral motherhood, which officials construed, as she had, in terms of her self-abnegation and willingness to suffer on behalf of her children, as well as the fact that the father, Aleksandr Baranovskii, "barely spends time with the children and hardly knows them." The relevant section of the decision reads as follows:

> Making all kinds of concessions, not sparing material means, often sacrificing her human dignity, suffering insult and injury from her husband, enduring a position sometimes worse than that of servant, she bore without complaint the yoke that fell on her shoulders, trying to hide her position not only from outsiders but even from the children. . . . Then, after she appealed, she accepted the compromise the chancellery worked out, in the hope that the interference of a higher authority would in some measure help to bring order to and render more endurable her family position. . . . but instead, in the course of six months, her situation grew worse.

The investigation revealed not one fact that could "sully her moral qualities," wrote Otto Rikhter, then head of the chancellery, in his summary report to the tsar.[12]

In the same vein, their decision faulted Aleksandr Baranovskii for failing to fulfill his parental responsibility to provide for the physical and moral needs of his children and to raise them in the proper Russian spirit. Of "low moral qualities," Aleksandr had "surrounded the children with non-Russian people" and forced the children to live in the unhygienic conditions of his estate, "threatening to destroy their already shaky health," while continuing to insist that Ekaterina Baranovskaia transfer her property to him—and when she refused, flying into a rage in the presence of the children and terrifying them. All this convinced officials that the father had not only proven untrustworthy to raise his children, but indeed "should be excluded from all influence on them, as in pursuit of his material interests, he exploits even his wife's maternal feelings." A man such as he "cannot give his children the moral rearing necessary for the interests of the family and the state," the report concluded, explicitly stating the convergence between the two. The chancellery's decision of February 12, 1892, deprived Aleksandr Baranovskii of custody and any authority over the children's upbringing and education, and left him only with the right to visit with his children at a time and place of the mother's choosing.[13]

This was not the end of the case, however. The curtailment of his paternal rights brought a swift response from Aleksandr Baranovskii, in which in a series of letters, he, too, endeavored to align the interests of the state with his own. First, aware of their key role in the outcome of his case, he directly challenged his wife's allegations concerning his ethnicity, religious faith, and lack of loyalty to Russia: "By birth and by belief, I belong to the Russian Orthodox nobility," he wrote early in 1893, providing a detailed genealogy to illustrate his point. He had not only graduated from the elite Imperial School of Jurisprudence, but had provided loyal service to the Russian state: first in the Ministry of Justice, then, between 1867–77 as a Justice of the Peace in the reformed court system, and finally, during the Russo-Turkish War of 1877–78, by working for the Red Cross, removing the wounded from the field of battle. At the same time, he sought to impugn his wife's moral integrity. Ekaterina had renounced "the family and the principles of religion," he alleged, and had taken a lover, "a man of Cossack origin" who had served as manager of her estates, and with whom she had openly conducted a sexual liaison.[14]

Although, as it quickly emerged, Aleksandr had bribed witnesses to testify falsely to his wife's sexual misconduct, his efforts eventually led to a modification of the initial decision. His noble birth, his personal connections in high places, and perhaps the fact that Ekaterina had misrepresented both his national allegiance and his, if not his family's, religious faith (the record is unclear on the latter score) surely played a role. In any event, Tsar Alexander III himself took an interest in the case. Brought to the tsar's attention, at his behest the case was reopened early in 1893 and a court of arbitration convened in January 1894. Instructed to resolve the question of child custody, the informal court, composed of two people, each selected by one of the spouses, delivered its verdict in mid-March 1894. Although they, too, found Aleksandr solely responsible for the breakdown of the marriage, the child custody arrangements they proposed differed from those decreed by the chancellery. Affirming maternal custody during the children's tender years, the two men nevertheless honored the father's abiding interest in the education of his children as set forth in the law, and especially the education of sons. The mother would raise and educate the children until they reached school age, "but under the supervision of the father," who would also choose the school his sons (although not his daughters) would attend. Thus, on the matter of the children's education—a source of considerable contention between the parents—the two men came down on the father's side. Their decision ensured that the boys would be educated as he wished (that is, in preparatory school and then the Imperial School of Jurisprudence) and follow in his footsteps.[15] With this agreement, the case came to an end. Ekaterina and Aleksandr Baranovskii never again lived under the same roof. After the end of his case, Baranovskii disappears from the record; we learn of Ekaterina Baranovskaia's later years from her brother Mikhail's memoir, which tells us that she died in France of cancer sometime after the Revolution of 1917, but does not tell us when.

In this final agreement, the cultural differences that had loomed so large in Ekaterina's appeal and the chancellery's decisions played no role. Was this because Ekaterina had misrepresented her husband's religion (although probably not his sister or brother's) and his Polish affinities? Or because neither mattered to the two men who mediated the case, Count Peter Geiden, director of the chancellery from 1886 until 1889, and Professor Aleksandr I. Chuprov (1842–1908), the distinguished economist and statistician? The record remains unclear.

What is certain is this: had the Baranovskii marriage not encountered difficulties for other reasons, the accusations of ethnic Otherness that figure so prominently in chancellery proceedings would never have been leveled. There is certainly no mention of such differences in the memoirs of Mikhail Sabashnikov, who otherwise has much to say about his former brother-in-law's shortcomings. Only when the marriage failed did ethnicity enter the picture. And it did so only because it mattered to others—in particular, to the tsarist officials whom Ekaterina had to convince of the merits of her case. Acting in the name of a tsar who made Russianness and Russian Orthodoxy a cornerstone of his rule, these officials proved highly responsive to claims of ethnic Otherness. The Baranovskii marriage thus suggests the ways that the policies of the state that defined ethnic difference might serve a private as well as public agenda.

## Notes

The source of the epigraph is Rossiiskii Gosudarstvennyi Istoricheskii Arkhiv (hereafter cited as RGIA), f. 1412, op. 213, d. 17, p. 3, 6. Research for this chapter was conducted with the support of the International Research and Exchanges Board (IREX) with funds provided by the National Endowment for the Humanities. I am grateful to Elena Nikolaeva for assistance with follow-up research.

1. Quoted in M. V. Sabashnikov, *Zapiski Mikhaila Vasil'evicha Sabashnikova* (Moscow, 1995), 58.

2. Barbara Alpern Engel, "In the Name of the Tsar: Competing Legalities and Marital Conflicts in Late Imperial Russia," *Journal of Modern History* 77, no. 1 (March 2005): 70–96.

3. Sabashnikov, *Zapiski*, 53.

4. Michelle Lamarche Marrese, *A Woman's Kingdom: Noblewomen and the Control of Property in Russia, 1700–1861* (Ithaca, N.Y.: Cornell University Press, 2002).

5. Sabashnikov, *Zapiski*, 135–36.

6. Paul W. Werth, "Empire, Religious Freedom, and the Legal Regulation of 'Mixed' Marriages in Russia," *Journal of Modern History* 80 (June 2008): 296–331.

7. RGIA, f. 1412, op. 213, d. 17, 6, 21, 146.

8. *Svod Zakonov Rossiiskoi Imperii*, vol. 10 (St. Petersburg, 1857).

9. RGIA, f. 1412, op. 213, d. 17, 144–46.
10. Ibid., d. 16, l. 76.
11. Ibid., 135–36, 145–46, 149.
12. Ibid., 131, 149–50.
13. Ibid., 145–50.
14. Ibid., d. 19, 6–7, 9–10, 11.
15. Ibid., d. 21, 164, 170–71.

Mannerheim as commander of the Thirteenth Wladimir Uhlan Regiment of the Life Guards at Novominsk. Reprinted with permission from the Mannerheim Museum, Helsinki, Finland.

# 20

# Carl Gustaf Emil Mannerheim

*(1867–1951)*

BRADLEY D. WOODWORTH

One of the great ironies of the history of Finland is that its most celebrated son, Baron Carl Gustaf Emil Mannerheim (1867–1951)—statues of whom stand throughout Finland—was less a product of Finland itself than of the tsarist empire. Mannerheim had two careers: one as an officer in the tsarist army; the other as Finland's first de facto head of state and greatest wartime hero. For Mannerheim, this was no contradiction; he was a man who disdained the exclusionist nature of ethnic nationalism and felt comfortable in a world in which loyalty to the land of his birth—Finland—and to his own aristocratic cultural background as a Swedish-speaking Finn—did not preclude loyalty to Imperial Russia.

In their steady rise in status, Mannerheim's forebears exemplified the permeable nature of the aristocracy in early modern Europe (not unlike that of Russia of the time) as well as the often flexible political loyalties among Europeans who were skilled, mobile, and ambitious. In 1768 Johan Augustin Mannerheim, grandson of a seventeenth-century Dutch immigrant to Sweden named Henrik Marhein, was elevated to the rank of baron for military services rendered the kingdom. His son, Carl Erik Mannerheim, survived a political tussle with the crown in the late eighteenth century and relocated to Finland, part of the Swedish realm from the thirteenth century. As Finland became established as a Russian-held grand duchy in the course of the Napoleonic Wars, this Mannerheim was present at the creation of the largely autonomous new Finnish state; in 1808 he led a delegation that met with Emperor Alexander I in St. Petersburg, and he later held high office in the Finnish Senate. He also purchased the large, dignified English-style estate not far from Åbo (Turku in Finnish) in southwestern Finland on which his great-grandson, Carl Gustaf Emil Mannerheim (called Gustaf by family and friends)—the future Grand Marshal of independent Finland—was born.

Swedish-speaking Finns made up just under 15 percent of Finland's population throughout the nineteenth century and comprised the bulk of the country's social and economic elite and virtually all of its aristocracy. The Finnish patriotism of both

Swedish Finns and ethnic Finns did not prevent them from volunteering for service in the Imperial Russian state as officers in the Russian military (or in the tiny army attached to the Finnish grand duchy) and also working as civil servants and professionals in Russia proper, especially in St. Petersburg. In the mid-nineteenth century over a fifth of all adult Finnish noblemen served in the tsarist armed forces.[1] There were advantages to Finland's status within the empire. As one Finnish historian put it, "Finns had actually got the best of two worlds: their own autonomous grand duchy and the tremendous opportunities offered within a world power."[2]

Eventually Gustaf Mannerheim would make the most of his opportunities, both in Finland and in Russia, using his social background as an asset in each case. Though not from a wealthy family, he still was an aristocrat from an advanced, Westernized part of the empire, and this helped him make his way in the cosmopolitan St. Petersburg aristocracy.

A tradition of ethnic diversity within the officers corps of the tsarist army also facilitated Mannerheim's career. Although "ethnicity" or "nationality" were not categories employed in tsarist record keeping until the twentieth century, the religious confession of officers was. In the 1860s, the decade of Mannerheim's birth, the percentage of officers who were Orthodox Christians never reached 78 percent (and in 1862 was only 69.4 percent).[3] As Russians were overwhelmingly Orthodox, as were most Ukrainians and Belorusians, and other non-Russians in the empire often were not (Georgians were an exception), it is clear that a fairly high percentage of officers were non-Russian. Germans were well represented, particularly Baltic Germans, who had a strong tradition of serving the Imperial Russian state. Even with efforts by the state beginning in the late nineteenth century to limit their numbers, non-Russian officers accounted for 12 percent of the officer corps in the years immediately before the outbreak of World War I, and officers from the Baltic provinces, Finland, and the Caucasus enjoyed the same status as their Russian counterparts.[4]

As a boy, Gustaf was willful and often reckless, and his mother, the daughter of a wealthy Swedish-speaking Finnish industrialist, was concerned about her son's "unbridled and boisterous nature." Once, when in the course of a snowball fight as a schoolboy in Helsingfors (Helsinki) Gustaf was knocked down by a horse-drawn sleigh, he picked himself up and declared to concerned onlookers: "My name is Mannerheim, and I am the general of the [younger school class]." Expelled from his school for breaking windows, he gained admittance to Finland's only military school, the Corps of Cadets, in 1882. He was a gifted student, excelling at French and horse riding, but he disliked the confined and isolated life of the school and chafed at its rules and regimentation. In 1884, he wrote his sister, "I look forward with joy to the moment I can turn my back on Finland for ever and go my own way—God knows where, but in any case my own master."[5]

With his father having abandoned the family for Paris and his mother dead from a heart attack in 1881, Gustaf felt there was little keeping him in Finland. He was attracted to the possibility of continuing his military training at the aristocratic School of Pages in St. Petersburg, but his record at the Corps of Cadets prevented this. Now almost without means, his future became even more clouded when in 1886 he left the Cadet Corps premises one evening without leave, which resulted in his expulsion. Facing a clear turning point, Gustaf realized he needed greater discipline. He spent the summer and part of that autumn in Kharkov, in what is now Ukraine, where a relative on his mother's side of the family worked as an engineer in charge of a factory. There he improved his Russian and spent time in a Russian military camp. Upon returning to Finland he studied hard for a year, with an eye toward passing entrance exams to the university and a possible civil career. But a military future was what he realized he wanted. He later wrote in his memoirs, "My disciplinary punishment [at the Cadet Corps] had spurred my ambition to show that . . . I was at heart a good soldier."[6] With the help of his godmother and her sister, who was married to a highly placed Russian aristocrat, Mannerheim was allowed to take the entrance exam for the two-year course at the Nikolai Cavalry School in St. Petersburg. After easily passing, he began a career in the Russian army that would last thirty years.

Mannerheim's regal appearance—he was six feet four inches in height and handsome—likely helped him in getting accepted by the Chevalier Guards, the most prestigious cavalry regiment. After an initial stint from 1889 to 1891 as a cavalry officer stationed near the border with Germany in Russian-held Poland, where he had to wait for a position as a Guards officer to open, Mannerheim served in the Guards's headquarters in St. Petersburg. Although scions of the most storied Russian aristocratic families served in the Guards, all the men were held as equals, regardless of background.

Unlike many of his fellow aristocratic officers, for whom a position in the Chevalier Guards was little more than a way to spend time when not indulging in the brilliant social life of the capital, Mannerheim took his duties very seriously. Some of the ostentatious pastimes of many guardsmen, such as fine dining, were beyond his means in any case. Although he found life in the city fascinating, much more so than that of provincial Finland, Mannerheim was never happier than when out riding or caring for horses. In 1895 he married Anastasia Arapova, the daughter of a wealthy former Guards officer and Moscow police chief. The marriage, which was likely arranged, produced two daughters but was loveless. Although warm and sociable, and a favorite with women, Mannerheim was not a success at domestic life and saw his immediate family largely as a burden. His relationship with Anastasia essentially ended by 1903, although divorce came only in 1919.

Tensions grew in Finland toward the end of the nineteenth century, when the Russian state, pressured by Russian nationalists and pan-Slavists, began infringing upon Finland's special status, limiting the purview of the elected Finnish Diet. Finland's elite was divided on how to respond. Growing unrest turned into civil disobedience and even violence after 1901, when the state announced a law that eliminated the Finnish army and obliged some Finns to serve in the Russian military. Mannerheim's relatives were liberals who felt the tsarist state was violating the constitution it had given Finland, and they were concerned about Gustaf's continuing military service, fearing he was becoming Russified. His elder brother Carl Erik Johan

Mannerheim was expelled from the empire for organizing public opinion against the conscription act (in 1908 he became a Swedish citizen). Gustaf explained to his family that he could fight for Imperial Russia without this meaning he supported autocracy. In fact, the social circle in Petersburg in which he moved was liberal, preferring a constitutional monarchy to autocracy. He believed constitutional change was on its way to Russia and that Finnish and Russian interests were inextricably intertwined.

Mannerheim's non-Russianness never seems to have hindered his career within the Imperial Army, even after the 1905 Revolution, when national tensions rose as minority peoples in a number of places in the empire rebelled against the tsarist order.

Another guardsman from Finland, Carl Enckell, who served in the Izmailovsky Guards Regiment in St. Petersburg from 1896 to 1899, wrote in his memoirs that while occasionally an ethnic Russian officer would point out the number of non-Russians at the officers' breakfast table, no sense of Russian nationalism existed to divide the officers. "The spirit of comradeship within the officers corps was irreproachable," he added. "In the distribution of tasks of high responsibility, the nationality of the individual was not taken into account, nor was praise from senior commanders the cause for envy."[7]

After 1905, debates took place within the military administration over quotas for non-Russians, particularly within the officer corps. District commanders reacted negatively to a draft project for restrictions produced by the Main Staff of the War Ministry in 1907. Their comments on the proposed limitations (which were not implemented) highlighted the importance of honor and duty in the outlook and behavior of non-Russian officers. Such a "patrimonial paradigm of service" was certainly characteristic of Mannerheim.[8]

For Mannerheim, service to the Russian state did not mean a shift in his core identity. Even though the world of politics and cultural and linguistic identities was changing around him, his personal worldview did not change. He remained a citizen of Finland (Finns had a special passport system that made them subjects of the grand duchy) and a Lutheran (non-Russian tsarist servitors who fully assimilated to Russian culture and language tended to convert to Orthodoxy). Mannerheim's fluency in the Russian language is disputed; he seems to have spoken it passably well—but not as well as French—and one of his World War I aides wrote that he had a "terrible Swedish accent."[9] He also did not stand out for his non-Russianness in an already diverse officer corps. Like other young men of various nationalities from throughout the empire, the young nobleman from the Grand Duchy of Finland had made a deep, personal commitment to the tsarist state, one that only ended when the state itself collapsed in 1917.

It is noteworthy that Mannerheim did not Russify, or allow himself to become Russified; this was by no means universal of natives of Finland in Russian state service. Like the rest of his family, Gustaf Mannerheim was a constitutionalist with regard to Finland's position within the empire; he gave his highest attention to Finland's interests and to Finnish-Russian relations. On several occasions, he sent to family members upset at Russian actions limiting Finland's autonomy advice on how most effectively to act. Well apprised of tsarist high politics as he was—an advantage proffered by his association with St. Petersburg high social circles—Mannerheim did not see Finland's future as deeply threatened as it appeared to many in Finland.[10]

Loyal to the army and state he was sworn to serve, Mannerheim did not hesitate to volunteer for a field assignment when war erupted in 1904 between Russia and Japan. The decision also reflected his ambition, as he sought to become a commander of men in the field. Only a squadron commander when he arrived in Manchuria, he rose rapidly in rank, ending the war as a colonel. Mannerheim's next assignment was a covert fact-finding mission in Xinjiang (Chinese Turkestan) and northern China from 1906 to 1908, undertaken at the request of the army's chief of staff. This extended gathering of geographic, ethnographic, and various kinds of statistical information and observation of nascent Chinese military reforms took him again far from St. Petersburg and Finland, but Mannerheim was attracted to the idea of exploring the East. As a child he knew of the exploits of an uncle by marriage, the Swedish (but Helsingfors-born) scientist and explorer Adolf Erik Nordenskiöld (1832–1901), who in the 1870s was the first to navigate the entire northern coast of Eurasia, following the Northeast Passage from Scandinavia to the Bering Strait. Although during the expedition Mannerheim often underwent considerable physical hardships, the extensive record he kept of his activities—which included an audience with the Dalai Lama—reflects the deep satisfaction he experienced as well as his inquisitive, perceptive mind.[11] Of greatest interest, surely, to his superiors were his recommendations on how to proceed with a Russian invasion of Xinjiang should Russia and China go to war, and his thoughts on the political utility of Russia's holding the region after an eventual Russian-Chinese peace settlement. Whether these were the sorts of details Mannerheim dwelled on during his audience with Nicholas II upon his return is not known. However, the report planned for just twenty minutes stretched before the impressed emperor to four times that length.

Mannerheim received a new position in 1909 as an Uhlan regimental commander in a small town in Poland. He had great success in raising the capabilities of the men under him, and in 1911 he was given a highly prized new command—that of His Majesty's Life Guard Uhlan Regiment in Warsaw—and was promoted to the rank of major general. He frequently socialized with Polish aristocrats, and although he did not discuss politics with them, he privately felt that Russia had mistreated Poland and the Poles. Mannerheim later recorded in his memoirs that as a native of a land that, like Poland, had been subjected to Russification, with Poles he had a "tacit understanding, which was a kind of freemasonry without vows."[12] Poland and Finland both would one day have greater autonomy, he believed, albeit within the ambit of a tsarist empire. A loyal servant of the tsar, Mannerheim's star continued to rise. In 1912 Nicholas II made him a major general à la suite (in the suite of His Majesty). In January 1914 he received yet another advancement, becoming commander of the Independent Guards Cavalry Brigade, which included his Uhlan regiment. The years Mannerheim spent in Poland (1909–14) were not only the apex of his career as a tsarist officer but also one of the happiest periods in his life.

Mannerheim fits rather well the stereotype held by Russian officers towards officers from Finland who served in their midst—ambitious, conscientious, and hardworking. One military historian of the mid-century campaigns in the Caucasus wrote of a general staff officer, Bernhard Indrenius (1812–84),

> He belonged to that category of officers whom we Russians refer to as being "honorable as a Swede." All of these officers from Finland were distinguished by their puritanical sense of honor, their conscientious attitude to their duties, a certain pedantry, a poor knowledge of Russian, various unremarkable abilities that set a man apart from the general mass, and a modest way of life. They were of the greatest help as workers and assistants in every branch of military service.[13]

In the specific case of Mannerheim, however, several caveats must be made. The hardships of his journey through China notwithstanding, Mannerheim was known to appreciate luxury (he loved fine clothes, fine dining and, especially, fine horses). More importantly, as biographer J. E. O. Screen points out, Mannerheim was "more than a conscientious officer with a devotion to horses and sport." The future grand marshal of Finland possessed not only a sharp intellect and analytical skills, but he also had a keen understanding of how political concerns affected the pursuit of state interests.[14]

Within a week of Austria's delivery of its ultimatum to Serbia in late July 1914, Mannerheim and his men were mobilized and ordered to the Austrian front. A bold tactician, Mannerheim in October was awarded the Order of St. George (fourth class) and in March 1915 was given command of an entire cavalry division, which was sent the following year to fight in Romania. "From day to day regard for Mannerheim increased, as did his authority," recorded an aide.[15] In 1917, shortly before the February Revolution, Mannerheim was the commander of 40,000 Russian and Romanian soldiers. When the revolution broke out Mannerheim was in Petrograd and, conspicuous in his officer's uniform, only narrowly escaped arrest by street demonstrators. Disgusted by the lack of discipline in the Russian army after February, and a convinced monarchist, he requested and was granted a transfer to the reserves in September, and shortly thereafter left for Finland.

Finland had not had its own military units since 1901, and in the polarizing chaos in 1917, separate armed White and Red forces formed. When civil war broke out in January 1918, the Finnish government, led by conservatives who in the previous month had obtained recognition for Finland's independence from Russia's Bolsheviks, named Mannerheim commander-in-chief of the Finnish Whites. For Mannerheim, there was little difference between Finnish Reds or Russian Reds; both were cancers that needed to be eliminated. Early in the war, tensions arose between some White Guard volunteers, whose native language was Finnish, and Mannerheim's headquarters, where Swedish was the primary language. A number of Mannerheim's Fenno-Swedish officers had, like him, served in the Russian army; for some Finnish Whites, who saw these officers as Russians, this was a source of suspicion. Mannerheim managed to quell dissatisfaction by creating a representative council—an act he surely would have preferred to avoid—where rank-and-file soldiers' views could be heard.[16]

When the Whites, who received significant assistance from the Germans, finally broke the resistance of Finnish Reds and allied Russian troops in May, some four thousand Finnish Whites and over twenty thousand Finnish Reds lay dead. Both sides engaged in terrorism and reprisals. Proportionally far more Reds died, including over ten thousand who perished from malnutrition and disease in White prison camps.

Emerging from the civil war as Finland's de facto head of state, Mannerheim believed that security for Finland could come only with defeat and removal of power of the Bolsheviks in Russia—an act he thought most Russians would be grateful for—and he was prepared to lead an interventionist army of nearly any composition (one of Western Allies or Russian Whites) to capture Petrograd. The support Russian peasants gave the Bolsheviks in the Russian Civil War caught him entirely by surprise.

Mannerheim mourned the Bolsheviks' rise to power in the Russian Revolution and for the rest of his life despised and hated the radical left, whether Russian or Finnish. He was convinced that the interests of Finland and Russia were deeply linked, and as late as the end of 1919 still sought a way to organize an army to attack Petrograd and oust the Bolsheviks.

Mannerheim made peace with the idea of representative government, although he perhaps never truly understood it. If Finland was to be a democracy, he wanted it to have a strong and confident government, preferably with himself as president. But his political career for the time being came to an end in the presidential elections of 1919, in which he lost overwhelmingly to the center-left candidate Kaarlo Juho Ståhlberg. Mannerheim was despised by Finnish socialists (and would be for decades), and many Finns were suspicious of both his Fenno-Swedish background and his experience as a tsarist Russian officer. (Mannerheim at this point in his life did not yet speak Finnish; later, in the 1930s, he worked on it diligently.) He also rejected the idea of becoming head of Finland's armed forces, as he found civilian control over the military unacceptable. He wrote to a Polish friend,

> I am again free, and am happy no longer to have any office of responsibility. I only regret that I did not finish off the Bolsheviks on our borders before returning to private life. The entire world would sleep much more calmly at night if at least in Petersburg this center of Bolshevism were destroyed.[17]

In the 1920s, Mannerheim avoided becoming identified with any political party; the party strongest among Fenno-Swedes—the Swedish People's Party—unsuccessfully courted him. Beyond his unwillingness to be associated with any interest group, party politics simply did not interest him—real power was what got his attention. With this in mind, in 1931 he agreed to become chairman of Finland's Defense Council, an advisory body that made recommendations to the president in matters of defense preparation. Mannerheim transformed the council, increasing its executive authority. In the 1930s he successfully pushed for larger military budgets, and to some degree was able to plan for the war effort he would eventually himself lead. He championed a pro-Scandinavian (instead of pro-German) foreign policy, but, to his dismay, no defensive alliance with Sweden was concluded.

By the mid-1930s Mannerheim had given up his dreams of overthrowing the Bolsheviks; his sought-after alignment with Sweden indicated he thought it best for Finland not to get embroiled in conflicts between Europe's major powers. He also relinquished his vision of a White Finland and came to accept that the socialists were also part of the Finnish nation. "If I could now make a gift to our people," he said in a 1937 speech, "it would be unity, mutual trust and contentment."[18] He was becoming a pan-Finnish figure.

When language politics rose in salience in Finland in the 1930s, Mannerheim intervened, albeit reluctantly, as he had a personal aversion to anything that smacked of national chauvinism. At issue was whether Finnish should hold clear primacy in society vis-à-vis Swedish (which language was to be used at the University of Helsinki was a particularly contentious problem), not questions of ethnicity or of divided national identity. Mannerheim was primarily concerned that rifts between Finnish-speaking and Swedish-speaking Finns could weaken the country during a period when a lack of domestic vigor and confidence could have grave security implications. The language conflict, he wrote to a friend, was an "absurd waste of the nation's strengths." In February 1935, Mannerheim and two ethnic Finnish former generals with whom he fought in Finland's civil war publicly called for the language divisions to end. In a text published in the country's newspapers they presciently wrote, "The moment is still coming when our people will need to concentrate all its powers. God grant that we may then find in our land a nation of one mind."[19]

Following Germany's invasion of Poland in the first days of September 1939 and the Soviet Union's request for political talks with Finland in early October, President Kyösti Kallio turned to the now seventy-two-year-old Mannerheim, appointing him commander-in-chief. Mannerheim was quite discouraged, believing that the country was insufficiently prepared to back up its rejection of Soviet demands for concessions, and submitted his resignation to Kallio on November 27. But when the Soviet Union invaded Finland three days later, Mannerheim resumed his post with vigor and confidence. One colonel who met with Mannerheim a few days before he set out to command the front in eastern Finland wrote, "The Marshal was as composed as God."

For three and a half months—from late November 1939 to mid-March 1940— the massively outnumbered Finns managed to hold off the Red Army, which attacked at a number of places along the shared border from the Gulf of Finland in the south to the Arctic Sea in the north, with especially heavy advances on the Karelian Isthmus between the Gulf of Finland and Lake Ladoga, most of which was on the Finnish side. In this "Winter War" the Finns were mostly on their own. Mannerheim was extremely loath to give up territory, afraid that once peace did come, any land already ceded for tactical reasons would never be regained. The German-Soviet Non-Aggression Pact signed in secret in August 1939 had placed Finland in the Soviet sphere, and the Germans held to it, remaining neutral. Some British and French military aircraft, weapons, and ammunition did manage to reach Finland, but no Allied troops;

Norway and Sweden denied transit rights. The Finnish government agreed to reopen negotiations in early March. The armistice came at a high cost, and all of Vyborg Province (the Finnish part of Karelia), including the city of Vyborg itself, was left to the Soviet Union.

When Hitler broke his alliance with the USSR and attacked the country in June 1941, Finland got an opportunity to regain its lost territory. Throughout the so-called "Continuation War" (June 1941–September 1944) Finland was an ally of Germany. This was a difficult orientation to assume for the former tsarist officer who had fought against Germany just over two decades earlier. But cut off from the Western Allies, Mannerheim had no other recourse: neutrality was impossible, as it could lead to a two-front war: with Germany in Finland's far north, where it coveted Finnish nickel, and with the USSR on the east.

Mannerheim was able to establish limits to German-Finnish cooperation: there was no unified German-Finnish command during the war, and he maintained his own separate command structure for Finnish troops. He refused Finnish collabora-tion in the German attack on Leningrad; when German generals brought the issue up Mannerheim would abruptly cease speaking and focus his eyes on a far corner of the room.[20] Mannerheim wanted the return of Karelia (a "land which we have cultivated for centuries with sweat and toil," as he called it), and did not want to be on the sidelines when Germany overthrew the Soviet Communist government. The seizure of lands in eastern Karelia by Mannerheim's army that had never been part of Finland was opposed by Social Democrats on the left and the Swedish People's Party on the right, and caused many outside Finland to see Finland's war aims as annexationist. For Mannerheim, who sensed early on that the Germans could not win in the east, the issue was one of security: he sought a buffer between Finland and what he feared and hated the most—the spread of Bolshevism. By early 1944 he knew the Germans would not win, and his goal became no more than to extract Finland from the war.

Mannerheim was not a perfect military leader. He did not delegate well, and he allowed the troops in parts of Finnish-occupied eastern Karelia to be less than fully prepared for the Soviet attack in June 1944. And yet his importance in the war can-not be overestimated. When the Finnish government saw that conditions for ending the war with the Soviet Union would be onerous, it realized it needed Mannerheim's personal authority to gain the country's acceptance. In March 1944, Finland's chief negotiator with the Soviets (and later Finnish president) Juho Kusti Paasikivi wrote him, "The only man whom the Finnish people trusts is you."[21] Accordingly, when Finland's wartime president Risto Ryti resigned in late July, the Finnish cabinet ap-pointed Mannerheim the country's sixth president a few days later.

The Soviet peace terms were indeed severe: a return to the borders of 1940, re-linquishing to the USSR its point of access to the Arctic Ocean, $300 million in repa-ration payments, long-term leasing of a peninsula near Helsinki for use as a Soviet military base, and the prosecution of Finnish "war criminals." Mannerheim was seen as the only figure that all groups in parliament could accept, the only person with sufficient popular authority to reach peace with the Soviets and to carry out their demands.

The Allied Control Commission in Finland, headed by Andrei Zhdanov (who had orchestrated Estonia's capitulation to the Soviet Union in 1940), pressed the Finns to include Mannerheim among those they would find in Finland guilty for the war, prosecution of whom was demanded by the armistice agreement. Ryti received a ten-year prison sentence, although he ended up serving only three years, and several others also served time in prison. But Mannerheim, who was central to Finland's role in both the Winter War and the Continuation War, was needed by the Soviets, just as he was needed by the Finns. Without Mannerheim, the conditions of the armistice could neither be accepted nor fulfilled.

With Finnish war guilt verdicts completed, Mannerheim could leave office, and he resigned in March 1946. He died in Lausanne, Switzerland, where he was writing his memoirs, on January 27, 1951.

In the crucial years between 1939 and 1945, Mannerheim's importance went far beyond the sum total of his personal accomplishments—his very person was important for the stability and success of Finland and its people. Although forever deaf to the siren call of ethnic nationalism, he was a loyal son of Finland. Yet it seems limiting to label Mannerheim as the most significant figure in all twentieth-century Finnish history—which he undoubtedly was—and also overly confining for any evaluation of Mannerheim as an individual. He was an exemplar of an era and a mindset for which there was no place in the twentieth century after World War I—a man who needed the political and cultural expansiveness of empire to flourish. He was "one of the last great aristocrats in European politics," in the words of one historian.[22] In Imperial Russia he found his first career and his life's calling. There his basic political views, his realism, his suspicion of ideologies, and his cosmopolitan outlook were formed. It is a great irony that it was revolution in Imperial Russia that propelled him at the age of fifty on to his second career, and in many ways his second life—this time as a Finn.

Mannerheim thus lived on a grand scale, his entire career revolving within two broad concentric circles. The first consisted of the territory of the multiethnic tsarist empire, a region that included Finland, which would later become one of its most successful successor states. The second was that of Eurasia itself, from China to Britain. In each of these orbits, Mannerheim made major contributions to the countries and peoples he served during his long imperial and postimperial life.

## NOTES

1. J. E. O. Screen, "The Entry of Finnish Officers into Russian Military Service, 1809–1917" (Ph.D. diss., University of London, 1976), 288. Beginning in 1888, the Russian general staff placed limits on the percentage of non-Orthodox officers permitted within all military units. The new policy, clearly intended to favor Russians, was intended to help ensure the reliability

of units that might be deployed to put down domestic unrest. As a result of the policy, Finns whose native language was Finnish could serve as officers only within Finnish units stationed in the Finnish grand duchy; the ban did not apply to Swedish-speaking Finns, who made up the majority of potential officers from Finland. See ibid., 264–65. The question of non-Russians serving as officers became an increasingly contentious issue for the Russian military in the early twentieth century. See Gregory Vitarbo, "Nationality Policy and the Russian Imperial Officer Corps," *Slavic Review* 66, no. 4 (2007): 682–701.

2. Max Engman, *Pietarinsuomalaiset* (Helsinki: Werner Söderström, 2004), 159.

3. S. V. Volkov, *Russkii ofitserskii korpus* (Moscow: Voennoe izdatel'stvo, 1993), 275.

4. See the table for the years 1910, 1911 and 1912 in Volkov, *Russkii ofitserskii korpus,* 354; M. fon Khagen [von Hagen], "Predely reformy: natsionalizm i russkaia imperatorskaia armiia v 1874–1917 gody," *Otechestvennaia istoriia* 5 (2004): 42.

5. The quotations appear in J. E. O. Screen, *Mannerheim: The Years of Preparation,* 2nd ed. (London: Hurst, 1993), 20–21, 24.

6. Carl Gustaf Emil Mannerheim, *Memoirs* (New York: Dutton, 1954), 5.

7. Carl Enckell, *Poliittiset muistelmani,* vol. 1 [translation from Swedish] (Porvoo: Werner Söderström, 1956), 14.

8. Quoted in Vitarbo, "Nationality Policy and the Russian Imperial Officer Corps," 697.

9. Screen, *Mannerheim: The Years of Preparation,* 32, 106.

10. Stig Jägerskiöld, *Nuori Mannerheim* (Helsinki: Otava, 1964), 272, 274–75, 286.

11. This was published in English translation as *Across Asia from West to East in 1906–1908* (Helsinki: Suomalais-Ugrilainen Seura, 1940). Mannerheim's diary is volume 1, and it runs 730 printed pages. The second volume comprises the annotated maps Mannerheim compiled of his route, descriptions and photographs of objects of anthropological interest and historical manuscripts and documents that he collected, and anthropological measurements and linguistic notes from the peoples he came into contact with while in China.

12. Mannerheim, *Memoirs,* 76.

13. Translation of passage in A. L. Zisserman, *Dvatsat' piat' let na Kavkaze (1842–1867)* II (St. Petersburg, 1879), 5–6, reprinted in J. E. O. Screen, *"Våra landsman": Finnish Officers in Russian Service, 1809–1917, A Selection of Documents* (Åbo: Åbo Akademi, 1983), 143. My translation of the Russian-language original is adapted from Screen's, which appears in *"Våra landsman,"* 184–85.

14. Screen, *Mannerheim: The Years of Preparation,* 81, 85, 90.

15. Screen, *Mannerheim: The Years of Preparation,* 110.

16. Stig Jägerskiöld, *Mannerheim 1918* (Helsinki: Otava, 1967), 80–82; Anthony F. Upton, *The Finnish Revolution, 1917–1918* (Minneapolis: University of Minneapolis Press, 1980), 309–10.

17. Letter to Marie Lubomirska, September 12, 1919, quoted in Eleonora Ioffe, *Linii Mannergeima: Pis'ma i dokumenty; Tainy i otkrytiia* (St. Petersburg: Zvezda, 2005), 181.

18. Quoted in Screen, *Mannerheim: The Finnish Years* (London: C. Hurst, 2000), 117.

19. Quoted in Stig Jägerskiöld, *Mannerheim rauhan vuosina, 1920–1939* (Helsinki: Otava, 1973), 281, 283.

20. Leonid Vlasov, *Mannergeim* (Moscow: Molodaia Gvardiia, 2005), 267.

21. Quoted in Screen, *Mannerheim: The Finnish Years,* 199.

22. Marvin Rintala, *Four Finns* (Berkeley: University of California Press, 1969), 35.

Photo taken by an unknown photographer at the Mariinsky Theatre, St. Peterbsurg, Russia of the Ballerina Mathilde Kshesinskaia in *The Talisman,* 1905. Wikimedia Commons.

# 21

## Mathilde Kshesinskaia

### (1872–1971)

KRISTA SIGLER

The essentialist view of nationality has by now been thoroughly rejected by the academic world. Instead, historians and other scholars have come to see national identity as a construct whose implications can vary widely depending on the individual. To be or feel national, in short, is akin to donning a costume in a play. Depending on the interpreter, the costume can express a variety of meanings and fit numerous roles. To a degree, one can also take the costume on and off, which allows whoever is wearing it the ability to signal inclusion or exclusion, difference or sameness.

Such was the case with Polish nationality in late Imperial Russia. In some social arenas, to be seen as Polish was an asset; in others, it meant association with the state's ultimate rival and nemesis, the bastion of liberalism that stubbornly refused to be assimilated into the triangle of Orthodoxy, autocracy, and nationality. For Poles within the empire, nationality, in fact, meant an identification that carried a host of implications, marking the individual as an insider or outsider.

We can see these tensions in the life of Mathilde Kshesinskaia, the Russian Empire's last great prima ballerina. Born in St. Petersburg to a Polish family and the product of the empire's most elite cultural form—the ballet—Mathilde Kshesinskaia danced in a world where her claims to nationality, both Polish and Russian, demonstrated the deep complexity of the Polish position in the last decades of the empire. Her successes and failures in both public and private life evoked nationalist responses from the Russian public, and her own interpretation of her life in her memoirs drew on national themes to explain her experience. That the various representations of nationality in play were ultimately contradictory mattered little. For people like Kshesinkaia, nationality often took on a quality of fantasy and was as much an element of self-fashioning as it was something placed upon them by society at large.

Kshesinskaia's life depicts these shifting connections between imagination and nationality. She leaned heavily on her Polish background as entrée into the cosmopolitan world of the nobility; her critics would later use that very same background to exclude her from Russian society altogether. In the world of the elites, her Polishness was a charming addition to her greater identity as a Russian imperial subject; for the Silver Age world of dance, her identity was as the star of a rising ballet, created by international artists under the banner of making a "Russian style." In the media, her initial supporters cheerfully overlooked her Polishness in order to claim her victories as Russia's own. Later, as revolutionary rage against the elites rose higher, street critics categorized her again as a simple Other, making Polishness a shorthand for non-Russian, and, thus, the enemy.

The story of Kshesinskaia was, in many ways, the story of Russian relations with Poland itself: a territory of continuing cultural conflict. As David Ransel and Bożena Shallcross have noted, from the seventeenth century onwards, the western border represented a threat to Russia's sense of self. First and most obviously, it was Poland-Lithuania that had conquered Moscow during the Time of Troubles.[1] With the ascendancy of the Romanovs did not come peace from a Polish threat, however; across their western borders, Russians saw that a church that was as strong as their own, a nobility that equaled almost a fifth of the population, and a reputation for culture that was admired by more Western nations. This specter, moreover, invaded their own territory: through the partitions of Poland (1772, 1793, 1795), Catholic territory was added to the Russian Empire, forcing a reconsideration of what made Russia Russia if Orthodoxy no longer was the norm.

At first, the tsars attempted to maintain Polishness as linked to, but separate from, Russianness. Alexander I, for example, created the Kingdom of Poland within the Russian Empire, giving Poland a constitutional monarchy and some semblance of autonomy. Catherine the Great herself had inaugurated the practice of giving Polish titles to the illegitimate children of Russian nobility. Her lover, Grigory Potemkin, even referred to himself as Polish, although he actually came from the Smolensk region.

Reactions to the 1830 Polish Uprising, however, disrupted that initial effort at finding a way to maintain a Polish sphere within the Russian territory. For many Russians, including the poet-hero Alexander Pushkin, the uprising was read as a betrayal. Even intellectuals sympathetic to Poland's political situation, such as Aleksandr Herzen, now found elements of Polish culture repulsive and ultimately incompatible with Russia. What the intellectuals began, the government finished, as the state increasingly repressed Polish liberties during the century. In Warsaw, for example, we see the government help to fund the reconstruction for Russian purposes of the historic Staszic building (later renamed "Palace") in central Warsaw.[2] This site, the resting place of a boyar-tsar, became an Orthodox school for Russians living in Poland. As if the palace's location and purpose were not enough to emphasize the Russifying message, the imperial government selected an architect well known for his mastery of the neo-Muscovite style. The potential for improving Polish-Russian relations, on the political level at least, was over.

Kshesinskaia positioned herself within Russian society against the backdrop of these tensions. Indeed, her family history went hand in hand with Russia's increasing absorption of Polish territory. In 1835, decades after the partitions of Poland and the Duchy of Warsaw, her Polish father danced for the meeting of Frederick William III and Nicholas I. So impressed was the emperor by the dance that he later invited the Polish ballet to send ten men and women to join his Russian troupe. Thirteen years before Russia clamped down on a rebellious Poland, Kshesinskaia's father, Adam Felix Krzesiński received one of these invitations and moved to Russia. From that moment on, while her grandfather and father would retain estates in Poland (and Kshesinskaia herself would own land there), Russia would be the family's home. A name change confirmed the permanence of the move: Upon his arrival in Russia, Adam Felix Krzesiński, the Pole, became Felix Kshesinsky.[3]

Those are the facts of the Mathilde Kshesinskaia story, a Polish family absorbed into Russia like the Polish territory itself. The reimagination of these facts, however, tells us something of the various ways in which nationalism could be framed in the later empire.

First, Mathilde Kshesinskaia herself used her Polish background as a means of social advancement. Although she was *prima ballerina assoluta* of the Mariinsky, a former mistress to tsar Nicholas II, and, at the time, the lover of at least one grand duke, Kshesinskaia herself existed in the same liminal social zone as an upscale shop-person today: both in and out of the most elite circles. As such, she had to constantly face the reminder that while elite by circumstance, she was not elite by blood. She danced before the highest aristocrats in the land, but she would not ever be invited to their private entertainments; although she dined with nobles after hours, she could not be acknowledged in public as their equal or even their associate.

Kshesinskaia turned to nationality to help smooth away this obstacle between herself and the society she kept. She did so by asserting that her family line was, in fact, Polish nobility. Within European nobility, nationality mattered; Baltic and Polish nobility ranked beneath the elite Russian families in the eyes of Russian aristocrats, but critically, they were still considered noble.[4] Class, however, mattered even more than nationality for the nobles. Suggesting she was a noblewoman (if from Poland) therefore was a plus for Kshesinskaia, at least within noble circles. In her memoirs, she crafted a detailed story to emphasize this noble provenance: in the first half of the eighteenth century, she claimed, the family Krassinsky lived in Poland. Her great-grandfather, the Count Krassinsky, was a child when his father died. His avaricious uncle then took control of the family fortune, and Krassinsky fell to the care of a kindly French tutor (significantly, the hallmark of an elite childhood among Russian nobles). The French tutor rescued the child from the shady plans of the uncle, carrying the infant Krassinsky off to Paris. Forced to live there, the child, Wojciech, received nothing of his family estate other than regular payments. Unfortunately, the tutor inadvertently helped break his claim to the estate by reregistering Krassinsky in Paris under a false name.[5] Despite this unfortunate, if romantic, background, Wojciech maintained his Polish loyalties, even marrying another Polish émigrée, Anna Ziomkowka, although their child did not gain access to the nobility. Instead, the child, Kshesinskaia's grandfather, had to work as a violinist, actor, and principal tenor of the Warsaw Opera, and this same fate then passed to Kshesinskaia's father, Adam Felix Kshesinsky, who became a dancer. Thus, by Kshesinskaia's generation, the family had ended up with an inheritance of art and culture rather than of landed wealth. All they held of this noble past, Kshesinskaia claimed, was a box holding a ring with the family seal—a box that was somehow lost, and with it, her proof of nobility.

This story, playing to popular associations of Polishness with Western culture, was Kshesinskaia's strongest claim to her Polish roots. According to our best evidence, none of it is true—other than that the Kshesinsky family did, indeed, come from the Polish arts world. Yet if this is the case, then why the lie? Kshesinskaia was not averse to her Polish identity and used it, in part, to help identify herself as a master of the mazurka, much like her father. Her writings showed how she used Polish culture to frame her life—her Polish Christmas Eve celebrations, for example, and her childhood years spent on a Polish country estate owned by her father (the estate was located near Siverskaia Station on the Warsaw Railway, overlooking the Orlinka River). As an adult, in 1898, Kshesinskaia visited Warsaw to pay homage to the Virgin of Czenstokov. In addition, she paid for a chapel for her grandfather in Warsaw, and had her father interred there as well.[6]

Mathilde Kshesinskaia's roots were Polish; however, her life was embedded within the Russian elite. For that reason, she remade her nationality to benefit her current connections. For all of her Polish background, Mathilde Kshesinskaia was much more interested in underscoring her belonging to the cosmopolitan order that surrounded her. Although her first diary was in Polish, her later writings, from recipes to guest lists to letters, were a mix of Russian and French.[7] Her birth name properly would have been Matylda Krzesińska; throughout her life (and even in her memoirs), she used the Russified Kshesinskaia (similarly, her brother and father did not go by "Krzesiński" in their imperial dance careers).[8] Although her mother came from a Catholic Polish background, just like her father, Kshesinskaia downplays this in her memoirs, spending six pages on a discussion of the mysterious Kshesinsky history but devoting just two lines to describe how her mother, Julia Dominksa, had been a ballet artist and came to the marriage with children from a previous union.[9]

Polishness to Kshesinskaia was, therefore, chiefly a social tool that she used to boost her position within international aristocratic society. Her disinterest in her Polish background otherwise is striking: After her son was born, she had the child baptized as Orthodox rather than Catholic. Her travels to Warsaw to visit the Virgin of Czenstokov were brief compared to her vacations in Italy. Indeed, as an adult, she never traveled to Poland for pleasure, despite her numerous travels outside of Russia. Her visits to Warsaw were for performance only. She did not even turn to Poland when it might have been her haven; in the highly dangerous year of 1917, Kshesinskaia did not even consider, let alone attempt, a flight to Poland. Although she later bemoaned the loss of the family's noble estate, she had sold the old Krasnitzy estate to Prince Henry of Wittgenstein—and it was not Kshesinskaia, but her lover, Grand Duke Andrei, who maintained property in Poland.

Kshesinskaia's Polish affectations were therefore just that—affectations. By asserting a Polish noble background, she was able to use nobility to elevate her social status. That is not to say her roots were forgotten by the elites she knew. Nicholas II frequently called her *Pani* or *Panochka,* or "Polish girl."[10] Courtiers, according to one witness, "smiled tolerantly at the tsar's passion for a Polish dancer."[11] At a family council over Nicholas's love life, a grand duchess reportedly praised the "beauty, elegance, passion, sentimentality, and tenderness" of Polish women.[12] For the elites, Polishness stood as a charming add-on to Russian nationality, a winsome combination of emotionality and artistry that had been bridled and glorified thanks to association with Russian power.

This association between Polishness and artistry had provided the basic platform for Kshesinskaia's entrée to the dance world: her father was a well-known mazurka expert who gave lessons to ambitious aristocrats, and Mathilde herself first appeared onstage, in *Le petit chevalier,* in a Polish folk costume. When she herself danced the mazurka, the critics hailed her as "adorable in her magnificent costume."[13] This indulgence toward Kshesinskaia's Polishness reflected the Russian theatrical world's image of Poland as a whole. Halina Goldberg has argued persuasively that, starting with Mikhail Glinka's classic *A Life for the Tsar* (1836), Russian theater frequently used the Polish Other as a device for defining Russianness. As Goldberg puts it, "In the course of modern musical history, 'defining Russia' very frequently meant 'appropriating Poland.'"[14]

Against this overlapping imagery of rebellion and nationalist pride, Kshesinskaia, daughter of the undisputed master of the mazurka and herself an expert in the same style, likewise became a symbol of the glory of the Russian empire. Although she insisted on her Polish nobility, and the elites remarked on her charming Polishness, the world of the Russian ballet—its audience, critics, and those who followed it via the press—knew her as a Russian, a proud representative of the country's cultural achievements. Ironically, her Polish background and identification with the mazurka only made her an ever-greater symbol of Russian pride, if only because Poland was itself a symbol of the empire's power.

Polishness therefore became a key element in asserting Kshesinskaia's Russianness in the world of international dance. The Russian ballet itself had foreign beginnings: The first master of the Russian School of Dance, founded in 1738, was the Frenchman Jean-Baptiste Landé.[15] Catherine the Great later reorganized the school along the lines of western dance academies, and the holy of holies of Imperial Russian ballet, the Mariinsky, was itself designed by an Italian. Just as the institutions of Russian dance had sprung of international roots, so, too, did the form of dance itself. By 1836, the dominating trend in ballet was French. The most famous ballerina in Petersburg was the Italian-Swedish Marie Taglioni, herself an import from the Paris ballet company. Nikolai Gogol even complained about what he saw as excessive French influence on the ballet of his times, arguing that Russians were not meant to dance like the French.[16]

The staff, like the theory behind Russian dance, nonetheless remained international: Kshesinskaia herself studied at the hands of Christian Johansson, "a Swede by birth, [who] . . . became Russian in St. Petersburg," according to the dancer. She was choreographed by Marius Petipa, a Frenchman who never achieved Russian fluency, and also worked with the great Italian dancer, Enrico Ceccheti.[17] Cecchiti's name is revealing. Athough our image of Silver Age dance emphasizes the role of Russian greats like Chaikovsky, and the later Ballets Russes, in reality, the theater of the turn of the century was dominated by the so-called Italian style, led by master dancers either from, or trained by, Italians. Kshesinskaia's Mariinsky was no different in this regard. At the time she began to assume lead roles, she was following the steps of Mariinsky prima ballerinas such as the Italians Pierina Legnani, Virginia Zucchi, and Carlotta Brianza.

Unlike Brianza and her Italian colleagues, Mathilde Kshesinskaia, born in St. Petersburg to a Polish family, had a definite claim to a Russian identity. As such, the Russian arts world found it easy to see her Polish background as nothing more than a minor element in her overall Russian identity. Three decades before Stravinsky's ballets showcased alternately a folkloric (*Petrushka*) or modernist (*Rite of Spring*) Russian style, individual dancers like Kshesinskaia bore the banner for Russia in dance. In particular, the dance writers found it quite convenient to celebrate her triumphs as victories for the Russian national ballet. An early biographer raved of her in 1892, "Our ballerina . . . owes these jewels to our model school. . . . Let me repeat that her debut may be considered a landmark in the history of our ballet."[18] The Russian reviewer A. Pleshcheev hailed her as "our dancer" and "the best Russian dancer of our time," when she performed in Warsaw in 1895.[19] Another critic identified her as a pivotal figure in Russian dance history: "On the eve of the twentieth century, our ballet can be proud of prospering thanks to national talent which no longer looks to the foreign dancer as ideal."[20] "She gradually opened the way for a complete conquest of the stage by Russian ballerinas. Zambelli [the lead dancer before Kshesinskaia] was the last foreign dancer invited to Russian," gushed another critic.[21] Her mastery of the mazurka was mastery of a Russian imperial—not Polish national—dance: "She danced with Slavic soul." Even the Polish press acknowledged her close association with the Russian ballet. During a tour in Warsaw in June 1895, *Gazeta Polska* listed her as a star of the St. Petersburg–based ballet troupe and did not mention her Polish background at all.

By World War I, however, Mathilde Kshesinskaia's national identity became much more problematic, in large part because she became an easy target in the heated wartime debate about the tsarist court and its failings. Eager to find a scapegoat for the government's shortcomings, the press lashed out with xenophobic claims against members of the court as would-be foreign agents working against the empire. Empress Alexandra suffered the most from these suspicions because of her German ties, but she was not alone. Kshesinskaia was also quickly turned by the press into a diabolical foreigner, bent on undermining the country through her grip on powerful Russian men. One courtier attributed her rise to the "Polish propensity for intrigue," which allowed her to make "an excellent position [for herself] in the world as well as earn a . . . fortune."[22] The boulevard view was that Kshesinskaia was a manipulator and a war profiteer who took advantage of her relationship with Grand Duke

Sergei Mikhailovich, then the inspector general of the Artillery, to line her pockets by taking a share of lucrative military contracts. It was even alleged that she sent her own representative to France to negotiate with the arms company Creuzat.[23] Thus, as despised as Grand Duke Sergei was as a member of the royal family and a symbol of the horrific failure of the Russian military in World War I, it was not the Russian-born Romanov who found himself accused, but his "Polish" lover.

Similarly, once the Revolution began, novellas, small books, and pamphlets pilloried Kshesinskaia for her history of close ties to what was seen as a corrupt, weak, and incompetent government, and her private life became a matter of public speculation. In one of the tales told in 1917, for example, we see the future tsar Nicholas cast as a fool for having frittered away his youth with her rather than dealing with problems of state.[24] In another work of the time, a salacious "secret" history of the many favorites of the Romanov dynasty, Kshesinskaia is presented as the last and most powerful favorites of Nicholas's court. Unlike the elite gossips, who did not hesitate to condemn her for her notorious behavior, the author of this particular history focuses exclusively on Nicholas's reign and his personal life, with no reference to Kshesinskaia's history after Nicholas or her relationships with Sergei and Andrei. We soon see why. The author is preoccupied with Nicholas's character failings, particularly his personal weakness. We thus read about how he falls to his knees before Kshesinskaia shortly after they meet and later "begins to cry" when his father orders him to marry Alexandra. Lest we sympathize with star-crossed lovers, the author shows the obscene wealth lavished upon Kshesinskaia by the doting Nicholas. "How much money was heaped upon her?" the author inquires pointedly. Her dressing room is depicted as an exotic den of seduction, a boudoir replete with "crystal bottles of champagne . . . luxurious vases, and . . . the sharp, alluring scent of spices." Although Nicholas married Alexandra (against his will), the author suggests he was too besotted with Kshesinskaia to break off the relationship and continued to dote on her by putting her up in a lavish mansion and offering her "heaps of wealth." We then learn that she has made even more treasure by selling military secrets to the Germans, working hand in hand with the "treasonous" Minister of War Vladimir Sukhomlinov.[25]

Other Revolution-era publications offer a similar picture, presenting Kshesinskaia, the Polish foreigner, as a dangerous force rocking the Russian throne. In the novel *The Love Affair of the Tsarevich: The Great Romance of the Life of Nicholas II*, the naïve Nicholas almost abandons his position as tsarevich to be with Kshesinskaia, proposing to his dying father that he will renounce the throne and leave for India to marry Kshesinskaia if only his father will give him his blessing. Although this love would be touching, author Maria Evgen'eva, like the anonymous author of *The Favorites of Nicholas II*, makes it clear Nicholas's affections were misplaced. Although the tsar generously recognizes his son by Kshesinskaia, granting him a title and a hefty bank account, Kshesinskaia "dreams of more." Although Evgen'eva does not accuse Kshesinskaia of selling secrets to the Germans, she repeatedly stresses her Polishness, suggesting that the ballerina urged the tsar to make Polish affairs as important to his rule as Russian ones, for "the blood of [Poland] runs in the veins of his natural son."[26]

Kshesinskaia's Polish background was dredged up, and linked with the idea of a "Polish son," because of wartime xenophobia. The war and imperial crisis clearly raised the amount of danger associated with competing concepts of nationality; in her life outside of Russia, Kshesinskaia would never be berated as she was for her heritage.[27] That she was not always described this way, however, brings us back to how this Polish dancer fit within the Russian Empire. As we have seen, her nationality was far from a fixed category but rather something plastic and changeable depending on the context and the observer. Kshesinskaia herself used her Polishness initially as an asset, a means to gain backdoor entry into the world of the nobility. For the cosmopolitan world of dance, meanwhile, her Polish heritage was simply a quirk in a woman who was otherwise the unrivaled icon of the greatness of Russian ballet. By the years of World War I and the Revolution, however, as far as the street readership and press were concerned, her Russianness had become insignificant and she was turned instead into one of the most visible symbols of the foreign interests that were supposedly corrupting the wartime empire. In every case, nationality proved to be a construct, a costume that Kshesinskaia either put on herself or had placed upon her by others. Rather than a rigid identity, nationality was a flexible garment to be tailored for multiple purposes.

## Notes

1. David L. Ransel and Bożena Shallcross, "Introduction," in *Polish Encounters, Russian Identity*, ed. David L. Ransel and Bożena Shallcross (Indiana University Press, 2005), 1–3.

2. Robert Pryzgrodzski, "Tsar Vasillii Shuiskii, the Staszic Palace, and Nineteenth-Century Russian Politics in Warsaw," in Ransel and Shallcross, *Polish Encounters:* 144–59.

3. The pronunciation of the family names would have been somewhat similar: in modern Polish, Krzesiński is pronounced "Ke-sha-shin-ski."

4. Dominic Lieven, "The Elites," in *The Cambridge History of Russia*, vol. 2, ed. Dominic Lieven (Cambridge: Cambridge University Press, 2006), 227–44.

5. Mathilde Kshesinskaia, *Dancing in Petersburg*, trans. Arnold Haskell (London: Gollancz, 1960), 14, 13.

6. Kshesinskaia, *Dancing in Petersburg*, 20, 70, 101.

7. Rossiiskii gosudarstvennyi arkhiv literatury i iskusstva (hereafter cited as RGALI), f. 2602, op. 1, ed. xp. 4.

8. Spellings of Kshesinskaia's name vary greatly because Kshesinskaia's preference was different from her family name's original spelling, and writers have transliterated both the Polish and Russian variants into other languages (including French and English.) These variants include Kshesinsskaia, Kshesinskova, Kchessinskaia, Kzecinsksaia, Krzesinskaia, Kschinsky, Kschessinska, Kressinska Krzesinska, Kschessinskaya, Kjzanski, Kschinskinska, Ksheshinsky, Krashinska, and the Princess Romanovsky-Krassinsky. For the sake of consistency, I rely upon the most direct transliteration of her name from Russian, Kshesinskaia.

9. Kshesinskaia, *Dancing in Petersburg*, 12.

10. Kshesinskaia, *Dancing in Petersburg*, 44.

11. Anatole Bourman and D. Lyman, *The Tragedy of Nijinsky* (New York: McGraw-Hill, 1936), 90.

12. Iurii Bezelianksii, *Vera, nadezhda, liubov'* . . . : *Zhenskie portrety* (Moscow: Raduga, 1998), 277.

13. A. Plessheeva, *Nash' balet', 1673–1896* (St. Petersburg: A. Benke, 1896), 446.

14. Halina Goldberg, "Appropriating Poland: Glinka, Polish Dance, and Russian National Identity," in *Polish Encounters*, ed. Ransel and Shallcross, 74–88. See also Kevin Bartig, "Rethinking Russian Music: Institutions, Nationalism, and Untold Histories," *Kritika: Explorations in Russian and Eurasian History* 11, no. 3 (2010): 609–26.

15. For a history of the ballet, see Tim Scholl, *From Petipa to Balanchine: Classical Revival and the Modernization of Ballet* (New York: Routledge, 1994); and Sergei Lifar, *A History of Russian Ballet From its Origins to the Present Day*, trans. Arnold Haskell (New York: Roy, 1954).

16. Nikolai Gogol, "Peterburgskie zapiski 1836 goda," *Polnoe sobranie sochinenii* (Leningrad: Akademiia nauk SSSR, 1952), 8:180, 184–85.

17. Kshesinskaia, *Dancing in Petersburg*, 21, 35.

18. E. Kartsova, *Nashi Artistki, Vypusk' 3: M.F. Kshesinskaia. Kritiko Biograficheskii Etiud* (St. Petersburg: Trud, 1900), 46.

19. Plessheeva, *Nash' balet'*, 99, and Kshesinskaia, *Dancing in Petersburg*, 45.

20. A. K. and V. O., *Matild'da Feliksovana Kshesinskaia: Desiatiletnie sluzheniia v balete* (St. Petersburg: T-vo Khudozhestvennoi Pechati, 1900).

21. E. A. Stark, *Our Ballet*, 128.

22. Count Paul Vasili, *Confessions of the Czarina* (New York: Harper and Brothers, 1918), 80–81.

23. *Rossiiskii imperatorskii dom* (Moscow: Perspectiva, 1992), 190–91. See also John Curtis Perry and Constantine Pleshakov, *The Flight of the Romanovs: A Family Saga* (New York: Basic Books, 1999), 124.

24. Anzhelika Saf'ianova (L. Nikulin), *O startse Grigorii i russoi istorii . . . Skazka nashikh dnei* (Moscow, 1917), 14.

25. *Favoritki Nikolai II: Vypusk' 1P* (Petrograd: 1917). Quotations on 4, 12, 14, 16.

26. Maria Evgen'eva, *Roman Tsarevicha: Bol'shoi Roman iz zhizni Nikolaia II* (Saint Petersburg: Interduk, 1990), 104, 29, 32. In both this text and the anonymously authored *Favorites of Nicholas II,* Kshesinskaia is said to have had sons by Nicholas II—here, ultimately, two sons.

27. Kshesinskaia left Russia for the French Riviera and later Paris. In her postimperial life, her national image was cut sharply downward; all critics and commentators refer to her as a Russian. To émigrés, Kshesinskaia herself continued, where possible, to mention her noble Polish background, but that was more to justify her marriage to Grand Duke Andrei Vladimirovich (1921) than to associate herself with Poland. For the rest of her life, she demonstrated little to no interest in Poland. Even her son Vladimir (popularly known as "Vova") indicated no interest in, or attachment to, Poland.

Stalin in 1902. Wikimedia Commons.

# 22

⌁

# Joseph Stalin

## (1878–1953)

RONALD GRIGOR SUNY

Three imperial leaders of modern Europe came from the peripheries of the empires they would rule and expand—Napoléon, Hitler, and Stalin. Born on December 6 (19), 1878, in the Georgian town of Gori, in a country exoticized as dramatically beautiful, fatally attractive, and savage as Corsica—and as far from the centers of political power as the hinterlands of Austria—Joseph Stalin (Ioseb Jughashvili) rose from impoverished son of a shoemaker to become one of the most powerful men in the world. He forged two empires—one internal between the metropole of Communist Party power in Moscow and the peoples and republics of the USSR (including the Russians!); the other in east Central Europe and Mongolia made up of subordinate satellite states ruled by communist satraps. Historians have linked his Georgian origins to his brutal political style, either as a "man of the borderlands" (Alfred Rieber) or as adolescent poet turned gangster (Simon Sebag Montefiore).[1] His dissolute father, Bessarion Jughashvili, and his religious mother, Ekaterina (Keke) Geladze, fought over their son's education; his mother ultimately triumphed, sending the boy to a Georgian Orthodox seminary. Stalin's first immersion in culture and politics was in a Georgian milieu, but in the cosmopolitan city of Tiflis (Tbilisi), young Joseph turned away from the church toward Marxism and a career as a professional revolutionary. Somewhat romantic as a youth—he wrote nationalist poetry in his native Georgian language—Soso Jughashvili embraced the hero of a Georgian novella, and to his closest friends and comrades he was known as "Koba."[2] As a member of the Marxist Social Democratic Party, he organized workers in the port town of Batumi, but his impetuous nature led to a reckless strike that ended with the police killing protesters. Never comfortable under the tutelage of the older generation of Georgian Marxists (Noe Zhordania and the *mesame dasi* [third generation]), Jughashvili gravitated after his first arrest and exile to Siberia toward the more militant wing of social democracy, the Bolsheviks, cutting himself off from most of his fellow Georgian revolutionaries, who preferred the more moderate Mensheviks.

From 1907 he worked largely outside Georgia, moving first to the oil-producing center at Baku, where he engaged in underground party work rather than the open labor movement. Taking the name "Stalin," from the Russian word *stal'* (steel), he met the Bolshevik leader Vladimir Lenin, whom he admired but not uncritically. Lenin commissioned Stalin to write a pamphlet on the problem of non-Russian peoples in the Russian empire, the so-called national question, and in 1913 he published his first major work, *Marxism and the National Question,* thus earning a reputation as an expert on the problem of the non-Russian peoples. Yet ethnic identification was unimportant to Stalin, like other Bolsheviks, and he projected a future state in which nationalism and national identity would eventually dissolve under the solvent power of socialism.

Liberated from his last Siberian exile by the Revolution of February 1917, he returned to Petrograd and soon became a leading figure in the Bolshevik party. At first his positions on key issues of the day were more moderate than Lenin's, but Stalin soon readjusted his views to conform to Lenin's line. After the Bolshevik seizure of power in October 1917, he was named people's commissar of nationalities, responsible for the policies of the new Soviet state toward the non-Russians. Although he preferred spending his time and energy on matters outside his commissariat, Stalin was a principal architect of what became the Soviet Union. Russian Bolsheviks repeatedly proclaimed the principal of national self-determination of peoples, which in Lenin's understanding permitted full secession of non-Russians from the Russian state. Stalin was more reluctant to permit the fragmentation of the country and pushed to have only the voice of the "proletariat" and its representatives count in the calculation of which peoples might go their own way. As Soviet power expanded thanks to the success of the Red Army, the actual resolution of the question came not in deliberation and negotiation, but on the battlefield. Some peoples—Finns, Poles, Estonians, Latvians, and Lithuanians—achieved independence in large part because of European support, whereas others—the bulk of the Ukrainians and Belorussians, Armenians, Azerbaijanis, Georgians, and the Muslims of Central Asia—experienced brief periods of statehood or autonomy before they were reintegrated into the Soviet sphere by force.

As the civil war came to an end, the Communists debated the shape of their new state. Just before a stroke incapacitated him in March 1923, Lenin proposed the maximal autonomy and equality for non-Russians. He was fiercely suspicious of "Great Russian chauvinism" and eventually concluded that the constituent peoples of the Soviet Union had to have their own territorial and cultural autonomy in a federal system. The program of "indigenization" (*korenizatsiia*) of national territories promoted schooling and publishing in local languages and the development of national cadres to fill the regional and republic state and party institutions. Stalin supported korenizatsiia, but he fought with Lenin over the degree of autonomy to be granted to non-Russians. Lenin preferred a genuine federation with greater autonomy left to the non-Russian republics, but Stalin pressed for a more centralized state with greater power in Moscow. Both men, however, understood that every part of the union would be ruled by a branch of a unified Communist Party.

Furious with Stalin, Lenin wrote to his comrades,

> Comrade Stalin, having become Secretary General, has unlimited authority concentrated in his hands, and I am not sure whether he will always be capable of using that authority with sufficient caution. . . . Stalin is too rude, and this defect, though quite tolerable in our midst and in dealings among us Communists, becomes intolerable in a General Secretary. That is why I suggest that the comrades think of a way to remove Stalin from that post and appoint in his place another man who in all respects differs from Comrade Stalin in his superiority, that is, more loyal, more courteous and more considerate of the comrades, less capricious, etc.[3]

Lenin's comrades did not heed his warning, and a decade and a half later most of them paid with their lives.

Even in Lenin's last years, Stalin accumulated enormous power within the party. In what at the time seemed to many to be a trivial appointment, the Eleventh Party Congress in the spring of 1922 elected Stalin a member of the party secretariat with the title "general secretary." Although he was not generally recognized outside party circles as one of the most influential leaders, his authority grew as his position at the head of the party bureaucracy provided the means to appoint and move party officials. Like other high-ranking party leaders, he took on a wide range of assignments—from people's commissar of nationalities (from 1917–23), people's commissar of state control (from 1919) and worker-peasant inspection [Rabkrin] (1920–22), to membership in the Military-Revolutionary Council of the Republic, the Politburo (the political bureau, the highest party council) and the Orgburo (organizational bureau, in charge of party workers)—from their creation in March 1919—and member of a variety of commissions set up to solve specific problems. Within the party political manipulation, Machiavellian intrigues, and a chilly ruthlessness were certainly part of Stalin's repertoire, but he also positioned himself in the immediate post-Lenin years as a pragmatic and cautious man of the center, a supporter of the compromises and concessions of Lenin's moderate, state capitalist New Economic Policy (NEP) unwilling to risk Soviet power to pursue elusive revolutions abroad.

By the time of Lenin's incapacitation in 1923, Stalin was fast becoming indispensable to many powerful figures. He allied with two others in the top leadership, Grigorii Zinoviev and Lev Kamenev, to prevent the growth of influence of the powerful and popular Leon Trotsky. On the eve of Politburo meetings, this *troika* would meet, at first in Zinoviev's apartment, and later in Stalin's Central Committee office, to decide what positions they would take on specific issues and what roles each would play in the meeting. In 1924–25 the group was expanded to seven, with the additions of Nikolai Bukharin, Aleksei Rykov, Mikhail Tomskii, and Valerian Kuibyshev. Power within the party steadily moved upward to the very institutions in which Stalin played a key role. He was the only person who was a member of all of the important committees and soon built up his own staff, which amounted to a personal chancellery. Despite his suspicious nature and his intellectual limitations (certainly exaggerated by political rivals and opponents), Stalin was able to attract a number of loyal subordinates, whose fortunes would rise with his.

Stalin was a master politician who understood earlier than many others the value of ideological orthodoxy. He positioned himself as a loyal follower of the revered Lenin, despite his principled disagreements with the leader. Immediately after Lenin's death a cult developed around his memory. The city of Petrograd was renamed Leningrad, and, against the wishes of his widow, the party ordered Lenin's body mummified and placed in a marble mausoleum in Red Square, a quasi-religious relic to be viewed by the faithful. In April and May, Stalin gave a series of lectures at Sverdlov University that were soon published as *Foundations of Leninism*. This association with the dead Lenin, even more than any past service, gave a political leader legitimacy and authority in the 1920s. In this new political environment, Stalin, who had seldom differed openly with Lenin, flourished, while Trotsky, whose prerevolutionary writings had often polemicized against Lenin, withered.

The Soviet government faced serious resistance in several regions to the imposition of central state and party control. In Central Asia the Red Army fought the so-called *basmachi*s (bandits), a collection of tribal, traditional Islamic, and Pan-Turkic warriors, well into 1923. But following the 1922 death of the former Ottoman minister, Enver Pasha, who had momentarily united many of the fighters, the movement disintegrated, and many radical Muslims gravitated to the Communist Party. In August 1924, a Menshevik-led insurrection directed from abroad broke out in Georgia, but the Communists quickly and brutally crushed the rebels. Stalin was even more directly involved in the convoluted case of Mirsaid Sultan-Galiev, a Tatar Bolshevik whom he had patronized earlier but had arrested in 1923 for secretly linking up with basmachis. Throughout the mid-1920s Stalin maintained strong support for the policy of korenizatsiia and resisted efforts by party "leftists" to denigrate the native cadres who joined the party in the non-Russian areas. At the same time he opposed "National Communists" whom he thought moved too far in the direction of nationalism and threatened to turn Russians against a policy that promoted non-Russians. He consistently held that ethnicity would not be eliminated in the Soviet Union until the complete victory of socialism worldwide. His nationality policy was contradictory (or, perhaps, in the language of the time, dialectical!), at once fostering the cultures and languages of dozens of peoples and trying to restrain tendencies to express nationalist political or even cultural aspirations. The Soviets were attempting to create internationalist, socialist ties between peoples, but simultaneously they were encouraging the development of more articulate, conscious nationalities. Yet national identity was Janus-faced: it was not only about what linked people of one ethnicity together but what separated and distinguished that nationality from another.

In 1924 Stalin and his close comrade, Nikolai Bukharin, adopted a moderate course favoring the concessions to the peasantry that Lenin had inaugurated in 1921 with the New Economic Policy. But Bukharin's pro-peasant policies went further than other Leninist stalwarts, like Zinoviev and Kamenev, thought appropriate for a proletarian dictatorship. Stalin proclaimed that the communists would build "Socialism in One Country," even though Lenin had always maintained that socialism could not be achieved in backward peasant Russia alone, but required support from an international revolution in more developed, industrial countries. When Zinoviev and Kamenev balked at his cautious policies and the growing bureaucratization of the party, Stalin broke with them and formed a new bloc with Bukharin.

This moderate, centrist policy was reflected in nationality policy as well—until 1930. The contradiction between the "nationalization" of non-Russians and the "internationalist" agenda of Soviet power was radically exposed during the "socialist offensive" of the *Velikii perelom* (Great Breakthrough). The years 1928–32 have been dubbed the "Stalin Revolution" or the "Revolution from Above," a five-year period of state-driven industrialization and massive violence against the countryside. The party/state forced millions of peasants into collective farms, seized their grain without adequate compensation, and exiled or killed the most productive peasants, the so-called kulaks. In March and April 1930, the secret police organized a massive show trial of Ukrainian nationalist intellectuals who were condemned as "anti-Soviet." This trial and others in Belorussia, Tatarstan, and Crimea signaled that the tolerance shown earlier toward "National Communists" was being curtailed. A year later Stalin introduced a novel theme into Soviet rhetoric—the conflation of Russian historical precedents into a more state-centered Russophilic narrative. In December 1931, the Politburo called a halt to the fast-paced Ukrainization programs that had been implemented in both the Ukrainian and Russian republics.[4]

Stalin's revolution with its forced collectivization of the peasantry and breakneck industrialization had its own unique characteristics—its own language, slogans, strategies, and costs. It was carried out as a massive military campaign, along "fronts," scaling heights, conquering the steppe, vanquishing backwardness, all while the country was encircled by hostile capitalist states. All obstacles, natural and technical, could be overcome. Stalin spoke of human will as the essential force to achieve the economic plan, proclaiming, "There are no fortresses Bolsheviks cannot capture!" For him the need to industrialize rapidly was connected with the dangers that the USSR faced from the great capitalist and imperialist powers. "One feature of the history of old Russia," he proclaimed in 1931,

> was the continual beatings it suffered because of its backwardness. It was beaten by the Mongol khans. It was beaten by the Turkish beys. It was beaten by the Swedish feudal lords. It was beaten by the Polish and Lithuanian gentry. It was beaten by the British and French capitalists. It was beaten by the Japanese barons. All beat it—because of backwardness, because of its military backwardness, cultural backwardness, agricultural backwardness. . . . Such is the law of the exploiters—to beat the backward and the weak. It is the wolves' law of capitalism. . . . That is why we must no longer lag behind.[5]

By linking forced-pace economic development to national security, Stalin construed any hesitation or foot dragging as "wrecking" or treason, crimes with heavy penalties. When the headlong rush to industrialization generated waste or breakdowns, rather than blaming the policy or the leaders, the police "uncovered" conspiracies and saboteurs. Contrived show trials imposed harsh sentences on innocent people. New dangers from Germany and Japan accelerated Stalin's étatist tendencies, and whatever autonomy non-Russian republics had enjoyed in the first decade of Soviet power rapidly eroded. The USSR was to be a unitary state, a pseudo-federation, with a monolithic party directing policy from Moscow and headed by an unchallenged autocrat. Stalin reversed the anti-imperialist and Russophobic direction of Lenin's time, launched ferocious attacks on the leaders of the national republics and regions, and submerged his centralizing project under the anodyne slogan "Friendship of the Peoples" (*Druzhba narodov*).

In a few short years the Soviet government had initiated a massive social transformation of society and the economy, founding the first modern non-market, state-run economy. Yet the Stalin revolution destroyed the regime's fragile relationship with the great majority of the population and created a new repressive apparatus that Stalin could use to consolidate his personal rule over the party and state. Stalin's rise was unexpected by most of his fellow Communists. He had little charisma, possessed no oratorical skills like Zinoviev, and was neither a Marxist theorist like Trotsky nor a likable comrade like Bukharin. Short in stature and reticent in meetings, Stalin did not project an image of a leader—until it was created for him (and by him) through the personality cult. For his closest associates, however, Stalin was indispensable, the solid center of the bureaucratic state and party apparatus, a generous patron, and a stern master. He turned the revolution inward, emphasizing the building of a militarized state and an industrial economy, and playing down international revolution. His ideology was a radically revised Marxism that grafted onto it a pro-Russian nationalism and a great power statism. As long as the country was challenged by enemies, it was claimed, state power had to be built up. When the Soviet Union was declared to be socialist by Stalin in 1936, the positive achievement of reaching a stage of history higher than the rest of the world was tempered by the constant reminders that the enemies of socialism existed both within and outside the country, that they were deceptive and concealed, and had to be "unmasked." Repeated references to dangers and insecurity and to the need for "vigilance" justified the enormous reliance on the secret police and the open exercise of political terror.

Stalin can be considered a "conservative revolutionary." The more radical tendencies in Bolshevism were shelved: instead of equalization of wages, Stalin promoted greater differentials between skilled and unskilled workers; instead of attacking "Great Russian chauvinism," he encouraged a new form of Soviet patriotism based on reverence for Russia's imperial past. Peter the Great, even Ivan the Terrible, became models of rulership. The USSR became a peculiar kind of internal empire with a developmentalist ideology that was supposed to legitimize the paternalistic dominance of the Communist Party over the population.

Stalin turned a political oligarchy into a personal dictatorship by the late 1930s. But as he rose to the pinnacle of power in the USSR, he became increasingly isolated. He narrowed his circle of friends and close comrades to those most loyal to him: his

sometime prime minister and foreign minister, Viacheslav Molotov; the industrial-
izer Sergo Orjonikidze; the economically savvy Anastas Mikoyan; the policeman and
executioner, Lavrentii Beria; and those loyal party workers ready to do his bidding—
Lazar Kaganovich, Georgii Malenkov, Andrei Zhdanov, and Nikita Khrushchev.
Suspicious even of these men, Stalin's personal life withered, especially after his young
wife, Nadezhda Allilueva, killed herself in November 1932. Outside of his work, late-
night dinners with his cronies, and the little time he spent with his daughter, Svetlana,
Stalin had no personal life. His suspicion of others matched their fear of him.

The height of Stalinist terror was reached in the Great Purges of 1937–38, when
approximately 700,000 people were executed and millions more were exiled, imprisoned, or died in labor camps. Among the victims were thousands of Communists,
including Lenin's closest associates—Zinoviev, Kamenev, and Bukharin. Angry and
upset at the turn that Soviet policy under Stalin had taken, Orjonikidze shot himself.
By the end of the 1930s, 3,593,000 people were under the jurisdiction of the secret
police; 1,360,000 of them were in labor camps. Whole peoples were deported from
border areas, among them Koreans, Poles, and Germans. Stalin personally initiated,
guided, and prodded the arrests and the show trials of 1936–38, and required his lieu-
tenants to sign off on executions. The bloodletting defies rational explanation. Here
personality and politics merged, and this excessive repression appears to be dictated
by the peculiar demands of Stalin himself, who could not tolerate limits on his will
set by the very ruling elite that he had brought to power. The purges eliminated all
rivals and potential rivals to Stalin's autocracy and produced a new, younger, Soviet-
educated political elite loyal to and dependent on the master. By 1938 the killings had
so destabilized government and society that the regime gradually brought them to
a halt, but the long arm of Stalin's police reached to Mexico, where in 1940 a secret
agent murdered his rival, Trotsky. Particularly devastating for the country on the eve
of war was the decimation of the highest ranks of the military.

By the outbreak of the World War II the central government, the military, the
republics and local governments, the economic infrastructure had all been brutally
disciplined. Obedience and conformity had eliminated most initiative and originality. After destroying the high command of the armed forces, Stalin's control over his
military was greater than Hitler's over his, at least at the beginning of World War II.
His control over politics was so complete that he was able to reverse completely the
USSR's "collective security" foreign policy that favored allying with Western capitalist democracies against the fascist states and sign a nonaggression pact with Nazi
Germany in August 1939.

Yet for all the human and material costs of Stalin's industrialization and state
building, the Soviet Union was not prepared for the onslaught of the German invasion of June 1941. Stalin did not expect Hitler to attack before subduing Britain,
and he was stunned when informed that German troops had crossed the border.
German fascism was virulently expansionist. Hitler's program included the creation of a vast German colonial empire in the east that would eliminate millions
of "degenerate" peoples and enslave millions of others. Rallying himself and his

countrymen to the colossal effort against the Nazis and their allies, Stalin stood at the center of all strategic, logistical, and political decisions. He was chairman of the State Defense Committee, which included the highest party officials (Molotov, Beria, Malenkov, Kliment Voroshilov, Kaganovich, and later Nikolai Voznesenskii and Mikoyan); the chairman of *Stavka,* the supreme military headquarters; general secretary of the party and chairman of the Politburo; chairman of the Council of Ministers and people's commissar of defense. Real business often took place in late-night meetings at Stalin's apartment or dacha, where he attended to the minutest details of the war effort.

Like Hitler, Stalin made major miscalculations early in the war. But when in October 1941 the Germans approached Moscow and many Muscovites panicked and fled the city, Stalin demonstrably stayed in Moscow and encouraged the resistance with a speech blending the heroic military traditions of the Russian Empire with the cause of Lenin and the Soviet Union. Ultimately the war was won by the tenacity and enormous sacrifice of the Soviet people, but Stalin provided both inspiration for many and fear that one step backward would end in death.

The Soviets bore the heaviest burdens of the war against fascism and lost some twenty-seven million people. To punish several small nationalities that he considered collaborators with the invading Germans, Stalin uprooted and deported Chechens, Ingush, Kalmyks, Crimean Tatars, and others. In the end the colossal sacrifices of Soviet citizens thwarted Hitler's imperial ambitions. The triumph over fascism provided the Communists with a new source of legitimation and Stalin with a new, uncontested authority. Now Russia and the Soviet Union were melded into a single image. Patriotism and accommodation with established religious and national traditions, along with the toning down of revolutionary radicalism, contributed to a powerful ideological amalgam that outlasted Stalin himself. In the postwar decades the war became the central moment of Soviet history, eclipsing the Revolution and the Stalin revolution of the early 1930s. After a brief attempt to work with his American and British allies to establish a condominium over Europe, Stalin reverted to a more traditional sphere of influence strategy and tightly tied east Central Europe to the Soviet Union. One by one the countries along the USSR's western border were brought under Stalin's rule, and an empire of "people's democracies" was consolidated. For the long years of the Cold War the Soviet Bloc stood face to face with the North Atlantic Treaty Organization, both armed with nuclear weapons and essentially preventing further expansion of the rival alliance.

Stalin's postwar policies were repressive at home and expansive abroad. There were sporadic uses of repression and terror against individuals or groups (such as the "Leningrad Affair" of 1947 and the "Doctors' Plot" of 1953), as well as another series of ethnic deportations of peoples from newly annexed territories (the Baltic republics, Western Ukraine, and Belorussia) as well as Kurds, Meskhetian Turks, repatriated Armenians, and others, but no massive terror on the scale of 1937 was employed after the war. Intellectuals suffered from the cultural crackdown known as the *Zhdanovshchina,* and a campaign against "cosmopolitanism" was directed against

Soviet Jews. The Soviet Union drew in upon itself, and grew more xenophobic and isolated from the capitalist world. The internal empire was firm but brittle. Although nationalization policies remained in place formally, the slightest expression of national sentiment might be arbitrarily punished as nationalism. Jews were particularly vulnerable as the "anti-cosmopolitanism" campaign targeted some of the most prominent Soviet intellectuals, artists, and professionals.[6]

In his last years, enfeebled by stokes, Stalin was arguably the most powerful man in the world. Not only did he control the USSR and much of Eastern Europe, but the communist leaders of China, North Korea, and Vietnam deferred to him. In 1950 he agreed that Korean leader Kim Il Sung could invade South Korea, thus opening the way to the Korean War. As Stalin deteriorated physically and mentally, the entire country—its foreign policy, internal politics, cultural life, and economic slowdown—reflected the shifting moods of its leader and his growing isolation, arbitrariness, and inactivity. No one could feel secure. The ruling elite was concerned with plots, intrigues, the rivalries between Stalin's closest associates, the rise and fall of clients and patrons. "All of us around Stalin," writes Khrushchev, "were temporary people. As long as he trusted us to a certain degree, we were allowed to go on living and working. But the moment he stopped trusting you, Stalin would start to scrutinize you until the cup of his distrust overflowed."[7] Ultimately, Stalin turned against Molotov and Mikoyan, and grew suspicious of Beria, Voroshilov, Kaganovich, and Malenkov. Khrushchev overheard him say, "I'm finished. I trust no one, not even myself." He died of a massive stroke on March 5, 1953.

Like his predecessors Ivan the Terrible, Peter the Great, and Catherine the Great, Stalin was both a state builder and an empire builder. Historically, Russia's "national" identity was an imperial one—nation, absolutist state, and empire intimately intertwined—and Stalin contributed to that tradition in an exceptionally brutal manner. His legacy was a hypercentralized state, a crudely industrialized economy, a country in which millions had died to build his idea of socialism, and other millions to defend their country against the enemies of Communism. Ironically, the Soviet Union's burden in World War II served both to preserve the power of the dictator and simultaneously to save Western liberalism and capitalism. By Stalin's death the Soviet Union was overextended politically, holding on with difficulty to its Eastern European possessions and facing a resurgent Western democratic capitalist camp far more powerful economically and militarily than Stalin's empires. Almost immediately after his passing, his successors began to dismantle many of the pillars of Stalinism. They ended the mass terror, closed down the slave labor camps, introduced a degree of "socialist legality," and opened the country to the West. In 1956, Nikita Khrushchev denounced Stalin's crimes and eventually, after an aging party official related a dream she had that Lenin was uncomfortable lying next to Stalin, the tyrant's body was removed from its place of honor in Lenin's mausoleum. But his real monument could not be so easily moved. So indelibly had Stalin put his mark on the Soviet system that each attempt to change it merely underlined how pernicious and pervasive had been his excision of the original emancipatory designs of the revolution.

NOTES

1. Alfred Rieber, "Stalin, Man of the Borderlands," *American Historical Review* 56, no. 5 (December 2001): 1651–91; Simon Sebag Montefiore, *Young Stalin* (London: Weidenfeld and Nicolson, 2007).

2. Ronald Grigor Suny, "Beyond Psychohistory: The Young Stalin in Georgia," *Slavic Review* 50, vol. 1 (Spring 1991): 48–58.

3. V. I. Lenin, *Polnoe sobranie sochineniia,* 5th ed. (Moscow: Institut Marksizm-Leninizma, 1958–65), 45:346; translation from Moshe Lewin, *Lenin's Last Struggle* (New York: Random House, 1968; repr. Ann Arbor: University of Michigan Press, 2005), 84.

4. The most thorough work to date on the shift from korenizatsiia to Stalin's *druzhba narodov* [friendship of the peoples] is Terry Martin, *The Affirmative Action Empire: Nations and Nationalism in the Soviet Union, 1923–1939* (Ithaca, N.Y.: Cornell University Press, 2001).

5. I. V. Stalin, *Sochineniia* (Moscow: Gosizpolit, 1951), 38–39.

6. On Stalin's last decade, see Yoram Gorlitzi and Oleg Khlevniuk, *Cold Peace: Stalin and the Soviet Ruling Circle, 1945–1953* (Oxford: Oxford University Press, 2004).

7. *Khrushchev Remembers,* trans. and ed. Strobe Talbott (Boston: Little, Brown, and Co., 1970), 307.

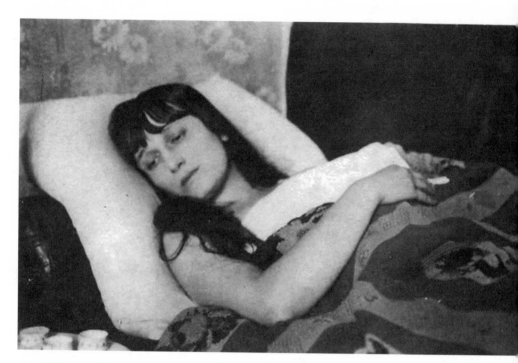

Akhmatova in 1924.

# 23

## Anna Akhmatova

### (1889–1966)

ALEXANDRA HARRINGTON

Anna Akhmatova is one of Russia's best-loved and most talented lyric poets. Yet her preeminent position in Russian cultural history rests on more than the quality of her writing. Through a combination of her poetry, the shape of her biography, and the force of her personality she has acquired a legendary status, becoming—even during her own lifetime—a larger-than-life, monumental figure, martyr against tyranny and preserver of prerevolutionary culture, a symbol of persecuted genius, and an example of moral courage. In short, she is a cultural icon. Early in Akhmatova's career, her contemporary Marina Tsvetaeva crowned her "Anna of all the Russias," which aptly reflects the fact that her life as a writer was, from the outset, intimately tied to Russian imperial experience. Akhmatova embodied the kind of cultural diversity that is an integral part of Russian identity: she was sympathetic to both Western and Eastern influences on Russian culture and her public image incorporates elements of each. This public image—not wholly invented but nonetheless carefully shaped—was a multicultural one, made up of a Tatar name and "Oriental" ancestry combined with a blend of southern (Ukrainian) and northern (Russian) heritage.[1]

She was born Anna Gorenko by the sea in Bolshoi Fontan, near Odessa in Ukraine, to an unexceptional gentry family. Akhmatova's mother, Inna Stogova, was a descendent of a rich Russian landowning family with strong links to Kyiv, and her father, Andrei Gorenko, was a Ukrainian naval engineer descended from Ukrainian Cossacks. He belonged to the minor aristocracy, hereditary nobility having been acquired by his father for his service in the navy. In 1890, Gorenko took up a position in the civil service in St. Petersburg and the family moved first to Pavlovsk and then to Tsarskoe Selo, just outside the capital, where the summer residence of the imperial family was located and many of the nobility kept their summer dachas. In her autobiographical prose, Akhmatova remarks that her first memories were of Tsarskoe Selo, which she calls in her poetry "my little toy town" and valued particularly for its associations with Alexander Pushkin. She was educated from 1900 to 1905 in the Mariinsky Gymnazium, whose richest young pupils had their lunch brought to them on silver trays by valets. Her recorded memories of this period are distinctly monarchist ones, and it was in Tsarskoe Selo that Akhmatova acquired the mannerisms and etiquette of an aristocratic young woman.

As a corollary to her development of an Imperial Russian identity, Akhmatova downplayed her Ukrainian origins and family to some extent, complaining with some bitterness in her autobiographical prose that people tended to think of her as Ukrainian. She said this was because of her obviously Ukrainian family name, because she was born in Odessa and graduated from the gymnasium in Kyiv (in 1907), and especially because her first husband, Nikolai Gumilev, wrote of her in a famous poem of 1910, "From the city of Kyiv, / From the serpent's lair / I took not a wife, but a sorceress." Akhmatova points out that she spent longer in Tashkent, where she lived in evacuation during the World War II (1941–44) than she ever did in Kyiv, where she spent three winters in total—at school and then university. This distancing from her Ukrainian background may have been prompted not only by her conscious assumption of a metropolitan identity, but in part also by her negative feelings towards her father, whose womanizing caused the breakup of her parents' marriage.

Akhmatova's childhood was, nevertheless, punctuated by the summers the family spent in the southern Russia, and she moved with her mother to the Crimean resort of Yevpatoria when her parents split up in 1905. As the poet herself noted, "Tsarskoe was the winter, the Crimea—the summer." Although Akhmatova recalled that she pined when in the south for Tsarskoe Selo, the Black Sea shore provided considerable inspiration for her poetry, as her richly descriptive long poem "Right by the Sea" (1914) demonstrates. Akhmatova's later characterization of herself in her autobiographical prose as the unconventional, tomboyish southern "wild girl" who went around barefoot, sunburned, and hatless, diving into the sea from a boat, provides a striking contrast with the more typically northern Russian refinement and restraint with which she came to be most closely associated. Nadezhda Mandelstam observed later, "Anna was not a Great Russian; she was from Southern Russia and of Petersburg stock, more or less," and "Behind the flimsy disguise of a lady [ . . . ] lived this feisty girl."[2] Akhmatova was ultimately the product of two very distinct environments, both of which influenced her character and poetry.

Akhmatova gave her image an additional multicultural dimension by adopting an Eastern-sounding pseudonym (apparently as a response to her father's concerns that she would bring shame on his family name). She took her exotic and un-Russian pen name, she claimed, from her maternal great-grandmother, whose forbear was Khan Akhmat, a descendent of Chinggis Khan and the last Tartar to receive tribute from the Russians; he was killed in 1481 by a hired assassin. This lineage, through which Akhmatova implied that royal Tatar blood flowed through her veins, is shrouded in legend. As though acknowledging this, she wrote of her name:

Tatar, dense
It came from nowhere.
Attaching to any misfortune,—
It itself—is misfortune.

It was an inspired choice (the poet Joseph Brodsky called it her "first poem"), because it added an exotic appeal to her image, yet remained well within the bounds of acceptability, since its dubious associations with the Mongol Yoke were offset by its Slavo-Turko-Finno-Ugric ring, which was demographically perfectly correct in the Russian Empire.[3]

In 1910, Akhmatova married fellow poet Nikolai Gumilev—by whom she subsequently had a son, Lev, in 1912—and the couple moved to St. Petersburg.[4] She and Gumilev belonged to a new group of poets, the Acmeists, who regarded themselves as heirs to the Russian and European poetic tradition of the past. In this respect they were typical products of the cultural atmosphere of Russia's westward-looking capital. Although Akhmatova retained her love of Tsarskoe Selo, she came to regard Petersburg as her "cradle" and her early poetry proclaims her as a fashionable young denizen of metropolitan life. She was living in Petersburg (then wartime Petrograd) when the February and October revolutions took place in 1917. Only a minority of the liberal intelligentsia supported the new regime, and many emigrated in the years immediately before and after the revolution. Akhmatova, unlike some of her poet acquaintances, such as Alexander Blok and Vladimir Mayakovsky, was steadfastly opposed to Bolshevism and the Revolution, but like them she chose to remain in her homeland. She seems to have regarded this as a moral duty: her worldview was shaped by traditional Russian Orthodox values of resignation and acceptance of suffering. Her patriotic poetry dealing with war and revolution is suffused with this sensibility, which gave her a wide appeal among the Russian readership. In one of her best-known poems of 1917 she dramatizes her resolve to remain in Russia:

A voice came to me. It called comfortingly,
It was saying: "Come here,
Leave your deaf and sinful country,
Leave Russia for good.

I will clean your hands of the blood,
From your heart I will dig out the black shame,
I will cover the pain of defeat and insult
With a new name."

But indifferently and calmly
I placed my hands over my ears,
So that this unworthy speech
Would not sully my sorrowful soul.

Akhmatova continued to publish in the years immediately following the Revolution. By the beginning of the 1920s she was at the height of her popularity, second only perhaps to Blok in the affections of Russian readers. Some fifteen thousand copies of her work were sold during the early years of the New Economic Policy. But this decade brought about an abrupt change in Akhmatova's fortunes. The brutal execution without trial of Gumilev by the Cheka in August 1921, a grossly disproportionate punishment for his failure to inform the authorities of a counterrevolutionary plot, was a devastating shock not only for Akhmatova but also for the educated classes in general. After the Revolution Gumilev had openly declared his monarchist sympathies, apparently believing that so long as he made no blatantly anti-Bolshevik statements he was in no real danger. His execution forced the intelligentsia to confront the truth about the new political reality.

Partly because of her association with the disgraced Gumilev and partly because her poetry now appeared outmoded, in subsequent months Akhmatova was vigorously attacked by critics. She was now regarded as an anachronism, a fossil from the past, despite the fact that she was still immensely popular and at the height of her talent. Her poetry was suffused with a traditional Orthodox spirituality and a concern with the private world of the individual, which were bourgeois anathema to Marxist critics. The critic Korney Chukovsky had admiringly described her in 1922 as "the last poet of Orthodoxy" with an "old-Russian soul." This view became the basis of the campaign against Akhmatova. She, perhaps more than anyone else, seemed to typify the old cultural values that the revolutionaries wished to sweep away. Her aristocratism and Tsarskoe Selo connections seemed too redolent of the Tsarist Empire and jarred uncomfortably with the new Soviet era. Her poetry was banned indefinitely by an unofficial party resolution of 1925 that was not announced publicly, and about which Akhmatova herself only learned in 1927.

The hiatus in Akhmatova's publishing career was to last until 1940. In the intervening years, she had no income other than occasional royalties from her early works, a pitiful and erratic state pension, and the little she earned from literary translation. Akhmatova approached translation with caution, once likening it to "eating one's own brain." She was particularly reluctant to translate poetry for fear that it might interfere with her own creative work. Her reservations notwithstanding, she was a gifted translator and went on later to translate the works of poets of various smaller Soviet nationalities, including Tatar, Ossetian, Armenian, Georgian, Latvian, and Lithuanian. Until 1956, her translations appeared anonymously.

In political terms, the 1930s were the most savage times the Soviet Union had yet seen. The murder of Sergei Kirov, the Leningrad party secretary, by a disaffected party member in 1934 was blamed on those who opposed Stalin, giving the leader an excuse to intensify his control on Soviet citizens. This led to the persecution in subsequent years of vast numbers of the population, including many of Akhmatova's friends and family members. Information which emerged after the collapse of the Soviet Union suggests that she herself only narrowly escaped arrest. Instead, she was persecuted by proxy, through the figure of her son, Lev. He was entirely innocent of counter-revolutionary activity: his only real offence was being the son of the two disgraced poets, Gumilev and Akhmatova.

Akhmatova's relationship with her son was a complex and often strained one. Lev, with some justification, complained of maternal neglect: as a child he had been brought up largely by his father's family in Bezhetsk, in the province of Tver, while Akhmatova pursued her career and bohemian lifestyle in the capital. In 1928 he went to live with Akhmatova, who was then involved with the art historian Nikolai Punin, because he wanted to enter Leningrad University to study Central Asian history. Lev was finally admitted to the history faculty of Leningrad University in 1933 but was expelled two years later after he was arrested for the first time. From them on, Lev spent most of the years until 1956, when he was released following Nikita Khrushchev's secret speech at the Twentieth Party Congress, in prison. He showed remarkable tenacity in pursuing his studies where possible, but his years in the camps, according to his mother, had a very negative impact on his personality. He came to believe that Akhmatova did not care enough about him to use her influence to get him out of prison. The evidence suggests otherwise: she did, in fact, manage to secure his first release in 1935, by writing personally to Stalin, but by the late 1930s she was simply not in a position to help him.

Akhmatova, according to Lev, also disapproved of his chosen career. It is unlikely, given that many of her close friends were academics, that she would have objected to his choice of profession as such, but many of Lev's views were fundamentally opposed to her own. His negative attitude towards Jews must have been particularly antipathetic. Akhmatova was open to cultural diversity to a degree unusual under both the tsarist and Soviet regimes. Throughout her life she was, by all accounts, entirely lacking in feelings of xenophobia or antisemitism. One young contemporary remarked in connection with this, "She was absolutely part of the old intelligentsia where such questions of nationality did not matter in the least."[5] Akhmatova evidently found it easier, at least at a superficial level, to share her son's admiration of Central Asian culture. Her letters to him in the camps take an active interest in his reading and she made efforts to send him the books that he requested. Memoirs record that when Lev was writing his first book, Akhmatova expressed sympathetic concern about the slow progress of his work. This book, upon its publication in 1961, provoked considerable controversy and hostility on account of its tendentious content: it examined the history of Siberia and Asia, emphasizing the positive influence of the Mongol Empire and Huns on Russian national history. Although Akhmatova proudly showed friends offprints of his ethnographic papers—and, despite her affinity with the East—Lev's pan-Asiatic, Eurasian stance was not shared by his mother, who was never aggressively nationalist in her outlook and who placed a high value upon the cultural heritage of Europe and Europeanized Russia.

During the mid-1930s, Akhmatova had begun to write again in a sustained way and she resumed her public appearances where possible. But this phase of her career was very different from the years of her early fame. She was only rarely given the opportunity to publish, and for the most part her poetry was kept secretly on scraps of paper, or memorized. At this time, Akhmatova started to write the lyrics that would form the center of one of her best-known and most openly dissident works, *Requiem* (1935–61). Inspired by the arrests of Lev and Punin, *Requiem* traces the speaker's psychological reactions to the imprisonment and sentencing of her son. It is a powerful and moving memorial both to the victims of the purges and to the relatives who waited in queues outside the prisons for news of them. Although the main setting of the poem is Leningrad, references to the Don and Enisei rivers expand its geographical reach. Akhmatova's speaker voices the suffering of the whole Soviet Union, writing of her "exhausted mouth / Through which one hundred million people scream."

In this poem Akhmatova also explicitly enacted a break with her past, asking that if ever a monument should be erected in her honor, it be placed not by the sea in the South, where she was born, and not in Tsarskoe Selo, where she grew up, but outside the Kresty prison in Leningrad.

It was impossible to contemplate publishing *Requiem* in the Soviet Union of the 1930s and the poem was preserved in the memories of a trusted group of friends. This method ensured the poem's survival: it went on to circulate widely in samizdat during the Thaw and was finally published in its entirety in Russia under perestroika in 1987.

Stalin had always kept a close eye on Akhmatova, as he did all prominent cultural figures. Her popularity and the prerevolutionary "Old Believer" aura that surrounded her placed her in a peculiarly vulnerable position, despite the fact that she had never been flagrantly disobedient. Her situation began to improve in the early 1940s as she benefited, as did others, from the relaxation of the hard line on culture as part of the war effort. She was invited to give a radio address to the citizens of Leningrad, and a well-known poem, "Courage," was even published in *Pravda*, the Communist daily newspaper:

> We know what lies in the balance today,
> And what is now taking place.
> The hour of courage has struck upon our clocks.
> And courage will not abandon us.
> We have no fear in the face of deadly bullets,
> We're not bitter, remaining without shelter,—
> And we will keep you safe, Russian speech,
> Powerful Russian word.
> Free and pure we will convey you,
> Give you to our grandchildren, and save you from captivity
> For ever and ever!

There is nothing particularly Soviet about this poem—it focuses on the safeguarding of the Russian language—but Akhmatova's dignified and stoical brand of patriotism was useful for boosting morale.

During the Siege of Leningrad Akhmatova was evacuated to Tashkent, along with other important cultural figureheads. The list of those to be moved to safety was approved by Stalin himself, indicating that he regarded her as important enough to be given special treatment. Akhmatova set off for Central Asia in September 1941, first traveling to Chistopol' in Tatarstan and then to Tashkent, capital of Uzbekistan, where she stayed until May 1944. Before leaving she told friends that she was hoping to be received well by the Tatars in view of her Tatar name and ancestry. She was not to be disappointed: despite the hardships of life in evacuation, Akhmatova was exhilarated by the surroundings and touched by the hospitality and kindness of local people, particularly when she was very ill with typhus. Tashkent was a lively place during the war, full of members of the Russian intelligentsia who kept up an active cultural program, complete with regular concerts, plays, and poetry readings.

Akhmatova's close affinity with the East is given expression in poetry inspired by her experience of evacuation:

I haven't been here for about seven hundred years,
Yet nothing has changed . . .
God's grace still pours in the same way
From indisputable heights,

The choirs of stars and waters are the same,
The vaults of sky are still as black,
And in the same way the wind carries the seeds,
And a mother sings the same song.

It is enduring, my Asiatic home,
And there is no need to be anxious . . .
I will come back again. Blossom fence,
Be full, clean reservoir.

In her magnum opus, *Poem without a Hero* (1940–65), Akhmatova implies that a turn to the East provided her with sanctuary from the horrors of war originating in the West.

The postwar years brought further hardships and a renewal of political repression. The authorities' discovery of a visit paid to Akhmatova by a Westerner, the liberal philosopher Isaiah Berlin, was to have serious consequences. In 1945, Britain and the Soviet Union were, ostensibly at least, allies. Berlin was attached to the British Embassy in Moscow from September 1945 until January 1946, assigned the task of preparing a dispatch about American-Soviet-British relations after the war. He had the advantage of being a fluent speaker of Russian and, indeed, his own childhood and the shaping of his political sensibilities were bound up with Russian imperial history: he was born in Latvia and lived in St. Petersburg as a child, where he was a horrified witness to the bloodshed of the Revolution. The circumstances of his meeting with Akhmatova are well documented. While browsing in a bookshop during a trip to Leningrad, he fell into conversation with a literary critic, who arranged a meeting with Akhmatova. Not long after he had arrived, Berlin's conversation with the poet was interrupted by the shouts of Randolph Churchill—son of Winston, who required Berlin's services as a translator—coming from the courtyard outside. What had begun as a discreet meeting with a foreigner was now a blatant transgression, reports of which reached the ears of Stalin himself, who apparently remarked, "Our nun is receiving foreign spies." Rumors circulated in Leningrad to the effect that Winston Churchill had organized a special aircraft to take Akhmatova to England.

Berlin returned to see Akhmatova later that evening and they talked for many hours. This encounter was enormously important to Akhmatova both personally and creatively. It gave her a sense of renewed contact with Western Europe, to the culture of which she felt closely tied, and from which the Soviet Empire was completely cut off.

Akhmatova, in somewhat idiosyncratic and grandiose fashion, repeatedly expressed to others her firmly held belief that she and Berlin were responsible for the onset of the Cold War. Churchill's famous Fulton "Iron Curtain" speech, denounced by Stalin as "war-mongering" and imperialist "racism," took place shortly afterward, in March 1946. Her theory, which ignores the role of events such as the Yalta Conference in causing the deterioration between the Soviet Union and Western powers, is difficult to take altogether seriously. Indeed, Berlin himself was highly skeptical about the major role in world history that Akhmatova assigned them both. Nonetheless, some (including Joseph Brodsky) have argued that Akhmatova's view has some foundation. As one commentator observes, she had "met a representative of an at least potentially hostile major power and meddled in international politics. This must have irritated if not enraged Stalin."[6] The evidence suggests that it did, and Berlin's visit undoubtedly had serious repercussions for both Akhmatova and her son. Lev was brutally interrogated about Berlin and his mother with demands that he admit that Akhmatova had spied for England, and a few days after Berlin's departure from the Soviet Union uniformed guards were posted outside Akhmatova's flat and microphones were installed in her ceiling. The punishment that she anticipated was meted out in August 1946, when the Party Central Committee passed a decree denouncing her work and that of the satirist Mikhail Zoshchenko, along with the two journals, *The Star* and *Leningrad,* that had published them. That September, Andrei Zhdanov, secretary of the Central Committee, gave a speech to the Union of Writers, attacking Akhmatova and Zoshchenko and announcing their expulsion from the Union. A flood of other condemnations followed. In subsequent months, the press repeatedly quoted Zhdanov's speech. This attack was the beginning of a broad campaign to compel creative artists to conform to official demands, which heralded a full-scale retreat from the relaxed cultural line of the war years. Akhmatova was not an arbitrary victim: she had incurred Stalin's personal displeasure by associating with a foreigner at a time when Stalin's xenophobia was mounting—and, more than this, she symbolized prerevolutionary culture and traditions and remained popular with the Soviet public.

The death of Stalin in 1953 brought a relaxation of cultural repression, and Akhmatova once again began to make public appearances. In her final decade, she was given a dacha and even permitted to visit the West. In 1964 she traveled to Italy to collect a prestigious literary prize, and in 1965 she was awarded an honorary doctorate from Oxford University. Her last book, *The Flight of Time,* was published in 1965. During this period of her life, Akhmatova provided a living connection to the past for a new generation of poets; the most notable among them was Brodsky. Brodsky was born in 1940 in Leningrad into a Russian-Jewish family. He came to the attention of the KGB partly because of his links with dissidents, partly because of his free-spirited, nonconformist attitude, and partly because of his apolitical poetry. Brodsky was brought to trial for parasitism in 1964 and sentenced to five years' hard labor in the Arkhangelsk region. Brodsky became something of an international cause célèbre when journalist Frida Vigdorova transcribed the court proceedings and disseminated them in the Soviet Union and abroad. The situation was extremely damaging to the reputation of the Soviet Union, and Brodsky was released a year later when the Soviet authorities bowed in the face of his massive international support. Akhmatova publicly supported Brodsky during his trial, sending letters and telegrams to the KGB and to the court in his defense.

Akhmatova died in 1966, in a convalescent home near Moscow. During her lifetime she had witnessed the end of the Tsarist Empire, and survived the difficult early years of the Soviet one, experiencing its worst excesses in the 1930s and then seeing the Thaw under Khrushchev. She occupies an almost unique position in Russian literary history in this respect. Her survival and undiminished reputation rest largely on her skill in shaping a public image with broad appeal and navigating her way back into official favor without seriously compromising her integrity. Those who met her and recorded their impressions frequently drew attention to her imperial manner and bearing in her later years. Abram Gozenpud, literary scholar and translator, described a meeting with Akhmatova in 1956 during which he told her that she resembled Catherine the Great. "You're not the first to say that," she replied. "I hope you're mistaken. I can't bear her. In general, I don't like famous women. There is something reeking of bad theatre in them. And what's more, they were invented by men."[7]

Akhmatova's response is disingenuous. She simultaneously accepts and distances herself from the remark: "you're not the first to say that," but "I hope you're mistaken." She carefully cultivated this imperial image and used it to shape herself as national poet. By the end of her life, after many years of almost complete suppression of her work, she was as celebrated in the Soviet Union as she had been under tsarism. Her enduring image, as Tsvetaeva's words seem to have predicted, is that of a kind of literary empress "of all the Russias."

NOTES

1. On Akhmatova's image making, see, especially, Alexander Zholkovsky, "Anna Akhmatova—piat'desiat let spustia," *Zvezda* 9 (1996): 211–27; and "The Obverse of Stalinism: Akhmatova's Self-serving Charisma of Selflessness," in *Self and Story in Russian History*, ed. Laura Engelstein and Stephanie Sandler (Ithaca, N.Y.: Cornell University Press, 2000), 46–68. Other studies relating to the poet's personal myth are Svetlana Boym, *Death in Quotation Marks: Cultural Myths of the Modern Poet* (Cambridge, Mass.: Harvard University Press, 1992); and *Creating Life: The Aesthetic Utopia of Russian Modernism*, ed. Irina Paperno and Joan Grossman (Stanford, Calif.: Stanford University Press, 1994).

2. Nadezhda Mandelstam, "Akhmatova," in *Anna Akhmatova and her Circle*, ed. Konstantin Polivanov, trans. Patricia Beriozkina (Fayetteville: University of Arkansas Press, 1994), 100–29 (quotations on 114 and 121).

3. Zholkovsky, "Scripts not Scriptures," *Slavic and East European Journal* 40 (1996): 135–41 (quotation on 137).

4. For a more complete account of Akhmatova's biography, see Roberta Reeder, *Anna Akhmatova: Poet and Prophet* (London: Allison and Busby, 1995); or Elaine Feinstein, *Anna of All the Russias: The Life of Anna Akhmatova* (London: Weidenfeld and Nicolson, 2005). For an English-language edition of Akhmatova's poetry, see *The Complete Poems of Anna Akhmatova*, trans. Judith Hemshchemeyer, ed. Roberta Reeder (Boston: Zephyr Press, 1997). For the original Russian texts, see Anna Akhmatova, *Sochineniia*, ed. M. M. Kralin (Moscow: Pravda, 1990).

5. The remark was made by Yevgeny Rein and is quoted in Feinstein, *Anna of All the Russias*, 251.

6. György Dalos, *The Guest from the Future: Anna Akhmatova and Isaiah Berlin* (New York: Farrar, Straus, and Giroux, 1999), 72.

7. Quoted in Reeder, *Anna Akhmatova*, 469–70.

A. V. Germano—A Sometimes Gypsy. From Aleksandr Germano, *Povesti i rasskazy* (Moscow: Sovetskii pisatel', 1960).

# 24

❧

# Aleksandr Germano

## (1893–1955)

BRIGID O'KEEFFE

"Am I a Gypsy or not a Gypsy?" Posed by Aleksandr Viacheslavovich Germano, the Soviet Union's most celebrated Gypsy (Romani) writer, the question is both surprising and puzzling—at least when taken at face value.[1] Yet the question remains: Who was Germano? A Gypsy? A Russian? Why did his nationality matter?

Three years before his death in 1955, Germano composed an autobiography and completed a short questionnaire in fulfillment of his duties as a member of the Union of Soviet Writers. He obligingly answered questions about his nationality, social origins, literary work, language proficiencies, party status, and Red Army service. Germano had performed this same routine many times before. As required of him by the Soviet state throughout his adult lifetime, he dutifully composed both long and short versions of his life story for bureaucratic consumption. As his writing career developed, Germano scrupulously updated his vita and tailored his autobiography to reflect the concerns of his bureaucratic inquirers as well as the ideological exigencies of changing times. In 1952, however, he made one significant edit to his autobiography. His status as the Soviet Union's leading Gypsy writer notwithstanding, Germano disavowed his Gypsy nationality and instead declared himself a Russian.[2]

Despite its bureaucratic provenance, Germano's 1952 narrative is a remarkably compelling read. In his own telling, Germano's life is the unexpected and inspiring tale of an orphaned provincial upstart who became a Soviet writer, and of a proletarian son who became the prophetic transmitter of Soviet light to the empire's benighted Gypsies. Germano is the self-made man whose triumph became possible only thanks to the Bolshevik Revolution. In 1952, he is the aging New Soviet Man—confident, but still weary seven years after the war. Naturally, he is Russian.

Born in 1893 in Orel, Germano described himself in his 1952 autobiography as the son of a worker father and an illiterate mother. The youngest of five children, Germano's early years were filled with sorrowful loss and crushing poverty. His father died of pneumonia while Germano was still in his mother's womb. Pregnant, uneducated, and penniless, Germano's mother sought factory work. Germano revealed little else about either parent. Although he mentioned that his mother lived until 1919, he credited his older sister with caring for him as a child and ensuring his education. Looking back, Germano envisioned himself as a young boy with a passion for story-telling. Otherwise, his childhood is a narrative blur.

For Germano, life began anew with his enlistment in the Red Army in 1919. Due to health complications, Germano did not serve as a soldier on the front lines. Instead, he adapted his love of literature to his commitment to Bolshevik victory in the civil war. In service of the army's cultural-enlightenment mission, he led political discussions and literary evenings for soldiers and civilians. Upon demobilization in 1921, Germano wrote, "I devoted myself completely to literary work." He published widely in his local press, volunteered at Orel's Turgenev Museum, and led the city's first workers' and soldiers' literary circle. In 1921, his satirical play, *In Some Bureaucratic Office,* premiered at the Orel Metropolitan Theater. A professional triumph for the young writer, the play was often staged locally in subsequent years. Spurred by his success, Germano devoted still more time to writing.

Germano soon became convinced that he and his literary talent had outgrown provincial Orel. In 1926, he relocated to Moscow with the naïve hope of quickly establishing himself as a great proletarian writer and Soviet literary icon. Moscow's editors, however, wanted nothing to do with his "provincial" talent. Without money, housing, or even a reasonable chance of fulfilling his professional dreams, Germano nonetheless refused to return to Orel and instead accepted menial work in a publishing office. His pittance of a wage afforded him a room in the capital and nourished his improbable literary ambitions.

Pockets empty, Germano relentlessly sought work as a writer until one day his life took a fateful turn. In 1926, Germano vaguely recalled, "Somehow someone among the Muscovites suggested that I apply to the All-Russian Gypsy Union [ARGU], where there was a need for a cultural worker and organizer of a publication in the Gypsy language." Unbeknown to Germano at the time, Romani youth activists had recently established the ARGU in the spirit of Soviet nationality policy.[3] Summarized in the slogan, "national in form, socialist in content," Bolshevik nationality policy promised to "liberate" the empire's minority peoples from their historic bonds of "backwardness" via expansive nation-building projects. Nationality policy entitled—theoretically, at least—non-Russians to the creation of their own national territories and institutions. Suffused with "socialist content," these "national forms" were intended by the state to assimilate minority peoples to a new, Soviet way of life. According to this same assimilationist logic, minority status also qualified Soviet citizens for preferential treatment in hiring and educational admissions.[4] Thus, when Germano assumed an ARGU leadership role in 1926, he joined Romani activists in their commitment to sovietizing the empire's "backward Gypsies." Reflecting in 1952 on his admission to the ARGU, however, Germano avoided the question as to why this anonymous "someone" suggested that he, a Russian, begin a career in Romani-language publishing. Germano only revealed that he accepted an editorial position at the ARGU and immediately immersed himself in serving "an unlettered people" as "an organizer in every regard."

In pursuit of the ARGU's enlightenment work, Germano meticulously researched Roma's language, history, and culture. He scoured the Lenin Library for clues on "their economy, everyday life, customs, survivals, [and] beliefs" while compiling his *Bibliography of Gypsies* (1930). Yet Germano soon decided that the library offered him only a superficial understanding of Romani language and culture. Therefore, Germano explained, "I undertook the collection of the nomads' folklore and the study of the Gypsy language by ear. Reincarnated as the original 'Aleko,' I spent weeks in the camps. All of this led to my fluent mastering of the language and I began to write poetry and prose in Gypsy as I became well acquainted with the life and aspirations of . . . the Gypsies."

Germano's narrative maneuver in this passage is subtle, yet powerful in its intended effect. Germano casts himself as Pushkin's Aleko—the Russian who, disenchanted with society, seeks haven in the wild and freedom-loving nomadic Gypsy camp. Germano identifies with Aleko, however, not because he shared with this literary character a sense of societal alienation or even a romantic desire to experience what Pushkin called Gypsies' "threadbare freedom of the road."[5] Instead, Germano casts himself as Aleko in an act of purposeful distancing. As Aleko, he is not a Gypsy, but an intrusive outsider in the Gypsies' strange world. He is a Russian.

Fearing that his sympathy with Aleko would not suffice to clarify his position as a Russian civilizer and ethnographer of Gypsies, Germano obviated any potential doubts about his own nationality: "I have dwelled on this explanation so that in the future there will not be the baffled questions: am I a Gypsy or not a Gypsy? I comprehended the language (I know the northern and southern dialects) and the Gypsy soul because otherwise I would not have been able to carry out political-enlightenment work among the nomads." Here again, Germano distanced himself from "the nomads" whose "Gypsy soul" only became legible to him once he mastered their foreign tongue. He emphatically storied himself as a stranger bringing enlightenment to a strange people. Germano insisted that he studied Gypsies, worked to transform them, and spoke their language, but was not one of them.

Nonetheless, Germano took pride in his dedication to the cause of sovietizing the empire's Roma. In a declared act of civic devotion, Germano married his literary ambitions to his duties as a socially useful citizen. He helped create a Cyrillic-based Romani alphabet, edited the world's first Romani-language journal, and printed his stories in its pages. While this work aided Roma on their path to Soviet redemption, it also allowed Germano to ingratiate himself in Moscow's widening literary circles. By the end of 1928, Germano had joined the "Worker's Spring" literary circle and the All-Union Society of Proletarian Writers (VOPP). These affiliations permitted him to study literary theory—especially the tenets of socialist realism—from respected Soviet authors. Germano soon published an array of Russian-language articles and short stories on the theme of Gypsies' cultural revolution.

In 1929, Germano spearheaded the creation of a national Romani literature, organizing a minority section of VOPP named "Word of the Gypsies." He mentored a group of young Romani writers while distinguishing himself as a prolific and versatile author. He wrote and edited the empire's Romani-language textbooks and literary almanacs. A founder of Moscow's State Gypsy Theater, Romen, Germano authored plays and songs for the new troupe. In addition to composing original prose and poetry in both Romani and Russian, Germano also translated hallowed Russian texts into Romani. His work appeared in a number of anthologies celebrating the literature of "the peoples of the USSR." In 1934, the Union of Soviet Writers welcomed Germano into its respected ranks.

Throughout the period of socialist construction, Germano served the cause of sovietizing the empire's Roma with more than his pen. "As a representative of the Gypsy press," Germano explained, "I actively participated in work among toiling Gypsies." He nestled into the Soviet bureaucracy as he aided the organization of Romani collective farms, schools, and industrial cooperatives. At Moscow's Gypsy Club, Germano performed readings and offered members advice on leading new, Soviet lives. He reached out to help the nomads about whom he so often wrote in his stories. "In the aim of becoming personally acquainted on the local level with the conditions and needs of Gypsies who settled on land and in order to carry out political-enlightenment work among them," Germano wrote, "I time and again traveled to the periphery"—that is, to the empire's nascent Romani collective farms. Saving the empire's "backward Gypsies" was not merely the party's mission, but also Germano's personal crusade. As his words testify, Germano pursued this mission not as a Gypsy, but as a "representative of the Gypsy press."

The Great Patriotic War necessarily interrupted Germano's civilizing mission. During the war's bleakest days, Germano served the Soviet Information Bureau, composed a poetry cycle on Romani partisans, recited his stories and poems to injured soldiers and civilians, and read letters from the front on the radio. Although crippled by bouts of writer's block and dwindling opportunities to publish, Germano kept writing throughout the war—about the war itself, about Roma in Russian literature, and about the Romani language.

Although the Soviet Union recovered from the war, Germano's vita reveals that his publication record did not. Germano did not comment directly on his own postwar diminishing literary returns, but the final paragraphs of his 1952 autobiography read superficially as a simple enumeration of works written for the Soviet public but fated for the author's desk drawer. Read another way, Germano's list of his own postwar writings provides subtle commentary on the author's willingness and perceived need to adapt to changing times. Emerging from the war hopeful that his Russian-language writings on Soviet Roma would interest his fellow citizens, Germano worked on three manuscripts between 1945 and 1948: *Fascism and Gypsies During the Fatherland War, A Short History of Soviet Gypsies,* and *A Short History of the State Gypsy Theater.* When these were not accepted for publication, Germano changed course. He wrote *A History of Orel Province* and collaborated on a collection of essays devoted to the history of Orel's party organizations. When it became obvious to him that Gypsies—a non-titular nationality that had long bewildered Soviet bureaucrats—were no longer even a theoretical state priority, Germano shrewdly repositioned himself as an author whose work reflected the postwar precedence of Russia, Russians, and Russianness.

Germano's autobiography also evidences his postwar refashioning of his non-professional life. Although Germano had earlier worked to transform "backward Gypsies" into enlightened workers and farmers, he endeavored after the war to transform himself into a more knowledgeable Soviet citizen. In the absence of any public need for him to carry out further political enlightenment work among Roma, Germano attended lectures organized by the Union of Soviet Writers on Bolshevism and socialist realism. Earlier, Germano's work educating Roma had served as his primary means of Soviet self-fashioning. After the war, Germano worked to perfect his Soviet self by trading his role as teacher of sovietism for that of student.

At the time he wrote his 1952 autobiography, Germano could boast a life made full by his dedicated participation in the construction of Soviet socialism. He could also delight in having fulfilled a dream that he had nourished since adolescence: Germano was an accomplished author. Looking back on his impoverished childhood, provincial origins, and rough start in Moscow, Germano recognized the fulfillment of his professional goal as a tremendous accomplishment. He thus "carefully preserved" his prized Union of Soviet Writers membership card as a precious sign of how much he had achieved.[6]

Following his death in 1955, the city of Orel memorialized Germano as an accomplished native son. The Museum of Orel Writers archived his writings and honored Germano alongside Turgenev, Bunin, and others. His colleagues in Orel and Moscow, meanwhile, sought to immortalize Germano as the empire's premier Gypsy writer. In 1960 and 1962, they translated Germano's Romani-language short stories into Russian and published his work in two separate anthologies. They honored Germano not only as a pioneer of "Soviet Gypsy literature," but also as a "Russian by upbringing and education" who had "devoted a large part of his work to the cause of developing and uplifting" a people that was "akin to him by birth."[7] Germano thus posthumously entered the pantheon of Soviet literature not precisely as he had defined himself in his 1952 autobiography. Whereas Germano had then declared himself a Russian and explained himself as a "reincarnated Aleko," his memorialists conceded that he was Russian only by dint of his "upbringing and education." His biographers pointedly detailed the fact that Germano was the son of immigrants—a Czech father and a "Moravian Gypsy" mother.[8]

Countless times in his adult life, Germano encountered the proverbial Soviet question: Who are you by nationality? Taken as a whole, Germano's self-authored paper trail reveals that he consistently approached this question as an opportunity to define, but also to revise his narrative of his own malleable Soviet self. Ultimately, however, his varying responses to the question—silence, creative elision, Gypsy, and Russian—reveal less about Germano than they do about the critical role nationality played in the forging of Soviet subjects in both the interwar and postwar periods.

Germano's refusal to identify himself as a Gypsy in his 1952 autobiography was not without precedent. In an autobiography commissioned by a provincial publisher in 1925, Germano wrote about his lineage without once employing the term "Gypsy." His parents, he revealed, were "foreigners who had wandered over to Russia from Austria-Hungary" as they "roamed" with a traveling camp of their metalworker and musician relatives. "Later, speaking broken Russian, they dispersed and settled in the towns of today's USSR." Admitting disinterest in his family tree, Germano traced his father to a village near Prague but provided a less clear account of his mother's origins. "My mother did not sit still anywhere," he explained, "She loved to travel and it was because of her that my father . . . aimlessly took to the road."[9]

Germano's veiled references to his Romani heritage only morphed into full-fledged assertions of his own Gypsy nationality once he joined the ARGU. The moment at which Germano first heard that the ARGU needed an organizer whose credentials included not only publishing experience but also Romani ancestors proved to be one of his life's most instructive and defining. From that time on, his claim to Gypsy nationality served as his springboard to fulfilling a professional goal that had once seemed unattainable. Germano gained work as a journal editor, ready outlets for the publication of his writings, and the cachet required for him to associate with esteemed Soviet writers. Thus, upon acceptance to the VOPP in 1928, Germano did more than openly identify as a Gypsy.[10] Claiming the ultimate in purported Gypsy authenticity, Germano noted in his application that as a child he had "sometimes wandered."[11] Further underscoring the political and social value that he now attached to his minority status, he soon traded the surname officially given to him at birth, German, for its Gypsy equivalent, Germano. Reincarnated as a Gypsy, he embraced nationality as his guarantee of Soviet success.

In his 1934 application to the Union of Soviet Writers, Germano further revised his autobiography. Here, he claimed that his writing career began in 1926—that is, "from the moment of the written Gypsy language's emergence."[12] In this retelling, Germano's professional life and socially useful work began only after he announced himself a Gypsy and joined the ARGU. Although in previous statements Germano had proudly itemized his relatively modest literary accomplishments in Orel, he now struck them from his vita as if only the creations of his reborn Gypsy self mattered. Excepting his *Bibliography of Gypsies,* Germano's 1934 vita enumerated merely his Romani-language poetry, prose, and translations of "Marxist classics." Germano rendered his Russian-language publications irrelevant—a choice that would be inexplicable outside the context of Soviet nationality policy. His application represents Germano's belief that his worthiness of membership to the Union of Soviet Writers would be judged against his credentials not simply as a writer, but as a Gypsy writer specifically. As the citizen of an empire that rigorously divided its population according to nationality and doled out opportunities as well tangible benefits to purported "backward" minorities, Germano underscored that he was first and foremost a Gypsy writer speaking to Gypsy readers "exclusively in the Gypsy language."[13]

Germano's embrace of Gypsy nationality ultimately survived the Soviet Union's termination of Romani-language publishing in 1938. In the spring of 1940, Germano reconvened his fellow Romani authors under the auspices of the Union of Soviet Writers. Openly pining for the days when the state had meagerly supported their literary efforts, Germano praised his Romani colleagues for helping the empire's benighted Gypsies to adapt to a settled, literate, Soviet way of life. Looking ahead with the hope that he and his fellow Romani writers could revive their aborted national literature, Germano agreed to organize and lead a new Gypsy section of the Union of Soviet Writers. Recognizing that his cohort's future work would necessarily be printed in Russian instead of in Romani, Germano optimistically promised that this new Russian-language Romani literature would prove a "revelation for the Soviet reader."[14]

Though the Nazi invasion interrupted his literary plans, Germano nurtured them throughout the war. In an autobiography composed after the war, Germano reiterated his longstanding commitment to the development of a Romani national literature. Reflecting on the start of his career in 1926, Germano recalled, "I gave myself completely to work among the backward Gypsy masses, and from that time forward I, as a Gypsy writer, have exclusively written in the Gypsy language. I am one of the founders of the world's only Gypsy script and an organizer of the Gypsy press. I established a core of Gypsy poets and writers." In the end, he declared, "I am happy and proud that, thanks to our party and Soviet power, I took the initiative and leading role in developing the new literature of Soviet Gypsies."[15]

Germano's shifting responses to his own personal "national question" can only be understood within the context of the evolution of the Soviet Union's ideology in general, and of its nationality policy in particular. In the 1920s, Germano and his fellow Romani activists awakened to the opportunities made available to them as a so-called backward nationality. By the dawn of World War II, he and his cohort had seen many of those same opportunities wither and disappear. Germano's cumulative autobiographic record not only reflects this trajectory, but provides a telescopic view of the changing priorities of the Soviet state and thus, of its Romani citizens. While his development as a Soviet citizen through socially useful work remained a constant focus of Germano's autobiographic narratives, his nationality could be and was revised. Nationality, however, was never merely incidental to the Soviet self whom Germano narrated and actively nurtured throughout his life. Rather, nationality was—as dictated by the Soviet state—a central ingredient of his Soviet self. Time and again, Germano met the state's demand that he define his citizen self in universal terms as Soviet, but also as a member of a distinctive nationality. Germano's own autobiographic statements, meanwhile, are the key to understanding why Germano variously elided, emphasized, and edited his Gypsy self in response to that demand.

As an ambitious writer steadily gaining status in his native Orel, Germano nodded briskly to his parents' shared history of "wandering" and to his mother's "love of travel." Yet in his 1925 autobiography, Germano prioritized neither his parents' idiosyncratic history nor his own nationality as central to defining himself as a Soviet citizen and writer. Instead, he emphasized his Red Army service as well as his efforts to educate Orel's soldiers and workers. Nearly ten years later, as an aspiring member of the Union of Soviet Writers, Germano embraced his stature as the empire's most accomplished Gypsy writer. In his 1934 autobiography, he enthusiastically declared himself a Gypsy and fashioned himself an enlightened Soviet shepherd to his flock of "backward" Gypsy brethren. In this telling, Germano's Soviet self took his first breath only at the moment of the Romani alphabet's creation. Soon after the war, Germano recounted his accomplishments as a Gypsy writer and declared himself "happy and proud" to have served his fellow Gypsies and the cause of socialist construction.

Only upon realization that the heyday of early Soviet nationality policy had passed did Germano edit Gypsiness from his storied self. By 1952, the breadbasket of opportunities afforded Germano *as a Gypsy* in the 1920s and 1930s had long been emptied. According to the Soviet Union's newly revised postwar history, the Soviet "first among equals"—the Russian nation—had already civilized the empire's "backward" Gypsies. Postwar Soviet ideology celebrated Russians not only as saviors of the homeland during the Great Patriotic War, but also as the natural-born leaders of the empire's economic, cultural, political, and social development.[16] Germano's 1952 autobiography could not have reflected these changes in Soviet ideology and nationality policy more clearly. In editing his nationality, Germano testified that for him, at least, Gypsiness no longer provided the political currency that Sovietness and now Russianness promised him.

Germano's autobiographical self encapsulates the process by which many minority citizens activated the distinctly ethnicized version of the Bolshevik civilizing mission in their embrace of Soviet nationality policy's offerings. In Germano's case, nationality operated precisely as the Bolsheviks hoped it would: as a plastic identity that could easily be discarded once the task of Soviet self-fashioning was achieved. Although Germano's colleagues and biographers refused to posthumously grant him the exalted status of Russian nationality, they praised him, above all else, as a faithful Soviet citizen who had devoted a lifetime to the cause of uplifting "backward Gypsies" to the heights of Soviet culture.

Who was A. V. Germano by nationality? Was he a Gypsy? A Russian? An examination of Germano's evolving autobiography provides clear answers to these questions. At times Germano was a Gypsy; at times he was a Russian. The Soviet nationality regime allowed for, and even encouraged, such shifts in his presentation of self. Yet throughout his adult lifetime, there remained one constant in his narrative self-fashioning: Germano was a Soviet citizen, proud of his empire in all its diversity.

## NOTES

1. As an official nationality, Roma were categorized in the Soviet Union as *tsygane,* or Gypsies. Soviet Roma self-identified and were identified by the state as Gypsies. The ethnonym

"Roma" was scarcely employed in the Soviet Union. In this text, I deploy both ethnonyms—Gypsies and Roma—with a distinct purpose in mind. In order to accurately reflect contemporaneous vocabulary as well as the stereotypes of Roma that prevailed in the Soviet Union, I reproduce the grammatical variants of "Gypsy" when reporting direct speech, referencing official state categories, and describing the documented perspectives of historical actors. When speaking for myself, I employ the terms "Roma" (nominative plural) or "Romani" (adjective).

2. Unless otherwise noted, all references are to the 1952 autobiography archived at Orlovskii ob"edinennyi gosudarstvennyi literaturnyi muzei I. S. Turgeneva (hereafter cited as OGLMT), f. 29, op. 1, d. 156.

3. See Brigid O'Keeffe, "'Backward Gypsies,' Soviet Citizens: The All-Russian Gypsy Union, 1925–28," *Kritika: Explorations in Russian and Eurasian History* 11, no. 2 (2010): 283–312.

4. See Terry Martin, *The Affirmative Action Empire: Nations and Nationalism in the Soviet Union, 1923–1939* (Ithaca, N.Y.: Cornell University Press, 2001).

5. Alexander Pushkin, *The Gypsies and Other Narrative Poems,* trans. and ed. Antony Wood (Boston: David R. Godine, 2006), 5.

6. A. V. Germano, *Povesti i rasskazy* (Orel: Orlovskoe knizhnoe izdatel'stvo, 1962), 6.

7. A. V. Germano, *Povesti i rasskazy* (Moscow: Sovetskii pisatel', 1960), 236.

8. See ibid., 237; Germano, *Povesti i rasskazy* (1962), 3; E. Sholokh, "A. V. Germano," in *Literaturnaia entsiklopediia* (Moscow: Izdatel'stvo kommunisticheskoi akademii, 1964), 2:138; and OGLMT, f. 29, op. 1, d. 214, l. 1 ("Aleksandr Germano"—Zanimatel' tsyganskoi sovetskoi literaturoi / k 80-letiiu so dnia rozhdeniia).

9. OGLMT, f. 29, op. 1, d. 137, ll. 1, 2.

10. See Rossiiskii gosudarstvennyi arkhiv literatury i iskusstva (hereafter cited as RGALI), f. 1638, op. 1, d. 92, ll. 2, 56.

11. RGALI, f. 1638, op. 1, d. 83, l. 76.

12. OGLMT, f. 29, op. 1, d. 136, l. 1.

13. OGLMT, f. 29, op. 1, d. 137, l. 4.

14. RGALI, f. 631, op. 6, d. 426, ll. 8–10.

15. OGLMT, f. 29, op. 1, d. 146, ll. 1–2.

16. See David Brandenberger, *National Bolshevism: Stalinist Mass Culture and the Formation of Modern Russian National Identity, 1931–1956* (Cambridge, Mass.: Harvard University Press, 2002).

Lazar′ Kaganovich in Tashkent, 1920. From Lazar′ Moiseevich Kaganovich, *Pamiatnye zapiski rabochego, kommunista-bol′shevika, profsoiuznogo, partiinogo i sovetsko-gosudarstvennogo rabotnika* (Moscow, 1996).

# 25

# Lazar' Moiseevich Kaganovich

## (1893–1991)

HIROAKI KUROMIYA

Lazar' Moiseevich Kaganovich lived for nearly a century: he was born in 1893 in the village of Kabany, near Chornobyl' (or Chernobyl' in Russian), Ukraine, and died a loyal Stalinist in Moscow in July 1991, six months before the Soviet Union collapsed. Perhaps he was fortunate not to witness the demise of the country to which he had devoted his entire adult life. He loyally and unswervingly served the country's dictator Joseph Stalin (1878–1953) as one of his most trusted associates. Like the man he served, Kaganovich was both extraordinarily energetic and capable, and extremely brutal and ruthless. Unlike Stalin, however, Kaganovich was not capable of independent thinking. If Stalin was a statesman, then Kaganovich was his trusted "vassal." Even though after Stalin's death in 1953, Kaganovich was politically discredited by his own erstwhile protégé, Nikita Khrushchev, he remained until the very end of his life a stubborn defender of Stalin. Kaganovich's devotion to Stalin and the state he had created was such that he was called by another loyal Stalinist Viacheslav Molotov (1890–1986) a "200-percent Stalinist."[1] Of Stalin's inner circle, he was the last to die. His remarkable life was part of the remarkable history of the Soviet Union, the first socialist state in the world.

Kaganovich was fifteen years younger than Stalin. So perhaps it was natural that Kaganovich looked up to Stalin. Like Stalin, he was not from Russia. Stalin was a Georgian from Georgia, and Kaganovich a Jew from Ukraine. Both reached the pinnacle of power from humble origins in the provinces of the Russian Empire. Neither Stalin nor Kaganovich had the intellectual flair of Stalin's archrival Leon Trotsky (1879–1940), but both surpassed Trotsky in playing power politics. In their political lives, neither Stalin nor Kaganovich allowed themselves to be swayed by personal sentiments such as anger, envy, vanity, and love. They lived by politics. This almost complete devotion to political life makes their personal lives so extraordinary.

One factor in Kaganovich's evolution into a professional revolutionary was his Jewish origins. Indeed, the Jewish community, a minority group subject to severe discrimination in the Russian Empire, gave birth to numerous revolutionaries. Late in his life, Kaganovich proudly maintained that all of his brothers (five including himself) had joined the Communist Party and fought for the victory of socialism.[2] Like Trotsky, a Jew from a village in southern Ukraine, Kaganovich grew up largely isolated from the ghetto life of shtetls. Unlike the relatively well educated and well off Trotsky, however, Kaganovich was born into a poor family and struggled to acquire even an elementary level of formal education: he was largely self taught. Trotsky, like Lenin and other prominent revolutionaries, lived a life of underground activity, arrest, exile to Siberia, desertion, and then foreign emigration; Kaganovich's early years appear much less glamorous. A move to Kyiv, the capital of Ukraine, at the age of fourteen was followed by unemployment and menial jobs. He was a good labor organizer, however, and joined the Bolshevik party in 1911 under the influence of his older brother Mikhail, who had joined six years earlier. Kaganovich was arrested twice, once in 1915 and again in 1917. Yet he never experienced prolonged exile. Nor is there any record that Kaganovich had ever been abroad or knew any foreign languages (apart from Russian, Ukrainian, and Yiddish, all of which he spoke from childhood).

All the same, Kaganovich, like Trotsky, became an "internationalist." Even though he had never traveled abroad, having growing among ethnic Ukrainians, he understood Ukrainian and Ukrainian peasant life well. Moreover, unlike Trotsky, Kaganovich was interested in Jewish traditions. He saw in Marxism an ideology that transcended national differences and afford a solution to the problems of poverty, exploitation, and injustice he saw all around him (including in the small Jewish colonies in his native village). Although he never denied his Jewish roots, he did reject Zionism (which he called "an imperialist and racist ideology") with the same resolve as he showed in his fight against antisemitism. (Kaganovich battled the chauvinistic and antisemitic Black Hundreds, especially strong in Kyiv, both before and after the 1911 Beilis affair, the Russian version of the Dreyfus affair.) Kaganovich claimed that he grew up in an environment of "natural internationalism."[3]

As the ruthless executioner of Stalin's brutal policies, Kaganovich allowed no room for what he considered narrowly national points of view. He later became known as the butcher of Ukrainians (especially for his role in curtailing cultural Ukrainization and the repression of Ukrainian and Kuban peasants at the time of the 1932–33 famine). Such a characterization is probably unfair. Ukrainian antisemitism accounted for part of his poor reputation in Ukraine. Moreover, there is no evidence that he was inherently anti-Ukrainian, any more than Stalin was inherently anti-Georgian. As convinced Marxists, Kaganovich, like Stalin and Trotsky, dismissed national issues as secondary to class issues.

This did not mean that they ignored national issues. On the contrary, Stalin came to the notice of Vladimir Lenin, the leader of the Bolshevik party, because of his expertise in national questions in the Russian Empire. Stalin then began his ascent in the party hierarchy. Kaganovich, for his part, first admired Stalin in 1917 when he listened to Stalin's reports on nationality affairs in the empire. Clearly, national issues were a common concern. Kaganovich was especially fond of Ukrainian literature and culture. In fact, Kaganovich revealed in a private conversation a few months before his death that his decision to become a professional revolutionary was deeply influenced by the Ukrainian writer and revolutionary Volodymyr Vynnychenko (1880–1951), whose national ideology Kaganovich had rejected and who, after the defeat in the civil war against the Bolsheviks, had emigrated abroad. Vynnychenko had been a political foe of Kaganovich's, and yet, more than three quarters of a century later Kaganovich fondly recalled the strong impact on him of Vynnychenko's short story "Talisman" in which Pinia, a humble man of Jewish descent, died a hero's death leading his fellow prisoners in an attempt to escape captivity.[4] Kaganovich's story is revealing: the Ukrainian writer Vynnychenko broke the mold of the stereotypical antisemitic Ukrainian in his creation of Pinia, and the Jew Kaganovich defied the stereotypical mold of anti-Ukrainian Jew. Clearly, Kaganovich's "internationalist" sentiments had deep roots in spite of the fact that he never left the country.

As an organizer of labor, Kaganovich excelled from early on. By 1914, at the age of twenty-one, he was already a central party figure in Kyiv. In 1917 he was busy organizing workers in various parts of Ukraine and Russia. Khrushchev, who first got acquainted with him in 1917, later recalled, "He was a real whirlwind. He might even chop wood, as the saying went, but he would carry out the task set by the Central Committee." He was, as Khrushchev put it, a "strong-willed man who didn't spare his own efforts or those of others": he "always found something to do" and "never had any spare time."[5] In 1917, according to some accounts, Kaganovich was inducted into the Russian army (and never deserted); according to others (including his own), he was sent by the party into the army "to undertake propaganda work."[6] In any case, he was soon arrested and sent to the front as punishment for his political sedition. He was released, however, owing to protests by local Bolsheviks. Thus, Kaganovich met the October 1917 Revolution near the front, in Gomel′ (Homel′) and Mogilev (Mahilew) in present-day Belarus, where he was instrumental in the Bolshevik party's seizure of local power.

He soon came to be recognized as an exceptionally capable party member. In 1918 he was put in charge of propaganda and recruitment among soldiers in the newly created Red Army in Moscow. After that, he was sent to Nizhnii Novgorod where he carried out Red Terror on Lenin's orders and with the assistance of Trotsky. Subsequently, he was sent by Moscow to other troubled areas such as Voronezh and Turkestan, where he supervised the brutal repression of *basmachi* ("bandit") rebellions. During the civil war Kaganovich ardently advocated the centralization of party and government affairs. In 1922, with his organizational skills widely recognized by the party leaders, Kaganovich began to work in the Central Committee Secretariat of the Communist Party in Moscow and as head of the Orgotdel (Organizational and Instruction Department). He worked side by side with Molotov, and reported to Stalin. By this time he had broken with Trotsky, with whom he had worked closely during the civil war.[7] In the ensuing power struggle between Trotsky and other party leaders (especially Stalin), Kaganovich clearly stood with Stalin. Why he sided with Stalin and against Trotsky, a fellow Jew and the hero of the Red Army is not difficult to understand. Trotsky was too much of an intellectual and too aloof and haughty; Stalin was just the opposite. Just as Stalin rose to power not through his intellectual prowess or theoretical acumen but through the practical work of managing seemingly boring party and personnel matters, so did Kaganovich. They must have had a mutual affinity. It was through the work in the secretariat in the first half of the 1920s that Kaganovich forged a strong alliance with Stalin. As Stalin beat one opponent after another in the fierce power struggle in the party, Kaganovich invariably took his side. With Stalin's rise, Kaganovich's star rose as well.

In 1925, Kaganovich returned to Ukraine as the first secretary of the Ukrainian Communist Party. As a staunch supporter of Moscow's centralized control, Kaganovich alienated many Ukrainian Communists whose national sentiments he considered parochial and even equated with dissidence and opposition. In 1928, he was called back to Moscow to work in the secretariat and in 1930 he became a full member of the Politburo, the highest organ of power in the country. From 1930 onward, Kaganovich managed the party organization of the capital city, Moscow, as its secretary. In that capacity, Kaganovich oversaw the destruction in the 1930s of numerous architectural legacies of old Moscow. Because many of these buildings were churches and cathedrals of the Orthodox Church, the role played by Kaganovich's Jewishness has been exaggerated. In fact, most Bolsheviks at the time, not just Kaganovich but many others—including Stalin, who had once dreamed of becoming an Orthodox priest—supported the massive destruction of the old and the construction of the new. They were all atheists and had little regard for anything religious. It was under Kaganovich's leadership that the construction of Moscow's magnificent subway was completed. Later, when Kaganovich's daughter became an architect, she was pressed by her colleagues for an explanation of her father's actions in the 1930s. She wrote to her father and, in response, Kaganovich penned a detailed description of the circumstances under which the destruction of old architecture took place in Moscow. Kaganovich insisted that it was a collective decision, fully justified.[8]

The 1930s were a truly turbulent decade in which the country was fundamentally transformed by Stalin's relentless drive for the collectivization of agriculture and rapid industrialization. Many difficulties such as peasant rebellions, worker strikes, and famine accompanied the process. Throughout the 1930s, Kaganovich served in various parts of the country as Stalin's troubleshooter. In 1932, Kaganovich was dispatched to the south of the country, Ukraine and the northern Caucasus, where millions were dying of starvation and where the peasants put up stiff resistance to Moscow's relentless seizure of grain. In the same year, Kaganovich was sent to Ivanovo-Voznesenk, in the north, where workers were striking to protest the food shortage, among other things; and to the Donbas, in the south, when it was falling behind in its coal production plans. Kaganovich was the man to go and break the bottleneck. All his visits were occasions for the application of extensive and brutal terror against presumed enemies of Stalin's policies. The terror solved the problems, at least in a short run, and Kaganovich's reputation rose as Stalin's troubleshooter. Similarly, when Stalin launched his bloody campaign of terror (the Great Terror) in 1937–38, it was Kaganovich who was sent to the provinces to ensure it was carried out. Nearly a million people were executed in the Great Terror. Kaganovich was also put in charge of railway transport and heavy industry, which he managed with his characteristic iron hand. Kaganovich thus came to be called "Iron Lazar'."

Meanwhile, Kaganovich played a vital role in the creation of the concept of "Stalinism" as equal to "Leninism." Stalin was immensely proud of the vast transformation of the Soviet Union, which he accomplished in the 1930s through terror and famine. It was Stalin's "revolution from above," comparable to Lenin's October Revolution. Kaganovich was an unapologetic defender of Stalin's "revolution from above" with all its terror. For Kaganovich as for Stalin, the most important accomplishment of the country was the transformation of the Soviet Union from a relatively backward, agrarian society into a mighty industrial power. Without rapid industrialization, the country would have remained a weak state that foreign capitalist powers could have beaten easily. Kaganovich reasoned that the great sacrifice the country made in the 1930s in the interests of industrialization was therefore justified. How else could the country have matched and surpassed Nazi Germany's tanks, fighter airplanes, bombers, and weapons? Kaganovich insisted that "only by means of the industrialization drive" was the country able to defend itself against external enemies.[9]

Kaganovich made a similar argument in justification of Stalin's terror: the survival of the country was at stake. Kaganovich insisted, even late in his life, that there were fifth columns in the country in the 1930s. Had they not been eliminated, according to him, the country would have been defeated in the war. The country had been under constant threat of attack. Internal divisions would have inevitably led to civil war in the Soviet Union, which then would have doomed the country to defeat. According to Kaganovich, former opponents of Stalin—such as Trotsky, Nikolai Bukharin, and others—engaged in clandestine activity to undermine Stalin's authority and even regarded it as their right. Although they may not have been foreign spies, Kaganovich maintained, they considered it acceptable to enter into an agreement with foreign powers against the Soviet Union. Therefore they had to be destroyed. Such was Kaganovich's argument until the very end of his life.[10]

Faced with the overwhelming evidence that innocent people were killed en masse, Kaganovich, like Stalin, had to admit that mistakes were made and innocent people sacrificed.[11] Nevertheless, Kaganovich, like Stalin and Molotov, remained absolutely convinced that Stalin's terror was correct and fully justified: their mistake was that they simply went too far. Clearly, Kaganovich admired Stalin as a leader forceful enough to kill untold numbers of people to ensure the survival of the country (that is, Stalin's power). Kaganovich insisted until the very end that Stalin was a "great man."[12]

Kaganovich's absolute devotion to Stalin was characterized by many around him as "bootlicking." Khrushchev, for example, noted after Stalin's death: "There is no question that Stalin singled Kaganovich out and regarded him as the one who correctly understood the critical role and merits of Stalin himself." Kaganovich, according to Khrushchev, "sensed what pleased Stalin and what did not" and behaved like a "real lackey."[13] Many observers accused him of abandoning his friends, and even his own brother, so as not to offend Stalin. It is true that Kaganovich, like everyone else in Stalin's inner circle, deserted his close friends in time of need. Stalin even made hostages of their wives and family members to test their loyalty. Whether Kaganovich actually failed to support his own brother is not proven (his brother Mikhail, faced with false accusations, committed suicide in 1941). Kaganovich's own story of these events is very different from the popularized version intended to show his lack of family loyalty. It is known, however, that "Iron Lazar'" was not entirely without sentiment: when one of his close friends was arrested, he was at a loss and "sobbed out loud." Yet he recovered from the breakdown quickly and chose to forget about him.[14]

This incident was perhaps characteristic of the lives of those who supported Stalin. They were not entirely devoid of human sentiment, but they sacrificed their sentiments and numerous individuals' lives in the interests of what they considered the higher cause of the state. In this sense, Kaganovich was a political man and a true Stalinist.

Like all others, Kaganovich fell out of favor with Stalin at certain points during his long political career, especially during World War II and afterward. There were times when Kaganovich returned to central stage, but toward the end of his life Stalin appeared to believe that Kaganovich's political utility had been largely exhausted. When Stalin died, Kaganovich wept. He was removed from the party when his unqualified support for Stalin stood in the way of Khrushchev's de-Stalinization campaign. He remained deeply suspicious of any criticism of Stalin (which provided "fodder for the anti-Soviet imperialists"). Likewise, he was extremely critical of Mikhail Gorbachev's campaign for glasnost' and perestroika, regarding it as a big mistake.[15] He died in 1991 the last of the Stalinists.

NOTES

1. Feliks Chuev, *Tak govoril Kaganovich: Ispoved' stalinskogo apostolov* (Moscow, 1992), 53.

2. Lazar' Moiseevich Kaganovich, *Pamiatnye zapiski rabochego, kommunista-bol'shevika, profsoiuznogo, partiinogo i sovetsko-gosudarstvennogo rabotnika* (Moscow, 1996), 34.

3. Ibid., 24.

4. "Dve besedy s L. M. Kaganovichem," *Novaia i noveishaia istoriia* 2 (1999): 120–21. Kaganovich did not tell this episode in his "official" memoirs.

5. *Memoirs of Nikita Khrushchev*, vol. 1, *Commissar (1918–1945)*, ed. Sergei Khrushchev, trans. George Shriver, supplemental material trans. Stephen Shenfield (University Park: The Pennsylvania State University Press, 2004), 31, 104, 113.

6. *The Stalin-Kaganovich Correspondence 1931–1936*, comp. and ed. R. W. Davies, Oleg V. Khlevniuk, E. A. Rees, Liudmila P. Kosheleva, and Larisa A. Rogovskaya (New Haven, Conn.: Yale University Press, 2003), 22.

7. On Kaganovich's career in the 1920s, see ibid., 22–24.

8. Kaganovich, *Pamiatnye zapiski,* 527–31.

9. Kaganovich, "Dve besedy," 106–107, 113–14.

10. Ibid., 114; Chuev, *Tak govoril Kaganovich,* 36, 45.

11. Kaganovich, "Dve besedy," 113; Chuev, *Tak govoril Kaganovich,* 35, 101; and Kaganovich, *Pamiatnye zapiski,* 562.

12. Chuev, *Tak govoril Kaganovich,* 27.

13. *Memoirs of Nikita Khrushchev,* vol. 2, *Reformer (1945–1964),* ed. Sergei Khrushchev, trans. George Shriver, supplemental material trans. Stephen Shenfield (University Park: The Pennsylvania State University Press, 2006), 136–37.

14. *Memoirs of Nikita Khrushchev,* vol. 1, 153.

15. Kaganovich, *Pamiatnye zapiski,* 568–70.

Dziga Vertov and Elizaveta Svilova at work, from the film *Goskino Review* (*Obzor Goskino,* 1924). Russian State Archive of Film and Photo Documents (11622).

# 26

❦

# Dziga Vertov

## *(1896–1954)*

JOHN MACKAY

A perpetually controversial figure in the history of cinema, Soviet filmmaker Dziga Vertov (b. David Abelevich Kaufman in Bialystok, Russian Empire [now Poland], January 15, 1896 [NS]; d. Moscow, February 12, 1954) has, since at least the early 1970s, figured centrally in debates about nonfiction cinema, avant-garde cinema, political propaganda film, and film theory worldwide. His work and thought present a number of apparently intractable paradoxes. Vertov was at once the most uncompromising advocate of documentary (or "non-acted") film as a means of showing "life as it is"—his neologism "kino-pravda" (film truth), as translated into French by Georges Sadoul, gave us the term "cinéma verité," a notion with a most problematic relation to Vertov's actual cinematic practice—and the most radical explorer of the possibilities of montage prior to the emergence of the European and U.S. avant-gardes in the late 1950s. He was both the implacable opponent of "scripted" documentary, and the most fanatically "formalist" micro-organizer of image and sound in the history of nonfiction film; he was at once a proud outsider, loudly defending his "kino-eye" doctrines as a bulwark of true revolutionary principle against the backsliding into bourgeois theatricality represented by dominant fiction film norms, and largely conformist in relation to the policies and rhetoric of the Soviet state. Beyond this, Vertov's famous writings, often fiercely manifesto-like in character, seem less than adequate keys to the singular complexity of his films, even as certain of their themes (the politicization of the distinction between fiction and nonfiction film, for instance, or the well-known "theory of the interval") continue to stimulate filmmakers and theorists alike.[1]

For its part, Vertov's biography, including his posthumous reception, presents us with, if not "paradox" exactly, certainly stark and sometimes bleak contrasts: specifically, the contrasts between his modest beginnings as a provincial student and war refugee, his rapid rise to artistic prominence between 1922 and 1929, his downward slide into total creative frustration and near-oblivion during the last twenty years of his life, and his legacy as a now canonical, if still provocative, giant of film history. To be sure, that legacy as articulated during the Cold War period was structured by familiar Vertovian paradoxes, as the "formalist" or "experimental" aspects of his work were downplayed or denounced in the Soviet Union (where he was recognized by the 1960s as the father of documentary and film journalism), and correspondingly valorized in the West.[2]

Vertov's life was an eventful one. His father, Abel Kushelevich Kaufman (b. 1868 in Grodno [now in Belarus], Russian Empire; d. sometime between 1941 and 1943 in Bialystok), after working as a librarian for the Bialystok city government, opened up a large bookstore (with an adjunct lending library) in that bustling industrial city at the beginning of 1893. A year later he married Chaya-Ester Rakhmielievna Gal'pern (b. 1873 in Zabludovo [now Zabludow, Poland] Russian Empire; d. sometime between 1941–43 in Bialystok), who worked alongside her husband in the bookstore and library. Extraordinarily, all of Abel and Chaya's sons—with the exception of Semyon (born 1900), who died in infancy—grew up to become significant figures in cinema history. Mikhail Kaufman (b. Moisei Abelevich on September 5, 1897 [NS], in Bialystok; d. March 11, 1980, in Moscow) was Vertov's main cameraman and close collaborator between 1922 and 1929, and later became an important documentary director in his own right; Boris (b. January 12, 1903 [NS], in Bialystok; d. June 24, 1980, in New York), who never practiced filmmaking in Russia, began to work as a cameraman and sometime co-director in France in the mid-1920s, eventually doing the cinematography for the early films of Jean Lods, all the films of Jean Vigo, and, still later in the United States, for films like Sidney Lumet's *Twelve Angry Men* (1957) and Elia Kazan's *On the Waterfront* (1954), for which he won an Academy Award. Evidently, the primary family stimulus to work with images was provided by Chaya's sister Masha Gal'pern (b. 1883 in Zabludovo; d. 1970 in Acre, Israel) who purchased Mikhail his first still camera; after 1924, Boris in France apparently corresponded with both Dziga and Mikhail about cinema, and Boris's early prose sketches for films are marked by a decidedly "Vertovian" interest in real-life processes, in montage fragmentation, and in speed.[3]

More interested in poetry and music than the visual arts in his youth, David (Vertov) was a pupil at the Bialystok Modern School [or Realschule: *real'noe uchilishche*] from August 1905 through June 1914, and studied music at the city's conservatory as well. Although the Kaufmans were Jewish (like most of the population of Bialystok), it is clear both from the overwhelmingly "secular" contents of Abel's library and from the kind of education that the sons received that the family was relatively nonobservant, liberal, and Russified. Among his classmates at the school was Mikhail Kol'tsov (b. Moisei Khaimovich Fridliand on June 12, 1898 [NS], in Kyiv; d. February 2, 1940, in Moscow), the future globetrotting Soviet journalist, who, like his brother, caricaturist Boris Efimov (1899–2008), began his journalism career producing anti-tsarist satire for "underground" school publications.

Starting in the fall of 1914, Vertov began a general course of study at psychologist Vladimir Bekhterev's famous Psychoneurological Institute in Petrograd, a preferred place for young Jewish *intelligenty* to get an education because of its indifference to prescribed quotas for Jewish students and its liberal, humanistic curriculum. By going to school in Petrograd, Vertov was also following in the footsteps of his beloved Masha Gal'pern, who had studied medicine at the Women's Medical Institute there from 1903–1906 and again from 1908–12, and remained to work as a doctor. (The hiatus in her studies in 1906 may have been prompted by the Bialystok pogrom in June of that year, which traumatized the city and left many dead and more wounded; Masha would later work for the Jewish relief organization in Minsk during World War I.) In 1915, Kol'tsov joined Vertov as a student at the Institute; other classmates included future journalist Larissa Reisner, future film historian and filmmaker Grigorii Boltianskii, and future director Abram Room.[4]

Meanwhile, with the advance of German troops into Bialystok in August 1915, Vertov's entire family (with the exception of Mikhail, who attended school in Mogilev [now in Belarus]) became refugees in Petrograd and later Moscow, not returning to Bialystok until 1918 at the earliest. Vertov was recruited—not into the regular army, but (on the basis of an audition) into a special musical section at a military academy in Chuguev, near Khar'kov, Ukraine—early in the fall of 1916, and never returned to his studies in the Psychoneurological Institute, although he may have intended to. He remained at the academy at least until the February Revolution of 1917, after which time he left for Moscow, the city that was to be his base for the remainder of his days.[5]

Virtually nothing concrete is known of Vertov's activities between September 1916 and May 1918, when his work in newsreel began. In 1917, he spent much of his time going to poetry readings and cafés frequented by the artistic *bohème*. Although he may have already been involved in the production of scientific film at Bekhterev's institute, he made his first major acquaintance with someone from the cinema world in the fall of 1917, when he met the nineteen-year-old cameraman and future collaborator Aleksandr Lemberg at Mayakovsky's "Poet's Café." 1916–17 may have also been the period Vertov was involved in experimentation with the recording, editing, and quasi-musical organization of nonmusical sound. This "laboratory of hearing," as he called it, was the forerunner of the innovative experiments in documentary sound montage Vertov would carry out for the soundtracks of *Enthusiasm: Symphony of the Donbass* (*Entuziazm: Simfoniia Donbassa,* 1930) and, to a lesser extent, of *Three Songs of Lenin* (*Tri pesni o Lenine,* 1934).[6]

It was somewhere around or just after 1918, too, that "David Abelevich Kaufman" became "Dziga Vertov," a moniker he previously used as an artistic pseudonym appended to poems. "Vertov" is a futurist neologism derived from the Russian verb *vertit'sia,* to spin or turn; "Dziga" is the Ukrainian word for a "(spinning) top," and may have been a nickname given him in his youth by the Kyivan Mikhail Kol'tsov. As an adult, he was formally addressed as "Denis Arkad'evich Vertov," and this sort of Russification of name was typical for the young members of the Russophilic Jewish milieu in which he grew up—his own parents had given their last two sons the Russian names "Semyon" and "Boris"—as a token of their entry into what historian Yuri Slezkine has called "the Pushkin religion."[7]

An important feature of Vertov's years of creative gestation (1917–22) is the way in which "experimental/avant-garde" and "documentary/propaganda" experiences and impulses overlap. Kol'tsov, who became acquainted with the Bolshevik intellectuals Anatoly Lunacharsky and Grigorii Chicherin shortly after the October 1917 events, and was named chair of the newsreel division of the All-Russian Cinema Committee of the People's Commissariat of Enlightenment early in 1918, hired Vertov as his secretary on May 28 of that year. (Kol'tsov was to remain a major patron for Vertov at least until the late 1920s, and wrote articles in *Pravda*, a publication supportive of Vertov throughout the '20s, about Vertov's films. The concrete extent of his patronage is unknown, however, for Vertov apparently purged his own archive of correspondence with Kol'tsov after the journalist was arrested at the end of 1938.) Although Vertov, unlike Kol'tsov, never joined the Bolshevik Party—indicating instead in a 1918 questionnaire that his political sympathies were "anarchist-individualist" in character—he clearly became committed early on to the Soviet cause, as both an administrator and a filmmaker.[8]

By the end of 1918, Vertov had taken over administrative responsibility for the first Soviet newsreel series, *Kino-nedelia* (Cinema week; forty-three issues between May 1918 and June 1919); in 1920 and 1921, he took part as administrator, programmer, and film presenter on the "October Revolution" agitational train, one of a number of such trains that went through territories recently captured by the Red Army during the civil war, propagandizing for the new regime, and often carrying various high-level representatives of that regime onboard. (It was in connection with his work on this train that he met his first wife, pianist and fellow activist Ol'ga Toom.) During this period, he made the acquaintance of many figures who would play important roles in Soviet fiction and nonfiction film—including actor and director Vladimir Gardin, director and pedagogue Lev Kuleshov, and cameramen Eduard Tisse and Aleksandr Levitskii. By 1922 he was one of those in charge of newsreel production at Moscow's Goskino studio, and remained at the center of nonfiction film work there until 1927.

At the same time, Vertov was a practicing, if non-publishing, futurist poet from at least 1917, and continued to be actively interested in linguistic experimentation of a futurist sort—involving explorations of the tension between sonic and graphic materiality on the one side, and signification on the other—for the rest of his life. Although the newsreel units Vertov worked for from 1918 onward operated independently of the other fledgling subdivisions of the People's Commissariat of Enlightenment, it is worth noting that those subdivisions were structurally if not physically adjacent. This situation probably created opportunities for conversation, if not collaboration, with experimental artists. The fine arts section in 1918, for instance, was headed by none other than the great proto-constructivist painter, sculptor, and designer Vladimir Tatlin, and counted among its members such distinguished figures as Vertov's collaborator-to-be Aleksandr Rodchenko, who was working at the time as painter Olga Rozanova's assistant in the "art-industrial" subsection. And after future documentary filmmaker Esfir Shub joined the newsreel group as an administrator in 1922—the same year, at the outset of NEP, that Vertov began work on the *Kino-pravda* newsreel series, the first works bearing his particular creative stamp—Vertov had the oppor-

tunity to make contact with Shub's partner, Aleksei Gan, probably the foremost ideologue and publicist of constructivism, and a major early promoter of Vertov's work.[9]

Thus Vertov's biography suggests a kind of lived intersection of avant-gardism
and newsreel from 1917 through at least the mid-1930s. Although his first experimental work was the lost *Battle of Tsaritsyn* (*Boi pod Tsaritsynym*) of 1919—about a
civil war battle in which future dictator Joseph Stalin was centrally implicated, and
the first film on which Vertov worked with the woman who would be his second
wife and main lifelong collaborator, Elizaveta Svilova—it was with the *Kino-pravda*s
(twenty-three issues between June 1922 and March 1925), and particularly from the
thirteenth issue onward, that Vertov was able to effectively experiment within newsreel. Although the initial idea for a major Soviet newsreel combining information and
agitation came from director Fyodor Otsep of the non-state-owned "Rus'" firm, the
Commissariat of Enlightenment decided to entrust the task to Vertov's documentary
group, who were soon to become known as the "kinoks" (from the Russian "kino"
[cinema] and "oko" [an archaic word for "eye"]). At the center of that group were
Svilova and cameramen Ivan Belyakov and Mikhail Kaufman; the latter had been
demobilized in 1922, after having served as a driver and mechanic in the Red Army
during the civil war, and was to be Vertov's close collaborator for the next seven years.

Though far too involved a process to be discussed in detail here, the evolution
of the *Kino-pravda* series was characterized both by the deployment of an increasingly rich repertoire of devices—including archival footage, news footage, anima-
tions, experiments with moving intertitles, reenactments, and (contrary to Vertov's
stated principles) staged sequences—and by increasing structural and thematic
unity; the series culminated in inventive treatments of single themes like the Young
Pioneer organization, the death of Lenin, or the visit of a peasant to the city. The fourteenth *Kino-pravda* (late 1922) includes mobile constructivist intertitles designed by
Rodchenko; it seems that Vertov, possibly under the influence of Gan, was attempting through their inclusion to align his work with developments in constructivism,
as a kind of "marketing strategy," in keeping with the spirit of the New Economic
Policy. After all, 1922 had seen major gatherings and exhibits of constructivist work
in Germany, involving such figures as El Lissitzky and Hans Richter, both of whom
later became good friends of Vertov's.[10]

It was also during the 1922–25 period that most of Vertov's most famous articles
were written. Hugely influential through the widespread dissemination in many languages of the Soviet collection published in 1966, these essays and manifestoes offer
a rhetorically brilliant if conceptually unstable compound of disparate arguments of
varying provenance. His emphasis on embracing the new at the expense of the old,
and on the need to modify perception and sensibility to bring them "up to speed"
with industrial modernity, recall the futurist provocations that had so influenced
him in his youth; his antagonism toward fictional ("acted") film recalls, in a radical-
ized and intransigent tonality, the left-liberal intelligentsia's hostility to the "vulgar"
fables purveyed through mass cultural channels—an attitude no doubt conditioned
by Vertov's bookstore upbringing. At the same time, Vertov's documentary insistence

on "showing the working class to itself" points at once to the emergence of a certain Soviet iconography of proletarian imagery and to the origins of the great left-wing, counter-normative, nonfiction tradition, while his stress on the camera's superior capacities of vision leads toward a "scientific" conception of cinema, whether the model for science be Marxist economics (as in *Kino-Eye* [1924]), energeticism (in *The Eleventh Year* [1928]), or some combination of these with philosophy and even linguistics (in *Man with a Movie Camera* [1929]).

The culmination of the *Kino-pravda* period is the feature-length *Kino-Eye: Life Caught Unawares* (*Kinoglaz: Zhizn' vrasplokh*, 1924), which comprises five autonomously structured reels joined only by the overriding theme of the activities of the Young Pioneer troops from Moscow's "Red Defense" factory and from the village of Pavlovskoe, located near the capital. 1924 and *Kino-Eye* also saw the culmination of Vertov's efforts to establish kinok groups throughout the USSR, mainly via the networks established by the still somewhat inchoate Pioneer organization. Although these attempts met with limited success, they generated interest among young people in Moscow and environs and as far away as Odessa; one of the products of this effort, Ilya Kopalin, became a major Soviet documentary director and pedagogue, and one of the main trustees of Vertov's posthumous legacy. *Kino-Eye* won a silver medal at the Exposition internationale des arts décoratifs et industriels modernes in Paris in 1925, but Sergei Eisenstein's *Strike* took the gold, helping to fuel an already-simmering hostility between the two filmmakers, a hostility that in Vertov's case seems to have been much conditioned by envy of Eisenstein's global fame.[11]

Vertov's success with the Lenin memorial film *Kino-pravda no. 21* led to two major commissions: *Stride, Soviet!* (*Shagai, Sovet!* 1926), an election-year promotional film for the Moscow City Soviet, and the grandiose *One Sixth of the World* (*Shestaia chast' mira*, 1926), a film commission by the state trade organization Gostorg to promote Soviet exports abroad. Both films became occasions for remarkable experiments in structure, audience address, and intertitle construction, and aroused considerable interest, controversy and, from some of those who commissioned the films, ire. In particular, *One Sixth of the World*'s combination of savage anti-capitalist satire, ethnographic cataloging, and ambiguous economic argumentation, all articulated across an arc of Walt Whitman–inflected poetic intertitles, proved difficult to assimilate, and the film was never, in fact, used for promotional purposes. Together with *Three Songs of Lenin*, *One Sixth of the World* is also Vertov's most explicitly "imperial" film, although its borrowings from Whitman's paeans to the globe (especially "Salut au Monde") usefully link Russo-Soviet ideologies of empire to the wider history of the colonialist and internationalist imaginations as such.[12]

Vertov was fired at the beginning of January 1927 from Moscow's Sovkino studio, following the release of *One Sixth of the World,* after a series of ferocious arguments with studio head Ilya Trainin. The disputes, centering on what was thought to be the excessive cost of the *One Sixth* production to the studio and on Trainin's decision to pass directorial control over the studio's planned found-footage film commemorating the tenth anniversary of the Revolution to Esfir Shub, reached the boiling point when Vertov, advocate of the non-scripted film, refused to present Trainin with a script for *Man with a Movie Camera*, footage for the never-realized first version of which Vertov had been amassing through 1925–26. After several months of melancholy unemployment (during which time he wrote a script for a fascinating, never-to-be-produced film on Jewish agricultural settlement in the Crimea that demonstrates his knowledge of Jewish issues like no other text), Vertov was hired by VUFKU (the All-Ukrainian Photo-Film Directorate, based in Kyiv and at this time staffed with artists and administrators sympathetic to Ukrainian futurism), under whose auspices he made three masterpieces in quick succession.

He was first contracted to make a film about industrialization in the Ukrainian SSR, with a focus on the construction of the Dnepr Hydroelectric Station—the film released in 1928 as *The Eleventh Year* (*Odinnadtsatyi*)—prior to resuming work on his pet project, *Man with a Movie Camera* (*Chelovek s kinoapparatom*, 1929). This work, shown in Germany, France, England, and the United States after its initial release, fell into almost total obscurity for the next thirty years. Now readily available on DVD and widely regarded as the most formally inventive and intellectually sophisticated film of the silent era, *Man with a Movie Camera* has become a touchstone for discussions of documentary, experimental practice in film, and cinematic self-reflexivity. The film was also, however, his last collaboration with Mikhail Kaufman: relations between the brothers had become strained during the production of *The Eleventh Year*, and they were not on speaking terms again until 1933.

Vertov's final Ukrainian—and first sound—film, *Enthusiasm: Symphony of the Donbass*, shot in the heat of the First Five-Year Plan in the mines and factories of Eastern Ukraine, is both one of his most politically problematic works—the film was shot during the inaugural stages of agricultural collectivization, although not during the most violent and destructive phases of that campaign—and one of his most artistically innovative, especially as regards its unprecedented and still astonishing use of documentary sound. During a screening in London in 1931 at which Vertov was present, Charlie Chaplin praised the film as "one of the most exhilarating symphonies [he had] heard"; much later, it served as an inspiration to such artists as Pierre Schaeffer, Peter Kubelka, and Richard Serra.[13]

1928–35 marked the apex of Vertov's worldwide fame and influence, and during those years, articles about his work were published everywhere from the United States and Argentina to Czechoslovakia and Japan. He took two trips to Europe—from the beginning of May through the beginning of August 1929, and from July 1931 to the beginning of 1932—during which time he showed his films in Germany, France, Holland, and England, and met Germaine Dulac, Léon Moussinac, and Joris Ivens, among others. Both trips were primarily lecture tours accompanied by film screenings: the 1929 visit was punctuated by the strange controversy surrounding found-footage filmmaker Albrecht Viktor Blum's appropriation of sections of *The Eleventh Year* for his *In the Shadow of the Machines* (1928); in 1931, *Enthusiasm*, after initially generating intense interest, was banned by the German government in October (while Vertov was still in Europe)—a prohibition that elicited protest from

Ivens, Hans Richter, Béla Balázs, and Lászlo Moholy-Nagy, among others. During the 1931 visit, he also managed to see his parents in Bialystok and Boris Kaufman in Paris for what was to be the last time.[14]

After his return from Europe, Vertov, now back in Moscow, was under fierce attack from the proletarian "cultural revolutionaries" of RAPP, but not for long (RAPP, along with all other artistic organizations, was liquidated in April 1932). By June 1932 he was working at the Mezhrabpomfil'm studio, and spent most of the next year and a half working on what was to be his greatest popular success, *Three Songs of Lenin*. A tribute to Lenin that integrates many of the tropes and even some of the footage from Vertov's 1920s films with "folk" music and poetry and innovative sync sound interviews, *Three Songs of Lenin* turned out to be the last film over which Vertov had relatively complete artistic control. The highly selective deployment in *Three Songs* of "folk" motifs from the Muslim regions of the USSR, together with his innovative sync sound interviews with workers, produced at once Vertov's most powerful representations of the coordination of national-ethnic and Soviet identities, and his most successful attempt to accommodate his experimental formal preoccupations with the new stress on narrative clarity and exemplary subjects typical of emergent socialist realism.[15]

He was awarded the Order of the Red Star in 1935 for *Three Songs,* and had the opportunity to rerelease the film in 1938, after adding a section of a speech by Stalin to the conclusion, and removing images of political luminaries who had in the interim become "enemies of the people." Unlike Mikhail Kol'tsov, Vertov and Svilova escaped the Terror of 1937–38 physically unscathed; they even received a modest new apartment at the end of 1938, but no other "perks" were coming their way, as it turned out. It seems that Vertov's loss of the patronage of Kol'tsov (and no doubt others) during the Terror, his inability to sustain a working collective, his often vocal obstinacy, and his gradually declining health all contributed to the waning of his productivity and influence from 1938 onward.[16]

A notable feature of Vertov's films, going as far back as some of the *Kino-pravda*s and in marked contrast to what we find in the work of other major filmmakers of the 1920s, is the unusual prominence he gave to women. For *Lullaby (Kolybel'naia,* 1937), he wrote a powerful script attacking the historical exploitation (particularly the sexual exploitation) of women, but his conception was altered almost beyond recognition during the course of production. In the end, *Lullaby,* which also enjoyed a U.S. release, ended up being less about women than about children and the "paternal care" offered to all Soviet citizens by the state, as personified by Stalin and given codified form in the 1936 constitution.

In the late 1930s and early 1940s, in the wake of *Lullaby,* Vertov and Svilova ended up wandering from one studio to another, working on films that either went unreleased (*Three Heroines* [*Tri geroini,* 1938: about the famous women pilots Raskova, Osipenko, and Grizodubova]), or unproduced altogether (*The Girl and the Giant* [*Devochka i velikan*], on which he worked in 1940–41 with famous children's author M. Il'in). Vertov's health had begun to fail from the mid-1930s, and while in Alma-Ata during World War II (where he made a remarkable film about Kazakh war production entitled *To You, Front* [*Tebe, Front,* 1942]), he suffered a nervous breakdown.[17]

During the war, the Nazis murdered Vertov's father, mother, and all his close relatives from Bialystok and the surrounding area sometime between 1941 and 1943. Along with Mikhail and Boris, Vertov attempted to uncover the details of his family's fate, but to no avail; it was left to Masha Gal'pern, who had already immigrated to Palestine, to provide documentation in the early 1960s about the Kaufman and Gal'pern family victims to the Yad Vashem archive. Significantly, Svilova was responsible for editing the very first documentary film about Auschwitz (*Osventsim,* 1945), and worked with Roman Karmen on a major documentary about the Nuremberg Trials (*Judgment of the Peoples* [*Sud narodov,* 1946]), which won a Stalin Prize; she herself had received this prize for her work with Yuli Raizman on *Berlin* (1945), which also garnered the best short film award at the 1946 Cannes Film Festival.[18]

Vertov's last noteworthy film, *The Oath of Youth* (*Kliatva molodykh,* about the commitment of Komsomol members to the war effort) was roundly criticized by studio supervisors in August 1944 and not accepted for wide release. In the months that followed, until the end of 1944, Vertov desperately proposed at least five different script ideas in rapid succession, but like virtually all the proposals he had offered since 1938, they went unproduced and virtually unnoticed. After this point—that is, from 1944 until 1954, when he died—Vertov stopped presenting ideas for films, or new ideas about film.[19]

The most significant speech of his last years was, alas, his self-defense against covertly antisemitic accusations of "rootless cosmopolitanism" and pro-Western sycophancy, delivered at an open party meeting of two hundred people at the Central Documentary Film Studio on March 15, 1949. Although he was not among the main group of cinema workers targeted during the slander campaign, the old "formalist" Vertov was singled out for abuse by none other than the deputy minister of cinema, V. Shcherbina, who had just published an attack on "aestheticizing cosmopolitans" in the pages of the official film journal *Iskusstvo kino* (Art of cinema). The major documentarian Roman Karmen, with whom Svilova had worked on *Judgment of the Peoples,* added his voice to the choir of denunciation, and Vertov's old friend and rival Esfir Shub attempted a coded defense. Vertov's own defense was to include self-lacerating attacks on *Man with a Movie Camera* as a "formalist mistake," but he fell suddenly ill and never completed it; he was guided away from the podium to a couch in a backroom by future documentary director Seda Pumpyanskaya, who had worked together with her husband, Boris, on *To You, Front.*[20]

After this point, Vertov, ailing and prematurely aged in appearance, rarely appeared in public; when he did, as in a 1952 lecture given to workers in newsreel, he offered defenses of principles diametrically opposed to those he had upheld in his heyday (for instance, defending the script as the basis of documentary). He returned, in a small way, to poetry, writing occasional cryptic verses that seem to combine accusation and self-critique in equal measure. In his diaries, he also produced some prose descriptions of the mindless bureaucratic obstructions he encountered when trying to put together some of the *News of the Day* newsreels, offering a level of detail that suggest he intended the descriptions for posterity. While his closest friend M. Il'in was dying of cancer at the end of October 1953, Vertov was diagnosed with incurable stomach cancer himself. Increasingly weak and depressed, he politely refused assistance freely offered by the famous surgeon Sergei Sergeevich Iudin, indicating that he was too feeble to endure the treatment.[21]

His death less than four months later, on February 12, 1954, was noted in a brief obituary in a single Moscow newspaper. Svilova, who retired soon after Vertov's death, dedicated the rest of her life to promoting his memory. Kopalin, too—by now teaching in the documentary section of the state film school and one of the grand old men of Soviet nonfiction film—began writing and publishing about Vertov's films as early as June 1955. Articles about and references to Vertov and his films started to appear with some regularity in the pages of official Soviet film publications from 1956 onward, and serious scholarship on Vertov (carried out by Nikolai Abramov, Sergei Drobashenko, Viktor Listov, Lev Roshal', and others) was well underway in the USSR by the mid-1960s.

Abroad, full retrospectives were staged as early as 1960 in Leipzig, followed by important screenings in Paris, Venice, and Vienna. The Western memory of Vertov was sustained by some of those who had known his work (Joris Ivens, Hans Richter, Léon Moussinac) and some who had not, like Georges Sadoul, whose unfinished book on Vertov (1971) preceded the major essays and books by Annette Michelson, Seth Feldman, Vlada Petric, and (later) Yuri Tsivian, Thomas Tode, Aleksandr Deriabin, Emma Widdis, Oleg Aronson and Elizabeth Papazian among others. Although the late 1980s and 1990s saw the beginnings of a reconsideration of Vertov in light of his propaganda work on behalf of Soviet power, his reputation has been complicated rather than undermined by new research; and recent assimilations of Vertov to media studies (Lev Manovich; the Vienna-based "Digital Formalism" project) promise to open still other avenues of historical and theoretical inquiry. Meanwhile, as major, career-spanning retrospectives (in Sacile in 2004; at New York's Museum of Modern Art in 2011) and new DVD releases bring the work of this stubborn, contradictory, and charismatic filmmaker to more audiences than ever before, we can safely assume that "Vertov studies," and the history of artistic responses to Vertov, have only just begun.[22]

NOTES

1. For an English translation of his writings, see Dziga Vertov, *Kino-Eye: The Writings of Dziga Vertov,* ed. Annette Michelson, trans. Kevin O'Brien (Berkeley: University of California Press, 1984). Vertov's works in Russian include *Iz Naslediia: Dramaturgicheskie Opyty,* ed. A. S. Deriabin (Moscow: Eizenshtein-Tsentr, 2004); and *Iz Naslediia: Stat'i i Vystupleniia,* ed. D. V. Kruzhkova and S. M. Ishevskaia (Moscow: Eizenshtein-Tsentr, 2008).

2. Two of the best works on Vertov exemplify this division: on Vertov as "avant-gardist," see Vlada Petric, *Constructivism in Film: The Man with a Movie Camera, A Cinematic Analysis*

(Cambridge: Cambridge University Press, 1987); for a major Soviet study characterizing Vertov exclusively as documentarian and film journalist, see V. Listov, *Istoriia smotrit v ob'ektiv* (Moscow: Iskusstvo, 1974).

3. See the wedding registration of Abel and Chaya Kaufman of January 30, 1894 (in archive 155, book 3 of the Jewish marriage registries); and registries for Jewish births for January 3, 1896 (David Abelevich [Dziga]), August 24, 1897 (Moisei Abelevich [Mikhail]), December 6, 1899 (Semyon Abelevich; died as an infant approximately six months later) and December 30, 1892 (Boris Abelevich) in the State Archive in Bialystok, Poland (all dates OS). See also the partially accurate records provided by Masha (Miriam) Halpern-Proginin to the Archive of Shoah Victims' Names on January 23, 1960, Yad Vashem website, yadvashem.org; Mikhail Kaufman, "Poet neigrovogo," *Dziga Vertov v vospominaniiakh sovremennikov,* ed. E. I. Vertov-Svilova et al. (Moscow: Iskusstvo, 1976), 74–76; Boris Kaufman Papers, Beinecke Rare Book and Manuscript Library, Yale University, GEN MSS 562.12.183, and the papers under the rubric "Paris Years."

4. For more on Vertov's early life, see Valérie Pozner, "Vertov before Vertov: Psychoneurology in Petrograd," in *Dziga Vertov: The Vertov Collection at the Austrian Film Museum,* ed. Thomas Tode and Barbara Wurm (Vienna: Austrian Film Museum/SYNEMA, 2006), 12–15. On the Bialystok pogrom, see Rebecca Kobrin, *Jewish Bialystok and Its Diaspora* (Bloomington: Indiana University Press, 2010), 58–59.

5. Tsentral'nyi gosudarstvennyi istoricheskij arkhiv Sankt-Peterburga (hereafter cited as TsGIASPb), f. 115, op. 2, d. 4048; and Kaufman, "Poet neigrovogo," 76.

6. On Vertov's possible prerevolutionary involvement in film, see John MacKay, "Film Energy: Process and Metanarrative in Dziga Vertov's *The Eleventh Year* (1928)," *October* 121 (Summer 2007): 41–78, especially 56–58.

7. V. M. Magidov, "Iz arkhiva Vertova," *Kinovedcheskie zapiski* 18 (1993): 161–64; Yuri Tsivian, ed., *Lines of Resistance: Dziga Vertov and the Twenties* (Pordenone: Giornate del Cinema Muto, 2004), 36–37; Yuri Slezkine, *The Jewish Century* (Princeton, N.J.: Princeton University Press, 2004), 127.

8. TsGIASPb, f. 115, op. 2, d. 9788, ll. 15, 22, 23, 39; A. Rubashkin, *Mikhail Kol'tsov: Kritiko-biograficheskij ocherk* (Leningrad: Khudozhestvennaia Literatura, 1971), 8; V.S. Listov, *Rossia, Revoliutsiia, Kinematograf* (Moscow: Materik, 1995), 87–94; Magidov, "Iz Arkhiva Vertova."

9. On Vertov's poetry, see Tsivian, *Lines of Resistance,* 33–37.

10. See John MacKay, "Vertov and the Line: Art, Socialization, Collaboration," in *Museum Without Walls: Film, Art, New Media,* ed. Angela Dalle Vacche (London: Palgrave, forthcoming).

11. On *Kino-Eye,* see L. Roshal', *Dziga Vertov* (Moscow: Iskusstvo, 1982), 103–11; Jeremy Hicks, *Dziga Vertov: Defining Documentary Film* (London and New York: I. B. Tauris, 2007), 15–20; MacKay, "Vertov and the Line." On Vertov's relationship to Eisenstein, see Petric, *Constructivism in Film,* 48–60; Tsivian, *Lines of Resistance,* 125–52.

12. On *Stride Soviet* and *One Sixth of the World,* see Tsivian, *Lines of Resistance,* 157–250; Oksana Sarkisova, "Across One Sixth of the World: Dziga Vertov, Travel Cinema, and Soviet Patriotism," *October* 121 (Summer 2007): 19–40. On Vertov and Whitman, see Ben Singer, "Connoisseurs of Chaos: Whitman, Vertov and the 'Poetic Survey,'" *Literature/Film Quarterly* 15 (1987): 247–58.

13. See Lucy Fischer, "*Enthusiasm*: From Kino-Eye to Radio-Eye," *Film Quarterly* 31, no. 2 (Winter 1977–78): 25–34; John MacKay, "Disorganized Noise: *Enthusiasm* and the Ear of the Collective," *KinoKultura* 7 (January 2005), www.kinokultura.com/articles/jan05-mackay.html.

14. On Vertov's European voyages, see Thomas Tode, "Ein Russe projiziert in die Planetariumskuppel: Dsiga Wertows Reise nach Deutschland," in *Die ungewöhnlichen Abenteuer des Dr. Mabuse im Lande der Bolschewiki,* ed. Oksana Bulgakowa (Berlin: Freunde der Deutschen Kinemathek, 1995), 143–51; Tode, "Ein Russe auf dem Eifelturm: Vertov in

Paris," in *Apparatur und Rhapsodie: Zu den Filmen des Dziga Vertov*, ed. Natascha Drubek-Meyer and Jurij Murashov (Frankfurt am Main: Peter Lang, 2000), 43–72; Tsivian, *Lines of Resistance*, 353–82; MacKay, "Disorganized Noise"; Rossiiskij gosudarstvennyi arkhiv literatury i iskusstva (hereafter cited as RGALI), f. 2091, op. 1, d. 71.

15. On *Three Songs*, see Annette Michelson, "The Kinetic Icon in the Work of Mourning: Prolegomena to the Analysis of a Textual System," *October* 52 (Spring 1990): 16–39; Mariano Prunes, "Dziga Vertov's *Three Songs about Lenin* (1934): A Visual Tour through the History of the Soviet Avant-Garde in the Interwar Years," *Criticism* 45, no. 2 (Spring 2003): 251–78; and John MacKay, "Allegory and Accommodation: Vertov's *Three Songs of Lenin* (1934) as a Stalinist Film," *Film History* 18 (2006): 376–91.

16. MacKay, "Allegory and Accommodation"; RGALI, f. 2091, op. 2, d. 392, ll. 50–58; f. 2091, op. 2, d. 425.

17. See Deriabin, *Dramaturgicheskie opyty*, 242–410; Roshal', *Dziga Vertov*, 238–54; RGALI, f. 2091, op. 2, d. 438.

18. Boris Kaufman Papers, Beinecke Rare Book and Manuscript Library, Yale University, GEN MSS 562.14.282; RGALI, f. 2091, op. 2, d. 274, ll. 678–739; f. 2091, op. 2, d. 392, ll. 103–15.

19. Deriabin, *Dramaturgicheskie opyty*, 424–76; Kruzhkova and Ishevskaia, *Stat'i i vystupleniia*, 345–76; Roshal', *Dziga Vertov*, 255–58; RGALI, f. 2208, op. 2, d. 622.

20. V. Shcherbina, "O gruppe estestvuiushchikh kosmopolitov v kino," *Iskusstvo kino* 1 (1949): 14–16; Lev Roshal', "Stenogramma odnogo zasedaniia," *Iskusstvo kino* 12 (1997): 124–33; Kruzhkova and Ishevskaia, *Stat'i i vystupleniia*, 377–79.

21. Marina Goldovskaya, *Woman with a Movie Camera* (Austin: University of Texas Press, 2006), 24–25; Kruzhkova and Ishevskaia, *Stat'i i vystupleniia*, 388–391; RGALI, f. 2091, op. 1, d. 269, ll. 66–76; f. 2091, op. 1, d. 308.

22. For a historical overview of Vertov reception, see John MacKay, "The 'Spinning Top' Takes Another Turn: Vertov Today," *KinoKultura* 8 (April 2005), www.kinokultura.com /articles/apr05-mackay.html.

Engraving of Mukhtar Auezov.

# 27

## Mukhtar Auezov

### (1897–1961)

MICHAEL ROULAND

With a life spanning the first six decades of the twentieth century, Mukhtar Auezov was a successful playwright, novelist, and scholar. His life provides a glimpse into the tumult of Central Asia in the twentieth century and raises questions about the constructed pantheon of Soviet intellectuals—their sacrifices, compromises, and ethnic diversity. Auezov, like many other prominent intellectuals of his time, struggled to avoid the purges while maintaining ideas of nationality, culture, identity, and modernity that ran counter to the socialist ethic prevalent in Moscow and Leningrad. Auezov transcended the Russian and Soviet paradigm that designated non-Russians as "native intellectuals" brought into the socialist fold and educated by the Soviet system. Significantly, his work illuminates the contradictions of the vague and antagonistic ideologies of nationalism and socialism.

Mukhtar Auezov was born in 1897 to an influential family in the village of Chingistan, near Semei (formerly Semipalatinsk). After completing his early education at the Semipalatinsk Teachers' Seminary, he spent the revolutionary era in several official Russian imperial positions from Semipalatinsk to Orenburg, where were located on the front lines of the late civil war. When the dust settled, local party officials sent Auezov, who already had been identified as a promising playwright, to study Russian philology at Leningrad University in the mid-1920s.

After this Russian studies interlude, he returned to the region in 1928 to pursue an advanced degree at the new Central Asian University in Tashkent, researching "eastern themes" and Kazakh epics until 1930. The study of Abai Kunanbaev became a central part of his research there; and a blend of scholarly and creative work filled the remainder of his life. As Auezov's work grew in prominence, he inevitably attracted the wrong kind of attention by avoiding socialist themes and focusing on pre-Soviet history and on traditional life in the village. Critics accused him of "reactionary romanticism" several times in the 1920s and 1930s; and ultimately Auezov was arrested for "bourgeois nationalism" in 1933. Fortunately, and owing to several compromises, Auezov survived the 1930s. He was soon rehabilitated and finished his work on two monumental historical novels on Abai Kunanbaev. In a reversal of fortunes, he won the Stalin Prize for Literature in 1949 and was appointed to the Soviet Academy of Sciences.

As the leading Kazakh literary scholar and a prolific writer, Auezov was the chief interpreter of Kazakh culture from the 1920s to the 1960s. But Auezov's life was also an echo of his mentor, the famed Abai Kunanbaev, a nineteenth-century Kazakh writer and intellectual figure who saw Russia as his model and Russian literature as his teacher. If we follow this path, through the lives of Abai and Auezov, we begin to perceive how Soviet ideology, Russian literature, and Kazakh traditional life intersected in the creation of a national narrative that was palatable for Russians and Kazakhs in the Kazakh Republic. It is a national narrative that remains a potent force today.

## AUEZOV AND HIS PLACE IN HISTORY

The life of Mukhtar Auezov reflects a significant moment in the history of Central Asia. As part of a new generation encouraged to pursue higher education and embrace socialism, Auezov provided an organic example of the compromises and intellectual conditioning of the Soviet system while maintaining a strong cultural awareness of his own Kazakh identity. There are several ways to approach a study of his life: to reveal the Soviet nationality experience through a native participant—not just through *vydvizhenie,* or "promotion," but engaging the Soviet intellectual elite directly; to present a literary figure and cultural embodiment of the Kazakh twentieth century; and to elucidate a Soviet intellectual who lived through the purges by locating a rationale for those who survived.

There exist many impressive biographies, bibliographies, and multivolume collected works of Auezov in Kazakh and Russian.[1] These works describe him with a diverse array of lofty ideals: "humanist," "artist," "thinker," and "ardent patriot." Enthusiasm for his work should not be surprising given its breadth: dramas, short stories, novels, ethnographies, histories, linguistic studies, and literary criticism. Auezov played a pivotal role in the development of modern Kazakh literature as a contributor and critic. And, like Chinghiz Aitmatov, Auezov became a model for the "Friendship of the Peoples" mantra of the postwar era.

Auezov's biography is particularly fascinating since his life was fashioned through a biography of his intellectual mentor, Abai Kunanbaev. Not only did his early work reflect a yearning to continue Abai's influence into the twentieth century but his major literary achievements were also celebrated through his award-winning historical novel of the life of Abai. Auezov even included his own brief autobiography as a preface to the 1950 edition of *Abai.*

Auezov envisioned himself traveling through time and history: from feudalism, to capitalism, and to socialism as Kazakhstan surged into the twentieth century. Auezov went against political endeavors to undermine tribal identity, extolling his Tobykty clan as a source of inspiration for his dilogy—*Abai* (1942–1949) and *Path of Abai* (1952–1958)—since Abai shared this designation. Linking his familial and tribal identity with a deep belief in modernity, education, and history formed Auezov's intellectual view of "internationalism through humanism."[2] This phrase was a way of negotiating the boundaries of the center-periphery divide by combining the Soviet internationalism of the metropole with the humanistic particularities of his national culture.

Zoia Kedrina's influential first biography of Auezov focused on the Abai phenomenon. This would become the standard for most biographies of the 1950s and 1960s. After his the publication of his *Abai* dilogy, his life was seen in a different light. He was seen as a twentieth-century reflection of the great nineteenth-century link of "friendship" between Russians and Kazakhs manifest in literature for the first time in Abai's writings. In an earlier response to Auezov's work, Kedrina wrote, "Today, observing the political, cultural, and material blossoming of Kazakhstan under the sunshine of the Stalin Constitution, we are convinced of the wise insight of Abai." And, according to Kedrina, Auezov links the popular sentiments of Abai with the achievement of Soviet literature to expose "the victory of Leninist-Stalinist national politics."[3] Yet the question of Russo-Kazakh ties, or collaborative annexation, remained unresolved in Auezov's work; he chose to reveal the positive and negative qualities of the Russian Empire. As a scholar and folklorist, Auezov did not like the term "the cursed past [*prokliatogo proshlogo*]"; instead, the past was a focal point for his professional and literary life.

## ABAI AND PATH OF ABAI

Mukhtar Auezov championed Abai Kunanbaev for several reasons: his contributions to Kazakh poetry, his preservation of the classical literature of the East, his moral certitude, and his respect of Russian "democratic" literature.[4] But we should question Auezov's place in interpreting Abai: Is Auezov an inheritor of Abai's attitudes and traditions? Or is his ideological view more in line with Soviet values? From his childhood, Auezov learned to read from his grandfather, and used Abai's writings as his first textbook. His own grandfather, Auez, was a close friend of Abai. Moreover, the confrontation between his early hatred of colonialism and his love for Kazakh music led Auezov to Abai. Abai represented to Auezov the moment of reconciliation between these two major forces in Kazakh life.

Looking back to the earliest scholarship on Abai, Ali Bokeikhanov, Akhmet Baitursunov, and Mir Yakub Dulatov celebrate Abai's work in the prerevolutionary pages of *Semipalatinsk listok* and *Kazak*. However, during the 1920s, so-called conservative intellectuals denounced Abai, along with folk and traditional culture broadly, because they considered them to be at odds with the new culture of Bolshevik agitators. Despite claims to the contrary, there were elements of Abai's and Auezov's literary lives that were attractive to Soviet policy in Central Asia. A new climate emerged in the 1930s that initiated a reevaluation of Abai.[5]

Abai opposed clerical conservatism, pan-Turkism, and pan-Islamism; he believed Russian cultural influences led to prosperity more directly. He was an early promoter of Russian language and literature, and often translated Russian lyrics and adapted them to music. Later, the Soviets viewed Abai as the epitome of social progress: he advocated the dismantling of the shari'a and rallied against the so-called tyranny of the *bais* (local Kazakh elite). Auezov supported these sentiments: "Abai already then realized the negative intentions of the pan-Turkic and pan-Islamic ideas, which in our day revealed in the end their intentions: bourgeois-reactionary nationalism."[6] It is sometimes difficult to interpret how far Auezov went to please his Russian audiences and tow the party line, but his Kazakh sources reveal the same sentiments. Moreover, by the 1970s, Auezov's *Abai* was regarded as a model for Central Asian writers. Presently, Abai Kunanbaev (1845–1904) is widely considered the founder of modern Kazakh literature.

Mukhtar Auezov began seriously researching the life of Abai Kunanbaev in the mid-1920s. It was not until 1937, however, that Auezov's conceptions of Abai were first revealed in print. A series of articles, entitled "How Tatiana's Voice Came to Be Heard in the Steppe," which ran in the Kazakh-language *Kazak adebieti* and *Adebiet maidany* and in the Russian-language *Literaturnyi Kazakhstan,* set out his biographical plot. Not only did Auezov reveal a deep spiritual affinity for his predecessor, but also he understood Abai to be a champion of social justice and intellectual awakening and as a window to the nineteenth century. Auezov portrayed the worlds of the village, *akïns* (renowned musicians), traditional elite, and provincial Russian authorities. In these pages, generational struggles between patriarchal, feudal forces and democratic, modern ones became clear. Auezov later described his project: "A historical novel will transform into a novel about modernity. The series begins with the story of a great poet, rushing into the future, and ends with portraying this future and becoming modern."[7] Here, Abai is a pro-Russian enlightener. But, to what extent did Auezov write events back into history? And who is the audience for these novels written in both Russian and Kazakh?

Auezov's historical novels presented an encyclopedia of Kazakh life in the nineteenth century. Even before Auezov set out to work on these novels, he studied Abai's life and works. He was the primary editor of Abai's complete works, wrote his biography, and collected historical material pertaining to Abai. Both novels, *Abai* and *Path of Abai,* trace the life of the poet through the history of his time. The biographical narrative begins as Abai returns from his Russian school in Semipalatinsk. It follows his moral and social struggles to bring Russian Enlightenment to the Kazakh steppe and ends with the establishment of his legacy. Moreover, Auezov exhibited the benefits of Russian culture to Kazakhs as well as the depth of Russian influences on Kazakhs to Russians. In his review of *Abai,* Boris Gorbatov explained, "Mukhtar Auezov managed correctly to represent two Russias. He showed the Russia of colonizers and bureaucrats and the Russia of democracy, the Russia of the great Russian people."[8]

While Auezov's glowing admiration has lasted to this day, Abai was not always revered in this way. Changes in the literary climate of the 1930s, for example, introduced Kazakh critics and officials seeking to conform to the prevailing socialist artistic movement. Earlier scholars dismissed Abai as "semi-feudal" and no longer as a positive hero. Auezov himself was declared a "counterrevolutionary" and "political enemy" in Gabbas Togzhanov and Ilias Zhansugarov's *Kazakhskii sbornik* (The Kazakh collection).[9] Abai's contemporaries criticized him for supporting the idea of sending Kazakh children to Russian schools in order to serve as interpreters and officials. To many Kazakhs of the late nineteenth century this plan was tantamount to a complete loss of national culture.

The experience of attending Russian school, however, was something that Auezov followed, even before the Bolsheviks arrived. And his historical novel sought to reconcile his own experiences with Abai's. Auezov explained, "While recreating the poet's image, I was mindful not only of his place in our history and his progressive role in the past, but of his dreams that linked him with our generation."[10] Thus, by transporting Abai's life into Auezov's conceptual milieu and through Auezov's imagination of Abai's historical past, Auezov could entwine their lives and lessons. Seeing his own life through the experience of his predecessor, Auezov led the conversion of Kazakh literature from an oral tradition to the Soviet novel and explored Abai's colonial experience within his new socialist intellectual space.

## PUSHKIN AND THE RUSSIAN FACTOR

Russian culture was more than a literary interest for Abai. "The writings of Pushkin, Lermontov, and Krylov became a school for [Abai]," Auezov clarified, "not only in artistic mastery but also in a code of ethics." Yet adopting a Russian worldview was a struggle famously exemplified in the musical synthesis of a Kazakh *kui* (instrumental musical composition) and *Eugene Onegin*. Auezov recounted this moment:

> [Abai] murmured quietly, his fingers caressing the dombïra, and though his eyes were fixed on the two peaks of Akshoky his gaze was turned inward. When he had gone to bed the previous night, he had the faint stirrings of a melody within him, but now it spoke more boldly. He tried to sing the air; the rhythm was much like that of the poem:
>
> You are my God-sent husband,
> I longed for you to be mine . . .
>
> Tatiana's lament as yet sounded uncertain in the Kazakh language; Abai urged his dombïra on, the chords flowing one after another. The final two lines were especially elusive, but at last fell in with the melody.[11]

This is a fascinating passage on several levels. First, we have a repetition of music melding with Tatiana's letter, which was important to Alexander Pushkin as well. "Music is the only medium for the Romantics," Monika Greenleaf explains, "that conveys intact the simultaneous multifariousness of inspiration." Auezov thus placed Abai within the romantic tradition and highlighted his contributions to Kazakh oral literature. Second, we can view Abai within the context of the Russian literary tradition (an act that Auezov extended through the repetition of Abai's life in novel form), claiming

Pushkin's lineage and proving a poetic mastery through his incorporation of Pushkin's words into his own work, what Stephanie Sandler calls an "act of possession."[12]

Auezov used Pushkin as his model in much the same way that Abai chose Pushkin. Rather than repeating Russocentrism, this act indicates continuity with the Russian tradition by identifying Pushkin as the ideal national poet. Chinghiz Aitmatov's comment in *Pravda* exemplifies Auezov's significance: "In the formation of the modern Central Asian artistic worldview and in all the spiritual life of our neighboring people, Auezov showed direction, such as Pushkin did in the development of Russian culture." Auezov himself often admitted, "I feel indebted to the Russian school as well as to Russian culture as such." At the same time, Auezov viewed Kazakh literature (and in the Soviet sense, "the Soviet East") through the lenses of Russian and Kazakh motifs. Even Abai asserted that the Russian language was crucial for him: "It provides a key to understanding the world."[13]

Highlighting Russian influences on nomadic Kazakh lives made them comprehensible to outsiders, as Russian writer Konstantin Fedin, attested: "In my youth I lived in the Kazakh steppe and saw quite a few Kazakh nomads. But only Mukhtar Auezov could make me understand the Kazakh people through his *Abai*, and I became closer to the steppe with its winds and aromas now brought to my own breath, as if I [myself] became Kazakh."[14] Rather than placing emphasis on the ethnic quality of a Kazakh national character, Auezov highlights the intersection of Russian and Kazakh values and influences that was well suited to the demographic realities of Kazakhstan following the war.

When we look at the history of Kazakh literature and Kazakh history broadly, we see that the lasting monuments of the nineteenth century for Kazakhs are expressed in the linkage of oral, musical, and literary genres. This contrasted with the new physical monuments of socialism. Auezov's biography draws on the new scale of socialist monumentalism and bridges the static identities of seminomadic and social democratic, past and present, Kazakh and Russian. After the Revolution, Kazakhs needed a national narrative to explain their past in the context of the Soviet present. This national narrative needed to describe the transformation of a people while providing some lessons about their historical experience. In the case of Auezov's *Abai* and *Path of Abai*, Abai Kunanbaev represented a Kazakh cultural ideal. We can read this narrative through the image of an optimistic Kazakh who viewed modernity through Russification while remaining committed to the cause of enriching Kazakh culture throughout this process. Ultimately, Auezov's view of Abai provided an essential national narrative that strengthened the Russian and Kazakh bond under the Soviets while infusing the particularities of the peripheral into the discourse of the center.

## LITERATURE AT CENTER AND PERIPHERY

There is a powerful draw toward European models of imperialism and intellectual Eurocentrism. Soviet history is complicit in this thinking. How, then, should we read the voices that struggle against imperialism in the twentieth century? Bill Ashcroft

has suggested the poignant image of "the Empire writing back." Internationally significant authors such as Naguib Mahfouz, V. S. Naipaul, Salman Rushdie, Wole Soyinka,
Gabriel García Márquez, and others have rewritten the backwardness and cultural
alienation imposed on them by engaging the "West" with a high level of literary discourse that pleases dominant artistic sensibilities but jars the mind through the view
of the "Native." Some argue that these writers have transcended Edward Said's challenge by turning a culture of imperialism, classification, and control into one of self-
reflection, magical realism, and empowerment.

Scholarship on Soviet history has underlined the importance of local studies to
interpret the contradictions between center and periphery. As Donald Raleigh has
argued, "Local studies actually help create and recreate the Center, because the relationship between center and periphery is symbiotic and dialectical. In seeking to
determine the inner mechanisms and perceptions of a locale, we ineluctably focus on
center-periphery contradictions and oppositions that often become the objects of our
research."[15] Whether observing non-Russian nationalities or provincial Russia, we see
that the process of adapting ideology from center to the particularities of the local
often leads to methods of evasion or outright conflicts.

The inequality (and unevenness) of these experiences should cause us to question the usefulness of center-periphery binaries. A great deal of recent scholarship on
British literature has sought to highlight such an ambiguity in the center-periphery
divide for writers of bilingual and postcolonial experiences. Describing her own bi-
furcated cultural background, between her mother's education of Persian, Arabic,
and Urdu poetry and her father's Cambridge education, Attia Hosain wrote, "There
was no division between the two elements in my home; rather a flow of life, acceptance and interdependence. We lived in many centuries, it seemed, moving across
them in moments."[16] Mukhtar Auezov, on the other hand, sees the driving force of
history "moving from feudalism to socialism" as deterministic rather than a mixing
of postmodern milieux. His life reflects a bridge between the folkloric past and the
"bright future."

While their *Weltanschauung* may differ, postcolonial discourse cannot be entirely
ignored in the case of Auezov. In particular, Homi Bhabha's concept of hybridity as a
response to the universalizing tradition offers a useful analytical tool. Addressing the
need to overcome binaries, Bhabha considers the liminal space of cultural production
on the margins. Choosing the space between colony and metropole, with its awkward
juxtapositions, he sees minority writers as the ideal subject of this hybridity. Bhabha
develops this further: "It is [the] double life of British minorities [that] makes them
'vernacular cosmopolitans,' translating between cultures, renegotiating traditions
from a position where 'locality' insists on its own terms, while entering into larger
national and societal conversations." Hybridity describes life lived precariously at the
cultural and political margins of modern society. Ultimately, it is a personal act of cultural survival in which "specific and local histories, often threatened and repressed,
are inserted 'between the lines' of dominant cultural practices." Thus, by transcending
boundaries and conventions, minority writers enter upon the discourse of dominant

(or imperialist) nationalities to forge their own path.[17] In the British case, we observe that scholarly admiration goes far beyond tokenisms to elevate Rushdie and Naipaul to the canon of contemporary literature.

Although the hybridity argument is particularly convincing in these specific examples, we should be cautious when extending the theory to the Soviet Central Asian case. Unlike Rushdie and Naipaul, who evoke a transfigured culture and experience of displacement that resulted from giving up their homelands, Auezov did not leave the steppe for the Moscow metropole. Still, the ideological displacement of Bolshevism, then Socialist Realism, alongside Auezov's own harrowing escape from the purges contributed to a dislocation that left Auezov always searching for his own cultural past.

Throughout his life Mukhtar Auezov published works in both Kazakh and Russian. While he tended to be more normative and descriptive in Russian, he was more analytical and contemplative in Kazakh original works. His ability to maintain his two lives, publishing for Russian and Kazakh audiences in journals in Alma-Ata and Moscow, was further complicated by translations of own work for alternate audiences. In the Bhabhian sense, Auezov was not dislocated by giving up his homeland and language, but he was, nevertheless, forced to engage the dominant cultural discourse of socialism and to locate himself within this system. As a folklorist and protector of the oral tradition, Auezov chose elements of his own cultural metaphors to replace the political loss of national autonomy while at the same time participating in Soviet rhetoric and writing within the system. Drawing upon comparisons with himself, Chinghiz Aitmatov recalled, "[Auezov] said that Soviet society creates a unified culture by incorporating all the best, the most progressive, and original of national cultures in itself while allowing space for their development." Rather than Russification, they advocated a pan-Soviet culture where "ideological, worldview, and political unity of a diverse, polylinguistic socialist culture" would emerge.[18]

## QUESTION OF THE SOVIET INTELLECTUAL

Operating at the intersection of academic and literary worlds, Russian and Kazakh, imperial and Soviet, Mukhtar Auezov expands our perception of the often-static interpretation of the Soviet intellectual. Russian-language authors, ethnically Russian or not, provide a rich tradition of exploring the dualities of writing on the edges of empire: in fact, Russian romanticism was deeply rooted in periphery relationships. In the twentieth century, increasing numbers of ethnic minorities embraced the Russian literary tradition and infused it with new metaphors. In our case, Auezov remained on the Kazakh periphery until the end of his life; yet his journey to the status of national intellectual also allowed Auezov to move freely between center and steppe. At times officials censured and punished Auezov for his writings, but they never could marginalize him.

In the Soviet context, one of the most important elements in the discourse on twentieth-century Soviet Central Asian intellectuals should be to place them into a broader discussion of Soviet intellectuals. For too long the intellectual paradigm of the Soviet intellectual has been dominated by émigrés and dissidents, poets and painters, who were purged by Stalin or escaped to Berlin, Prague, Paris, and New York. Their strong personal links across increasingly isolating but permeable borders maintained a sense of continuity with the intellectual community within Russia during the Soviet era. But Central Asian intellectuals, such as Baymirza Hayit and Mustafa Chokaev, who traveled through Istanbul to Berlin and Paris, were drawn into an ideological and polemical struggle with the Soviet Union that ruptured relations with the intellectual communities of Alma-Ata, Tashkent, and Bishkek (Frunze).

In Marxist terms, the Soviet intelligentsia was an "inter-class stratum" of journalists, engineers, and writers who represented the workers if they were not originally drawn from that group.[19] In Soviet parlance, the intelligentsia was chosen from the Soviet masses to lead as the "productive-technical intelligentsia."[20] The openness of the definitions and the desire to document encouraging statistics brought non-Russians into this new intellectual designation. The promotion of ethnic minorities has been lauded as a method of inclusion, reaching out to non-Russians through a kind of "Affirmative Action Empire."[21] Finding the voices of these policies is useful in perceiving the Soviet intelligentsia on an individual level, transcending empty Soviet rhetoric while problematizing it.[22] Mukhtar Auezov was a classic Soviet intellectual who lived in a tumultuous time: he sought to preserve a cultural legacy that was quickly being destroyed and to create continuities between imperial nostalgia and socialist idealism.

## NOTES

1. Zoia Kedrina, *Mukhtar Auezov: kritiko-bibliograficheskii ocherk* (Moscow, 1951); Mukhtar Auezov, *Mysli raznykh let* (Alma-Ata, 1961); Aikin Nurkatov, *Mukhtar Auezov tvorchestvosy: Maqalalar* (Alma-Ata, 1965); Mukhamedzhan Karataev, *Mukhtar Auezov: Zametki o tvorchestve* (Alma-Ata, 1967) and *Istoriia kazakhskoi sovetskoi literatury* (Alma-Ata, 1967); Evgeniia Lizunova, *Masterstvo Mukhtara Auezova* (Alma-Ata, 1968); Kerimbek Syzdyzkov, *Mukhtar Auezov: Literaturnyi kritik* (Alma-Ata, 1972); Leilia Auezova, ed., *Mukhtar Auezov v vospominaniiakh sovremennikov* (Alma-Ata, 1972); *Bizding Auezov* (Alma-Ata, 1976); Leilia Auezova, *Problemy istorii Kazakhstana v tvorchestve M. O. Auezova* (Alma-Ata, 1977); Mukhtar Auezov, *Zhiyrma tomdyq shygharmalar zhinaghy* (Alma-Ata, 1979–85); Azilkhan Nurshaiykov, *Eki estelik: Mukhtar Auezov pen Sabit Mukanov turaly khikaia, esseler* (Alma-Ata, 1985); Altai Taizhanov, *M. O. Auezov: Myslitel'* (Alma-Ata, 1991) and *Mukhtar Auezov: Oishyl, ghalym, ustaz* (Almaty, 1998). The most recent biography is Nikolai Anastas'ev, *Mukhtar Auezov: Tragediia triumfatora* (Moscow, 2006; Almaty, 2007).

2. Mukhtar Auezov, "Kultura i natsiia," *Abai* 10 (1918): 1–3.

3. Zoia Kedrina, "Torzhestvo kazakhskoi literatury," *Novyi mir* 5 (1949): 279–80, 282.

4. Abai Kunanbaev, *Izbrannoe* (Moscow, 1981): 14. This was argued by Auezov in the 1930s.

5. The 1920s effort was led by Il'ias Kabulov in the pages of *Enbekshi Kazak, Kyzyl Kazakhstan,* and *Sovetskaia step'.* On the 1930s climate, see, for example, Isa Baizakov, "Abai,"

*Qazaq adebiet* 30 (November 29, 1934); Orynbai Taimanov, "Abai," *Adibiet zhane iskusstv* 9 (1934): 94; Narmambet, "Ode to Abai," *Izbrannye stikhi Narmambeta* (Alma-Ata, 1939), 46. Also, Abusagit Zhirenchin, *Abai i ego russkie druz'ia* (Alma-Ata, 1949), 4, notes that this work is the culmination of ten years' research.

6. Mukhtar Auezov, "Zhizn' i tvorchestvo Abaia," *Novyi mir* 7 (1954): 238.

7. The original stories appeared in *Qazaq adebieti* (February 10, 1937), "Tat'janan'ng q'rdaq' ani," *Adebijet majdan'* 4 (1937): 57–69, and "Kak zapela Tat'iana v stepi," *Literaturnyi Kazakstan* 2–3 (1937): 50–60. Mukhtar Auezov, "Avtobiographiia," in *Abai* (Moscow: Sovetskii pisatel', 1955).

8. Kedrina, *Mukhtar Auezov*, 82; quotation from *Literaturnaia gazeta*, December 18, 1948.

9. Togzhanov and Zhansugarov, *Kazakhskii sbornik* (Moscow, 1934): 3–11.

10. Mukhtar Auezov, *Abai: Tarikhi roman* (1953): 13.

11. Mukhtar Auezov, "Narodnost' i realizm Abaia," *Uchennye zapiski KazGU* 19 (1955): 16. Also see *Literaturnaia gazeta* (7 September 1954), *Tandamaly* (1997): 410–13; Mukhtar Auezov, *Abai: Tarikhi roman* (Alma-Ata, 1953): 402.

12. Monika Greenleaf, *Pushkin and Romantic and Fashion: Fragment, Elegy, Orient, Irony* (Stanford, Calif.: Stanford University Press, 1994), 256; see Stephanie Sandler, *Commemorating Pushkin: Russia's Myth of a National Poet* (Stanford, Calif.: Stanford University Press, 2004).

13. See Chinghiz Aitmatov, "*Otvet' sebe*," *Pravda*, August 5, 1967; Abai Kunanbaev, *Slova neizdaniia* (Alma-Ata, 1982): 66–67.

14. Fedin, *M. Auezov v vospominaniiakh sovremennikov* (Almaty, 1997): 7–8.

15. Donald J. Raleigh, ed., *Provincial Landscapes: Local Dimensions of Soviet Power, 1917–1953* (Pittsburgh, Pa.: University of Pittsburgh Press, 2001), 6.

16. Attia Hosain, "Deep Roots, New Language," in *Voices of the Crossing: The Impact of Britain on Writers from Asia, The Caribbean, and Africa*, ed. Ferdinand Dennis and Naseem Khan (London: Serpent's Tail, 2000): 20.

17. Homi Bhabha, "The Vernacular Cosmopolitan," in *Voices of the Crossing*, 139; Bhabha expresses a triumphant optimism that their dual cultural identity is maintained and that ultimately "the margins of the nation displace the centre; the peoples of the periphery return to rewrite the history and fiction of the metropolis" (*Nation and Narration* [London: Routledge, 1990], 6). This success depends on the cultural and linguistic conversion of minorities into the dominant culture.

18. Chinghiz Aitmatov, "Slovo ob Auezove" in *Mukhtar Auezov: Klassik sovetskoi literatury*, ed. B. Tulepbaev (Alma-Ata: Nauka, 1980): 35.

19. Sheila Fitzpatrick, "Stalin and the Making of a New Elite, 1928–1939," *Slavic Review* 3 (1979): 377–402; and Kendall Biales, *Technology and Society under Lenin and Stalin: Origins of the Soviet Technical Intelligentsia, 1917–1941* (Princeton, N.J.: Princeton University Press, 1978).

20. M. Protsko, "Intelligentsiia strany sotsializma," *Bolshevik* 6 (1949): 11.

21. See Terry Martin, *The Affirmative Action Empire: Nations and Nationalism in the Soviet Union, 1923–1939* (Ithaca, N.Y.: Cornell University Press, 2001). For statistics on non-Russian *vydvizhenie* into the intelligentsia, see Liudmilla Ivanova, *Formirovanie sovetskoi nauchnoi intelligentsii, 1917–1927* (Moscow, 1980).

22. Tomohiko Uyama raised some of these questions in his study of the geographical indicators of Kazakh intellectualism. Short biographies reveal in his work the personal associations and tribal backgrounds as a signifier of political beliefs in the early twentieth century. This is particularly interesting for the transitional Central Asian elite, whose mature lives straddled the Russian imperial and Soviet experiences. Tomohiko Uyama, "The Geography of Civilizations: A Spatial Analysis of the Kazakh Intelligentsia's Activities, from the Mid-Nineteenth Century to the Early Twentieth Century," in *Regions: A Prism to View the Slavic-Eurasian World; Towards a Discipline of "Regionology*," ed. Kimitaka Matsuzato (Sapporo: Slavic Research Center, Hokkaido University, 2000), 70–99.

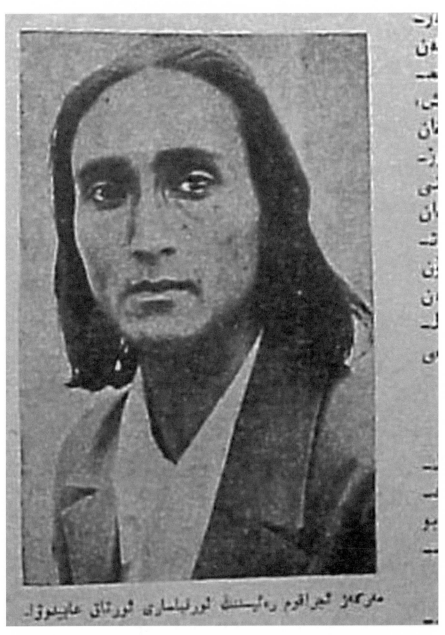

Central Executive Committee Vice Chairperson comrade Obidova. *Yer Yuzi*, 1929.

# 28

# Jahon Obidova

## (1900–1967)

MARIANNE KAMP

Looking back along the path I've trod, one cannot help but recall the Russian wom-en—Communist activists—Artiukhina, Kollontai, Liubimova . . . They were the ones who, in those hard years, explained to us, Uzbek women, the party's policies, and helped us understand the laws of the new life. They helped us with everything . . . we were taught to work among Uzbek women, to bring them out of seclusion on the road to freedom, equality, and light. Those remarkable daughters of the Russian na-tion, humble, attentive, with wide open souls, came to Turkestan in the struggle for liberation of the women of the East. . . . And one recalls the first Uzbek women activ-ists—Burnasheva, Shodieva, Narbayeva . . . and many, many others. Different in age and character, they were united by one idea—the idea of the party, which called for the liberation of the woman of the Soviet East. It was they who, in the first years, and continually, fought for strengthening and consolidating Soviet power in Uzbekistan.[1]

These words were written by Jahon Obidova, a Communist Party activist from Uzbekistan, in 1960. They reflect a Soviet ideology of the brotherhood (or sisterhood) of nationalities, and they highlight the importance of Soviet efforts to create equality for Central Asian women in the 1920s.

Obidova's early life gave no hint that she would work with others in the Communist Party's Women's Division to change women's lives. Born in a Central Asian village, Obidova at first entered a trajectory similar to that of most Central Asian women who lived under Russian imperial rule. Russia's conquest of Central Asia between the years 1865 and 1891 expanded the Empire into a very large terri-tory that shared neither a political history nor a common culture with Russia. After Russia conquered the Emirate of Bukhara, the Khanate of Kokand, and the Khanate of Khiva, Russian adventurers became colonial administrators, deciding how to gov-ern lands whose population consisted almost entirely of Muslims, whose native lan-guages were either Turkic or Tajik, and whose livelihood was based on nomadic ani-mal husbandry, farming irrigated lands, or trade. Although administrators in Central

Asia argued that controlling the territory was worthwhile because it would produce a profit for Russia, in fact, running distant colonies was expensive, and the government in St. Petersburg pressured its forces in Central Asia to keep its interventions limited. By creating the Turkestan territory in Central Asia, Russia extended a practice that it had established in the Kazakh steppe—organizing land under a military governor-general, making its government distinctive from, and less comprehensive than, the forms followed in most Russian provinces. The Russian administration established Russian-style schools for Turkestani boys, in part to train bilingual local administrators. These schools challenged traditional Muslim understandings of education and its purposes, and Turkestanis who sought change and progress began establishing their own modernist, or Jadid, schools—again, mostly for boys.[2]

Turkestan territory, where Jahon Obidova was born in 1900, was valuable as the primary producer of raw cotton for textile factories in central Russia. Russian rule increased trade in Central Asia's cities, bringing new sources of wealth to Central Asian merchants and landowners, and a flood of Russian settlers to the southern Kazakh steppe and to some districts around Tashkent. Russian administration rebuilt the larger cities, tying them to the empire's network of railroads, and opening factories, but in Obidova's hometown of Nanay, Russian rule was distant.[3] Nanay, a mountain village northeast of Tashkent, in the present-day district of Bustonliq, Tashkent Province, Uzbekistan, was home to a Tajik-speaking population, and Uzbek speakers lived in villages across the Pskem River; Obidova grew up knowing both languages. Russia encouraged Russian migration to the nearby city of Chirchik, between Bustonliq and Tashkent, but not to the area around Nanay. The Russian administration's attention focused on irrigated lands appropriate for cotton growing, but the highlands around Nanay sustained only grain, fruits, and vegetables. Villages like Nanay felt few of the Russian Empire's economic and political effects. However, Russian rule established peace in a region that had been a zone of contest. Residents of Nanay still refer to their town as Kala (fortress), because of the village's long dependence on its walls for defense against invaders, a need obviated by Russian dominance.[4]

Jahon Obidova described her life thus: she was the oldest among a poor peasant's many children. Obidova's age at marriage, thirteen, was not unusual among Tajik families, but due to her parents' poverty, they arranged her marriage into poor circumstances. Her husband was "Inagamjan Irmatov, a rich man who already had three wives," who lived in a distant village in Tashkent province. Obidova's father arranged Jahon's marriage to this sixty-five-year-old man in exchange for debt relief. Jahon wrote that in her husband's household, "I was not only his slave, without contradiction, silent, obedient, but I was also the slave of his wives, his children, who repaid all my service daily with kicks, curses, and abuse, because I was still a child who could not stand up for herself, and besides, I was from a poor family."[5]

Obidova explained her transformation from abused fourth wife to politically active Communist in this way: in 1915, she ran away to the city of Tashkent, where she found work as a household servant, and where she also became aware of dramatic political events. In 1916, Turkestan's native population rose up in violent demonstra-

tions against colonial administration, because of a suddenly imposed military conscription order to raise forces for the Russian army in World War I. In 1917, there was
talk of revolution, and in October, the Bolsheviks took control in Tashkent. Obidova
described running away from her husband: "when [Obidova] was about seventeen,
she fell seriously ill because of her prematurely begun sexual life . . . she ran away from
her 'master' to Tashkent. There she was picked up by a Russian passer-by . . . taken to
a hospital, and so at last received medical treatment." A Tatar nurse found Obidova
employment with a family in the old-city. Within four years, she "learnt to read and
write and divorced her husband, who had discovered her whereabouts and was constantly threatening to murder her."[6]

Zahida Burnasheva, an Uzbek woman teacher from Tashkent who herself had
gained education in a Jadid (Muslim modernist) school during the late Imperial period, opened a school and recruited young Uzbek women to fill the first class. Obidova
entered the first class, but before long, she transferred to a different, newly opened
educational institution, the "worker's school," or "rabfak." Rabfak schools, which were
first founded in Russia and then spread to other parts of the Soviet Union, sought
to educate, and politicize, the urban working classes. This move suggests some of
the ways that Obidova's own marginal status shaped her opportunities. Burnasheva's
teachers' school for Uzbek women became a very important institution in Soviet
Tashkent, attracting the daughters of the urban intelligentsia, and contributing to the
creation of the new Uzbek elite.[7] Obidova, from a poor, rural Tajik village, a runaway
who had worked as a servant, instead built her career from the springboard of the
workers' institute, where party membership was strongly encouraged.

The Bolsheviks declared their government in Tashkent in December 1917, but in
reality, they faced difficulty establishing authority over Turkestan. Many Bolsheviks,
new joiners to the party after its seizure of power, were Russian settlers who wanted
to maintain colonial dominance in Turkestan. Uzbeks and other native ethnic groups
divided their political support among various parties, many of them turning against
Soviet/colonial power. A brief attempt to challenge Tashkent Bolshevik dominance
failed when the Tashkent Soviet sent military forces to conquer the rival Turkestan
autonomous government in Kokand in early 1918. Opposition to Bolshevik rule
continued through the 1920s as the Soviet government established a new order in
Central Asia through force and consent, fighting its opponents and rewarding its
supporters.

Obidova was one of the supporters of the new Soviet state. At the Rabfak, she
joined the Komsomol (Communist Youth League), participated in grain requisition
campaigns that went to the countryside to force farmers to turn wheat over to the
state, and she worked with the Cheka, or secret police, to track down enemies of the
Bolsheviks. What made Obidova join the Soviet side in this struggle? She depicted
herself as one of the party's natural supporters, because of her poor peasant origins
and her association with the working class. The Bolsheviks sought supporters among
marginalized, powerless people in Central Asia—including women whose family
situations were unstable—by offering them a living, a new locus of loyalty, and a way

to share in the party's power. Obidova was such a woman, but perhaps she became an ardent supporter of the party because it also offered her a chance for adventure.

In Central Asia, the Bolsheviks fought against various groups whom they labeled collectively as *basmachi* (bandits). Obidova worked with the Cheka to entrap opponents, occasions that offered her risk and challenge. In one case, she boarded a train in order to spy on a group of wealthy Central Asian men who were traveling, ostensibly for trade, but—as Obidova learned through her conversations with them— actually smuggling weapons for the basmachi. On another occasion, Obidova went to a men's prison in disguise: she cross-dressed. As she emphasized in her memoir, "My voice at that time was low, like a bass, so the imitation was complete." She pretended to be the son of a wealthy man from a well-known family. In prison, she sat in a cell with a wealthy Central Asian man for days in order to elicit his story, which she then reported to the Cheka, enabling them to accuse him of specific crimes against the state.[8]

The Communist Youth League assigned Obidova to work with women. She became director of the women's section of the Tashkent district Koshchi, or union of poor and landless peasants. From this position, she worked her way up through the Communist Party ranks. She headed the party's women's division (*zhenotdel*) in Samarkand old city.[9] The party had great difficulty recruiting women members from the indigenous nationalities in Central Asia, but Obidova, an indigenous woman who was unfettered by family ties, eagerly took on party work.

In 1922, the Bolsheviks declared that the entity they governed would henceforth be known as the Union of Soviet Socialist Republics, and in 1924, the Soviet government created new divisions in Central Asia, designating territories there as the Uzbek Soviet Socialist Republic, the Turkmen Soviet Socialist Republic, and the Tajik, Kazakh, and Kyrgyz Autonomous Soviet Republics. Samarkand became the capital of the new Uzbekistan, and Obidova, already working there in the women's division, was well placed for advancement. She gained membership in the Communist Party of Uzbekistan in 1927, and she served on the Samarkand commission for land reform. She went to remote villages to make decisions about how much land the rich would lose, and which poor farmers would benefit from redistribution. Obidova's own utility to the party was based in part on the fact that she was a woman, and in part on her multilingualism: she spoke Tajik and Uzbek and had also become a Russian speaker. She was committed to the Party's goals, and she could speak to any audience in Uzbekistan, male or female, in their own language. She recalled going to Urgut region on a land reform commission: there a large landowner who was also a Muslim religious leader made a speech declaring that Islam encourages all Muslims to live together in harmony, and therefore he agreed with the idea of land reform. Obidova responded, speaking to the crowd in the market: "You said that according to shariʻa, exploitation is forbidden, and all Muslims should live in conditions of equality. So, then, why do you yourself own about 70 percent of all the land in the district, and hundreds of oxen, sheep, cows, and horses, while the peasants don't own even a plot of land?"[10]

Obidova stood resolutely on the side of the Communist Party, and she earned enmity from a wide array of society in Uzbekistan. The Soviet government embarked on a massive, and violent, transformation in Uzbekistan in the late 1920s. Land reform (1925) led to collectivization of agriculture (1930), and the accompanying dekulakization campaign arrested leaders in rural communities. An anti-religious campaign (1927) closed mosques, Islamic schools, and Islamic courts; and arrested mullahs. The "Attack" (or *Hujum*) campaign (1927–29) tried to improve women's status rapidly by convincing or forcing women to unveil and penalizing violations of women's rights: "The brave fighter Jahon Obidova frightened the rich and the mullahs, and was not afraid of their insults but continued her struggle. Her vow before women, that they would unveil, and they would enter work in factories, work on kolkhozes, and in soviet organizations, became more and more a reality."[11] Although Obidova believed in these efforts, they produced mixed results. People from Obidova's hometown still recall that women's division activists told the women of Nanay to march to the nearby town of Bogustan to unveil publicly. They say that there were some women who, "unable to come to peace with this fate, threw themselves over the cliffs instead."[12] Nonetheless, by 1928, Obidova's activism and outspokenness made her one of Uzbekistan's delegates to Moscow, for the Communist Party's All-Union Conference of the Women's Division.

In 1929, Uzbekistan's political leaders decided that they needed to advance indigenous women to leadership positions, in order to give force to decisions about women's rights. Jahon Obidova was elected vice president of Uzbekistan's Central Executive Committee, the group that set the agenda for the party and the government. This gave Obidova a very prominent platform: the leading party newspaper, *Qizil O'zbekiston*, published her frequent speeches on collectivization, agriculture, women, and the Communist Youth League. In 1930, she became one of the state prosecution's voices in a prominent trial of Uzbeks who were members of the judiciary and who were accused of distorting government policies by protecting criminals, including those who had murdered unveiled women.[13]

Obidova became mayor—director of the Tashkent City Soviet Executive Committee in official Soviet terminology—of Tashkent (1934–38), and in this context, foreigners met her. She made a strong impression on Fannina Halle, a German socialist who was interested in the Soviet Union's efforts to change women's lives. Halle wrote that Obidova possessed "Such burning, flashing eyes, reflecting not only all the hardship and despair of past centuries, and the succeeding revolt, rebellion, struggle, and readiness to die of an Eastern woman." Halle watched Obidova in action as mayor: "[S]he was conferring with three male 'responsible,' but nevertheless rather slow-witted, Uzbek officials. . . . [S]he smoked one cigarette after another. I saw how she brought them all to book, and at the same time not only talked down two telephones standing beside her, but also kept her secretary busy."[14] African American poet Langston Hughes, who traveled in Central Asia in the early 1930s, described Obidova as "short and dark. Her olive complexion is not unlike that of an American mulatto. Her face is plain and strong, her hair bobbed and very black. She is slight and dynamic. . . . But Jahan Abinova [*sic*] must have been made for freedom. She was made, too, with an ardent desire for inspiring freedom in others. It became her mission to spread the new life among the veiled women of Uzbekistan, to arouse the timid ones to come out of their harems, cast off their veils, and take advantage of new Soviet laws."[15] Soviet accounts, foreigners observations, and Jahon Obidova's own words express the wonder that someone born into her circumstances was able to rise to such prominence; and all credited this both to Obidova's own abilities, and to the Communist Party's policy of drawing women into activism.

As mayor and in her continuing position on the Central Executive Committee, Obidova worked with economic planners to bring factories to Tashkent, to increase Uzbekistan's cotton production, and to bring in funds for new hydroelectric dams. In 1938, she was summoned to Moscow—at a time when such a summons for a high-ranking party member often meant an accusation of wrongdoing, a trial, and sentencing. But Obidova did not become a victim of the Great Terror; instead, she stepped down from her political roles to take a position as the deputy director of Uzbekistan's trade commission. From 1938 until her retirement in 1958, Obidova was involved in Uzbekistan's industrialization. During World War II, she was named director of the trust that owned food preservation factories in Uzbekistan, involving her directly in the USSR's war supply effort. She continued working in this sphere, and ended up the director of Tashkent's tobacco factory. During her years of managing factories, Obidova took pride in hiring and promoting women.[16]

Obidova had begun her political career working in the Communist Party's Women's Division. The party disbanded the women's division in 1930, ostensibly because all issues of women's inequality were resolved. Many of the women's division leaders, across the Soviet Union as well as in Uzbekistan, moved to other spheres of activity, and they no longer gave a clear voice to women's interests. Some of Uzbekistan's Communist women activists were arrested during the Great Terror and spent years in prison and exile.[17] Obidova, who moved from politics to management in 1938, continued to draw attention to women's issues throughout her career. In 1958, two years after Khrushchev's denunciation of Stalin and the beginning of the post-Stalin Thaw, Uzbekistan's Communist Party held a women's conference. At that conference, activists from Russia who had worked for the women's division in Central Asia during the days of the unveiling campaign renewed acquaintances with activists from Uzbekistan whom they had not seen for decades, and they published their remembrances of the 1920s in a collection called *Probuzhdennye Velikim Oktiabrem* [Awakened by Great October]. Obidova's words at the beginning of this chapter come from that collection, and reflect the pride and solidarity of the former Women's Division activists. When Obidova died in 1966, her laudatory obituary was signed by those activists, as well as by Uzbekistan's Communist Party leaders.

Jahon Obidova, a Tajik woman, became an exemplary Soviet Communist. The Communist Party created the conditions for her to emerge as an activist and a leader. In the process, she broke every one of her own society's gender conventions. She left her husband, became educated, went to work, unveiled, took leadership positions, used the those positions to attack and arrest enemies, and played a key role in the party's programs to undermine all traditional forms of authority. On some occasions she cross-dressed. Unlike almost all other women in Uzbekistan, including Communist women who entered similar public careers, she never remarried and never had children. Some of those who recalled Obidova's later years described her as "masculine," a word that captured their ambivalence about her.[18] She had accomplished much in modernizing and developing Uzbekistan, and she brought fame to Nanay. The village was even renamed Jahonobod in the 1970s, although it later reverted to its original name. Although she was a source of pride, Obidova was far from their concept of a normal woman; she transgressed gender boundaries. Moreover, she had been at the forefront of political actions that brought change, turmoil, and anguish to many.

Jahon Obidova probably never thought of herself as a subject of empire. When she was a young Communist activist, the party declared that the Soviet Union was a new sort of state, one in which the formerly colonized peoples were equal to their former Russian masters, and where Great Russian chauvinism would disappear.[19] Obidova placed party loyalty above all other loyalties: in the 1930 Kasimovshchina trial, she attacked Uzbek judges as nationalists who distorted the law to favor their fellow Uzbeks. The new political order, with its national republics and affirmative action policies, created all of Obidova's opportunities. In Imperial Russian Central Asia, an urban girl from an Uzbek Jadid or merchant family might have been able to avail herself of education and experience the limited reforms of Russian rule. But such opportunities were unthinkable for a rural girl like Jahon Obidova; she became reality because the Communist Party of the Soviet Union engineered a social revolution in Central Asia.

## Notes

My thanks are due to Shakhnoza Madaeva, Doctor of Philosophy, Uzbekistan Academy of Sciences, who contributed extensively to the research for this chapter, and to Ulfat Abdurasulov, Ph.D., History Institute, Uzbekistan Academy of Sciences, who provided lengthy notes about Nanay.

1. D. Abidova, "Davno minuvshee," in *Probuzhdennye Velikim Oktiabrem: Sbornik ocherkov i vospominanii* [Awakened by Great October: a collection of notes and remembrances], ed. I. I. Finkel'shtein and Kh. S. Shukurova (Tashkent: Gos. Izdat. UzSSR, 1961), 109–25, quotation on 124–25.

2. On Russian rule in Central Asia, see Daniel Brower, *Turkestan and the Fate of the Russian Empire* (London: Routledge Curzon, 2003); Adeeb Khalid, *The Politics of Muslim Cultural Reform: Jadidism in Central Asia* (Berkeley: University of California Press, 1998).

3. On Russia's role in Central Asian cities, see Jeff Sahadeo, *Russian Colonial Society in Tashkent, 1865–1923* (Bloomington: Indiana University Press, 2007); Alexander Morrison, *Russian Rule in Samarkand: A Comparison with British India* (Oxford: Oxford Historical Monographs, 2008).

4. A description of Nanay and its economy, location, and population come from personal correspondence with Ulfat Abdurasulov, an Uzbek historian with family ties to the village.

5. Abidova, "Davno minuvshie," 109–10. Fannina Halle, *Women in the Soviet East,* trans. Margaret Green (New York: E. P. Dutton, 1938), 300.

6. Obidova's autobiographies do not discuss sexuality so directly. This account comes from a 1934 conversation that Obidova had with Fannina Halle, a German socialist who was visiting Uzbekistan. Halle, *Women in the Soviet East,* 300–301.

7. Marianne Kamp, *The New Woman in Uzbekistan: Islam, Modernity and Unveiling under Communism* (Seattle: University of Washington Press, 2006), ch. 4.

8. Abidova, "Davno minuvshie," 111–12.

9. F. Z. Zvedeniuk, "Dzhakhon Abidova," in *Khudzhum znachit' nastuplenie,* ed. Kh. T. Tursunov et al. (Tashkent: Izdatel'stvo Uzbekistan, 1987), 163.

10. Abidova, "Davno minuvshie," 114–15.

11. Qodir Fozilxo'jaev and Filiura Zvedeniuk, *Jahon Obidova* (Tashkent: Yo'sh Gvardiia nashriyoti, 1977), 18.

12. Notes from Ulfat Abdurasulov, recounting stories passed down from his grandmother.

13. The trial was called the Kasimovshchina. Obidova referred to, and took pride in, her own role as a member of the prosecution, but contemporary public accounts of the trial do not present her as playing a major role in it. Obidova's accounts appear in Abidova, "Davno minuvshie," 118–19; Fozilxo'jaev, *Jahon Obidova,* 25–26. *Qizil O'zbekistan* coverage from April to August 1930 does not mention Obidova prominently. On the murders of unveiled women, see Kamp, *The New Woman,* ch. 8.

14. Halle, *Women in the Soviet East,* 299, 302.

15. Langston Hughes, originally published as "Farewell to Mahomet: The New Women of Soviet Asia, Tragedies of the Harem, Young Uzbeks at Work," *Travel* (February 1935): 28–31, 47; edited by David Chioni-Moore for a revised and expanded edition of Hughes, *A Negro Looks at Soviet Central Asia* (forthcoming).

16. Fozilxo'jaev, *Jahon Obidova,* 38–45.

17. Among Obidova's Uzbek colleagues in women's division work, Tojixon Shodieva and Sobira Xoldarova spent years in Siberian prison camps. Kamp, *The New Woman in Uzbekistan,* 101, 106; on disbanding the women's division, 217.

18. This description comes from a summer 2009 interview with F. Y., a ninety-year old Nanay man, collected indirectly by Shakhnoza Madaeva, an Uzbek researcher, and from Ulfat Abdurasulov's summer 2009 conversation with his father, who met Obidova and recalled her as a "women of masculine appearance, with a short haircut, smoking 'Kazbek' cigarettes."

19. For an explanation of these policies, see Terry Martin, *The Affirmative Action Empire: Nations and Nationalisms in the Soviet Union, 1923–1939* (Ithaca, N.Y.: Cornell University Press, 2000).

Olzhas Suleimenov. Photo IA Fergana.ru.

# 29

## Olzhas Suleimenov

### (1936–)

MARLÈNE LARUELLE

Olzhas Suleimenov has been a key representative of Kazakh culture since the 1960s. A Russian language writer and poet impassioned by history, he expressed during Soviet times a Kazakh national feeling within the framework then set by "peoples' friendship," which implied the superiority of the Russian "big brother." Since Kazakhstan's independence in 1991, his adopted aim has been to rehabilitate the Turkic cultures of the steppes by proving their ancient status and their major role in world history. His life, but his thought even more so, on the history and identity of the Eurasian steppes, reflect the multiple intersections of faiths, geographies, and ways of life that have characterized Russia and its empire for several centuries.

Suleimenov's commitment in literature is revealing of the inspiration that has followed him throughout his life: to give meaning to humanity in its totality. A geologist by training, in April 1961, Suleimenov proposed to the editor in chief of *Kazakhstanskaia pravda* a poem written for the glory of Yuri Gagarin, who had only just undertaken the first inhabited space flight in the history of humanity. The poem enjoyed such success that it rapidly propelled Suleimenov to the status of representative of Kazakh literature. He was employed by *Kazakhstanskaia pravda* the following year, and was sent to the famous Moscow Institute for Literature, where he associated with the great Soviet writers of the time, such as Mikhail Sholokhov, Vsevolod Ivanov, Ilia Ehrenburg, and Yevgeny Evtushenko. The atmosphere of the *shestidesiatniki,* the 1960s liberals who, in the wake of de-Stalinization, challenged the Soviet ideological stranglehold on arts and letters, had a decisive influence on his intellectual and political development. He then accumulated prestigious prizes and honors, including the Komsomol Prize for Kazakhstan, State Prize of the Kazakh Soviet Republic, and National Poet of Kazakhstan.

But Suleimenov is not simply a writer; he has always been a major figure of public life in Kazakhstan. As a member of the Communist Party, he joined his republic's central committee in the 1970s and was named president of the Union of Writers of Kazakhstan in 1983. In 1989, he was elected deputy of the Supreme Soviet of the

USSR and started a political career as leader of the Nevada-Semipalatinsk ecological movement, which was instrumental in bringing about the closure of the nuclear polygon in Kazakhstan. After 1991, he took up the leadership of the party that he founded, the People's Congress of Kazakhstan, and was appointed parliamentary speaker, a position he held until 1994. He thus did not show any reluctance to engage in several political struggles against President Nursultan Nazarbaev over national identity and the political and economic decisions being taken in the new state. As one of Nazarbaev's potential rivals, he was discreetly removed from the political elite in 1995 by being appointed ambassador to Rome and permanent representative to UNESCO in Paris. Although he quickly became politically marginalized, Suleimenov has continued to seek shelter in a cultural role, enabling him to remain a popular figure without having to stand up against Nazarbaev's authoritarianism. Indeed, he continues to elaborate new ideological guidelines for contemporary Kazakh national narrative. In 2004, the Atamura publishing house published an eight-volume set of his complete works.

Suleimenov is part of an old intellectual tradition that has promoted, since the nineteenth century, the cultural syncretism of Kazakh society, its being at the crossroads of the great world civilizations since antiquity. From this heritage Suleimenov draws much inspiration, a heritage which includes, among others, Chokan Valikhanov (1835–65), a former student of the Omsk Cadet Corps who entered into the service of the empire and participated in several ethnographic expeditions in Central Asia; Abai Kunanbaev (1845–1904), the son of one of the leaders of the Middle Horde, a great translator of Western works into Russian, and the author of *The Book of Words*, a lyrical reflection that expressed his belief in the possibility of building closer ties with Russian culture in a way that would not undermine Kazakh identity; and Ibrahim Altynsarin (1841–89), one of the major figures of Kazakh pedagogy and founder of the first system of modern Russo-Kazakh schools. Suleimenov also owes much to Mukhtar Auezov (1897–1961), whose renowned *Path of Abai,* devoted to Abai Kunanbaev, is considered to be a major text of Soviet Kazakh literature. Lastly, Suleimenov can be seen in parallel to Chinghiz Aitmatov (1928–2008), a celebrated Kyrgyz who also sought to write the history of his nation within the larger one of Eurasian peoples.

The book *Az i Ia,* published in 1975 in a print run of sixty thousand copies, unleashed a heated debate in the Soviet Union. It may be considered Suleimenov's manifesto, to which he was to remain faithful throughout his life. This book brought about a profound change in his career and forced him into a semi-dissident position until perestroika. The book received immediate and vehement criticism from Russian nationalist journal *Molodaia Gvardiia.* The author of the article, Apollon Kuz'min, who had also spoken out against Lev Gumilev, accused the author of hostility toward Russians, of Turkic nationalism, and of pro-Zionism. After another attack in a different nationalist journal, *Russkaia literatura,* the debate reached the culture subdepartment of the Communist Party Central Committee's ideology department. In February 1976, it forced Suleimenov to explain himself to the Academy of Sciences, which condemned his writings for national chauvinism and for glorifying feudal nomadic culture. The director of the publishing house was fired, and Suleimenov's publications, as well as all books quoting him, were withdrawn from bookstores and libraries. He received an instruction to write a self-critical letter, which was published in *Kazakhstanskaia pravda* on March 19, 1977, in which he acknowledged his errors and historical inaccuracies but refused to repudiate his conclusions. Suleimenov was restricted to publishing poetry for many years. Only the intervention of the first secretary of the Communist Party of Kazakhstan, Dinmukhamed Kunaev, who took up the matter with Leonid Brezhnev, saved him from more serious problems.

In this polemical book, Suleimenov attempted to rehabilitate Turkic nationalism: *Az i Ia* is a refutation of the official view of the Turkic peoples' place in history. One of its aims was to denounce Soviet orientalism, and, more generally, Russian historiography, much of which, Suleimenov argued, is based on a denial of the antiquity of Turkic peoples.[1] In the 1970s, both supporters and opponents perceived the book as a work of historiography, even if its scientific worth was questioned by Suleimenov's adversaries. Yet the Kazakh writer was clearly influenced by the linguist Nikolai Marr (1864–1934) and by the poet Velimir Khlebnikov (1885–1922). An aesthetic reading of this prima facie historical work thus seems warranted. Literary historian Harsha Ram has even proposed an interpretation of the book as a work of literature, suggesting that the confusion of genres—poetry, history, and linguistics—was intentional: Suleimenov, Ram argues, needed the metaphor of *Az i Ia* in order to elaborate a new science of language.[2]

Suleimenov argued that Russia became part of the steppe in a cultural sense, and that in order to survive it had no historical choice but to become more Turkic. The first part of the book is devoted to the famous *Tale of Igor*, a medieval Russian text supposed to have been written in the twelfth century. It recounts the defeat of Prince Igor of Novgorod at the hands of the Polovtsians, and contains numerous appeals for political unity addressed to the Russian principalities of the time. The original manuscript, discovered at the end of the eighteenth century, perished in the Burning of Moscow in 1812, and hence could not be dated using modern techniques. Although its authenticity was corroborated by Soviet historiography, it remains highly contested; in fact, the document is probably a forgery, perhaps written in the fourteenth century.[3] Because of its appeals for Russian unity, *Tale of Igor* remains central to Russian nationalist narrative. This is why Suleimenov mounted a frontal attack on this monument of literature to support his case against Russia and his acculturation thesis. Although he does believe in the manuscript's historical authenticity, he proposes an iconoclastic interpretation that stands in stark contrast with the Russian reading.

Suleimenov argues that the text's numerous stylistic and lexical borrowings from Turkic languages show that the political and economic elites of the time were bilingual and that there was an ethnic and cultural symbiosis between the Slavs and the Turkic peoples. He considers this as proof of an early fusion between Kyivan Rus' and the steppe; the Turks, he argues, built the political and military structure of the first Russian state. According to him, the famous Polovtsian incursions into Kyivan territory, decried in medieval Slavic chronicles for being calamities sent from Heaven, were merely a response to a demand from the Russian princes, who were fighting amongst themselves. The only defense Russia, and hence Europe, had against the Mongol invasion and the onslaught of Islam, he argues, was the peoples of the steppe. He thus seeks to dissociate two worlds that are too often assimilated in the minds of Russians: the Turkic peoples of the steppes, who have been Russian allies for centuries, and the more distant Mongols—the only ones, he claims, that had relations of conflict with Russia.

This analysis places Suleimenov in the so-called Eurasianist line of thought: in the 1920s, certain great figures of the Russian emigration such as Prince Nikolai Trubetzkoy (1890–1938), Piotr Savitsky (1895–1968), Piotr Suvchinsky (1882–1985) and Georges Vernadsky (1887–1973) had tried to demonstrate that Russia belonged more to the world of the steppe than to European culture. They sought to minimize the conflicts between the Kyivan Rus' and the peoples of the steppes, by pointing up their still unconscious cultural symbiosis, which heralded future Eurasian unity.[4] Indeed, the title of Suleimenov's book may be read as the Russian term for Asia (*Aziia*). It also stands for the first letter of the Old Slavonic alphabet and the last letter of the modern Russian alphabet, which, in addition, means "I" in each language, respectively. This pun introduces the book's two chapters, the first being devoted to the Russian/Slavic world, and the second to criticizing Indo-European linguistics. Thus, for Harsha Ram, what the book's title signifies is at once "the Slavs and the Turks" and "me and I," and is hence a subtle synonym for "Eurasia."

Since the implosion of the Soviet Union, Suleimenov has not concealed his Eurasianist convictions: he states that although the communist regime was destined to disappear, the unity it brought between Eurasian peoples can only temporarily be destroyed. The future, he asserts, belongs to a Eurasian Union, and this has led him to support all the various logics of post-Soviet integration, in particular that pertaining to the Russia-Belorussia Union that was signed in 1996, and to the Eurasian Economic Community initiated by Vladimir Putin and Nursultan Nazarbaev in 2000. From this point of view, Suleimenov is not in disagreement with the policies implemented by the Kazakh president; on the contrary, he lends them his support by inviting Russia, Belorussia, and Kazakhstan to serve as the motors of a new Eurasian integration. As he stated in 2005, "We are destined to live together, by each other's sides; there is no force that can move one of the countries to another continent. We are all Eurasian, our continents cannot be separated. Historically, geographically, and in all other respects, we ought to be together. Our economies and our cultures form a united space."[5]

The second part of *Az i Ia* is a more poetic reflection on the Turkic peoples' place in the world and their universality. Once again, it is through linguistics, and more precisely etymology, that Suleimenov seeks to rehabilitate Turkology by endowing the Turkic peoples with a prestigious ancestry. He is violently critical of Soviet linguistics—inspired by Western linguistics of the nineteenth century and, thus, of its Eurocentrism—which privileges Indo-European languages and consigns the equally as prestigious saga of Turkic languages to the dustbin of history. The rivalry between these two linguistic families seems to him revealing of the historical inequality of relations with the peoples of Europe, who appropriated for themselves the history of the world by dispossessing other peoples of it. In order to show that the Turkic populations have a lineage that is just as ancient and as prestigious as the Europeans, a category in which he includes the Russians, Suleimenov has sought to base himself on research that is mainly phonetic and philological. He has thus contributed to the rehabilitation of linguistic theories dating back to the early nineteenth century, drawing on a current of romanticism that attempts to appropriate the prestige of the ancient languages through the study of sonorities.

From this linguistic study, Suleimenov draws the conclusion that the Turks are the worthy heirs of the ancient Eastern civilizations, especially of the magnificent culture of Sumer. He claims that Sumerians spoke a Turkic language and that their writings are close to the Runic alphabet discovered in Siberia. The importance of the allusion to Sumer can be explained by the need to have some reference to a prestigious state—by the search for what is called "statehood" (*gosudarstvennost'*). This requires resurrecting state and cultural affiliations in order to assert the unique antiquity of the present-day Kazakh state. Suleimanov also emphasizes the cultural proximity of Turkic peoples to the Scythians, who were some of the first "state builders" on Eurasian territory. He thereby forms part of an old tradition, in which, since the Western, and especially Hungarian, orientalism of the end of the nineteenth century, Turkic peoples—including Huns, Kipchaks, Seljukids, and Ottomans—have always insistently been presented as "state builders."

Since Kazakhstan's independence, Suleimenov has pursued the Sumerian and "statist" line of argument that he first elaborated in the 1970s. In three books, *The Language of Writing* (1998), *The Turks in Prehistory* (2002), and *Intersecting Parallel Lines* (2002), he advances new etymological arguments in support of the claim that Sumerian and Etruscan are Turkic languages. What he thereby hopes to demonstrate is that Kazakhstan is not a recent state born of a Russo-Soviet construction, but rather the last stage in a long Turkic history in which the state has always constituted the matrix of national identity. Suleimanov is not the only one to take an interest in the affiliation with Sumerian: it is still to be found today in Turkish nationalism, but also among the great names of what in post-Soviet space is called "alternative history" (that is, alternative to Western and Russo-Soviet historiography), such as Murad Adzhi. Aimed at the general public, this "alternative history" reconstructs dubious historical, linguistic, and ethnic filiations that affirm that the people in question (such as the Russians in Russia, the Kazakhs in Kazakhstan) are at the origin of all the great cultures on the old continent.

Among the supporters of Tengrism, a religious trend that rehabilitates the ancient cult of the god Tengri and presents Islam as a faith foreign to local populations, one finds a similar Kazakho-Sumerian genealogy. In this vein, the Kazakh philosopher Nigmet Ayupov, for example, argues that Tengrism was the ancient religion of Sumer.[6] And according to Dastan Sarygulov, who is Tengrism's main exponent in Kyrgyzstan, the kings of Sumer were called *Tengir*. Moreover, he says, if all the great ethical teachings were born in the Orient, it is because Tengrism was dominant there until the eighth–sixth millennia BC.[7] Suleimenov shares with these theorists the vision of an ancient Kazakh religion that existed before Islam. In *Az i Ia*, he became one of the first Soviet scholars to reintroduce the term Tengrism (*tengrianstvo*) into Russian, presenting it as "the most ancient religion in the world, elaborated as a philosophical teaching four thousands years ago."[8]

However, notwithstanding his fervent Kazakh nationalism, Suleimenov does not share any fascination with the notion that the Turks had an original Altaic cradle, nor for their links with the Mongols. Imbued as he is with classical culture, his historical writings are focused on the Mediterranean; for him, Turkic grandeur can only be confirmed by Mesopotamian civilizations, whose legacy is also important for the West. Indeed, his ultimate aim is to put an end to the battle of memory that Europe has won till the present day by altogether changing the perspective on world history. Accordingly, on 2008, he opened a large conference organized at UNESCO called "Large-scale Migration of Peoples in Prehistory and Protohistory," and enthused about the possible areas of study the monogenetic theory has opened up in fields such as linguistics: he is, in fact, persuaded that there exists some "truly remarkable coincidences about discoveries in the languages and cultures of Africa, Eurasia, Australia, and the Americas"[9] that confirm the existence of a primitive speech and writing of humanity. And precisely this, he thinks, will aid our clarification of some of the neglected aspects of the history of global migrations, aspects that will highlight the role played by the Eurasian steppes in the passage of peoples from the Middle East toward Asia.

This will to grasp the history of humanity in its totality—spatial as much as temporal—is registered in Suleimenov's fundamentally humanist convictions, but also in his essentialist understanding of nations. For him, peoples are living persons, hence the importance he grants to biological metaphors. Every civilization has a transcendent idea of its own and is the bearer of a portion of divine truth; should such a unique character disappear, all of humankind would be left impoverished. This is why the Turkic peoples ought not internalize a Eurocentered vision of their history but uphold their national specificities, conceived as atemporal, and thus as unchanged from the first empires of the steppes through to contemporary Kazakhstan. Although Suleimanov is part of the Eurasianist line of thinking, he also bases himself on cosmist postulates, as was announced in his first poem, devoted to Gagarin. Cosmism, which formed one of the main streams of Russian religious philosophy during the first half of the twentieth century, claims that humankind is intrinsically linked to the cosmos, that its historical and political development is governed by physical or chemical laws which apply to the totality of living beings, and that humanity is only ever on the right path when it moves within an awareness of this belonging to the cosmos.

Suleimenov's personal trajectory is revealing of Russia's experience as a multinational and multiconfessional polity and culture. Soviet culture provided an extraordinary cultural incubator to intellectuals like Suleimenov: starting out in the physical sciences, he was then able to pursue a brilliant literary career, to associate with the great names of Russian literature of the 1960s, to engage in politics during perestroika over questions concerning ecology and peace, and then to get involved in solving the difficulties that emerged after Kazakhstan's independence by serving large international organizations such as UNESCO. Suleimenov is thus the embodiment of a specific contemporary Kazakh culture: he is Russophone and not Kazakhophone; he is nostalgic about the lost unity of Eurasian peoples rendered possible by the Soviet regime; not much interested in Islam, he prefers a postmodern and ecumenical vision of religions; and he is quite convinced of the major historical role that the Kazakh steppes played in ancient and contemporary world history. To his mind, Kazakhstan has a message of national and religious tolerance to spread throughout the rest of the world. This he bases on a conception of the Soviet/Eurasian space as fundamentally accommodating, a space which he thinks provides a model for the harmonious development of humanity in its diversity. This is perhaps not the last of his paradoxes: claiming a Kazakhness that is unashamed of its Russification and of its sovietization, he devotes his work to the rehabilitation of the ancient global role of Turkic peoples.

## NOTES

1. F. Diat, "Olzhas Sulejmenov: *Az i Ya,*" *Central Asian Survey* 1 (1984): 101–21.

2. H. Ram, "Imagining Eurasia: Olzhas Suleymenov's AZ i IA," *Slavic Review* 60, no. 2 (2001): 289–311.

3. See Edward L. Keenan, *Josef Dobrovsky and the Origins of the Igor' Tale* (Cambridge, Mass.: Harvard University Press for the Harvard Ukrainian Research Institute and the Davis Center for Russian and Eurasian Studies, 2003).

4. M. Laruelle, *Eurasianism in Russia: The Ideology of Empire* (Washington, D.C.: Woodrow Wilson Press/Johns Hopkins University Press, 2008).

5. O. Suleimenov, "Kazhdyi poet sozdaet svoi globus," *Rossiiskaia gazeta* 233 (September 22, 2005), www.rg.ru/2005/09/22/suleymenov.html.

6. N. G. Ayupov, "Tengrianstvo," *Izvestiia Akademii nauk respubliki Tadzhikistan* 3–4 (2002): 86.

7. M. Laruelle, "Religious Revival, Nationalism and the 'Invention of Tradition': Political Tengrism in Central Asia and Tatarstan," *Central Asian Survey* 26, no. 2 (2007): 203–16.

8. O. Suleimenov, *Az i Ya* (Alma-Ata: Zhazushy, 1975), 271.

9. O. Suleimenov, "How Man Spread over the Earth," June 19, 2008, www.firstgreatmigrations.org/letter.php.

Boris Akunin (Grigorii Chkhartishvili) Playing with Imperial History. From Boris Akunin, *Smert' na brudershaft 2* (Moscow: 2008).

# 30

# Boris Akunin

## (GRIGORII SHALVOVICH CHKHARTISHVILI, 1956-)

### STEPHEN M. NORRIS

The most famous living author in a country that has long worshipped its literary stars, Boris Akunin is really two people—both products of empire. The first Akunin is his creator, for Akunin is a pseudonym used by a Georgian literary scholar of Japan named Grigorii Chkhartishvili. The second Akunin is the creator of an alternate empire, a place described by the author as "a country resembling Russia," where the forces that sustained and ultimately dissolved the empire of the Romanovs are turned into playful points of debate and the basis for a good detective story. The first Akunin is a product of the Soviet empire and the specific milieu of late socialism, and the second is a product of the post-Soviet cultural desire to understand the Russia that may have been lost in 1917.

### TURNING JAPANESE

Born in a significant year in a significant place, Grigorii Chkhartishvili's Soviet life was in many ways a typically atypical one. The son of a Georgian father and a Jewish mother whose families had long since become assimilated Muscovites, Grigorii arrived on the scene in May 1956. The fact that he was born in Tbilisi was part coincidence, for Chkhartishvili's father was at the time a member of Stalin's Red Army Georgian unit, created as an imagined Praetorian Guard and as a symbol of the Georgian acceptance of Soviet socialism (or perhaps the Soviet acceptance of Georgian socialism). Chkhartishvili's unit was stationed in Central Asia and then in Georgia; thus, Grigorii was born in his ethnic homeland. Just three months before Grigorii's birth, however, Soviet Premier Nikita Khrushchev delivered his Secret Speech at the Communist Party's Twentieth Party Congress, where he denounced Stalin's cult of personality in a packed special session. Fearing a revolt among the supposedly Stalinist loyalists who made up the Georgian guard, Khrushchev eventually had the unit disbanded. The Chkhartishvilis moved back home, to Moscow, within a year of Grigorii's birth. Chkhartishvili senior did not protest.

Grigorii maintained no connections with his homeland, nor did his parents encourage him to do so. He does not speak Georgian and has returned to Tbilisi only
once. However, in many ways, because of the way Soviet nationality policies worked,
Grigorii Chkhartishvili was deemed "Georgian," not "Russian," and therefore had to
claim Georgian nationality on his Soviet passport. Soviet nationality experts, beginning with Stalin himself (a fellow ethnic Georgian), viewed Georgians as one of the
great power nations within the larger Soviet empire of nations. Georgians, the Soviet
state decided, oppressed and exploited their Ossetian and Abkhazian minorities but
also had acquired a sense of national consciousness by the twentieth century. Georgia
became a Soviet republic because of this perceived enlightenment, but ethnic minorities within Georgia gained special rights. Within each national republic and among
other nationalities, the Soviet state encouraged the national minorities to develop
their own "national cultures." Georgians were encouraged to learn their own history, folklore, and culture while also learning about the other national groups within
the Soviet empire of nations. In sum, as Yuri Slezkine has defined it, the Soviet state
functioned like a communal apartment. Each nationality got a room next to other
nationalities. Although the Russians got the biggest room (metaphorically speaking), the Ukrainians and Georgians got the next best rooms. As Slezkine has argued,
however, Soviet encouragement to develop a sense of nationhood also encouraged
ethnic particularism: Georgians quarreled with Armenians and Russians within the
apartment.[1] Because of the stress on "nationality," the Soviet state ultimately viewed
Grigorii Chkhartishvili, despite his Muscovite roots, as "Georgian."[2]

Being Georgian may have meant occupying a nice place at the table of Soviet nationalities, but it also meant coming from the Caucasus. Many Soviet citizens viewed
Caucasians as swarthy bandits predisposed to corruption and violence. Soviet society
certainly revered Georgian artists such as the film director Georgii Daneliia and the
singer Bulat Okudzhava. At the same time, as Georgii Chkhartishvili was well aware,
films such as the 1967 comedy *Kidnapping Caucasian Style* and Daneliia's 1977 comedy *Mimino* depicted Georgians and other Caucasian peoples as scheming, boorish,
and criminal. Being Georgian—even if one thought of oneself as Russian—carried
certain connotations.

Chkhartishvili grew up Georgian and Russian amid the cultural relaxation of the
Thaw, nuclear brinksmanship with the United States, the Soviet conquest of space,
and the stagnant stability of the Brezhnev era. As a child in this environment, Grigorii
turned inward—first to the safety and excitement of books; he devoured virtually
everything he could find, from Walter Scott to Fëdor Dostoevsky. He also developed
an interest in Japan after attending a Moscow kabuki theater. This introverted aspect of his Soviet childhood informed his decision to major in Japanese history and
languages at the Institute of Asia and Africa at Moscow State University, which he
entered in 1973. The interest in Japan, as Chkhartishvili later claimed, came because
it "seemed so exotic and so unlike the Soviet Union."[3] In this sense, Grigorii followed
the course of many young Soviet citizens of the 1970s—not fully dissidents, not party
enthusiasts, but people who simply carved out spaces in which they could pursue

their own interests. As a product of the late Soviet empire and therefore late socialism itself, by the 1970s Chkhartishvili was typically atypical, representing a strange embodiment of the way the Soviet empire worked and shaped its citizens: Georgian by ethnicity and on his passport, a Muscovite by inclination and upbringing, a devotee of Russian literary classics and world literature, an enthusiast of Japanese culture and history, and a Soviet citizen who had no strong political views but a general sense of "slight discontent." This strange mix of selfhood may only be explained by simply stating that the person who united these seemingly disparate elements lived in Brezhnev-era Moscow, a sentiment later articulated by Chkhartishvili: "It's Moscow and everyone has different roots. My life and education was typically Muscovite and typically Soviet." As a child in the 1960s, Chkhartishvili mused, "I was a happy kid in the happiest country in the world. Then in the 1970s, when I got older, I started to think, to compare things in the Soviet Union with what I read and heard about other places, and to see the lies all around. I was not as happy and neither was my country."[4]

After graduation, Chkhartishvili worked as an academic and literary expert. He published articles on Japanese literature and translated works from Japanese and English (including Yukio Mishima and Malcolm Bradbury), although some of these translations could not be published until the Gorbachev era. For the most part, Chkhartishvili remembers the Brezhnev era as "boring."[5] And then, as is the case with many of the last Soviet generation, Gorbachev arrived and everything changed. For Grigorii Chkhartishvili, the cultural changes that glasnost' unleashed brought exciting career opportunities. His work appeared in print and his reputation rose enough for him to become deputy editor of the prestigious journal *Foreign Literature* (*Inostrannaia literatura*). Chkhartishvili headed the publication's oriental literature section, and helped to further the journal's reputation as a source of real information about the world outside the Soviet empire. Chkhartishvili had been attracted to Japan because it was exotic and not like the USSR; readers looked to the journal for the same reasons. When the reforms unleashed by Gorbachev eventually caused the collapse of the Soviet Union and the Soviet empire, Chkhartishvili remained with *Foreign Literature* and watched it—like most Soviet-era journals—drop in subscriptions and significance. The journal survived, but its importance as an escape, as a source of the world outside the USSR, no longer mattered as much.

During the 1990s, Chkhartishvili, like many of his compatriots, experienced an existential crisis. To deal with it, he researched and wrote *The Writer and Suicide* (*Pisatel' i samoubiistvo*), which appeared in 1999 with Novoe literaturnoe obozrenie, a well-respected Moscow publisher. Aimed at a broad audience, the book examines literary suicides in a number of works, showcasing Chkhartishvili's longstanding habit of reading voraciously and broadly. Konstantin Klioutchkine has characterized the book's intention as "not to generate profound or original philosophical insight but, rather, to amass valuable information, on the basis of which readers can make their own ethical choices. The salient feature of the book is the exceedingly tactful, albeit firm, way in which Chkhartishvili espouses his views—a manner of presentation indicative of his own ideology. An agnostic, Chkhartishvili believes that each individual has the right to make any decision whatsoever on the matter of suicide, provided that he does not impose his views on others."[6] The book in many ways has Chkhartishvili putting into print typically atypical views—his arguments are unconventional in the Russian context (for, as Klioutchkine notes, he focuses on restraint, on divisions between public and private selves, and on individual values—all anti-Soviet by definition), yet his personal crisis and search for meaning in the 1990s is all too typical among former Soviet citizens. Chkhartishvili's musings were not those of a chauvinist who longed for the empire to be restored, nor were they brought about by the collapse of Soviet ideology. Rather, as *The Writer and Suicide* articulates, they were simply a search for some sort of meaning in a rather chaotic world.

Chkhartishvili admitted that the research for his work on suicide took a toll on him. For kicks he decided to indulge his love of detective stories and his increasing interest in genre-bending works by writing a series of detective scripts and novels. This therapy, it turned out, provided the cure for his ailments, for Chkhartishvili decided to keep his writing a secret and to assume another persona, that of Boris Akunin.

## Reimagining the Russian Empire

The second person of empire that inhabits Chkhartishvili is his literary alter ego, Boris Akunin. Chkhartishvili chose the name for two reasons: first, to pay homage to Mikhail Bakunin, the founder of modern anarchism (B. Akunin = Bakunin). Second, *akunin* means "bad person" (or "villain") in Japanese. Thus, Chkhartishvili draws on several strands of Russian and imperial memories in order to play with the past, to cause chaos and anarchy in the accumulated memories of the nineteenth century in particular and the baggage of the Russian imperial project over the centuries. In the chaotic 1990s, when bad guys could do good and vice versa, Chkhartishvili's choice of Akunin for a pseudonym worked perfectly.

Akunin is best known for his detective series starring Erast Fandorin, a Moscow member of the tsarist police force. He began the series in 1998 and has since published thirteen books, which became a sensation by the time the fifth book, *Special Assignments,* appeared in 1999. In just one year, Akunin went from a complete unknown (in all senses) who had never written a novel before to a literary and cultural sensation. Since 1998, the Fandorin series has sold millions of copies (the first in the series, *Azazel* alone has sold about fifteen million), and its individual books often sell two hundred thousand in their first week of release. Boris Akunin, it is fair to say, is a celebrity, a phenomenon that has not been seen before in Russian literary culture. His books are bestsellers, his film scripts are blockbusters, and his rewriting of Chekhov's *The Seagull [Chaika]* even sold out the Moscow Arts Theater when it premiered in 2000.

It is hard to categorize Akunin's prodigious output. In addition to the Fandorin series, he has published a three-part series starring a nineteenth-century mystery-solving nun, Sister Pelagia; four novels starring Nicholas Fandorin, Erast's London-based grandson; four novels in his "genre series" that each employ a different literary genre; five books in his new "cinema novels" that imitate a particular style of silent film; a collection of short stories; and two plays in addition to *The Seagull*. It is fair to say, however, that all of Akunin's works play with Russia's past, particularly the Romanov and Soviet empires. Much as his name has two meanings, his works deliberately distort the history of Russia's empire in order to challenge widely held views about this entity.

Let us take a look at two examples. The Fandorin novel *The Turkish Gambit* [*Turetskii gambit*], which was later adapted into a 2005 blockbuster movie, revolves around the Russo-Turkish War of 1877–78, when Panslavist sentiment raged through Russia and, after a bloody siege of the Turkish fortress at Plevna, when Russian forces nearly captured Constantinople. The spectacular Russian successes in the war and the subsequent Treaty of San Stefano shook European leaders enough that Otto von Bismarck called the special Congress of Berlin and brought all the major heads of state to the Prussian capital in order to revise Russian gains. For a few months in 1878, however, Russian imperialists rejoiced, seemingly having reached a new zenith in imperial expansion and Russian cultural influence. The Panslavist dream of making Constantinople into Tsargrad seemed a near reality for the first and only time in the nineteenth century.

Set amid this complex and often heady period, Akunin's "spy-detective novel" has Fandorin at the Turkish front attempting to uncover the machinations of a shadowy spy named Anwar Effendi, an urbane enemy who seemingly slips unseen in and out of both Russian and Turkish headquarters. Effendi's gambit is to draw Russian forces farther and farther into the war and into Turkey, in the end by playing on General Mikhail Sobelev (modeled on the popular hero of the war, the "White General" Mikhail Skobelev) and his dreams of becoming a new national hero. As Sobelev confesses to Varvara, the feminist volunteer who helps Fandorin, "[M]y true passion is my ambition, and everything else comes second. That's just the way I am. But ambition is no sin if it is directed to an exalted goal." Anwar Effendi sees this view for what it is—a puffed-up desire to be worshipped—and lures Sobelev into Constantinople to provoke a general European war and the end of Russian power on the continent. Sobelev follows, and in the end thwarts Effendi's gambit.

Effendi tells Varvara that he plays chess as the white pieces—and Russia is the black—but at the close of the novel we are not certain who has played their pieces better. In the Turkish spy's words, "[Y]our immensely powerful state constitutes the main danger to civilization. With its vast expanses, its multitudinous, ignorant population, its cumbersome and aggressive state apparatus. . . . The mission of the Russian people is to take Constantinople and unite the Slavs? To what end? So that the Romanovs might once again impose their will on Europe? A nightmarish prospect indeed! It is not pleasant to hear this, *Mademoiselle Barbara*, but lurking within Russia is a terrible threat to civilization. There are savage, destructive forces fermenting within her, forces that will break out sooner or later, and then the world will be in a bad way. It is an unstable, ridiculous country that has absorbed all the worse features of the West and the East. Russia has to be put back in its place; its reach has to be shortened."[7] The novel closes with Anwar Effendi dead but seemingly proven correct, for the announcement of the Congress of Berlin is printed in the press. Is Akunin's reimagined empire, then, a romantic setting when spies and detectives played elegant games and where Fandorin, a committed monarchist, is a true hero and nostalgic reminder of the "Russia we have lost"?[8] Or are Effendi's words a reminder that the Romanov Empire was a dangerous creation that in turn produced the "destructive forces" unleashed by the Bolsheviks; a reminder that the Russia of 1998 continued to harbor "aggressive and cumbersome" ideas? The reader is left to wonder these questions, for Akunin provides no clear answers.

A second snapshot of Akunin's reinvented Russian empire can be glimpsed in the first novel of his Pelagia series, *Sister Pelagia and the White Bulldog* [*Pelagia i belyi bulldog*], which appeared in Russian in 2000. Set in a fictional Volga town named Zavolzhsk, the novel introduces the redheaded nun Pelagia, a Miss Marple–like provincial woman living in the late nineteenth century. Pelagia struggles to retain her vows of humility and remember her "place" as a woman (and a nun at that), and is simultaneously reined in and let loose by her benefactor, Bishop Mitrofanii. Mitrofanii had become known throughout his district as having a talent for "unraveling all sorts of baffling mysteries," largely because of his use of Pelagia's gifts for detective work and his ability to take credit for her gifts. In the plot of the novel, the beloved bulldog of Mitrofanii's rich aunt has been poisoned, and Mitrofanii dispatches Pelagia to take care of things. The nun soon uncovers a more sinister plot that involves high politics, nihilist radicalism, and a seemingly murderous religious sect bent on causing unrest in Russia by causing problems in the provinces.

In the middle of the novel, though, Akunin includes a curious and yet revealing interlude about the relationship between the center and the periphery in tsarist Russia, an aside that clearly echoes Russia in 2000, the first year of Putin's presidency. Among other things that Pelagia's investigations have uncovered, we learn that "the name of our province thundered resoundingly throughout the length and breadth of Russia, even echoing beyond its borders. The newspapers of Petersburg and Moscow took to writing about us almost every day, separating into two camps, with the supporters of the first asserting that the Zavolzhsk region was the location of a new Battle of Kulikovo Field, a holy war for Russia, our faith, and the church of Christ, while their opponents, in contrast, characterized the events that were taking place as medieval obscurantism and a new Inquisition." Among the "solutions" to the murderous provocations of the sect, Akunin wrote, included a special government commission to deal with the problem headed by a police inspector sent from St. Petersburg, Vladimir Lvovich Bubentsov. The Petersburg policeman set up a special commission to deal with the case "with a membership consisting of special investigators sent from St. Petersburg, and also a few local investigators and police officials—each of whom was selected by Vladimir Lvovich himself. The commission was not subordinated either the governor or the district procurator and it did not have to report to them about its activities." Ultimately, the new policies meant that "in the course of [a] month the entire edifice of our province's life had been twisted awry, although it had appeared to be soundly and intelligently constructed." The real way to govern the provinces,

Mitrofanii claims, was "less management, and then things would manage themselves. One needed only to lay a firm foundation and everything else would follow of its own accord." As for the foundation, Mitrofanii also was clear: "One has to cultivate and foster the dignity in people. So that people will respect themselves and other people. A man who understands dignity will not steal, act meanly, or live by deceit."[9]

The "digression" at the heart of Pelagia's world, in other words, is a not-so-thinly veiled attack on Vladimir Putin's early policies to deal with alleged Chechen provocations in Moscow and later his plan to end the autonomy of Russia's governors. Vladimir Putin, like Bubentsov, was a St. Petersburg policeman called to Moscow to clean up a problem and offered the solution of bringing in his own men. Bubentsov/Putin, in other words, did not cultivate and foster dignity, but fanned the flames of extremism and xenophobia, the "destructive forces" within Russia that Anwar Effendi warned against.

Akunin openly admits these connections, responding to an Italian interviewer that "the problems that Russia faced at the end of the nineteenth century are essentially the same problems we have in Russia today. I don't want to go on at great length about the political and economic aspects of these problems. That's not really the point. Right now there is an ongoing debate in my country about which values deserve the highest priority: whether individual values need to be emphasized, or whether we should return to social and collective interests. Last century, Russia chose an answer to this question that led to the tragedies of the twentieth century. Now we find ourselves at a similar crossroads, but we don't know yet which road will be taken this time." As for Fandorin, Akunin told his interviewer, "I don't believe that Fandorin would have taken part in Putin's military campaign against Chechnya. Yes, Fandorin is a detective in the tsar's police force, but he is above all a man of solid moral principles. The war against Chechnya is taking place in an atmosphere of immorality."[10]

Not surprisingly, because of his popularity and his provocative suggestions on Russian history, Akunin has received a lot of critical attention. When the Fandorin series became a phenomenon, some critics believed that Akunin romanticized tsarist Russia, creating a positive hero out of a policeman and an elegant empire that gave way to a brutal dictatorship. In this view, Akunin can even be seen as a conservative xenophobe, a charge leveled by Roman Arbitman.[11] Other critics see another Akunin, one that created a "self-indulgent individual who scorns everything Russian."[12] Because of his repeated critiques of Russian power in the past, some critics claim that Akunin is a Russophobe and that he hates his homeland.[13]

Other critics such as Lev Pirogov praise Akunin for popularizing Russian history, whereas Elena Diakova writes that Akunin's nineteenth-century empire is a fascinatingly complex place.[14] Akunin embraces this latter view, referring to himself as a "belletrist" and not an "author [*pisatel*]," thereby publicly scorning the mantle of prophet that has often accompanied important Russian writers of the past. Although Akunin does not want to be read and championed in the tradition of Gogol, Dostoevsky, Tolstoy, or Bulgakov (to just name a few), many of his readers want to see him as the latest incarnation of the artistic genius who lays bare all the essential meanings of life and of Russia. Russian academics such as Georgii Tsiplakov see Akunin—because of Chkhartishvili's interest in Eastern culture and his preference for postmodern literary games with the reader—as a "cunning and masterful Taoist who demonstrates to the heroes of his books the inexorability of the Tao. . . . He [Akunin] has fun with his villains, but he himself in the principal villain. It is he, not his criminals, who is the master of the chess gambit."[15] Ultimately, Akunin's recreated empire is a space where the author can "set Taoism against romanticism, East against West, inaction against the desire to act and create" and where Fandorin—like Akunin—is a passive mediator, a perfect blend of the age-old belief that Russia is both East and West.[16] Western academics have tended to view Akunin as an embodiment of the supposedly widespread nostalgia for the Romanovs in post-Soviet Russia (if a remarkably gifted nostalgic, as Elena Baraban and Sofya Khagi depict him),[17] or as a writer who articulates "homosexual panic" by writing about the "perverted leanings" of characters in novels such as *Turkish Gambit* (as Brian Baer has explored).[18]

The diversity of views about Akunin and his use of the imperial past seem to be appropriate responses, given the tangled memories and histories of the Russian imperial project and the people who have made it over the centuries. As a product of one empire—the Soviet—and a literary commentator on another—the Romanov—Boris Akunin/Grigorii Chkhartishvili captures the dynamics and contradictions of the Russian imperial experience personally and in his prose.

## Epilogue: August 2008

Boris Akunin faced off with Grigorii Chkhartishvili when Russian troops invaded Georgia in August 2008. Although famous for his Akunin and therefore "Russian" persona, Chkhartishvili remained "Georgian" in the eyes of many of his countrymen because of his ethnicity and the lingering effects of Soviet nationality policy; once a Georgian, always a Georgian, in other words—even if he had lived his entire life in Moscow, spoke only Russian, and wrote bestsellers under a Russian name.

Appearing on the radio station Echo Moscow during a segment of the "Culture Shock" program devoted to the conflict, Akunin was introduced by the host Ksenia Larynina as "our famous writer who exists under two names." In the ensuing discussion about the relationship between Georgian and Russian culture, Chkhartishvili championed cosmopolitans like himself who had lived between the two cultures: "Once again the television stations have begun to show us program about Georgian thieves, Georgian saboteurs, and now the entire country is beginning to hate Georgians. If they were to replace them with the films of Georgii Daneliia and allow the guitar of Bulat Okudzhava to play, then the country would again love Georgians." For Akunin the Russian, being a Georgian named Chkhartishvili meant being stereotyped in traditional ways. As for the conflict and how he saw it, Akunin took a split view: dealing with President Saakashvili was one thing, but "as soon as *we* crossed the Georgian border and *they* began to speak that *we* wanted to replace the President of Georgia, immediately *we* provoked the historical memory of the entire world about

Budapest, Prague, Afghanistan. Aha! They did not change, there was a Soviet military threat and now the same Russian military threat. *We* are now located on the fragments of our foreign policy. . . . You understand, in this conflict, Russia gained a small military victory and suffered a large political defeat. Here is the sum of this conflict, if *we* don't speak emotionally, but from a reasonable point of view [my emphasis]."[19] In this debate, one that was internal as much as anything, Chkhartishvili sided with the cosmopolitan Russia created by Akunin, not the Soviet empire that created the assimilated Georgian.

NOTES

1. See Yuri Slezkine, "The USSR as a Communal Apartment, or How a Socialist State Promoted Ethnic Particularism," *Slavic Review* 53, no. 2 (1994): 414–52; Ronald Grigor Suny and Terry Martin, eds., *A State of Nations: Empire and Nation-Making in the Age of Lenin and Stalin* (New York: Oxford University Press, 2001); and Francine Hirsch, *Empire of Nations: Ethnographic Knowledge and the Making of the Soviet Union* (Ithaca, N.Y.: Cornell University Press, 2005).

2. See Ronald Grigor Suny, *The Making of the Georgian Nation* (Bloomington: Indiana University Press, 1994).

3. Grigorii Chkhartishvili, interview by Stephen M. Norris, July 13, 2008, Moscow.

4. Chkhartishvili, interview. Chkhartishvili's views correspond to those of his generation, explored best by Alexei Yurchak in *Everything Was Forever, Until It Was No More: The Last Soviet Generation* (Princeton, N.J.: Princeton University Press, 2005).

5. Konstantine Klioutchkine, "Boris Akunin (Grigorii Shalovich Chkhartishvili)," in *Russian Writers Since 1500*, ed. Marina Balina and Mark Lipovetsky (Detroit: Thompson Gale, 2004), 4.

6. Ibid., 5.

7. Boris Akunin, *The Turkish Gambit,* trans. Andrew Bromfield (New York: Random House, 2005), 202.

8. Stanislav Govorukhin's 1992 documentary film, *The Russia We Have Lost,* romanticized the Romanov empire and since has become a symbol of post-Soviet nostalgia for the prerevolutionary past.

9. Boris Akunin, *Sister Pelagia and the White Bulldog,* trans. Andrew Bromfield (New York: Random House, 2006), 130–35.

10. Ibid., 271–72.

11. Roman Arbitman, "Bumazhnyi oplot prianichnoi derzhavy" *Znamia* 7 (1999): 217–19.

12. Pavel Basinskii, "Shtil' v stakane vody: Boris Akunin: pro et contra" *Literaturnaia gazeta* 21 (May 23–29, 2001): www.lgz.ru/archives/html_arch/lg212001/Literature/art6.htm.

13. See Tatiana Blazhova, "Nu chto, brat Fandorin? Ili igry patriotov," *Moskovskaia pravda,* May 19, 1999.

14. See Lev Pirogov, "Konets tsitaty," *Literaturnaia gazeta* 15 (April 11–17, 2001), www.lgz.ru/archives/html_arch/lg152001/Literature/art10.htm; and Elena Diakova, "Boris Akunin kak uspeshnaia otrasl' rossiiskoi promyshlennosti" *Novaia gazeta* 45 (July 2, 2001), color.novaya-gazeta.ru/data/2001/45/34.html. For more on the Russian views of Akunin, see Elena Baraban, "A Country Resembling Russia: The Use of History in Boris Akunin's Detective Novels," *Slavic and East European Review* 48, no. 3 (2004): 396–420.

*Stephen M. Norris*

15. Georgii Tsiplakov, "Evil Arising on the Road and the Tao of Erast Fandorin," *Russian Studies in Literature* 38, no. 3 (Summer 2002): 48. The article appeared originally in Russian in *Novyi mir* 11 (2001): 159–81.

16. Ibid., 51–52.

17. Baraban, "A Country Resembling Russia"; Sofya Khagi, "Boris Akunin and Retro Mode in Contemporary Russian Culture," *Toronto Slavic Quarterly* 13 (Summer 2005): /www .utoronto.ca/tsq/13/khagi13.shtml.

18. Brian Baer, "Engendering Panic: Homosexual Panic in the Post-Soviet *Detektiv*," *Slavic Review* 64, no. 1 (Spring 2005): 24–42.

19. Kseniia Larina, "Rossiia i Gruziia: Esli u nas obshchee budushchee?" *Ekho Moskvy,* August 16, 2008, www.echo.msk.ru/programs/kulshok/534013-echo.phtml.

Vladislav Surkov in 2010. Wikimedia Commons

# 31

# Vladislav Surkov

## (1964–)

KAREN DAWISHA

Many details of Vladislav Surkov's life remain a mystery. What is undisputed is his absolute centrality in Kremlin politics since Putin came to power in 2000. His private role as the center of the spoke of the vast wheel of relationships directed by the Kremlin, and his public persona as the ideologist of the Russian revival are equally deserving of focus.

## EARLY LIFE: BIOGRAPHICAL NOTES AND SILENCES

Vladislav Surkov has had several incarnations. His official Kremlin biography lists him as having been born in the village of Solntsevo, in the Lipetsk region in southern Russia, near Tambov and Voronezh, on September 21, 1964. However, in a 1995 interview with the German newspaper *Der Spiegel* he admitted publicly for the first time what had long been rumored, that he was born in Chechnya of a Chechen father and had spent his first five years there. Other information lists him as being born not in 1964 but in 1962 in the Chechen village of Duba-Yurt, twenty miles from Grozny.[1]

This biography suggests he was a true son of empire. The village of Duba-Yurt, founded in 1859, was named after the Chechen general Duba, whose valorous service to Alexander II earned him these lands when he joined the Russians in capturing the legendary Chechen leader Shamil in that year.

Duba-Yurt was almost completely razed to the ground during the second post-Soviet Chechen war, when Russian soldiers carried out a punitive aerial and land bombardment, followed by the burning of the entire village of six thousand inhabitants, on charges that they had sheltered rebels. This bombardment started on December 31, 1999—the day that Yeltsin handed over power to Putin—and continued for two months. Vladislav Surkov was already working in the presidential administration for a year at this point, with responsibility also for links with the Chechens, although he had not yet revealed publicly that Duba-Yurt was the place of his birth.

Anna Politkovskaya, a legendary Russian journalist who was assassinated in 2006, visited Duba-Yurt and the neighboring village of Chiri-Yurt in 2001, and wrote,

> Duba-Yurt resembles a huge scarecrow: dead, ragged, riddled with holes from "hail" and artillery shots. . . . The same can be said about the Duba-Yurtans. They are a lost tribe, unclear as to how to restore their lives, 98 percent of which has been bombed and burnt. . . . People ran from Duba-Yurt to Chiri-Yurt for shelter in small groups. . . . The Duba-Yurtans planned to wait nearby until the battles were over and come back right away. But . . . on February 6, when not a single person was left in Duba-Yurt, the Feds started to burn down the houses that had survived the bombing. . . . The destruction of Duba-Yurt was shocking even for the soldiers of the military unit that was stationed there after that fiery pogrom. [The new Russian commanders] issued a report . . . on Duba-Yurt. It stated that "the military convoys that pass through the village systematically rob and burn the houses of civilians."[2]

Surkov's Chechen relatives had been well entrenched in key Chechen clan structures in and beyond Duba-Yurt. Surkov's grandfather was Danilbek Dudaev, a member of the Zandakkhoi clan, or *taip*, of the Nokhchmakhkkhoi, the largest of the nine *tukkhums*, or non–kin based tribes, that make up the Chechen nation. The Kremlin has used Vladislav Surkov as the point man in its relations with the Chechens, and Surkov comes from the same tukkhum as the Putin-appointed president of Chechnya, Ramzan Kadyrov, who is from the Benoi taip of the Nokhchmakhkkhoi tukkhum. Under both Ramzan Kadyrov and his father, Akhmad, who ruled Chechnya from 2000 until his assassination in 2004, there has been an increased focus on appointing members of his own taip.[3] During Putin's presidency, Surkov was used as an intermediary between Kadyrov and Putin, and he assumed the role of accompanying to Grozny visiting Kremlin officials such as presidential hopeful Dmitry Medvedev, whose preelection visit to Chechnya brought Kadyrov's public assurance that the Kremlin could count on a 99.9-percent vote in favor of Medvedev.[4]

Surkov's family was well educated and Russia-oriented. Surkov's grandfather, Danilbek Dudaev, was trained as a lawyer, and his father, Andarbek Dudaev, graduated from Rostov University. Andarbek Dudaev, who was also called by the Russian name Yura (thus, Surkov's mother used the patronymic Yurevich rather than Andarbekovich after she changed his birth certificate), returned to Duba-Yurt after graduation to become a teacher, and this is where he met his future wife, then a twenty-three-year graduate of the Tambov Teachers' College, in 1959. Mutual friends recall everyone spilling out onto the streets of Duba-Yurt to celebrate the launching of Yuri Gagarin into space.[5] It seems that the Chechen inhabitants of this small village at the time yearned indeed to be part of the larger family of Soviet nationalities, and any rebelliousness in the village was clearly overtaken by gratefulness for having been recently allowed to return to their homes from the Central Asian steppes to which they and a half million other Chechens had been forcibly relocated by Stalin during World War II.

Surkov's mother, Zoya Antonovna Surkova, was a talented singer, and she and another local teacher, Abdelbeki Bachaev, formed a singing duo that took first prize in a regional competition. It was in 1962 that Zoya gave birth to Vladislav, who at that time was named Aslambek. Five years later, the extended family moved to Chechnya's capital, Grozny; at the same time, Surkov's father, Andarbek, went to work at a military training facility in Leningrad, and cut all ties with the family—reportedly never again writing home. Zoya returned to Lipetsk, even though she had enjoyed good relations with her Chechen in-laws, and continued to be in touch with them and other Chechen friends in Duba-Yurt; she even wrote them a letter in 2003, after they had returned to their destroyed village, commiserating with their "bitter fate" and remembering the Chechens as an "excellent people," and "kind and welcoming."[6]

It was in 1969 that Zoya changed her son's name formally from Aslambek Andarbekovich Dudaev to Vladislav Yuriyevich Surkov, and may also at this time have registered his birthday as 1964 instead of 1962. It is not publicly known whether he has or had brothers or sisters or whether his father was ever a part of his life. He has admitted to spending his first five years in Chechnya, but has never talked publicly about his family or his background. His father's fate has never been mentioned publicly by Surkov. However, it is clear from his subsequent biography that he inherited his mother's musical ability; he took up writing poetry and then lyrics at an early age.

## EARLY FAILURES AND OPPORTUNITIES

Much of Vladislav Surkov's education was in the Soviet period. He studied at the Moscow Institute of Steel and Alloys, where he famously met the oligarch Mikhail Fridman, one of the founders of Alfa Group. He failed to graduate from the Institute, and was conscripted into the Soviet military, where he served from 1983–85. His Kremlin biography states he was a part of the southern group of Soviet forces in Hungary, but in a November 2006 television interview, Russian Defense Minister Sergey Ivanov revealed what he called a "secret"—that Surkov, like Presidential Plenipotentiary to the Southern District Dmitry Kozak, had served as part of the special forces (Spetsnaz) of Soviet military intelligence, the Main Intelligence Administration (GRU) of the Ministry of Defense.[7] No more information about this interlude, nor Ivanov's reasons for revealing such sensitive and classified information at this time, has ever been published.

After his military service, Surkov enrolled in the Moscow Institute of Culture to follow a course in theater directing, but he also did not complete this course. In 1987, four years before the collapse of the Soviet Union and at the very beginning of the Gorbachev political reforms, he set up the advertising department for a new cooperative venture formed by Mikhail Khodorkovsky. Between 1987 and his ascent into a political position in the Kremlin, he was at the very center of creating an image of the oligarchs that the Russian population would accept. He became head of the Russian Association of Advertisers, joined the board of Mikhail Khodorkovsky's Menatep Bank, then became the first deputy chairman of Fridman's Alfa Bank; as well as becoming a vice president of Rosprom and head of its department for relations with state organizations. In 1998–99 he had a brief stint as director of public relations for the Russian state television company ORT. At this time, he also became an assistant to Aleksandr Voloshin, the head of the Presidential Administration. From there he was appointed deputy chief of staff of the president of the Russian Federation in 1999. Thereafter he has worked as either deputy chief of staff or senior deputy chief of staff under Presidents Putin and Medvedev, and has had primary responsibility for domestic policy.[8]

It is central in Surkov's earlier biography that he rose to elite status as a result of helping two of Russia's richest, most dynamic, and youngest oligarchs build their empires and shape their images. Naturally, it ultimately proved difficult to control the public personae of these oligarchs given their profligate behavior and the commensurate descent of the Russian population into widespread poverty during the 1990s. Yet Surkov, unlike others in the Putin circle who were identified as members of the so-called *siloviki* (elites who had risen up through, and represented, the intelligence, defense, and heavy industry sectors—and who often had a negative view of the entire process of economic liberalization), was intimately involved in this process and understands its logic from the inside. He was also linked by marriage to Anatoly Chubais (his first wife is the sister of Chubais's wife), the one early architect of privatization who has remained in the Kremlin inner circle. This first wife, Yulia Vishnevskaya, with whom he had a son, subsequently moved to London. He then married Natalya Dubovitskaya, a former employee of Menatep, with whom he has two additional children. By 2009, Dubovitskaya was listed on the Kremlin website reporting salaries of Kremlin officials and their wives as having the highest income of all Kremlin wives in 2009—16.8 million rubles. Surkov, in line with common practice within the Kremlin since Putin, kept many of his connections in the private sphere alive after beginning work for the Kremlin, and resigned his position as president of the board of directors of the open joint stock oil company AK Transnefteprodukt only in February 2006, on orders from newly appointed Prime Minister Mikhail Fradkov. It is, therefore, probably impossible to judge the correct balance between heartfelt loyalty on the one hand, and cynicism and irony on the other hand, in his remarks in to *Der Spiegel,* in which he said he could not comment on Khodorkovsky's ten-year prison sentence: "I'm biased because I respect him, which is one reason I prefer not to comment."[9]

While he publicly distanced himself in a delicate way from some of the excesses of the 1990s, excesses he undoubtedly personally benefited from, he has never been part of the group who publicly stated that they missed the USSR. Even when Putin himself waxed nostalgically about the USSR, calling the collapse of the Soviet Union "the greatest geopolitical catastrophe of the century," Surkov responded soon after, saying that while "many were terribly disappointed at the way things turned out and are now saying Russia made the wrong decision, . . . personally, I believe that renunciation of the Soviet Union was an expression of the free will of the Russian people. I still remember my own feelings at the time very well. I felt an enormous sense of relief, as if a huge leech had dropped from my back." Even as Surkov has attempted to advocate for, and construct, a new ruling party, and with it a system for recognizing and promoting elites, he has rejected any talk that this new system was rebuilding the

Soviet Communist Party's *nomenklatura* system: in his view, during the Soviet period, all the old CPSU and KGB elites had succeeded in doing was the "mobilization of their own grave diggers."[10]

## MOVING UP

Almost immediately after moving into the Kremlin, Surkov assumed a position of importance both by virtue of the nature of his assignments, and by his contribution to the ideological direction of the Putin regime. Since then, he has been officially responsible, above all, for all aspects of domestic policy, federal policy, and interethnic relations; he has supervised the interaction between the Kremlin and the legislature, political parties, the Central Electoral Commission, the media, and all public organizations. He has organized the Kremlin's relations with religious organizations and cultural institutions, and coordinates the awarding of all state prizes for education, culture, literature, and art. The official Kremlin website at one point even listed him as having responsibility for disposing of funds in accordance with the Kremlin budget. And if there were some other area he wanted to involve himself with, he also was officially listed as the official who "coordinates activity of advisory and consultative bodies under the President," without limitation as to area.[11] One cannot imagine a person with greater behind-the-scenes power since the rise of Joseph Stalin began under Lenin.

Not only did Surkov have a substantial position under Putin, he also has a distinctive style. Often animated and smiling in public settings, and ever present at Medvedev or Putin's side, he is nevertheless unafraid in closed sessions to deliver a blunt message on behalf of the Kremlin. In summer 2004, after the 2003 Duma elections, Surkov called new legislators to his office and berated them for "behaving like they were elected representatives," according to Anatoly Yermolin, one of the group present and himself a former FSB colonel. Yermolin wrote to Boris Gryzlov, the head of United Russia, and to the Constitutional Court complaining that Surkov had told them, "Just vote like you're told." Those thinking otherwise "should have a good look at what's happening to Yukos," referring to Mikhail Khodorkovsky's arrest and imprisonment. Yermolin complained in a formal letter to prosecutors that "it was like a mafia sit-down."[12] Yet the "mutiny," as the press called it, was quelled: Yermolin was kicked out of United Russia within days, and was not on the party list for the December 2007 Duma elections.

Even beyond these assignments—which make Surkov the cog in the reassertion of central Kremlin control over all aspects of daily politics—it is his role as lightning rod for ideological innovation that has been fundamental. He has consistently advocated for a more centralized state; for a political path that deemphasizes Western-style democracy; for a reassertion of a ruling idea or ideology in Russian political culture; and for an economy in which the state controls the "commanding heights," but which is nevertheless based on liberal economic principles. He would certainly assert that he is merely reflecting the wishes of the president, whether Medvedev or

Putin. Yet his comments in favor of a strongly centralized state are often more blunt than those of either Medvedev or Putin.

When Putin came to power in 2000, he had been concerned about the ever-weakening state, but events took a sharp turn in autumn 2004. In September, Chechen separatists took 1,100 women and children hostage at School number one in Beslan North Ossetia, leading to three days of siege and one hour of carnage in which 700 were freed, but over 334 died—an event known throughout Russia by the single word "Beslan." All political insiders accept that the massive political recentralization that was announced in the immediate aftermath of Beslan had been prepared well in advance, reforms that included the ending of direct elections of governors, the elimination of single member districts as the method of electing half of the Duma (which had assured the election of many independents) and the calling for the reestablishment of a strong "vertical of power" to protect the state and the country from terrorism. When challenged by the statement, "One such opinion exists that Putin is using events in Beslan for strengthening his personal power and for the liquidation of democracy," Surkov replied cynically: "Our country is unique and requires its own system of governing. . . . Putin is strengthening not himself, but the state. His authority is sufficiently high and he has no problems with regional leaders. And the new system will work not immediately and not for Putin personally."[13]

At the same time, it was clear that for Surkov, Russia required recentralization because of the threat it faced from a myriad of enemies, at the forefront of which was Chechen-inspired terrorism, but which included all forms of political opposition. As he stated in 2006,

> The virus of terrorism attacked the state at the point when regions, shut in their operetta-type sovereignties, and weak disposable parties were unable to oppose the chaos which ruled in the country then. . . . I think mobilization of the nation to fight against terrorism is the most important part of the president's program announced on Sept. 13 [2004]. We must all understand that the enemy is at the gates. The front line runs through every town, every street, every house. . . . Now we have a fifth column in the besieged country—left-wing and right-wing radicals. Now lemons and apples grow on the same branch [a reference to the political alliance at that time between the liberal Yabloko—apple—party and the right-wing National Bolsheviks of Eduard Limonov—lemon—to defeat the Kremlin]. False liberals and true Nazis have more and more in common as time goes by. They have common sponsors of foreign origin, common hatred towards "Putin-ruled Russia."[14]

Only after Medvedev became president in 2008 and United Russia held a constitutional supermajority in the Duma did Surkov tell party workers that they needed to accept that at some point they were going to have to transfer power to another party. He told the young people gathered for the 2008 annual conference of Nashi, the Kremlin-created youth movement, that they needed to continually accept the need for innovation in politics, that democracy was like a bicycle—if you stopped pedaling you would fall off. At the same time, he complained about the lack of qualified cadres coming up through the system, especially among young people and especially from the regions. This is ironic, since Surkov had himself been a key official in the formation of the youth movement Nashi, designed to prevent youth from getting swayed by the pro-democracy movements in Ukraine and Georgia. He had worked to expunge any independence at the lower levels, saying that Russia needed innovation, but not anything that he described as "merciless and pointless."[15] Similarly, President Medvedev was quick to point out that top leaders in the Kremlin were constantly racking their brains looking for good people to appoint in the regions, forgetting that it was precisely the center that had created this problem by eliminating the bottom-to-top transmission of elites that was produced by direct election of local officials. As the person responsible for relations with the regions, Surkov above all was responsible for controlling governors' access to the president, access that is given to those who are compliant with central directives and denied to those who continue to lobby for a return to greater autonomy.

When President Medvedev came to power as part of the Putin-Medvedev tandem, Surkov was left in place in the Kremlin administration, acting as one of the linchpins in the connection between the president and the prime minister. He also came to voice support for Medvedev's plan to modernize the Russian economy. His conception was geopolitical—that Russia stood between rapidly expanding and technologically innovative countries, and without modernization itself, it would not survive. However, the model was not free enterprise, but state-guided and state-centered development. He openly advocates the use of authoritarian methods to achieve economic transformation. As he stated, "A fundamental and to-the-point debate is underway here. We have a school, which teaches that political modernization, by which it means lack of political discipline, 'can do anything'—it is the key to economic modernization, the first precedes the second. There is another blueprint, which I follow, which considers the consolidated state a tool of the transition period, a tool of modernization. Some people call it authoritarian modernization. I do not care what it is called. Spontaneous modernization is a cultural phenomenon (and it is cultural, not political), and it has only been achieved in the Anglo-Saxon countries. Not in France, not in Japan, and not in Korea. Modernization was accomplished there by dirigiste methods. The nineties in Russia showed: the splitting of society does not in itself engender positive energy."[16] Continuing this debate in an open forum in Yaroslavl in 2010, Anatoly Chubais, one of the creators of the free-market system in Russia, who had become head of the state firm RosNano, criticized Surkov's notion that the state could be a motor of modernization, saying, "If the state does not interfere, that would be the best state support of the innovation business." Chubais also stated, "Economic modernization can create prerequisites for political modernization that in turn can provide conditions for democracy that we are currently lacking." At that point Surkov interrupted: "There is our national democracy in Russia. . . . One person has a nice car; another person has a car that does not work well. But both are cars." And he protested that at least his own car works well: "I do not know whether I am a Democrat. However, I am confident that I am free."[17]

Vladislav Surkov has stood at the center of all these behind-the-scenes efforts not only at recentralization, but also at the massive curtailing of free and fair elections and a genuine multiparty system, at the construction of Nashi and other anti-democratic and pro-Kremlin social movements, and at the creation of an ideological glacis over authoritarianism named first "sovereign democracy" and then, beginning in 2010, simply "authoritarian modernization."[18]

He represents possibly the highest-ranking member of the Russian elite who had no known party background, no known previous career in the power ministries, no favored family connections, no elite university credentials. On the contrary, he was a half-Chechen dropout who was entirely responsible for his own invention and reinvention.

More than that, since beginning his work in the Kremlin, he has pursued his interests in arts and culture, even while tightening cultural life for others. He has, for example, written lyrics for several albums by the Russian hard rock band Agata Kristi. Lyrics for one song, entitled "Don't Speak," ironically released just prior to the December 2003 Duma elections, read, "Are your days unnumbered? / Is your December really yours? / Was your laughter even once / As clear as water?" Another song, "We'll Be like Everyone Else" uses many references to the devil: "Our Master is Lucifer, we recognize his style. / For Christmas instead of snow he sends us dust. / We wind ourselves in the rear of his endless horde. / I'll be like you. You'll be like him. / We'll be like everyone. / He's always in the front, in scarlet silk on a pale steed. / We follow him, up to our knees in mud and to our throats in wine. / And along our road burn houses and bridges. / I'll be like you. You'll be like him. / We'll be like everyone."[19]

In 2009, he published a novel titled *Okolonolya* (Close to zero), written by a pseudonymous Natan Dubovitskiy (drawn from his wife's name, Natalya Dubovitskaya) about the corrupt world of Kremlin elites, governors, publishers, and law enforcement. The novel, once its author's true identity was revealed, was hailed in the Russian press as "combining the language of Nabokov and the tragedy of Shakespeare."[20] Authors complained that the text heavily plagiarized existing novels by Pelevin, Sorokin, and Bykov. But Kremlin insider Stanislav Belkovsky cynically defended such plagiarism:

> In the last ten years, the Kremlin ideological machine that the godfather of Natan Dubovitskiy [Surkov] embodies has been working exactly like that and only like that. It does not produce original ideas. All the ideas are taken from elsewhere—in the present or the past, and afterward are declared to be its own—and later are gradually emasculated and in the end lose any meaning at all. . . . So the novel *Okolonolya* was written specifically in the style of their main administration of domestic policy. In no way different. . . . [T]he new superman is conceited, small-minded, petty, selfish, vengeful, shallow, base, sneaky, and certainly not ready for any brave deed—such is the age . . . , such is the messiah.[21]

For Surkov as a public figure, it is the "new Russian idea," not any kind of Eurasian family of peoples that motivates his political thinking. In "Russian Political Culture: The View from Utopia," he makes his disdain for all but the Russian idea clear:

From the heights of utopia we clearly see that the old liberal dogma of liberating creative energy exclusively by means of mechanistic fragmentation, division, and dismantling of social structures is not wholly correct, that the holistic approaches and methods of social synthesis, preservation, and unification intrinsic to Russian political culture are also suited to the development of democracy. We see that the inevitable complication and differentiation of social institutions are balanced by the opposite process of the reintegration of fragments into a complex whole. We see that culture is of significance, of decisive significance and Russian culture predetermines a worthy future for Russia. . . . Commenting on the disagreements between Slavophiles and Westernizers Herzen said: "We were opponents, . . . but we shared a single love, . . . a single strong feeling of boundless . . . love for Russian life and the Russian cast of mind." I am sure that the unifying work of President Putin is successful and widely acclaimed precisely because it is guided by a Russian mind, respect for Russian political culture, and love for Russia.[22]

The late 1980s and 1990s were a different time in the former Soviet Union. Young people of all nationalities could make their way, as Surkov did, working in a variety of positions for a slew of rising stars. He benefited from the USSR's having been a multinational state, one in which, however, his own mother "bettered" his chances by giving him a Russian identity. He benefitted from the Gorbachev and Yeltsin periods' being a time of upward mobility and reinvention. What a pity that although Surkov rejected his communist and Yeltsin-era past, he has held so tight to the more unsavory aspects of both of these systems. He has been the chief pen behind the violation of law in the name of order; the ending of democracy in the name of its establishment; the criticism of Yeltsin-era oligarchs despite his having been the direct beneficiary of that era and being at the center of the current pay-to-play system; the harnessing of the population's energies in the name of innovation; and the promoting, directly and through Nashi, of a xenophobic, anti-immigrant view of the Eurasian space.[23] That he vilified the USSR as a "leech" and saw the post-Soviet system as one of unequaled opportunity is interesting; that he has single-handedly done so much to serve as the handmaiden for the reestablishment of a vast Russian empire based on the venality of elites who rule from within thick Kremlin walls is tragic.

NOTES

1. His official biography appears on the Kremlin website, kremlin.ru/state_subj/27815 .shtml. The German interview is "The West Doesn't Have to Love Us, Spiegel Interview with Kremlin Boss Vladislav Surkov," *Spiegel Online,* June 20, 2005, http://www.spiegel.de/inter national/spiegel/0,1518,361236,00.html. His 1962 birth was reported by Maksim Marinin and Irina Kosareva, "The Chechen Childhood of Surkov," *Zhizn,* July 13, 2005, reprinted in *Compromat,* www.compromat.ru/main/surkov/detstvo.htm.

2. Anna Politkovskaya, *A Small Corner of Hell: Dispatches from Chechnya* (Chicago: University of Chicago Press, 2003), 45–46.

3. Maksim Marinin and Irina Kosareva, "The Chechen Childhood of Surkov," *Zhizn,* July 13, 2005, reprinted in *Compromat,* www.compromat.ru/main/surkov/detstvo.htm. Enver Kisirev and Robert Bruce Ware, "After the Referendum: Changing Trends in Chechnya," *Russia and Eurasia Review* 2, no. 15 (July 22, 2003): 4–7. For a breakdown of all the Chechen clans, see www.chechnyafree.ru; and Kevin Daniel Leahy, "A Medvedev Presidency: Implications for Chechen-Russian Relations and Ramzan Kadyrov," *Central Asia-Caucasus Institute Analyst* 10, no. 3 (February 6, 2008): 8–10.

4. Nabi Abdullaev, "Putin will be Medvedev's Premier," *Moscow Times,* December 18, 2007.

5. Marinin and Kosareva, "The Chechen Childhood of Surkov."

6. Ibid.

7. Sergei Ivanov on Evgeniy Rozhkov's program *News of the Week,* November 12, 2006, quoted in "Surkov, Vladislav," Lenta.ru, November 22, 2006, lenta.ru/lib/14159273/full.htm.

8. "Surkov, Vladislav Yuriyevich," *Russia Profile,* November 26, 2004, www.russiapro file.org/resources/whoiswho/alphabet/s/surkov.wbp; and Surkov's own Myspace page, www .myspace.com/vladislavsurkov.

9. "The West Doesn't Have to Love Us."

10. The full text of Putin's annual address to the Federal Assembly, April 25, 2005, is available on the Kremlin website, www.kremlin.ru/appears/2005/04/25/1223_type63372 type63374type82634_87049.shtml. Surkov's response appeared in "The West Doesn't Have to Love Us." Surkov's "gravediggers" remarks were delivered at a speech to the United Russia conference on June 23, 2008, and were reprinted in Igor Romanov, "Social Lifts of Surkov," *Nezavisimaya Gazeta,* June 24, 2008, www.ng.ru/politics/2008-06-24/3_surkov.html.

11. Quoted on the Kremlin website, kremlin.ru (accessed April 15, 2008). This detailed information was subsequently removed.

12. The event became a cause célèbre in the Russian press: see "The Evolution of Vladimir Putin's Image: 'President of Hope' or 'Clumsy Dictator,'" *Politruk,* November 16, 2004; www .wps.ru/en/pp/politruk/2004/11/16.html; Gregory L. White and Alan Cullison, "Putin's Pitchman Inside Kremlin as It Tightens Its Grip," *Wall Street Journal,* December 19, 2006.

13. Quoted in Edward Limonov, "The Fellow Named Surkov," *The eXile,* October 15, 2004, www.exile.ru/print.php?ARTICLE_ID=7484&IBLOCK_ID=35.

14. Surkov briefing for foreign reporters, June 28, 2006, quoted in "Surkov: In His Own Words," *Wall Street Journal,* December 19, 2006.

15. For his words to workers, see Igor Romanov, "Longing for Opposition, Sociologists Claim that Society Longs for a Multiparty System," *Nezavisimaya Gazeta,* July 31, 2008. On Surkov speaking at the Nashi annual conference, see Sergei Krinitsyn, "The Mood is Changing: Surkov Sets Out Some New Objectives," *Nezavisimaya Gazeta,* July 23, 2008.

16. "Interview with Vladislav Surkov: 'A Miracle Is Possible,'" *Vedomosti,* February 15, 2010.

17. Vera Sitnina, "Our Own Democracy: Russian Officials Complain about the National Economy's Excessive Governmentalization; The International Political Forum in Yaroslavl Estimates Changes in Russia's Economy and Democracy," *Vremya Novostei,* September 10, 2010.

18. For more on his views, see *Russkaya politicheskaya kul'tura: Vzglyad iz utopii; Leksiya Vladislava Surkova; Materialy obsuzhdeniya v "Nezavisimoi gazete"* (Moscow: Izdatel'stvo NG, 2007).

19. The lyrics appear in Caroline McGregor, "Surkov Writes the Songs in the Kremlin," *The Moscow Times,* November 6, 2003; and Gregory L. White, "Kremlin Official's Other Job: Rock Music," *Wall Street Journal,* December 19, 2006.

20. Confirmation that Surkov was the author came from the publisher, Ruskiy Pioner, appeared in "Novel About Corruption and Crime May Be Work of Kremlin Official" *The*

*Telegraph,* August 14, 2009, www.telegraph.co.uk/news/worldnews/europe/russia/6025615/ Novel-about-corruption-and-crime-may-be-work-of-Kremlin-official.html. The review by Kirill Reshetnikov appeared in *Izvestiia;* quoted in Stanislav Belkovskiy, "In the Kremlin," *Yezhednevnyy Zhurnal,* September 1, 2009.

    21. Belkovskiy, "In the Kremlin."

    22. Vladislav Surkov, "Russian Political Culture: The View from Utopia," *Russian Politics and Law* 46, no. 5 (September–October 2008): 26.

    23. For a wonderful discussion of the many strategies used in the governance of empires, see Jane Burbank and Frederick Cooper, *Empires in World History* (Princeton, N.J.: Princeton University Press, 2010). I wish to thank Jane Burbank for her excellent comments on this draft.

# Contributors

**Edyta Bojanowska** is Assistant Professor in the Department of Germanic, Russian, and East European Languages, Rutgers University.

**Karen Dawisha** is the Walter Havighurst Professor of Political Science and Director of the Havighurst Center for Russian and Post-Soviet Studies at Miami University (of Ohio).

**Barbara Alpern Engel** is Distinguished Professor of History at the University of Colorado.

**Michael D. Gordin** is Professor of History at Princeton University.

**Rebecca Gould** is Assistant Professor in the Department of Asian and Slavic Languages and Literatures, University of Iowa.

**Alexandra Harrington** is Senior Lecturer and Head of Russian in the School of Modern Languages and Cultures at the University of Durham (UK).

**Hilde Hoogenboom** is Assistant Professor of Russian at Arizona State University.

**Marianne Kamp** is Associate Professor of History at the University of Wyoming.

**Charles King** is Professor of International Affairs and Government at Georgetown University.

**Mara Kozelsky** is Associate Professor of History at the University of South Alabama.

**Hiroaki Kuromiya** is Professor of History at Indiana University.

**Marlène Laruelle** is Senior Research Fellow with the Central Asia–Caucasus Institute and Silk Road Studies Program, Johns Hopkins University.

**John MacKay** is Professor of Film Studies and Slavic Language and Literatures at Yale University.

**Alexander M. Martin** is Associate Professor of History at the University of Notre Dame.

**David McDonald** is Professor of History at the University of Wisconsin.

**Erika Monahan** is Assistant Professor of History at the University of New Mexico.

**Stephen M. Norris** is Associate Professor of History at Miami University (of Ohio).

**Brigid O'Keeffe** is Assistant Professor of History at Brooklyn College.

**Donald Ostrowski** is research advisor in the social sciences and lecturer at Harvard University's Extension School.

**Maureen Perrie** is Emeritus Professor of History at the University of Birmingham (UK).

**Sean Pollock** is Assistant Professor of History at Wright State University.

**Michael Rouland** is Visiting Scholar and Professorial Lecturer at Georgetown University.

**David Schimmelpenninck van der Oye** is Professor of History at Brock University (Canada).

**Krista Sigler** is Assistant Professor of History at the Raymond Walters College, University of Cincinnati.

**Charles Steinwedel** is Associate Professor of History at Northeastern Illinois University.

**Richard Stites** was Professor of History at Georgetown University.

**Willard Sunderland** is Associate Professor of History and Chair, Department of History, at the University of Cincinnati.

**Ronald Grigor Suny** is Professor of History at the University of Michigan.

**Theodore R. Weeks** is Professor of History at the University of Southern Illinois.

**Bradley D. Woodworth** is Assistant Professor of History at the University of New Haven.

**Ernest A. Zitser** is Librarian for Slavic and East European Studies at Duke University.

# Index